THE COMPLETE SHANE WARNE

Cricket books by Ken Piesse

Great Triumphs in Test Cricket (1978)

Prahran Cricket Club Centenary History (1978)

Cricket Digest Annual (ed.) (1980)

Cricket Year Annual (ed.) (1980–83)

Calypso Summers (with Jim Main) (1981)

The Great Australian Book of Cricket Stories (1982)

The Golden Age of Australian Cricket (ed.) (1982)

Duel for Glory, England Tours of Australia 1861–1982 (with Jim Main) (1982)

Donald Bradman (Famous Australians series) (1983)

Cartoonists at the Cricket (ed.) (1983)

The A to Z of Cricket (1983)

Bradman & the Bush (with Ian Ferguson) (1986)

Hooked on Cricket (with Max Walker) (1988)

Match Drawn (ed.) (1988)

Simply the Best: The Allan Border Story (1993)

Warne: Sultan of Spin (1995)

Cricket Skills & Secrets (1995–99)

One Day Magic (1996)

The Big Australian Cricket Book (1996)

Wildmen of Cricket Vol. 1 (with Brian Hansen) (1998)

TJ Over the Top (with Terry Jenner) (1999)

The Taylor Years (1999)

Steve & Mark Waugh (2000)

Cricket's Greatest Scandals (2000) (in preparation)

THE COMPLETE
SHANE WARNE

KEN PIESSE

VIKING

Viking
Penguin Books Australia Ltd
487 Maroondah Highway, PO Box 257
Ringwood, Victoria 3134, Australia
Penguin Books Ltd
Harmondsworth, Middlesex, England
Penguin Putnam Inc.
375 Hudson Street, New York, New York 10014, USA
Penguin Books Canada Limited
10 Alcorn Avenue, Toronto, Ontario, Canada M4V 3B2
Penguin Books (N.Z.) Ltd
Cnr Rosedale and Airborne Roads, Albany, Auckland, New Zealand
Penguin Books (South Africa) (Pty) Ltd
5 Watkins Street, Denver Ext 4, 2094, South Africa
Penguin Books India (P) Ltd
11, Community Centre, Panchsheel Park, New Delhi 110 017, India

First published by Penguin Books Australia Ltd 2000

10 9 8 7 6 5 4 3 2 1

Designed by Tony Palmer, Penguin Design Studio
Typeset in 11/16 pt Berkeley by Midland Typesetters, Maryborough, Victoria
Printed and bound in Australia by Australian Print Group, Maryborough, Victoria

National Library of Australia
Cataloguing-in-Publication data:

Piesse, Ken.
   The complete Shane Warne.

   Includes index.
   ISBN 0 670 89232 7.

   1. Warne, Shane. 2. Cricket – Australia. 3. Cricket
   players – Australia – Biography. I. Title.
796.358092

www.penguin.com.au

CONTENTS

AUTHOR'S NOTE

The best young cricketers are easily identified for their poise, enthusiasm and skill. In Shane Warne's case, he stood out for his generous size, wide infectious grin and a handshake that was genuine and caring.

As a 17-year-old playing for his school, Mentone Grammar, against the Crusaders, a Melbourne-based band of ex-cricketers with the knack of scheduling some free time each Wednesday afternoon, Warne demanded attention. Not only did he make 38 and hit the ball as hard as any of us, he took several wickets with leg-breaks which genuinely spun – including yours truly, stumped.

Not so long afterwards, Shane was at Melbourne's delightful Albert Ground, in a trial match involving the Australian Cricket Academy. As the players were coming off for lunch, I asked if he would mind returning to the centre to bowl a few balls for our *Sunday Herald Sun* photographer.

He readily obliged, the first ball gripping and spinning past the off stump and thudding into my hands, leaving a healthy seam imprint. The second spun even further and hit my hands even harder. The bounce and rip were extraordinary. Here, clearly, was a young player of infinite potential, already excelling in the hardest of all cricketing arts.

Within weeks he was named for Victoria and all of us began to dine out on the time we played against the likeable, blond-haired schoolboy who even then had class with a capital C.

ACKNOWLEDGEMENTS

The Complete Shane Warne pays homage to Australia's new Test wickets record-holder, a natural, likeable young man who emerged in spectacular fashion to inspire and establish new standards of excellence in the most fascinating and difficult cricketing art of all.

In compiling a match-by-match record of Warne's career, I've been fortunate to have access to some of the most diligent statistical minds of them all. Ken Williams spent weeks over the records section and happily embarked on fresh, specific research tracking never-before-published information like, for example, the percentage of Warne's top-order victims and his strike rate against left-handers – a surprisingly healthy figure given his perceived weakness against them.

The sourcing of original scores at both international and state level would not have been possible without the generous assistance and support of Mike Walsh, the Australian Cricket Board's official scorer, and Peter Binns and staff from the Victorian Cricket Association.

Statisticians including Aslam Siddiqui, Pieter Barnard, Bill Frindall, Peter Griffiths, John King, Charlie Wat, Ric Finlay and others from the Association of Cricket Statisticians have been very kind with their time in answering queries, as have many players with their reminiscenses.

The researches of Allan Miller and his *Allan's Cricket's Annual* were invaluable. No genuine cricket lover's library can be complete without a set.

Most of the photographs supplied have come from Patrick Eagar, David Munden, Ken Rainsbury, Sergio Dionisio and Stephen Laffer.

Shane Warne's management was asked if Shane would like to have an involvement. They said no.

PREFACE

Shane Warne was hosting a party at his million-dollar Brighton Beach property for some old friends when one saw his red Ferrari and said: 'Mate, you've done alright for a fella who used to cart beds.'

Warne stared, suddenly serious. 'I've taken my chance and run with it,' he said. 'Everyone gets a chance at some time. It's a matter of taking it when it comes.'

No longer was Warne the happy-go-lucky, social butterfly who treated cricket as a diversion.

He may have been the Chosen One, fast-tracked like no one before or since and enjoying more than his share of life's luxuries, but he'd deserved it and was grateful. For all his extroverted ways, over-exuberance and good fortune, his commitment, focus and hard work ethic have been absolute.

He may have been blessed with the ability to rip prodigious leg-spinners with a flick of a wrist, but it could all have ended prematurely years ago, when thumped on debut by the Indians in Sydney, or more recently after career-threatening operations.

For a roly-poly, hesitant rookie afraid to bowl his googly in his maiden Test in case it bounced twice, Warne's advancement has been as extraordinary as his start. In Auckland earlier this year, he became Australia's all-time Test wicket record-holder, surpassing the feats of his childhood idol Dennis Lillee.

He has made mistakes and has genuine regrets, but few have so consistently exerted such a matchwinning influence or so rejuvenated what seemed to be a lost art.

Challenging convention with his dyed-blond hair and liking for custom jewellery, Warne has enlivened cricket with his flamboyance and personality.

He's also showed great courage to bowl and keep bowling, despite the deleterious effect it was having on his body. Win-at-all costs it might have been, but had his first captain, Allan Border, not bowled him into the ground so often, Warne's very best years would surely have extended longer.

For all the warts, millions of cricket fans around the world are privileged to have seen Warne bowl. Without his ability to demoralise, Australia would not today be the reigning World Cup champions.

No one, not even Lillee, has intimidated or so consistently confounded opposing batsmen. Like kangaroos dazzled by headlights, opposing batsmen have been powerless to stop his momentum.

A spinner with a fast bowler's psyche, Warne's genius in perfecting a series of menacing, mysterious deliveries like the flipper and the zoota and the spitting leg-break others can only dream about has led to a rare celebrity status and levels of adulation unparalleled since the Bradman era.

Before he finishes, body withstanding, he may even become the first to take 500 Test wickets, one of world cricket's previously unobtainable records. Maybe by then even the non-believers will have been converted.

Warne may not be everybody's idea of a national treasure, but without him over the last ten years, the game would never have been as irresistible or diverting. Like a young Don Bradman who lifted spirits during the Depression with his fabulous runmaking feats, Warne has given cricket a kiss of life which should endure for years.

PART ONE

FIRST-CLASS CRICKET

1990–91

IN THE WINTER of 1990, Shane Warne at 20 was little more than a precocious young hopeful, living away from home for the first time and struggling to adjust to the disciplines required at Australian cricket's just-established finishing school, the Australian Cricket Academy in Adelaide.

Showy, fun-loving and with a larrikin streak, he'd been plucked from the anonymity of Melbourne club ranks with little pedigree or performance, and found himself working daily with the most feted young cricketers in the country, including budding internationals Greg Blewett, Justin Langer, Damien Martyn and the 16-year-old Tasmanian prodigy Ricky Ponting.

Had he been a batsman or a fast bowler, the interest in him would have been passing and in all probability he would have been playing with his mates in the lower grades at St Kilda, or back in sub-district ranks on the beach at Brighton. But as a young spin bowler in an era so besotted by pace that spin bowlers were rapidly becoming redundant, Warne was treated as something special and fast-tracked like no other slow bowler in the history of Australian cricket.

Impressed by the kid's rare ability to bowl effortless, big-spinning leg-breaks, the Academy's head coach Jack Potter regarded him as an immediate find. He showed him some variations including the flipper – the faster, skidding delivery aimed at deceiving even the most eagle-eyed batsman – and marvelled at his ability to absorb it all.

Warne's improvement and temperament to rise to the challenge was first on show in two limited-over friendlies with the touring Englishmen at St Peter's College. He took just one wicket, but was the only one to make double figures twice. Clearly he enjoyed the heat of the battle and was undaunted by the challenge of confronting big names.

Even more significantly, he'd established a rapport with Terry Jenner, the former Test leg-spinner dabbling in coaching as part of his own rehabilitation after a prison sentence. They were kindred spirits – impulsive, rebellious and brilliant. From the time they made eye contact and shook hands, there was an affinity between them, Jenner rating Warne's ability to rip his leg-break as a gift from God and Warne warming to Jenner's knockabout honesty, knowledge and punchlining stories.

The first leg-spinner Warne bowled to Jenner in the nets at Adelaide No. 2 spun so sharply that Jenner wondered if it had hit a pebble. When the second one bit just as much, he smiled to himself and said: 'Jeeeesssuus Chrrrriiisst, we've got something here.' For an old leg-spinner it was manna from heaven. Here was a natural with the ability to be a world-beater.

The Academy was only in its infancy and the teething problems with programs and accommodation sometimes led to a shortfall in humour, especially from some staff members. Many of the inductees, Warne included, were staying in hotels yet were barred from even entering the front bar. Fines were commonplace, for latecomers and even for indiscretions as trivial as farting on the mini-bus.

Still overweight after a winter of club cricket in England, Warne rebelled against the regimentation and so offended authority that Robert de Castella, the head of the Australian Institute of Sport in Canberra, became involved.

As a disciplinary measure, Warne was omitted from an Academy-based tour of Sri Lanka and after a week training by himself and with the South Australian Sheffield Shield squad, he penned a note of resignation, left it at Academy headquarters and promptly drove back to Melbourne, determined to show how much he had improved, despite the hiccups.

In a club game, he was bowling to ex-Test fast bowler Rodney Hogg, who at 40 was in his farewell senior season. After a third giant leg-break hummed past his outside edge, Hogg turned to St Kilda's captain Shaun Graf at slip and wide-eyed said, 'This bloke is going to play for Australia.'

The following week, in his column in *Truth* newspaper, Hogg said he'd just played against a kid who could easily take 500 Test wickets. He was immediately sacked.

IN AUSTRALIA

1. **Victoria v Western Australia**, at St Kilda Cricket Ground, Melbourne, 15, 16, 17 & 18 February 1991.
SCORES
WESTERN AUSTRALIA 418 for 6 wickets dec. (G. M. Wood 166, M. P. Lavender 118, D. R. Martyn 68 not out) and 197 for 4 wickets dec. (T. M. Moody 73, G. M. Wood 50); VICTORIA 342 (G. M. Watts 81; M. J. McCague 5/105) and 64 for 1 wicket. **Drawn**.
S. K. WARNE
1st inns: 18 overs – 7 maidens – 61 runs – 0 wickets.
2nd inns: 19–6–41–1. Dismissed: T. M. Moody c D. W. Fleming 73.

Just weeks after bailing out of the Cricket Academy, ending his tumultuous eight-month stay, Warne, 21, was named at Sheffield Shield level for the first time, ahead of Victoria's two senior slow bowlers, left-arm finger-spinner Paul Jackson (who was made 12th man) and fellow leg-spinner Peter McIntyre.

With nine wickets in two maiden games with the Victorian second XI, Warne had shown promise and some poise, but the step-up in class was defining. He may have been one of the few young wrist-spinners in the country, but he'd served the barest of apprenticeships. He was overweight and with his flowing, shoulder-length blond hair and ear-stud looked more like a surfie than an aspiring first-class cricketer.

As reassuring as it was to be playing at the Junction Oval (St Kilda's home ground and the temporary stronghold for Victorian cricket with the Melbourne Cricket Ground's Great Southern Stand under construction), Warne was nervous and uptight. Having been a third XI club-standard player just 18 months previously, the pressure so enveloped him he felt like a novice.

Senior Victorians Merv Hughes and Dean Jones had left for the Caribbean and Warne was one of two Victorians making their debut, alongside rangy seam bowler Peter Smith, 23, from South Melbourne via Geelong. Three West Australians were also chosen for the first time: opening batsman Mark Lavender and pace pair Martin McCague and Mark Wasley.

Introduced from the city end just before the lunch break, Warne saw his opening two deliveries smashed to the boundary by Lavender and his fourth hit for three. His first over cost 11 and when re-introduced later, his next went for nine.

So overcome by nerves was he that he could hardly feel the ball in his hand. And so wide was he stepping on the return crease, that umpire Len King several times had to warn him he was on the verge of being no-balled.

Lavender made 118 and veteran Graeme Wood 166, the pair adding 195 for the second wicket. Warne improved his line but still conceded 61 runs from 18 overs in three spells.

By batting almost five sessions, WA ensured the game would be fought only for first-innings points. Warne made 20, batting at No. 9, before being stumped by Tim Zoehrer from the left-arm orthodox slows of WA captain Wayne Andrews.

In the second innings, WA international Tom Moody lifted Warne for a huge six down the ground into the dirt mounds at the Fitzroy Street end of the ground. Two balls later, attempting another big hit, he skied a steepling catch to Damien Fleming at long-on. After 30 overs for the match, it was Warne's first major wicket. While he'd felt more relaxed in the second innings, his match figures were an unflattering 1/102 from 37 overs. However, he did have one catch grassed, Wood (on 49), early on day one, by captain Simon O'Donnell at shortish midwicket.

'It was straight in and straight out,' said O'Donnell. 'I picked it up and threw it back to Warnie and said, "C'mon fellas, keep at it," just trying to put doubt into people's minds that perhaps it was a bump ball. It wasn't. It was a very easy catch.'

Wood, a veteran of 59 Tests, became Western Australia's highest run-scorer during the game. It was the only time he ever opposed Warne. 'It was a good deck and he was quite uptight and nervous and didn't have the variety he's got now,' said Wood. 'My son, Christopher, asks me now if I faced Shane Warne and I say, "Yeah, I've always had the better of him" and show him the one scoresheet!'

It was to be Warne's only Victorian match of the season. A week later, he was back at St Kilda . . . and in a quirk of selection, playing in the second XI!

SUMMARY, 1990–91 (Australia)

	Mts	Overs	Mdn	Runs	Wicks	Ave	BB	5wI	10wM
Sheffield Shield match	1	37	13	102	1	102.00	1/41	–	–

1991–92

THE START OF THE 90s was a period of euphoria for the Australian XI, triggered by the team's resounding back-to-back victories against traditional foe England. However, seeking bigger game, the national selectors had reinforced their priority to find a quality spin bowler. The West Indies had paraded as world cricket's champion force for more than ten years, their battery of fast bowlers and champion batsmen producing an enviable, unsurpassed run of success.

Their only apparent weakness was against slow bowlers capable of spinning the ball from the leg, either a right-arm leg-spinner like Queensland's Trevor Hohns or a left-arm finger-spinner à la Allan Border.

After some important contributions in England, Hohns had been asked to continue into the 1990–91 Ashes summer with a view of touring the West Indies the following autumn. But at 36, he felt obligated to his family and business and while he did captain Queensland throughout the domestic summer, it was to be his farewell season.

Border, also in his 30s, had always been a reluctant slow bowler, even after his astonishing, career-best double of 7/46 and 4/50 to trigger the Windies' only loss of the 1988–89 Test summer, in Sydney.

He'd fill in as a fifth or sixth bowler at one-day level, but never seriously rated himself at first-class level. In the five Tests against the 1990–91 Englishmen, he'd given himself only 28 overs and taken just one wicket. In 1989, he'd bowled even less.

Peter Taylor, a specialist off-spinner from Northern District in Sydney, had shown promise, but he bent the ball back into the right-handers and at 34 was only ever going to be short term.

From being members of a threatened species, wrist-spinners around the country were suddenly being eyed with fresh benevolence. However, not all were prepared to look at the big picture and when Warne and fellow leg-spinner Peter McIntyre were chosen for the Australia 'B' team tour of Zimbabwe in September, Victorian coach Les Stillman said the selections were not only premature and unwarranted, it placed abnormal pressure on the Victorian selectors back home.

Hohns' unavailablity had so thinned Australia's spin bowling ranks that the national selectors had little choice but to experiment on the six-match, 21-day tour of Zimbabwe, then only a cricketing fledgling without full Test status.

No specialist leg-spinner had been ranked highly enough to deserve a place in the No. 1 team to the West Indies the previous autumn. Instead, the NSW finger-spinners Greg Matthews and Taylor toured and had been thrashed.

With Hohns and fellow veteran, 34-year-old South Australian Peter 'Sounda' Sleep out of the equation, Warne, McIntyre and Western Australia's multi-gifted Tim Zoehrer, who'd been combining wicket-keeping with some leggies and googlies, were among the few wrist-spinning prospects.

As keen as the selectors were to test Warne, it was considered preferable to blood him on the bigger grounds of Zimbabwe against a far less intimidating set of batsmen, even if he had been successful in the Caribbean before, on a youth tour 12 months earlier.

Warne was match-fit and full of momentum having taken 73 Lancashire League wickets with Accrington during his second winter in

England. At The Oval Test he'd also had an inpromptu chat with Richie Benaud, Australia's most celebrated wrist-spin bowler.

The Australian 'B' team, the first to be captained by Mark Taylor, featured several other Test players including Steve Waugh and Tom Moody. It was prelude to an extraordinary summer for the rising young spinner from bayside Melbourne.

AUSTRALIA IN ZIMBABWE

2. **Australia B v Zimbabwe**, at Bulawayo Athletic Club, 16, 17, 18 & 19 September 1991.
SCORES
AUSTRALIA B 483 (T. M. Moody 141, S. R. Waugh 119, P. R. Reiffel 54 not out, M. G. Bevan 54) and 20 for no wicket; ZIMBABWE 193 (G. W. Flower 74) and 309 (G. W. Flower 84, K. J. Arnott 60; P. R. Reiffel 5/43). **Australia B won by ten wickets**.
S. K. WARNE
1st inns: 20–5–42–0.
2nd inns: 24.4–8–76–3. Dismissed: A. J. Pycroft lbw 30; D. L. Houghton b 5; M. P. Jarvis c P. R. Reiffel 17.

A first-ball duck and a wicketless first innings on his Australian representative debut was followed by 25 overs in the second innings and 3/76, including David Houghton, Zimbabwe's captain and master batsman, bowled by a flipper. Warne also unveiled his 'Derryn Hinch' expect-the-unexpected ball, a deliberate head-high full toss, aimed at forcing a surprised batsman into a mishit.

Writing in *Time to Declare*, Australian captain Mark Taylor said Warne, even then, was an exceptional talent: 'In those days the most famous blond in cricket had more of a "bluey" look about him: his hair had more of a reddish tinge than it does today. For a young leg-spinner he just about had it all. Warne 1991 was not too different from Warne now – a bit of a larrikin and an outstanding talent.'

Taylor was impressed that he could hear the ball hum as it came down the wicket, a sure sign that the rookie Victorian was trying to extract as much sideways spin as possible.

3. **Australia B v Zimbabwe**, at Harare Sports Club, 21, 23, 24 &
25 September 1991.

SCORES

ZIMBABWE 239 (D. L. Houghton 105 not out; D. J. Hickey 5/72) and 179
(D. L. Houghton 57 not out; S. K. Warne 7/49); AUSTRALIA B 383
(S. G. Law 94, T. M. Moody 85, R. J. Tucker 62; E. A. Brandes 6/95)
and 36 for 1 wicket. **Australia B won by nine wickets**.

S. K. WARNE

1st inns: 17–5–40–1. Dismissed: A. G. Huckle lbw 1.
2nd inns: 36–10–49–7. Dismissed: K. J. Arnott b 47; G. W. Flower lbw 27;
A. D. R. Campbell c T. M. Moody 7; A. Flower b 6; N. P. Hough
c T. M. Moody 5; M. G. Burmester c M. A. Taylor 5; A. G. Huckle lbw 0.

Taking eight wickets for the game, including a career-best 7/49 from
36 overs in Zimbabwe's second innings, Warne inspired the Australia
B team's second victory of their campaign. Four of his victims were
bowled or lbw and a fifth caught at slip by Taylor. Peter McIntyre,
with four first-innings wickets, was also effective.

'Shane spins the ball sharply and with the bounce in the pitch he
was able to produce some nice variation which did the job for [Mark]
Taylor,' Australian team manager and national selector John Benaud
said. 'He's also got a good sense of humour for a leg-spinner, which is
just as well as they get thrashed around a bit.'

Warne also made his most notable batting contributions of the
tour, with 35 not out from 45 balls in the first innings (2 fours and
2 sixes) and 18 not out, opening the innings in the second. The first
three deliveries he faced from paceman Eddo Brandes were hit to
the fence as the Australians took just 3.3 overs to score 36 runs for
victory.

SUMMARY, 1991–92 (ZIMBABWE)

	Mts	Overs	Mdn	Runs	Wicks	Ave	BB	5wI	10wM
All First-Class matches	2	97.4	28	207	11	18.81	7/49	1	–

In Australia

4. **Victoria v Tasmania**, at Melbourne Cricket Ground, 1, 2, 3 &
4 November 1991.
Scores
Victoria 434 for 8 wickets dec. (D. M. Jones 243 not out) and 109 for
no wicket (D. J. Ramshaw 58 not out); Tasmania 372 (J. Cox 82,
D. J. Buckingham 73). **Drawn**.
S. K. Warne
Only inns: 47–14–75–4. Dismissed: B. A. Cruse b 25; R. J. Tucker
c D. S. Berry 7; J. Cox c D. S. Berry 82; D. R. Gilbert c S. P. O'Donnell 2.

Having at the eleventh hour baulked at an offer to play in Sydney
with the Bankstown club, home of the Waugh twins, Warne was
named ahead of the more-experienced McIntyre and Paul Jackson
(12th man) for the opening match against Tasmania as Victoria
defended its Sheffield Shield.

On a rock-hard Melbourne Cricket Ground batting track, Dean
Jones made an unbeaten 243 and Victoria amassed 8/434 declared.
So impressed were the workers on the MCG's new Southern Stand
that, in pink paint, they christened it the Dean Jones Stand.

In addition to scoring 41 and 43 not out on his debut, Northcote's
Gerard Dowling made an immediate name for himself by bringing
sandwiches and fruit in a lunch-box from home. 'No one told me that
we'd get lunch at the ground,' he said.

Given immediate responsibility as first-change bowler ahead of
Paul Reiffel and captain Simon O'Donnell, the reigning International
Cricketer of the Year, Warne bowled Tasmanian opener Bruce Cruse
before having David Boon (0) dropped at slip by O'Donnell.

Extracting consistent spin and drift, Warne was impressively accurate, O'Donnell ringing the Tasmanian batsmen with close-in fieldsmen. His first 11 overs cost just nine runs and he conceded little more
than a run an over for the first 30 overs, extraordinary bowling for a
wrist-spinner.

On the final day he triggered a Tasmanian collapse when Jamie Cox (82) was caught behind at the second attempt by Darren Berry. 'On the surface he looks okay,' said Tasmanian captain Boon. 'He's extremely tight and has a lot of control for a leg-spinner. He's going to have to bowl on different types of wickets. Halfway through the year when he's bowled everywhere, we can really make a calculation on where he's going.'

---

5. **Victoria v New South Wales**, at Sydney Cricket Ground, 8, 9, 10 & 11 November 1991.
Scores
NEW SOUTH WALES 459 (G. R. J. Matthews 139, S. R. Waugh 88, S. M. Small 79); VICTORIA 260 (D. M. Jones 68, D. J. Ramshaw 53) and 394 for 6 wickets (D. M. Jones 144, D. S. Lehmann 66, D. J. Ramshaw 60). **Drawn**.
S. K. WARNE
Only inns: 22–3–76–0.

Bowling in front of national selector John Benaud, Warne went wicketless on his first visit to the Sydney Cricket Ground, suddenly minus the last patch of grass on its once-famous Hill. In conceding more than three an over, despite sending down only one full toss and no discernible long-hops, he showed a frailty against the left-handers.

Test off-spinner Greg Matthews was particularly keen to assert his authority and in Warne's 18th over, shortly before the introduction of the second new ball, Matthews lifted him for 2 sixes and 1 four on his way to a three-hour 139. The following day, when Warne came in at No. 11, Matthews welcomed him with a bumper, or in cricket-speak, a 'Kuala'.

Warne's control, however, was commendable and he had two chances fumbled: Steve Waugh (at 36) to a leg-side stumping attempt by Darren Berry and Trevor Bayliss (0) by Dean Jones on the cut shot.

'He showed promise as an exuberant cricketer constructed along generous lines,' said Peter Roebuck in the *Sydney Morning Herald*.

'But it seems premature to cast Warne as Australia's leading spinner. Sometimes the heart runs far ahead of the brain.'

Replying to headlines that Warne's early efforts could see him rewarded with immediate Australian selection, Victorian captain Simon O'Donnell replied: 'If you bowl leg-spin in this country, people go a bit onky-ponky. I just hope people have enough sense to let people learn their art before they start hailing them as national heroes.

'Shane has played only three or four games. You've got to give kids like him a chance to mature. I hope the public expectation is not there that there's the robot, send him out there and he'll bowl out Imran Khan, Viv Richards and the rest around the world.'

NSW clinched first-innings points, but not before Victorian opener Darrin Ramshaw (53 in five-and-a-half hours) had made the slowest half-century by an Australian in first-class cricket. It took him two hours to go from 1 to 14. Warne (16) added 57 for the 10th wicket with Paul Reiffel (42 not out).

'Just four matches and 16 wickets into his first-class career, Victorian leg-spinner Shane Warne is on the verge of a Test berth. Crazy as it may seem on those figures, 22-year-old Warne could find himself in the Australian side for the opening Test against India in Brisbane later this month.' TRENT BOUTS, *Herald Sun*, 8 November 1991

---

6. **Victoria v South Australia**, at Melbourne Cricket Ground, 15, 16, 17 & 18 November 1991.

SCORES

VICTORIA 514 for 8 wickets dec. (D. M. Jones 214, W. N. Phillips 121); SOUTH AUSTRALIA 244 (A. M. J. Hilditch 103) and 246 (J. A. Brayshaw 90, A. M. J. Hilditch 50). *Victoria won by an innings & 24 runs*.

S. K. WARNE

1st inns: 25.3–3–67–3. Dismissed: J. A. Brayshaw b 23; J. D. Siddons st D. S. Berry 2; D. J. Hickey lbw 13.
2nd inns: 17–6–43–0.

Another MCG run-spree led by Jones, who increased his season aggregate to 669 runs for just three times out, set up Victoria's outright win, Warne again central to the success with three key wickets in the first innings which caused South Australia to follow on. Drifting the ball appreciably, he had Jamie Siddons, in his first year as SA captain, stumped down the leg side to a full-length ball for two.

He also batted aggressively, hitting Tim May for 2 sixes over midwicket on his way to 30 from just 14 balls as Victoria, sent in to bat, declared at 8/514.

While Warne was wicketless in the SA second innings, all ten wickets being taken by the pacemen, his national prospects seemed buoyant. Australian selection chairman Lawrie Sawle confirmed that Warne was 'short-listed' for the Test team. 'We flagged to Victoria our interest in him by picking him for Zimbabwe,' he said. 'We're delighted Victoria are playing him and have stuck with him.'

Siddons had his jaw fractured when struck in the face by the fifth ball he faced from Merv Hughes, who said he felt sick having injured his old team-mate.

Emerging SA all-rounder Joe Scuderi withdrew from the game after a bout of influenza, saying he would not have passed a drug test after all the prescribed medicine he'd had.

'There may well be a need later in the season to induct one or two young bowlers into the side with an eye to the future, to give them a bit of exposure to international cricket. The old guard can't carry the bowling attack forever.'

Australia's chairman of selectors, LAWRIE SAWLE

---

7. **Australian XI v West Indies**, at Bellerive Oval, Hobart, 20 (no play), 21, 22 & 23 December 1991.
SCORES
WEST INDIES 235 (B. C. Lara 83) and 133; AUSTRALIAN XI 461 for 9 wickets dec. (T. M. Moody 70, S. G. Law 68, C. D. Matthews 63, M. G. Bevan 58,

W. N. Phillips 51). *Australian XI won by an innings & 93 runs*.
S. K. WARNE
1st inns: 5.1–1–14–3. Dismissed: B. C. Lara c W. N. Phillips 83;
A. C. Cummins b 23; B. P. Patterson c P. R. Reiffel 2.
2nd inns: 15.2–6–42–4. Dismissed: C. L. Hooper c M. G. Bevan 33;
R. C. Haynes c. C. D. Matthews 1; H. A. G. Anthony c sub (J. Cox) 15;
B. P. Patterson st I. A. Healy 0.

After serving as Victoria's 12th man in Brisbane, when four fast bowlers were chosen at the exclusion of a specialist spinner, Warne was named for an Australian XI against the touring West Indians, maintaining his reputation as the country's most promising young spinner.

In their only first-class fixture of their tour, the West Indians were beaten inside three days after the first had been rained out. Six tourists made their Australian debut, including 22-year-old Brian Lara, whose enterprising 83 in three-and-a-half hours confirmed his status alongside India's Sachin Tendulkar as one of the game's emerging champions.

Warne was the fifth bowler used in the first innings. He wasn't introduced until 59 overs had been bowled. In the second, he was on at first change. While he took seven cheap wickets, only two were in the top order, Lara in the first innings and Carl Hooper in the second.

Adding fuel to suggestions that he was about to be called up, the Australian selectors named a team only for the Melbourne Test against India, rather than also releasing a squad to include the Sydney Test starting just days afterwards.

'Warne is just the sort of boy to put a breath of excitement into the Australian attack and he could swing the series . . . I almost needed ear muffs when the ball came out of his hand [at the Academy nets]. It was really humming. I hadn't heard a ball come out of a leggie's hand quite like that before.'

Australian Cricket Academy head coach and wicketkeeping great
ROD MARSH

8/1. **Australia v India**, Third Test Match, at Sydney Cricket Ground,
2, 3, 4, 5 & 6 January 1992.
Scores
Australia 313 (D. C. Boon 129 not out, M. A. Taylor 56) and 173 for
8 wickets (A. R. Border 53 not out); India 483 (R. J. Shastri 206,
S. R. Tendulkar 148). **Drawn**.
S. K. Warne
Only inns: 45–7–150–1. Dismissed: R. J. Shastri c D. M. Jones 206.

TEST

Warne's seven-wicket haul at Bellerive was enough to convince the national selectors that he was 'ready', despite his minimal apprenticeship. Having played just four games of Sheffield Shield cricket, he was included in the 12 for Sydney ahead of home town hero Greg Matthews and Peter Taylor, who'd taken just one wicket in the opening two Tests.

'Hopefully I can look after him and not expect him to come on after five or six overs and start knocking blokes over,' said captain Allan Border. 'If we use him properly and well, he'll develop into a very good leg-spinner. It's more of a development process than expecting instant results.'

Other than a one-off appearance in the annual Prime Minister's XI game at Manuka Oval a fortnight earlier, Warne had not opposed the Indians. He hadn't even met several of his new team-mates.

There was prolonged applause as he walked onto the Sydney Cricket Ground early on the second day and the electronic scoreboard flashed: CONGRATULATIONS SHANE WARNE, AUSTRALIA'S 350TH TEST PLAYER. It remains one of his all-time favourite career moments. Fewer than 14 000 were present but it felt and sounded like a capacity crowd.

In at No. 10, Warne shared a 44-run ninth-wicket stand with centurion David Boon, before he was caught behind for 20, having batted for more than an hour.

The wicket was slow and devoid of bounce. Walking out, Border wished Warne luck and as an aside quipped, 'Just don't do a Johnny Watkins on us,' a reference to the Newcastle leg-spinner overcome by nerves in his infamous one and only Test match at the SCG almost 20 years previously.

Bruce Reid's breakdown after just four overs forced Border to reassess his pre-match strategies. To another huge reception, he introduced Warne in the 18th over of the innings, from the Randwick end. Ian Chappell, in the Channel Nine commentary box, rang Terry Jenner, Warne's coach, in Adelaide and turning up the effects microphone said, 'Listen to this mate. And this for a leg-spinner . . .'

Warne says he was panicking as Border set the field and as he took a deep breath and walked in to bowl, he hoped it wouldn't bounce twice.

The striker, Sanjay Manjrekar, struck Warne's fourth ball through the covers for four, but played the rest defensively and with respect. Swapped to the Paddington end, he bowled another long hop in his third over which was also dispatched. Throughout several lengthy spells, he relied almost exclusively on his leg-break with the occasional flipper. He didn't trust himself to bowl a genuine googly.

The Indians are masterful players of spin and both Ravi Shastri and a teenage Sachin Tendulkar were superb, Shastri's inside-out drives peppering the extra cover boundary. He had scored 206 before he went down the ground once too often and sliced the ball high to extra cover and a fleet-of-foot Dean Jones, who had dashed in from the boundary. It had taken Warne 41 overs and 244 balls to break through. Earlier he'd dropped Shastri at 66 to a sharp caught and bowled chance.

The Indians amassed 483 and Australia had to fight hard on the fifth afternoon to save the game. Warne's figures of 1/150 from 45 overs mirrored his feelings of inadequacy. He may have been Australia's 350th Test player, but he and everyone else knew his selection had been a brave one and was based more on potential than performance.

One veteran observer remained convinced of Warne's worth. The legendary Bill 'Tiger' O'Reilly, then 86, wrote in the *Sunday Age*, 'I am prepared to accept him with open arms to the important spin society . . . there are tonnes of easy pickings waiting out there along the track . . .' As always, the Tiger was right on the money.

9. Victoria v Tasmania, at Bellerive Oval, Hobart, 17, 18, 19 &
20 January 1992.

SCORES

VICTORIA 200 (W. N. Phillips 67; C. D. Matthews 5/48) and 246 for
5 wickets dec. (W. G. Ayres 100 not out, A. I. C. Dodemaide 53 not out);
TASMANIA 157 (A. I. C. Dodemaide 5/34) and 211 for 8 wickets. ***Drawn.***

S. K. WARNE

1st inns: 14–7–26–2. Dismissed: C. D. Matthews c D. S. Berry 15;
D. R. Gilbert c D. S. Lehmann 0.

2nd inns: 22–6–66–1. Dismissed: G. A. Hughes c S. P. O'Donnell 18.

With the finals of the World Series Cup taking precedence, Warne
returned to Sheffield Shield ranks where Victoria, the ladder leaders,
could only draw against Tasmania.

Warne took 2/26 in the first innings and 1/66 in the second. His sixth
over on the second day went for ten, courtesy of a six and a four by Dene
Hills. Team-mate Tony Dodemaide claimed six wickets for the game,
including the remarkable figures of 5/34 from 35 overs in Tasmania's
laborious first innings which produced just 157 runs from 99 overs.

'Basically I wanted to be a footy player. It wasn't until I was 13 or 14
that I started playing junior cricket and was shown the basics of leg-
spin. I've no idea why I stuck with it. I could never land the bloody
thing then.'   SHANE WARNE

10/2. Australia v India, Fourth Test Match, at Adelaide Oval, 25, 26, 27,
28 & 29 January 1992.

SCORES

AUSTRALIA 145 and 451 (D. C. Boon 135, M. A. Taylor 100, A. R. Border 91
not out; Kapil Dev 5/130); INDIA 225 (Kapil Dev 56; C. J. McDermott 5/76)
and 333 (M. Azharuddin 106; C. J. McDermott 5/92). ***Australia won by
38 runs***.

TEST

S. K. WARNE

1st inns: 7–1–18–0.

2nd inns: 16–1–60–0.

The Adelaide Test, Warne's second, was notable for the dramatic final day in which Allan Border, in true Captain Grumpy style, initially refused to take the field after learning that his long-time deputy Geoff Marsh and Mark Waugh had been dropped from the fifth Test team.

Set 372 to win, India played superbly, captain Muhammad Azharuddin making a classical 106, including 80 between lunch and tea. Warne went for 47 runs from 12 overs as India marched back into the game. However, once Azharuddin fell to Craig McDermott and the second new ball, the Indians collapsed, handing Australia the match.

A week later, in Perth, Warne was 12th man, the Australians winning comfortably with Michael Whitney, one of four pacemen included in the XI, taking a career-best 4/68 and 7/27.

---

11. **Victoria v New South Wales**, at Melbourne Cricket Ground, 13 (no play), 14, 15 & 16 February 1992.
SCORES
NEW SOUTH WALES 280 (M. A. Taylor 158) and 273 for 6 wickets dec.
(M. E. Waugh 76, M. G. Bevan 70, M. A. Taylor 53); VICTORIA 338
(P. C. Nobes 61, D. M. Jones 54) and 17 for no wicket. **Drawn**.
S. K. WARNE
1st inns: 10–2–35–0.
2nd inns: 20–8–78–1. Dismissed: T. H. Bayliss c W. N. Phillips 7.

Victoria's return game against New South Wales was drawn after unseasonal rains washed out the entire first day's play. Faster bowlers claimed all but three wickets to fall, Victoria taking the first-innings points despite a six-hour marathon from Mark Taylor who batted through the NSW innings and was last out for 158.

Warne's second ball of the match was hit for six by Greg Matthews and he was used only sparingly. However, he bowled 20 overs in the second, taking 1/78. Three of his first four overs were maidens, 13 came off his 11th and 17 from his last (4 6 . 4 3 .), courtesy of an in-command Michael Bevan. His only wicket, Trevor Bayliss, was caught at point.

12. **Victoria v South Australia**, at Adelaide Oval, 21, 22, 23 &
24 February 1992.

SCORES

VICTORIA 461 for 9 wickets dec. (A. I. C. Dodemaide 117 not out,
D. S. Lehmann 112, S. P. O'Donnell 87) and 175 for 4 wickets dec.
(P. C. Nobes 76 not out); SOUTH AUSTRALIA 316 for 7 wickets dec.
(J. A. Brayshaw 101, A. M. J. Hilditch 63) and 299 for 9 wickets
(J. D. Siddons 65, J. C. Scuderi 57). ***Drawn.***

S. K. WARNE

1st inns: 35–15–67–1. Dismissed: J. D. Siddons c A. I. C. Dodemaide 21.
2nd inns: 11–1–36–0.

In David Hookes' Adelaide farewell, during which he created a new
high for the most runs in Sheffield Shield cricket, Warne was outbowled by Paul Jackson, playing only his second game of the Shield
season, and first alongside the chubby leggie. Bowling all but ten of
his 46 overs·from the northern end, Warne took just one wicket and
Jackson five, with South Australia forcing a draw with one wicket in
hand.

In Victoria's first innings Warne (14) and Tony Dodemade (117 not
out) added 57 for the ninth wicket.

Warne finished his tumultuous, topsy-turvy first full season as Victoria's 12th man in the final match of the summer against Queensland
at the MCG, the Vics' failure to force an outright costing them a place
in the Shield final, ultimately won by Western Australia in Perth.

SUMMARY, 1991–92 (AUSTRALIA)

	Mts	Overs	Mdn	Runs	Wicks	Ave	BB	5wI	10wM
All First-Class matches	9	312	81	853	20	42.65	4/42	–	–
Test matches v India	2	68	9	228	1	228.00	1/150	–	–
Australian XI v West Indies	1	20.3	7	56	7	8.00	4/42	–	–
Sheffield Shield matches	6	213.3	65	569	12	47.41	4/75	–	–

1992–93

IT WAS APRIL and Shane Warne walked into friend and mentor Terry Jenner's small unit in Adelaide sure of his welcome and armed with a slab of beer and two bottles of red, one for Jenner and the other for Australian Cricket Academy head coach Rod Marsh.

The normally affable Jenner was noticeably quiet and the atmosphere tense.

'Are we going to have a beer?' said Warne.

'No, we're not going to have a beer.'

'Why . . . what's wrong?'

'I'm angry, Shane,' said Jenner. He'd been waiting for the opportunity to let him have it.

'If you want to play Test cricket again, you have to make sacrifices,' said Jenner. 'You have to get fitter and be more focused.'

Warne stared at the floor and said nothing.

'What sacrifices have you made, Shane? Can you name even one?'

Again there was dead silence. Warne was a chain smoker, a drinker and loved partying.

'Shane,' said Jenner, 'you have to be the best you can possibly be.

Don't make the mistakes I did. You have a gift and you have the opportunity. But unless you work harder than you ever have before, you're going to disappear and regret it the rest of your life.'

Two weeks later Brigitte Warne, Shane's mother, phoned from Melbourne. 'I don't know what you said, Terry, but it's working,' she said. 'He is running every morning bar Tuesday when he goes to golf. He has already lost four kilograms.'

By the start of Australia's springtime tour of Sri Lanka, Warne had lost 13 kilograms thanks to his dawn runs around Half Moon Bay and a new, health-conscious diet, including no alcohol or fatty foods of any description.

At Tullamarine, waiting for the flight to Colombo's Bandaranaike International Airport, captain Allan Border looked at the once-chubby Warne and nodded approvingly. Here was a kid desperate to play for Australia.

Australia in Sri Lanka

13/3. **Australia v Sri Lanka**, First Test Match, at Sinhalese Sports Club Ground, Colombo, 17, 18, 19, 21 & 22 August 1992.

Scores

Australia 256 (I. A. Healy 66 not out) and 471 (D. C. Boon 68, G. R. J. Matthews 64, M. E. Waugh 56); Sri Lanka 547 for 8 wickets dec. (A. P. Gurusinha 137, R. S. Kaluwitharana 132 not out, A. Ranatunga 127, R. S. Mahanama 78) and 164. **Australia won by 16 runs**.

TEST

S. K. Warne

1st inns: 22–2–107–0.

2nd inns: 5.1–3–11–3. Dismissed: G. P. Wickremasinghe c M. E. Waugh 2; S. D. Anurasiri c M. E. Waugh 1; M. A. W. R. Madurasinghe c G. R. J. Matthews 0.

Allan Border had never been renowned as a gambler, especially on anything as serious as a cricket match. But his role in helping trigger Australia's greatest-ever comeback at the Sinhalese Sports Club in Colombo is underrated.

Trailing by 291 runs on the first innings, the Australians fought hard to avoid an innings defeat and with tailenders Craig McDermott (40), Warne (35) and Mike Whitney (10 not out) adding some valuable late-innings runs (including 40 for the last wicket), Australia's lead increased to 180.

From early afternoon, however, Sri Lankans in the stands and on the terraces began to chant in anticipation of a Sri Lankan victory, the country's first ever against Australia. Busloads had been arriving from late morning from outside Colombo in anticipation.

Even the dismissal of Aravinda de Silva, with 54 runs still needed, wasn't overly concerning. But when captain Arjuna Ranatunga and Marvan Atapattu also fell, the Sri Lankans were suddenly 6/141, still 40 short.

Warne had spun the ball from his opening overs in Sri Lanka's first innings, but on the unforgiving slow wicket and in searing heat and humidity, he struggled to penetrate the defences of opener Roshan Mahanama or either of Sri Lanka's champion left-handers Gurusinha and Ranatunga. Mahanama took 13 from his third over, including three boundaries in a row, all from long hops. 'We never found him that difficult then,' said Mahanama.

When reintroduced, having bowled only four of the first 72 overs, Warne was struck for 2 sixes in four balls by Ranatunga, the premier batsman against slow bowling in the world.

Sharing a near-record double-century stand, both Ranatunga and Gurusinha used their feet to hit Warne on the full, or their pads to protect their off stump when he pitched wide. Dispirited at his lack of success, Warne told Border afterwards that all his hard work over winter had been wasted. He was simply not up to it. 'Mate, I'm a big believer in guys who keep trying, keep putting in, keep working hard,' said Border. 'If you keep hanging in there, one day it'll just click for you.'

By bringing Warne back with just 36 runs needed on the final afternoon, Border was risking everything. Typically, there were no great lectures. 'Warm up, Warnie. You're on next over,' he said.

After his first-innings pasting, Warne's Test figures had blown out to 1/335 in 90 overs. His first over on the last day had cost nine. He feared this was going to be his one and only overseas Test.

Known as 'Mr Concrete' amongst his own team-mates, Gurusinha was again well set and threatening to win the game himself. When Warne was re-introduced, this time from the scoreboard end, Sri Lanka was 6/145 from 43 overs. With Gurusinha still not out, the chanting had hardly lulled.

'The Guru' took a couple of early singles, but never got to face him again as Warne, in a dramatic turnaround, rushed through the tail, spinning his leg-break prodigiously from the bowler's footmarks.

In a dramatic ending, Warne snared the last three wickets to fall for 0 from only 13 balls, the Australians taking the last eight wickets for just 37 runs to snatch an incredible victory by 16.

The scorebook entries read:

Over No. 4: X . . . . .
Over No. 5: . . . . X .
Over No. 6: X

'I only got to face two or three balls from him,' said Gurusinha. 'He was bowling at the tail and the pressure was too much. The shots they played were ridiculous. Shane did the right thing. He bowled at the patches and the ball turned, almost at right angles.

'The ground was packed. Thousands of people had come in from around and outside Colombo. They all expected a Sri Lankan win. We expected it to be a cakewalk. We learnt a very good lesson. You can take nothing for granted in cricket.'

It was only the second time the Australians had won a Test after trailing on the first innings by more than 200 runs. In 1949–50 in Durban, having conceded a lead of 236, they defeated South Africa by five wickets thanks to a Neil Harvey masterpiece.

'He [Warne] could have just crawled into a corner and died. But he won us a Test match. And he didn't win it darting them in. He won it giving them a rip and tossing them up. He put his hand up when it mattered most.'   Australian all-rounder GREG MATTHEWS

---

14. **Australia v Southern Province**, at Uyanwatte Stadium, Matara, 24, 25 & 26 August 1992.
SCORES
AUSTRALIA 312 for 9 wickets dec. (M. E. Waugh 118, I. A. Healy 78 not out, D. R. Martyn 61) and 204 (D. C. Boon 57); SOUTHERN PROVINCE 164 and 34 for 2 wickets. *Drawn*.
S. K. WARNE
1st inns: did not bowl.
2nd inns: did not bowl.

This was the first-ever major match to be held at Matara's Uyanwatte Stadium, on the southern tip of the island. Developing inflammation in the arch of his right foot, Warne did not bowl a ball or take any part in the final two days of the game.

15/4. **Australia v Sri Lanka**, Third Test Match, at Tyronne Fernando Stadium, Moratuwa, 8, 9, 10, 12 & 13 September 1992.
SCORES
AUSTRALIA 337 (A. R. Border 106, I. A. Healy 71, G. R. J. Matthews 57; C. P. H. Ramanayake 5/82) and 271 for 8 wickets (G. R. J. Matthews 96, A. R. Border 78); SRI LANKA 274 for 9 wickets dec. (H. P. Tillekeratne 82, P. A. de Silva 58, R. S. Mahanama 50). *Drawn*.
S. K. WARNE
Only inns: 11–3–40–0.

TEST

Relegated to 12th man in the rain-ruined second Test after continuing worries about his injured ankle, Warne was re-included for the third and final Test at the Tyronne Fernando Stadium in Moratuwa. He played only an inconsequential role behind No. 1 spinner Greg Matthews, bowling just 11 of 100 overs in Sri Lanka's only innings.

After becoming only the sixth cricketer – and first recognised batsman – to make a pair of ducks in consecutive Tests, Mark Waugh presented all his clothes and equipment to the room attendant. Allan Border notched his first century for four years.

By drawing the match, Australia won its first series in Sri Lanka since 1969–70 and were full of confidence for the soon-to-start West Indian tour, truly believing they could finally unseat the world champions.

SUMMARY, 1992–93 (Sri Lanka)

	Mts	Overs	Mdn	Runs	Wicks	Ave	BB	5wl	10wM
All First-Class matches	3	38.1	8	158	3	52.66	3/11	–	–
Test matches v Sri Lanka	2	38.1	8	158	3	52.66	3/11	–	–

'Until then [the Sri Lanka tour], Shane knew little about taking wickets, relied on his natural talent and bowled without great expectation. His body language was poor and he seemed to feel he'd done the job when the ball left his hand. I instilled in him the importance of following through aggressively, which gave him even more spin and bounce and put greater pressure on the batsmen.'

Australian coach Bob Simpson

In Australia

16. Victoria v New South Wales, at Sydney Cricket Ground, 6, 7, 8 & 9 November 1992.

Scores

New South Wales 377 for 8 wickets dec. (M. A. Taylor 102, M. E. Waugh 88, M. G. Bevan 68, T. H. Bayliss 64; M. G. Hughes 6/83) and 179 for 7 wickets (G. R. J. Matthews 54); Victoria 547 for 9 wickets dec. (W. N. Phillips 205, S. P. O'Donnell 67, A. I. C. Dodemaide 53 not out, S. K. Warne 52). **Drawn**.

S. K. Warne

1st inns: 18–1–94–1. Dismissed: M. G. Bevan c W. N. Phillips 68.
2nd inns: 26–7–73–2. Dismissed: M. A. Taylor c D. S. Berry 42; M. E. Waugh st D. S. Berry 2.

Having again missed selection for Victoria's one-day team, Warne was slammed for 4 sixes from his first ten overs in a humbling start to

Victoria's new season in the Sesquicentennial match against New South Wales at the Sydney Cricket Ground. After rain forced a late start, new Blues captain Mark Taylor and Mark Waugh both struck Warne for 2 sixes as the Victorian's early overs cost more than five an over.

Waugh was missed behind by wicketkeeper Darren Berry attempting a third six, the ball beating him in flight and spinning so wickedly from outside the leg stump that the normally sure Berry fumbled with Waugh stranded. When he finally did gather the ball, his backhand flick at the stumps missed. He had his revenge in the second innings, however, Waugh (2) being stumped from a quicker one and Taylor (42) feathering a googly on a rapidly deteriorating pitch.

Victoria took first-innings points thanks to a marathon 205 from opening batsman Wayne Phillips, the controversial replacement for Geoff Marsh in the final Test of the Indian series in Perth. Used as a nightwatchman for the first time at interstate level, Warne responded with a half century in less than an hour-and-a-half. He shared a bright and breezy 90-run stand for the second wicket with Phillips. He was particularly pleased to lift 'Mo' Matthews over the top of midwicket for six.

Poor light ended the game early, the umpires not being empowered to call for artificial lighting which would have allowed the scheduled final dozen overs.

Warne conceded 16 runs (. . 4 4 6 2) to Trevor Bayliss from his 16th over and 17 runs (4 . 4 4 4 1) to Matthews from his 19th.

---

17. **Australian XI v West Indies**, at Bellerive Oval, Hobart, 14, 15, 16 & 17 November 1992.

Scores

Australian XI 341 (S. R. Waugh 95; C. L. Hooper 5/72) and 293 for 4 wickets dec. (S. R. Waugh 100 not out, D. S. Lehmann 54 not out, M. L. Hayden 53); West Indians 382 (P. V. Simmons 106, K. L. T. Arthurton 76) and 213 for 5 wickets (D. L. Haynes 79). **Drawn**.

S. K. WARNE
1st inns: 33–8–104–4. Dismissed: P. V. Simmons c D. C. Boon 106;
C. L. Hooper c C. D. Matthews 22; A. L. Logie c sub (D. F. Hills) 15;
J. C. Adams lbw 4.
2nd inns: 17–2–80–1. Dismissed: R. B. Richardson c D. A. Freedman 32.

Selected for the Test trial against the West Indies at rapidly developing Bellerive Oval for the second consecutive year, Warne took five
frontline wickets to enhance his chances of playing in the first Test in
Brisbane. Enjoying the breeze from the nearby Derwent River, Warne
dipped and drifted the ball and gained considerable turn.

Phil Simmons, who made 106 from 126 balls, was particularly
aggressive against Warne, but should have been out at 94 when
Damien Martyn, fielding short on the leg side, dropped a skied
catch.

For the first time in a first-class match in Australia, Warne was
twice no-balled for overstepping.

---

18. **Victoria v Queensland**, at St Kilda Cricket Ground, Melbourne,
20, 21, 22 & 23 November 1992.
SCORES
QUEENSLAND 222 for 9 wickets dec. (A. R. Border 71, M. L. Hayden 51) and
144 for 9 wickets dec.; VICTORIA 195 (P. C. Nobes 70; A. R. Border 5/46)
and 95 for 9 wickets (G. J. Rowell 5/31). *Drawn.*
S. K. WARNE
1st inns: 21–3–59–1. Dismissed: T. J. Barsby c W. G. Ayres 35.
2nd inns: 13–0–48–1. Dismissed: M. L. Hayden c D. S. Lehmann 28.

In association with Test fast bowler and fellow tailender Merv Hughes,
Warne helped save a rain interrupted game against Queensland at the
Junction Oval. Set 172 to win, the Victorians slumped to 9/84 before
finishing at 9/95 from 32 overs, Hughes and Warne batting 35 minutes
and safely negotiating the final 52 balls to force a draw.

For the first time in a match, Warne bowled at Allan Border but
could not dismiss him. Matthew Hayden and Peter Goggin took 14

from his third over in Queensland's second innings. On the third day of the game, Border grabbed the first five Victorian wickets to fall.

---

19. Victoria v Western Australia, at St Kilda Cricket Ground, Melbourne, 4, 5, 6 & 7 December 1992.

SCORES

WESTERN AUSTRALIA 212 (J. L. Langer 70, D. R. Martyn 51; S. K. Warne 5/49) and 337 for 3 wickets (D. R. Martyn 116 not out, G. R. Marsh 101); VICTORIA 352 (S. K. Warne 69, D. S. Lehmann 60, A. I. C. Dodemaide 50; B. P. Julian 5/84). *Drawn*.

S. K. WARNE

1st inns: 17.3–4–49–5. Dismissed: G. R. Marsh b 26; J. L. Langer c D. S. Berry 70; T. J. Zoehrer c D. S. Lehmann 0; J. Angel c A. I. C. Dodemaide 0; B. A. Reid c G. J. Allardice 4.

2nd inns: 27–4–74–2. Dismissed: M. R. J. Veletta b 20; J. L. Langer b 44.

To his disappointment, Warne missed the drawn first Test at the 'Gabba but there was a consolation when Allan Border, at the conclusion of the game, said that Australia could easily have won had a leg-spinner of Warne's calibre been chosen.

Instead of wearing the baggy green, Warne played a light-hearted Puma Cup one-day game for his club team St Kilda at White Hills, Bendigo, and in Victoria's next Sheffield Shield game against Western Australia at the Junction.

With seven wickets for the match, including 5/49 in WA's first innings and a career-best 69, featured by some clubbing 'on the up' drives over cover from the bowling of WA's comeback fast bowler Bruce Reid, Warne had a leading impact from the opening day. TYPHOON WARNE SWEEPS WA AWAY was the headline in Melbourne's *Sunday Herald Sun* after WA had been dismissed for 212, with Warne taking 3/7 from his last 13 balls. He took wickets in his 2nd, 9th, 16th, 17th and 18th overs and led the Victorians from the field. WA wicket-keeper and Test leg-spinning aspirant Tim Zoehrer again alternated with Mike Veletta behind the stumps. He took 3/66 from 24 overs of tidy leg spin.

In just a few months, Warne had fine-tuned his run-up, his arm slightly higher at delivery. He was tending to bowl slower and flight the ball more. He was also learning his lessons, how to defend when necessary and when to bowl his variations. 'The more you play the better you bowl,' he told Mark Ray of the *Sunday Age*.

The following week, he was chosen for Victoria's one-day team for the first time – taking 3/31 against Tasmania in Devonport – and for Australia for his first-ever Christmas Test against the West Indies in his home town of Melbourne. He'd fulfilled his most cherished ambition.

20/5. **Australia v West Indies**, Second Test Match, at Melbourne Cricket Ground, 26, 27, 28, 29 & 30 December 1992.

SCORES

AUSTRALIA 395 (M. E. Waugh 112, A. R. Border 110) and 196 (D. R. Martyn 67 not out); WEST INDIES 233 (K. L. T. Arthurton 71, B. C. Lara 52) and 219 (P. V. Simmons 110, R. B. Richardson 52; S. K. Warne 7/52).

Australia won by 139 runs.

S. K. WARNE

TEST

1st inns: 24–7–65–1. Dismissed: C. E. L. Ambrose c C. J. McDermott 7.
2nd inns: 23.2–8–52–7. Dismissed: P. V. Simmons c D. C. Boon 110;
R. B. Richardson b 52; K. L. T. Arthurton st I. A. Healy 13; C. L. Hooper c M. R. Whitney 0; D. Williams c M. E. Waugh 0; I. R. Bishop c M. A. Taylor 7;
C. A. Walsh c M. G. Hughes 0. Man of the match.

As nervous as he'd ever been leading into a match, an ill-at-ease Warne was racked by self-doubt at his ability to successfully make the transition from interstate to Test cricket. Thrilled by a hero's welcome when he came in to bat for the first time in a home Test, it also reminded him of his responsibilities.

Introduced late on the second day, his first over was a maiden and his first six cost just three runs, before he struggled against a West Indian middle order featuring left-handed trio Brian Lara, Keith Arthurton and Jimmy Adams. On his way to top score of 71, Arthurton lifted him for a big six. Warne's only wicket in 24 overs was tailender Curtly Ambrose. His leg-break spun only slowly, his googly was telegraphed and every time he tried his flipper it was either wide or over-pitched.

Walking through Yarra Park towards the Melbourne Cricket Club members' entrance on the final morning with Australia well placed for a rare win against the world's No. 1 team, Warne mused on his career figures: five wickets in five Tests at almost 100 runs apiece. Even a motivating talk with Ian Healy about his right to be in the Test team was only of partial comfort.

Sensing his young team-mate's distress, Healy asked: 'What are you thinking about, Shane?'

'I'm worried about being thumped all around the ground in front of my friends and never playing for Australia again.'

On a well-worn, fifth-day wicket, he was expected to perform. His time had come and he knew it. Healy reassured him of his stature in the team, told him to relax, have faith and to simply go out and enjoy himself.

Set 359 to win, the Windies started buoyantly with cavalier Trinidadian Phil Simmons lifting a Merv Hughes slower ball high over the backward square leg boundary before repeating the shot to a third ball of a new spell from Mike Whitney.

Introduced from the members' end in the 25th over, Warne was into his ninth over when he bowled a flipper which skittled a champion, changed the direction of a Test match and re-energised a career. Sighting Warne's change-up too late, the West Indies' master batsman Richie Richardson was beaten for pace, caught on his crease and lost his off stump. The No. 1 batsman in the world lingered momentarily, glanced at the wicket and slowly trudged off. For Warne it was an unforgettable highpoint and one of the deliveries of a lifetime. Fifteen thousand fans, including normally staid MCC members, rose in acclaim, debating just which of Warne's 'mystery' balls had been employed to knock over the captain of the West Indies.

'It was like someone took the air out of the ball,' said wicketkeeper

Ian Healy. 'I remember thinking "too late Richie" when he didn't get his bat down in time.'

From being the hunted, unsure and sensitive of his right to be in Australia's elite XI, Warne was suddenly the hunter and in a dramatic afternoon, achieved fairytale-type figures, improving from 0/31 to 7/52, including 4/3 in 38 balls when switching ends. As Merv Hughes was circling under the last catch of the match, Warne was already gathering a souvenir stump in excitement. The last leg-spinner to take five wickets in an innings in an MCG Test had been Bill O'Reilly against England in 1936–37.

From 1/143, the Windies slumped to 219 all out and were beaten by tea-time.

Five of Warne's wickets were caught, one stumped and one bowled. The world champions had been humbled by a kid some north of the Divide had claimed was an impostor. VICTORY IN A FLIP OF THE WRIST headlined the *Age*. VIC HERO said the Melbourne *Herald Sun*. Only 12 months previously Warne had been at the Christmas Test, having a pie and a few beers in the members with Dean Waugh, younger brother of the twins. 'I'll wake up soon,' he quipped, winking at a mate.

The biggest Melbourne Test match crowds (138 555) in 10 years witnessed the game.

'Shane is always prepared to try something and think in the positive. He's always receptive to me trying to winkle batsmen out. That's why I like him. He's prepared to back himself.'

Australian captain ALLAN BORDER

21/6. **Australia v West Indies**, Third Test Match, at Sydney Cricket Ground, 2, 3, 4, 5 & 6 January 1993.

SCORES

AUSTRALIA 503 for 9 wickets dec. (S. R. Waugh 100, G. R. J. Matthews 79, D. C. Boon 76, A. R. Border 74, M. E. Waugh 56) and 117 for no wicket

TEST

(D. C. Boon 63 not out); WEST INDIES 606 (B. C. Lara 277,
R. B. Richardson 109, J. C. Adams 77 not out). *Drawn*.
S. K. WARNE
Only inns: 41–6–116–1. Dismissed: C. L. Hooper b 21.

A high-scoring game in which Allan Border became only the second player to amass 10 000 Test runs and Brian Lara (277) made the highest score in an Australian Test match since 1965–66, Warne's impact was minimal despite the pre-match predictions of a spinning wicket.

Drizzling rain on the third day softened the seam and made it difficult for Warne and his spin partner, the reinstated Greg Matthews, to grip the ball adequately. Repeated requests to the umpires to have the ball changed were rejected. Warne and Matthews bowled 100 overs and took 3/285 between them as the Windies made a near-record 606.

While there was turn, it was very slow, the rain helping bind the wicket together. Warne said afterwards he'd never bowled on a less-responsive wicket, or with a seam so flattened.

Lara played so superbly that Richie Richardson (109) was made to look like a bystander as the pair added 293, the best-ever partnership for the third wicket in a Sydney Test.

---

22. Victoria v Western Australia, at WACA Ground, Perth, 8, 9, 10 & 11 January 1993.
SCORES
WESTERN AUSTRALIA 440 (G. R. Marsh 129, M. P. Lavender 103, T. M. Moody 54); VICTORIA 265 (S. P. O'Donnell 62, D. S. Berry 57; J. Angel 6/71) and 457 for 7 wickets (A. I. C. Dodemaide 123, S. P. O'Donnell 99, N. D. Maxwell 64 not out, L. D. Harper 58). *Drawn*.
S. K. WARNE
Only inns: 29–5–89–0.

Making his debut at the pace-friendly WACA Ground, Warne went wicketless as Western Australia batted into a fifth session with openers Mark Lavender and Geoff Marsh starting with 223. Figures of 0/89 and a sixth-ball duck were unflattering in a first-innings loss; however, a slick slips catch to dismiss Tom Moody was an indication of his sharp reflexes and sure hands.

23/7. Australia v West Indies, Fourth Test Match, at Adelaide Oval, 23, 24, 25 & 26 January 1993.

SCORES

WEST INDIES 252 (B. C. Lara 52; M. G. Hughes 5/64) and 146 (R. B. Richardson 72; T. B. A. May 5/9); AUSTRALIA 213 (C. E. L. Ambrose 6/74) and 184 (J. L. Langer 54). **West Indies won by one run.**

S. K. WARNE

1st inns: 2–0–11–0.

2nd inns: 6–2–18–1. Dismissed: R. B. Richardson c I. A. Healy 72.

TEST

Having captured their sixth World Series title in only eight attempts, the West Indies were motoring back into top form. They won a cliffhanging Test by just one run at the Adelaide Oval after Australian No. 11 Craig McDermott was given caught behind evading a bouncer from Courtney Walsh which tipped only his helmet.

Instead of building an insurmountable 2–0 lead with a Test to play, captain Allan Border buried his head in a white towel after McDermott's controversial dismissal squared the series 1–1. It was to be the closest Australia's normally indomitable leader was to get to his world championship dream. Later he said the West Indian summer was the most exciting of all the 34 series he'd contested.

In a match of riveting highlights, including Justin Langer's debut heroics and off-spinner Tim May's extraordinary second-innings analysis of 5/9 from 6.5 overs, Warne made 0 and 9 and was required to bowl just eight overs. However, he did bat for more than an hour in Australia's fourth-day run-chase, while his dismissal with a sharp-turning leg-break of West Indian topscorer Richie Richardson for 72 was similarly important in the context of the low-scoring match.

Richardson had earlier hit Warne for 2 sixes and if he hadn't been caught at the wicket, he was so far down the pitch he would have been stumped.

24/8. **Australia v West Indies**, Fifth Test Match, at WACA Ground, Perth, 30, 31 January & 1 February 1993.

SCORES

AUSTRALIA 119 (C. E. L. Ambrose 7/25) and 178 (D. C. Boon 52; I. R. Bishop 6/40); WEST INDIES 322 (P. V. Simmons 80, K. L. T. Arthurton 77). *West Indies won by an innings & 25 runs*.

TEST

S. K. WARNE

Only inns: 12–0–51–0.

The deciding Test finished before lunch on the third day, the West Indies winners by a massive margin after man of the series Curtly Ambrose's first-day assault in which he captured 7/1 in 32 balls, the most dynamic, destructive spell in the history of Test cricket.

Winning the toss and batting, the Australians were bowled out in less than 50 overs in their first innings and 57 in their second. Warne's 13 in the first innings was equal second-top score before he was last man out in bizarre fashion, run out off a no-ball. He made a second-ball duck in the second, having been sent in as a nightwatchman, at No. 5. His 12 debut Test overs in Perth cost 51.

Allan Border, in his 138th Test, made his first-ever 'pair'. Both he and fast bowler Merv Hughes had to front International Cricket Council referee Donald Carr to answer charges of dissent. They were severely reprimanded.

SUMMARY, 1992–93 (AUSTRALIA)

	Mts	Overs	Mdn	Runs	Wicks	Ave	BB	5wl	10wM
All First-Class matches	9	309.5	57	983	27	36.40	7/52	2	–
Test matches v West Indies	4	108.2	23	313	10	31.30	7/52	1	–
Australian XI v West Indies	1	50	10	184	5	36.60	4/104	–	–
Sheffield Shield matches	4	151.3	24	486	12	40.50	5/49	1	–

Australia in New Zealand

---

25. **Australia v New Zealand Board XI**, at Pukekura Park,
New Plymouth, 16, 17 & 18 February 1993.
Scores
New Zealand Board XI 264 for 9 wickets dec. (M. D. Crowe 163;
P. R. Reiffel 5/78) and 150; Australians 348 (J. L. Langer 89, I. A. Healy
87 not out) and 69 for 1 wicket. *Australia won by nine wickets*.
S. K. Warne
1st inns: 16–1–60–0.
2nd inns: 12.5–7–21–2. Dismissed: C. Z. Harris c J. L. Langer 8; M. B. Owens
c M. E. Waugh 0.

After only a week off, a 13-man Australian squad began its first full
tour of New Zealand for seven years at New Plymouth, continuing
their hectic international program which was to continue unabated
for a further 14 months with tours of England and South Africa and
a full home summer of six Tests.

Opposed by New Zealand's master batsman Martin Crowe for the
first time at scenic Pukekura Park, Warne's entry to the crease was
deliberately delayed by captain Allan Border. He advised Warne not to
bowl anything but leg-breaks, rather than previewing to Crowe and
the other leading New Zealanders his variations, especially his now-
deadly flipper.

Looking to assert an immediate psychological presence, Crowe, in
at No. 4, was 52 at lunch and 136 at tea before falling to Paul Reiffel
for 163 after an exhilarating, chanceless display. In three spells Warne
conceded 60 runs from 16 overs, including nine from his third and
eighth overs. He bowled only one flipper, to Crowe after he'd passed
three figures, which brought a nod of appreciation. In the second
innings Warne, running in slower and with increasing rhythm,
claimed his first wickets on tour and, in one stretch, bowled four
maidens on end as Australia clinched a comfortable nine-wicket win.
Mark Taylor took five catches for the game.

26/9. **Australia v New Zealand**, First Test Match, at Lancaster Park, Christchurch, 25, 26, 27 & 28 February 1993.

SCORES

AUSTRALIA 485 (A. R. Border 88, M. A. Taylor 82, J. L. Langer 63, S. R. Waugh 62, I. A. Healy 54); NEW ZEALAND 182 (K. R. Rutherford 57) and 243 (K. R. Rutherford 102). *Australia won by an innings & 60 runs*.

TEST

S. K. WARNE

1st inns: 22–12–23–3. Dismissed: J. G. Wright lbw 39; K. R. Rutherford b 57; M. B. Owens lbw 0.

2nd inns: 26–7–63–4. Dismissed: K. R. Rutherford c I. A. Healy 102; C. L. Cairns c M. A. Taylor 21; A. C. Parore c D. C. Boon 5; D. N. Patel b 8.

Man of the match.

Man of the match in a game in which Allan Border surpassed Sunil Gavaskar's all-time Test runs record, Warne took seven wickets and conceded under two runs an over at spacious Lancaster Park as New Zealand was beaten by an innings with a day to spare – their first home loss to Australia since 1981–82.

It was the third time in as many Test wins Warne's emerging spin talents had been a decisive factor in Australian victories.

From the time opener Mark Greatbatch fell third ball after Australia had started with 485, the Kiwis were under pressure. Warne's first seven overs were maidens, a personal record. A sparkling half-century from Ken Rutherford ended when he was bowled by a leg-break behind his legs in Warne's ninth over, Warne's figures to that stage being 8.4–7–2–1.

Going for a sweep shot, John Wright was surprised by the pace of a flipper and adjudged lbw, having made a painstaking 39 in four and a half hours.

With four pacemen in their XI, the NZ tail was lengthy, despite the all-round capabilities of Chris Cairns.

Following on, more than 300 runs behind, the Kiwis were bowled out a second time for 243, with Rutherford again top-scoring with 102, including a straight six down the ground against Warne. He was eventually caught behind when Warne, going around the wicket, induced an edge to a big-spinning leg-break which pitched in foot-

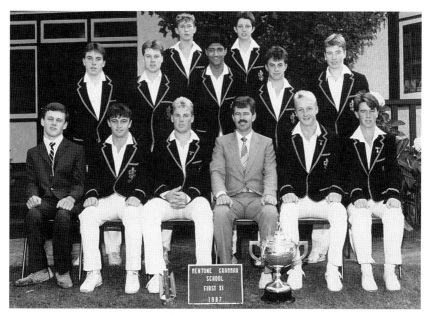

Captain of Mentone Grammar, 1987 (Warne is in the front row, third from left). The team won the Crusaders' outstanding school award.

After a near miss two summers previously, Warne and St Kilda won the 1991–92 Victorian Premier League title, Warne taking 2/65 from 49 overs in the final. The team: (back row, left to right) Lachlan Stonehouse, Mark Osborne, Jacon Jacoby, David 'Bagga' Robinson, Laurie Harper, Ivan Wingreen, Freddie Fitchett (12th man); (front row) Shane Warne, Warren Whiteside, Jack Edwards (president), Shaun Graf (captain), Darren 'J.B.' Walker, Jamie Murphy.

He may have had a gift for bowling big-spinning leg-breaks, but without the hard work element, he would have remained a 'coodabeen'.

2ND INNINGS OF WEST INDIES — BOWLING ANALYSIS

BOWLER	OVERS	MDNS	RUNS	WKTS
McDERMOTT	17	2	46	1
HUGHES	18	7	41	1
WHITNEY	10	2	32	1
WARNE	23.2	8	52	7
M. WAUGH	3	0	23	0
B, LB/RO	—	—	5	—
TOTAL	71.2	19	219	10

30 December 1992: the day Warne's career changed once and for all. In an astonishing collapse, the mighty West Indies were bowled out for 219 to lose by 139 runs, after Warne took 7/52 from 23.2 overs.

Patrick Eagar

At Edgbaston, during his first tour of England in 1993. The umpire is ex-England No. 5 John Hampshire.

Warne was a revelation from the opening Test in 1993, his outstanding performances crucial in Australia's successful defence of the Ashes.

Patrick Eagar

Lord's 1993, the match-turning moment: Mike Atherton is bowled Warne for 80, after more than four hours of the fiercest concentration.

That ball: Mike Gatting is bowled by Warne's very first delivery in Anglo-Australian Test cricket at Old Trafford, Manchester. Gatting was so stunned he stood at the crease for almost 10 seconds wondering if the ball had hit a stone.

Grand Final day 1993. After a lap of honour to the roars of more than 95 000 adoring Melburnians, Warne indulged in a kick-to-kick session with fellow Victorian Merv Hughes. Shane played football with St Kilda reserves and under 19s before concentrating on cricket.

marks and spun wickedly across the New Zealander. A mortified Martin Crowe offered his immediate resignation as NZ captain. And coach Warren Lees questioned the commitment of his players, saying many didn't sufficiently treasure the honour of wearing the NZ cap.

Warne's spells, 22 overs in the first innings and 26 in the second, were interrupted only by lunch and tea breaks on the third and fourth days. Cantabrians had never seen leg-spinning like it.

27/10. Australia v New Zealand, Second Test Match, at Basin Reserve, Wellington, 4, 5, 6, 7 & 8 March 1993.

SCORES

NEW ZEALAND 329 (M. D. Crowe 98, J. G. Wright 72, M. J. Greatbatch 61) and 210 for 7 wickets (T. E. Blain 51); AUSTRALIA 298 (S. R. Waugh 75, M. A. Taylor 50; D. K. Morrison 7/89). **Drawn.**

S. K. WARNE

1st inns: 29–9–59–2. Dismissed: W. Watson c M. A. Taylor 3; M. B. Owens b 0.
2nd inns: 40–25–49–2. Dismissed: A. H. Jones lbw 42; T. E. Blain c I. A. Healy 51.

TEST

Warne's mastery over the Kiwis was the highlight of the drawn second Test at the Basin Reserve, the most personal of all New Zealand cricket grounds, noted for its marvellous cricket museum and the homage administrators pay their favourite sons.

After five hours was lost on the opening day through rain, the Kiwis batted into the third day, taking almost nine hours to score 329 with top scorer John Wright labouring six hours over 72, the fifth-slowest half-century by a New Zealander in Test cricket.

Warne bowled almost 70 overs and conceded fewer than 100 runs, only Martin Crowe showing the inclination to readily attack. After taking 2/59 in the first innings, Warne took 2/49 in the second in another remarkably accurate showing. From the time he spun his first ball, a leg-break, past Andrew Jones' probing bat, he commanded unstinting respect, seven of his first ten overs being maidens. Later he bowled six maidens in a row.

So far was he turning that wicketkeeper Ian Healy suggested he pitch outside leg stump to have a chance of hitting off.

28/11. **Australia v New Zealand**, Third Test Match, at Eden Park, Auckland, 12, 13, 14, 15 & 16 March 1993.
SCORES
AUSTRALIA 139 (D. K. Morrison 6/37) and 285 (D. R. Martyn 74, A. R. Border 71, D. C. Boon 53; D. N. Patel 5/93); NEW ZEALAND 224 and 201 for 5 wickets (K. R. Rutherford 53 not out). *New Zealand won by five wickets*.
S. K. WARNE
1st inns: 15–12–8–4. Dismissed: K. R. Rutherford st I. A. Healy 43; C. Z. Harris c M. A. Taylor 13; D. N. Patel c I. A. Healy 2; M. L. Su'a c S. R. Waugh 3.
2nd inns: 27–8–54–2. Dismissed: A. H. Jones b 26; M. D. Crowe c J. L. Langer 25.

TEST

Australia's dramatic first-day collapse, during which they lost 6/10 to slump from 0/38 to 6/48 minutes after lunch on day one in the third and final Test at Eden Park, was the catalyst behind a five-wicket defeat.

Swinging the ball late and at pace, Danny Morrison's six-wicket haul took him to 100 Test wickets, as Australia was bowled out at NZ's premier ground in virtually two sessions for 139. Captain Allan Border was given out in unusual fashion after a Morrison delivery clipped his off-stump, without a bail being dislodged. Thinking he'd been bowled, Border went to walk off only to notice his wicket still intact. By then umpire Chris King had raised his finger for caught behind!

Warne's 4/8 from 15 overs in NZ's first innings continued his remarkable mastery over the leaden-footed Kiwis. It was almost as if he was bowling hand grenades. After an initial over from the northwest end, he switched to the south-east end and had top scorer Ken Rutherford stumped second ball.

In the second innings, with New Zealand chasing 201 for victory, Warne claimed two more top-order wickets, including Martin Crowe, for 25 with a wrong'un, before Rutherford and Tony Blain ensured the victory with an unbroken 67-run stand in even time for the sixth wicket. Blain hit consecutive Warne deliveries for four, which was as many runs as Warne conceded in 15 first-innings overs.

With 17 wickets in three Tests, Warne had produced the most consistent form of his fledgling career and was named man of the series. In 12 months, Warne had reduced his Test average from 228 to 30. Crowe was so impressed he rated him superior even to Pakistan champion Mushtaq Ahmed. 'He has the mark of a potentially great leg-spin bowler,' he said.

Included for his first one-day international, at Wellington at the conclusion of the tour, Warne took 2/40. He was only the fourth leg-spinner chosen by Australia in more than 20 years of limited-overs cricket.

SUMMARY, 1992–93 (New Zealand)

	Mts	Overs	Mdn	Runs	Wicks	Ave	BB	5wI	10wM
All First-Class matches	4	187.5	81	337	19	17.73	4/8	–	–
Test matches v NZ	3	159	73	256	17	15.05	4/8	–	–

1993

HAVING HOSTED THE menacing march of Pakistani pace pair Wasim Akram and Waqar Younis in 1992 and watched in horror as all four of the wintertime Tests in India and Sri Lanka were lost, England's pride as well as its Test team had taken a hammering leading up to the arrival of Allan Border's 1993 tourists, the 33rd to land on British shores.

A rain-free summer in which less than an hour's play was lost in four of the first five Tests fuelled opinion that officials had deliberately ordered a series of dry, featherbed wickets, rather than the fast bowling friendly green-tops of previous years.

Five fast bowlers were named in Australia's XVII, including one of the world's premier speedsters, Craig McDermott, who was considered at the tour start a bigger menace than either of the specialist spinners, first-time tourist Shane Warne (Test average 30.81) and Tim May (29.53).

Despite his advances in New Zealand, Warne's reputation was more of a sun-loving beach-boy than a matchwinning wrist-spinner. With just one delivery, however, his first in Anglo-Australian Test contests, he was to change everything, forever.

Australia in England

29. **Australia v Worcestershire**, at New Road, Worcester, 5, 6 &
7 May 1993.

Scores

Australia 262 (D. C. Boon 108) and 287 for 5 wickets (D. C. Boon 106,
M. L. Hayden 96); Worcestershire 90 and 458 for 4 wickets dec.
(G. A. Hick 187, S. R. Lampitt 68 not out, T. S. Curtis 67, A. C. H. Seymour
54 not out). *Australia won by five wickets*.

S. K. Warne

1st inns: did not bowl.
2nd inns: 23–6–122–1. Dismissed: D. B. D'Oliveira b 27.

Ever since 1930 when Don Bradman previewed his mammoth feats in
the Tests with a double century on debut, Worcester has been the traditional starting point for touring Australian teams. New Road is an
entrancing ground, small, intimate and ringed by the River Severn,
historic churches and the magnificent medieval Norman cathedral,
rebuilt in 1158.

After two inconsequential warm-up matches at Radlett and Arundel, the Australians enforced the follow-on and then won their first
major game in a thrilling run-chase, with just one ball to spare. David
Boon scored twin centuries and newcomer Wayne Holdsworth took
five wickets. Warne, however, suffered the biggest pummelling of his
career, taking 1/122 and conceding almost a run per ball.

In an exhilarating warm-up for the Tests, Worcestershire and England top-order specialist Graeme Hick slammed 187 with 24 fours and
6 sixes, including a record 19 runs from Warne's 2nd and 22nd overs.

Warne's only wicket was Damian D'Oliveira, son of the former
headlining South African-born English all-rounder Basil D'Oliveira.

The Australian tactics had again been for Warne to ease into the
tour, concentrating on his leg-break, without telegraphing his vari-
eties to anyone likely to bat in the first six in the Tests.

But so good was Hick and so small the English boundaries that it
seemed even mishits found the rope. MURDER AT THE CATHEDRAL was

one of the headlines after Hick's big 100, his 69th in first-class cricket.

Having conceded 96 runs from just 77 balls to the aggressive Hick, Warne was crestfallen and despite a pep talk from captain Allan Border, privately wondered if the slower wickets which even Richie Benaud had taken three tours to adapt to, might also be his undoing.

On the last morning, when Hick accelerated to 187, with his last 26 in just 17 minutes, he lifted Warne, operating from the scoreboard end, for 4 sixes and 2 fours. Three overs cost 33. The young man was unable to defend himself. As much as visiting mates from Melbourne like Shaun Graf tried to make light of the mauling, he was left punch-drunk and unsure, hardly remembering New Zealand, let alone his flippering of Richie Richardson in Melbourne.

---

30. **Australia v Somerset**, at County Ground, Taunton, 8, 9 & 10 May 1993.
Scores
Australia 431 (M. J. Slater 122, M. E. Waugh 68, A. R. Border 54) and 40 for no wicket dec.; Somerset 151 for 4 wickets dec. (C. J. Tavaré 62) and 285 (A. N. Hayhurst 89). *Australia won by 35 runs*.
S. K. Warne
1st inns: 6–3–5–1. Dismissed: N. A. Folland lbw 1.
2nd inns: 28–6–77–4. Dismissed: A. N. Hayhurst b 89; C. J. Tavaré c M. A. Taylor 31; N. A. Folland st T. J. Zoehrer 32; A. van Troost c S. R. Waugh 8.

Somerset's only international-class batsman was their veteran captain, 38-year-old Chris Tavaré, who'd been out of Test cricket for years. Realising how fragile Warne's confidence was after the Hick hammering at New Road, Border used him sparingly in the first innings, at third change behind off-spinner Tim May. In the second, May and Warne bowled virtually all afternoon on the final day as Somerset, set 321 to win in 84 overs, was bowled out for 285 in just under five hours. May took 4/75 from 23.3 overs and Warne 4/77 from 28, top scorer Andy Hayhurst being bowled around his legs at 89 by a big leg-break.

It was the first pairing of a combination which was to prove as deadly and destructive as many of Australia's most-vaunted postwar new-ball pairings from Lindwall and Miller onwards.

Somerset unveiled the fastest bowler the Aussies faced all tour in Adrianus van Troost, a Dutch-born right-arm express ineligible for England until the year 2000. His 23 overs for the match went for five an over.

---

31. **Australia v Surrey**, at The Oval, London, 25, 26 & 27 May 1993.
SCORES
AUSTRALIA 378 for 9 wickets dec. (M. E. Waugh 178, D. R. Martyn 84) and 171 for 4 wickets dec. (M. A. Taylor 80, M. J. Slater 50); SURREY 231 and 144. *Australia won by 174 runs*.
S. K. WARNE
1st inns: 23.5–8–68–3. Dismissed: M. A. Lynch b 48; M. A. Butcher lbw 4; G. J. Kersey lbw 1.
2nd inns: 19.1–6–38–4. Dismissed: G. P. Thorpe c T. J. Zoehrer 23; M. A. Butcher st T. J. Zoehrer 10; J. E. Benjamin st T. J. Zoehrer 2; A. J. Murphy c W. J. Holdsworth 5.

After a two-week playing break, during which the Australians contested and won all three Texaco Cup games, Warne returned at The Oval for the build-up to the first Test.

With more than 40 overs and seven wickets for the match, he was in immediate rhythm, despite being hit for 16 runs in one incomplete over by tailender Tony Murphy which enabled Surrey to avert the follow-on.

In the second innings, Warne's accuracy was again a talking point. He also spun the ball markedly, the highlight being the dismissal of rising left-hander Graham Thorpe to a fine catch down the leg side by wicketkeeper Tim Zoehrer, who equalled the Australian record with eight dismissals in a single innings.

Surrey was without its captain and Test wicketkeeper/batsman Alec Stewart. Leading fast bowler Waqar Younis was rested. Mark Waugh hit 8 sixes in his even-time 178 on the opening day.

32. **Australia v Leicestershire**, at Grace Road, Leicester, 29, 30 &
31 May 1993.
SCORES
AUSTRALIA 323 for 3 wickets dec. (D. C. Boon 123, M. J. Slater 91) and 88 for
4 wickets dec. (M. J. Slater 50 not out); LEICESTERSHIRE 168 for 7 wickets dec.
and 146. *Australia won by 97 runs*.
S. K. WARNE
1st inns: 12–5–31–3. Dismissed: P. E. Robinson c I. A. Healy 11;
B. F. Smith b 0; P. A. Nixon c M. L. Hayden 5.
2nd inns: 13–7–27–3. Dismissed: P. E. Robinson b 31; B. F. Smith lbw 31;
V. J. Wells b 9.

Australia won their fourth county game in five matches in just two-
and-a-half days, Warne passing 100 wickets in first-class cricket with
his second-innings dismissal of Ben Smith. In the first he dismissed
Phillip Robinson and Smith with consecutive first-over deliveries.

Warne and spin partner Tim May bowled more than half the overs,
May finishing the game with three wickets in four balls. Batting only
once in the game, Warne hit his first ball for six before being stumped
off the second.

His English haul of 19 wickets in four first-class matches guaranteed his place for the opening Test in Manchester. After Worcester and
the savagery of Hick's onslaught, it had been a mighty fightback.

'In cricket, there is no better sight than an innocuous slow bowler
making total fools of big names with wide bats and respectable averages 22 yards down the pitch.

Melbourne *Age* journalist PETER MCFARLINE

33/12. **Australia v England**, First Test Match, at Old Trafford,
Manchester, 3, 4, 5, 6 & 7 June 1993.
SCORES
AUSTRALIA 289 (M. A. Taylor 124, M. J. Slater 58; P. M. Such 6/67) and
432 for 5 wickets dec. (I. A. Healy 102 not out, D. C. Boon 93,

TEST

S. R. Waugh 78 not out, M. E. Waugh 64); ENGLAND 210 (G. A. Gooch 65)
and 332 (G. A. Gooch 133). *Australia won by 179 runs.*
S. K. WARNE
1st inns: 24–10–51–4. Dismissed: M. W. Gatting b 4; R. A. Smith
c M. A. Taylor 4; G. A. Gooch c B. P. Julian 65; A. R. Caddick c I. A. Healy 7.
2nd Inns: 49–26–86–4. Dismissed: M. A. Atherton c M. A. Taylor 25;
R. A. Smith b 18; A. J. Stewart c I. A. Healy 11; C. C. Lewis c M. A. Taylor 43.
Man of the match.

It was a ball of dreams, a spitting, unplayable, jaffa of a leg-break
which pitched 18 inches outside leg stump and glanced the off. A
nonplussed Mike Gatting, acknowledged as the best player of spin in
England, stared at the wicket, hardly believing a ball could have drifted or spun so much. It was the first Warne had ever delivered in a Test
against England and within 24 hours it had been given exalted status
as THAT BALL, THE BALL FROM HELL and even THE BALL OF THE CENTURY. It
once and for all ensured Warne's reputation as a matchwinner of
uncommon ability and set the tone for the entire summer, with both
Warne and his spinning partner Tim May weaving a mesmeric spell
against leaden-footed opponents unwilling to leave their crease and
take the attack to the bowling. The spin twins complemented each
other, one liking the breeze coming over his left shoulder, the other
being happiest coming into it.

England was 1/80 after 27 overs when Warne was introduced at
3.05 p.m. from the Warwick Road end. With a casual couple of paces
and a wheel of his arm, he delivered a leg-break, his signature ball, the
delivery which had so excited Terry Jenner in the nets at Adelaide only
a few winters previously.

After it deviated drunkenly from a good length and glanced Gatting's
off stump, Warne clenched his fist in a prolonged mid-pitch celebration before being engulfed by equally ecstatic team-mates.

Gatting had stood at the wicket for almost ten seconds, thunder-
struck, before slowly departing with a shake of his head. 'The last time
I saw that look on Gatt's face, someone had nicked his lunch,' said
England spinner Phil Tufnell.

Gatting had only just regained his place in the English top order, having missed the entire home series with Pakistan 12 months earlier. After play that night, the players shared a drink and Gatting approached Warne. 'Bloody hell, Warnie. What happened?'

'Sorry, mate. I just got lucky.'

Years later Gatting said it wasn't a bad shot. 'It's nice now to look back at it and know I'm part of Test history.'

At the non-striker's end, Graham Gooch was just as amazed. 'That ball would have got anybody out,' he said. 'It was the perfect ball.'

England's manager Keith Fletcher reckoned Warne's dramatic opening delivery had drifted two feet, before spinning three. While there was a fair degree of exaggeration, it *was* a remarkable ball, right up there with 'Chuck' Fleetwood-Smith's chinaman to Walter Hammond which won a Test match in Adelaide in 1936–37 and Eric Hollies' fabled googly which castled Don Bradman and denied him a 100-plus average in his last Test at The Oval in 1948.

Minutes later, to the first ball of Warne's following over, Robin Smith edged a catch to slip from a delivery which spun almost as much. And Gooch, 39, was out to a waist-high full toss which he lifted straight to mid-on. With 4/51 from 24 overs, Warne, a virtual unknown, had made a dramatic Boys' Own entry into Anglo-Australian Test cricket.

Australia built a huge lead, setting England 512 to win in eight-and-a-half hours. With Gooch making 133, the Englishmen batted well into the last session before being bowled out for 332, the last wicket falling with less than ten overs remaining. In the longest stint of his career, Warne took 4/86 from 49 overs, including three of the top six. Introduced in the 14th over from the scoreboard end just after tea on the fourth day, he started with five maidens in his first six overs and bowled unchanged for a personal record 41 overs until almost tea on the fifth day.

England was 0/51 when he started and 6/248 when he was rested. Captain Allan Border was using him both to attack and defend.

Mike Atherton was caught at slip, Smith bowled by a topspinner and Alec Stewart caught behind off a zoota, his just-perfected back-spinning slower ball bowled from the front of the hand. Throughout both innings, Warne bowled with intimidating purpose and aggression, his confidence ballooning with the early dismissals of Gatting and Smith. None of the Englishmen bar Gooch was able to cope with his variations. Warne also held a wonderful juggled catch at backward square leg to dismiss Andy Caddock, who had defied the Aussies for almost an hour-and-a-half.

With eight wickets for the game, the best return by an Australian spin bowler in a Test in England since 1938, Warne was named man of the match. 'He has proved that he can bowl long, long spells,' said Border. 'He doesn't seem to get tired or weary. We're on a winner here.'

'It was an amazing ball. Long after we've all retired, that one delivery will be etched in the memory of everyone who witnessed it.'

STEVE WAUGH

'Warne has startling talent and simply petrified the English batsmen as he whirred and howled through the match.'   DAILY MAIL

'Shane Warne was a nobody, so far as the majority of Englishmen were concerned. A boy off the beaches, bleached and bronzed as if auditioning for *Neighbours*.'

Prominent English cricket writer and author ALAN LEE

---

34. Australia v Gloucestershire, at County Ground, Bristol, 12, 13 & 14 (no play) June 1993.
SCORES
GLOUCESTERSHIRE 211 (B. C. Broad 80; S. K. Warne 5/61); AUSTRALIA 400 (D. C. Boon 70, M. E. Waugh 66, M. L. Hayden 57, D. R. Martyn 51).
Drawn.

S. K. WARNE

Only inns: 28–9–61–5. Dismissed: B. C. Broad c M. L. Hayden 80;
T. H. C. Hancock c M. L. Hayden 37; A. J. Wright c M. A. Taylor 23;
R. I. Dawson b 1; R. C. Russell c D. R. Martyn 26.

After a match off during which he proposed to his girlfriend, 23-year-old Simone Callahan, while on a boat trip in the Lake District, Warne returned his best English analysis of 5/61 from 28 overs, including four of the top six on a slow and low wicket at Bristol, where he'd first played League cricket as a teenager in 1989. In mid-innings, his 13th over cost 12 runs before he took 3/0 from 14 balls, including top scorer and ex-Testman Chris Broad. Play was possible on only two of the scheduled three days.

35/13. **Australia v England**, Second Test Match, at Lord's, London,
17, 18, 19, 20 & 21 June 1993.

SCORES

AUSTRALIA 632 for 4 wickets dec. (D. C. Boon 164, M. J. Slater 152,
M. A. Taylor 111, M. E. Waugh 99, A. R. Border 77); ENGLAND 205
(M. A. Atherton 80) and 365 (M. A. Atherton 99, G. A. Hick 64,
A. J. Stewart 62, M. W. Gatting 59). *Australia won by an innings & 62 runs*.

TEST

S. K. WARNE

1st inns: 35–12–57–4. Dismissed: M. A. Atherton b 80; C. C. Lewis lbw 0;
N. A. Foster c A. R. Border 16; P. M. Such c M. A. Taylor 7.
2nd inns: 48.5–17–102–4. Dismissed: G. A. Gooch c I. A. Healy 29;
M. W. Gatting lbw 59; P. M. Such b 4; P. C. R. Tufnell b 0.

Beaten only once at Lord's, the acknowledged 'home' of cricket in almost 100 years, the Australians batted into a third day and declared at 4/632, with Mark Waugh going within a run of being the fourth centurion for the innings.

The English slumped to 9/193 at the close on day three and had lost by mid-afternoon on day five, despite fast bowler Craig McDermott not being able to bowl in either innings with a twisted bowel. Warne was again central in England's capitulation. He claimed 4/57 and 4/102 and again bowled lengthy opening spells, 19 overs in the first innings and 18 in the second.

Spin partner Tim May took six wickets and, like Warne, extracted extravagant turn on a wearing wicket which increasingly favoured the slower bowlers. Again Gatting fell to spin, to May in the first innings and to Warne, lbw, attempting a cut shot in the second. He'd spent four hours for 59.

Warne finished the game by bowling Peter Such and Phil Tufnell around their legs with successive balls before both teams were presented to Her Majesty, Queen Elizabeth. The game was a virtual sellout, more than 110 000 attending over the five days. With 16 wickets in the opening two Tests, Warne had claimed more wickets than any Australian leg-spinner to tour England since Bill 'Tiger' O'Reilly in 1938.

So big a gulf was emerging between the sides that few took seriously English chairman of selectors Ted Dexter's bold promise that his team would turn the series around and win 4–2. 'We are competing,' he told newspapermen. 'It's always assumed that if somebody plays poorly, someone else would have played better.'

---

36. **Australia v Combined Universities**, at The Parks, Oxford, 23, 24 & 25 June 1993.

SCORES

AUSTRALIA 388 for 5 wickets dec. (D. R. Martyn 138 not out, M. J. Slater 111, M. L. Hayden 98) and 233 for 6 wickets dec. (M. E. Waugh 84, M. A. Taylor 57); COMBINED UNIVERSITIES 298 for 7 wickets dec. (R. Q. Cake 108, R. R. Montgomerie 52) and 157. **Australia won by 166 runs**.

S. K. WARNE

1st inns: 22–7–45–3. Dismissed: R. R. Montgomerie st D. R. Martyn 52; R. Q. Cake c B. P. Julian 108; G. B. T. Lovell st T. J. Zoehrer 20.

2nd inns: 12–6–21–2. Dismissed: J. R. Wileman c M. A. Taylor 48; S. F. Shephard lbw 0.

A light-hearted game against the Combined Universities saw Michael Slater become the first Australian since Bob Cowper in 1964 to start with a century before lunch. Warne took five wickets, including the top scorers Russell Cake (108) in the first innings and Jonathan Wileman (48) in the second. For a time Warne bowled in sunglasses and in tandem with wicketkeeper and fellow leg-spinner Tim Zoehrer.

Cake, a Cambridge man, dominated the headlines, especially after announcing he could 'read' all of Warne's variations.

37/14. **Australia v England**, Third Test Match, at Trent Bridge, Nottingham,1, 2, 3, 4 & 5 July 1993.

SCORES

ENGLAND 321 (R. A. Smith 86, N. Hussain 71; M. G. Hughes 5/92) and 422 for 6 wickets dec. (G. A. Gooch 120, G. P. Thorpe 114 not out, R. A. Smith 50); AUSTRALIA 373 (D. C. Boon 101, M. E. Waugh 70) and 202 for 6 wickets (B. P. Julian 56 not out). *Drawn*.

TEST

S. K. WARNE

1st inns: 40–17–74–3. Dismissed: M. A. Atherton c D. C. Boon 11; A. J. Stewart c M. E. Waugh 25; N. Hussain c D. C. Boon 71.

2nd inns: 50–21–108–3. Dismissed: M. N. Lathwell lbw 33; R. A. Smith c I. A. Healy 50; G. A. Gooch c M. A. Taylor 120.

After seven consecutive Test defeats, England's delayed declaration, 40 minutes into the fifth morning, cost the home team a realistic chance of victory with Australia 6/202 at the close, having been set 371 to win in five hours. At a tea-time 6/115, Australia was struggling to avoid defeat before England ran out of time and answers to an unbeaten 87-run stand between Steve Waugh and Brendon Julian.

In the heaviest workload of his career, having replaced opening bowler Merv Hughes at the Radcliffe Road end after just 12 overs on the opening morning, Warne bowled more than 30 per cent of Australia's overs for the match: 40 in the first innings and 50 in the second. His biggest spells were 22 overs in the second innings and 17 in the first. Many were again delivered from around the wicket, with Warne aiming directly into the opposite footmarks created by the heavyweight Hughes, Australia's frontline paceman in the absence of Craig McDermott.

England included four debutants in its team with a fifth newcomer, Martin Bicknell, 12th man. Not since the England–India Test in Delhi in 1951–52, when five newcomers played, had a set of English selectors introduced so much untried talent. One of the first-gamers, left-hander Graham Thorpe made a century to nullify at least some of the Warne menace.

---

38. **Australia v Derbyshire**, at County Ground, Derby, 13, 14 & 15 (no play) July 1993.
SCORES
DERBYSHIRE 305 (K. J. Barnett 114. D. G. Cork 56; W. J. Holdsworth 5/117 inc. hat-trick); AUSTRALIANS 268 for 1 wicket (M. J. Slater 133 not out, M. E. Waugh 60 not out). *Drawn.*
S. K. WARNE
Only inns: 10–5–20–0.

A hat-trick from Wayne Holdsworth, the first by an Australian in England since 1912, and another century-in-a-session from Michael Slater were the highpoints of a rain-affected draw at Derby. Warne didn't bowl until the 40th over of Derbyshire's innings and had just ten overs without taking a wicket.

39/15. **Australia v England**, Fourth Test Match, at Headingley, Leeds, 22, 23, 24, 25 & 26 July 1993.
SCORES
AUSTRALIA 653 for 4 wickets dec. (A. R. Border 200 not out, S. R. Waugh 157 not out, D. C. Boon 107, M. J. Slater 67, M. E. Waugh 52); ENGLAND 200 (G. A. Gooch 59, M. A. Atherton 55; P. R. Reiffel 5/65) and 305 (A. J. Stewart 78, M. A. Atherton 63). *Australia won by an innings & 148 runs.*
S. K. WARNE
1st inns: 23–9–43–1. Dismissed: M. J. McCague c M. A. Taylor 0.
2nd inns: 40–16–63–0.

TEST

For once Warne was nullified, but England still slumped to their eighth loss in nine Tests at the Yorkshire cricketing capital, Australia reclaiming the Ashes by mid-afternoon on day five.

Starting with 4/653 declared, Australia bowled England out for 200 and 305, pace reinforcement Paul Reiffel taking eight wickets for the match and big-hearted fellow Victorian Merv Hughes six, including his 200th Test wicket. Mark Waugh's one-handed catch to dismiss Alec Stewart on the final day was a gem.

With 63 overs for the match, Warne again bowled lengthy spells, his accuracy unerring. The most runs he conceded was seven, from his opening over of the match.

However, he took only one wicket, compared with five by spinning partner Tim May. There were signs that by going around the wicket so often, his action was suffering and he was placing abnormal stress on his shoulder.

In the second innings, his 40 overs were stretched over four spells. He was introduced in the tenth over of the game and bowled 22 overs unchanged.

Graham Gooch announced his resignation as captain after the match. He was to be replaced by Mike Atherton.

---

40. **Australia v Lancashire**, at Old Trafford, Manchester, 28, 29 & 30 July 1993.

SCORES

AUSTRALIA 282 for 3 wickets dec. (M. A. Taylor 122, D. R. Martyn 70 not out, M. L. Hayden 61) and 194 for 8 wickets dec. (M. L. Hayden 79); LANCASHIRE 250 for 7 wickets dec. and 228 for 5 wickets (J. P. Crawley 109).
Lancashire won by five wickets.

S. K. WARNE

1st inns: 32.4–12–54–3. Dismissed: G. D. Mendis b 29; N. J. Speak c & b 48; P. A. J. DeFreitas c W. J. Holdsworth 1.

2nd inns: 24–7–61–1. Dismissed: G. D. Mendis c M. A. Taylor 24.

With the Ashes won, a five-wicket Australian loss, the first of the tour, to Lancashire at Old Trafford was an indication of a less-than-full focus in between Tests. Three declarations were made, emerging right-hander John Crawley sparking the win with a three-hour century on the final afternoon.

Captaining the team in the absence of Allan Border, Mark Taylor allowed himself five overs of wrist-spin in Lancashire's first innings. Wicketkeeper Tim Zoehrer also bowled. With four wickets, Warne was again Australia's most successful bowler.

---

41. **Australia v Glamorgan**, at The Gnoll, Neath, 31 July, 1 & 2 August 1993.

SCORES
AUSTRALIA 414 for 4 wickets dec. (M. E. Waugh 152, D. C. Boon 120, M. J. Slater 72) and 235 for 7 wickets dec. (A. R. Border 52); GLAMORGAN 363 for 8 wickets dec. (M. P. Maynard 132, P. A. Cottey 68) and 169 for 6 wickets. *Drawn*.

S. K. WARNE
1st inns: 26.2–6–67–4. Dismissed: P. A. Cottey b 68; D. L. Hemp b 40; R. D. B. Croft lbw 17; S. D. Thomas st I. A. Healy 9.
2nd inns: 17–3–44–2. Dismissed: A. Dale c I. A. Healy 31; D. L. Hemp b 16.

A high-scoring draw saw Warne bat at No. 5 in the Australian second innings. Earlier, in the Australian first innings, Mark Waugh (152 not out) hit 17-year-old debutant Stuart Phelps for 4 sixes in a row and 25 runs from the over.

Warne took six wickets for the game, including bowling Glamorgan's No. 6 David Hemp in both innings.

42/16. **Australia v England**, Fifth Test Match, at Edgbaston, Birmingham, 5, 6, 7, 8 & 9 August 1993.

SCORES
ENGLAND 276 (M. A. Atherton 72, J. E. Emburey 55 not out;

TEST

P. R. Reiffel 6/71) and 251 (G. P. Thorpe 60; S. K. Warne 5/82, T. B. A. May
5/89); AUSTRALIA 408 (M. E. Waugh 137, I. A. Healy 80, S. R. Waugh 59) and
120 for 2 wickets (M. E. Waugh 62 not out). ***Australia won by eight wickets***.
S. K. WARNE
1st inns: 21–7–63–1. Dismissed: A. J. Stewart c & b 45.
2nd inns: 49–23–82–5. Dismissed: G. A. Gooch b 48; M. A. Atherton
c A. R. Border 28; R. A. Smith lbw 19; A. J. Stewart lbw 5; G. P. Thorpe
st I. A. Healy 60.

Edgbaston had always been England's 'lucky' ground, just like
Bridgetown is for the West Indies and Karachi for Pakistan. They'd
been beaten only once there in eight Tests against the Australians, but
by now, so superior were Warne and Co. that even hoodoos were
meaningless. The Australians won comfortably by eight wickets and
Warne equalled Clarrie Grimmett's record spin mark of 29 wickets in
the 1930 Ashes series. His 5/82 from 49 overs in the second innings
was his first 'five-for' in a Test outside Australia. Almost half his overs
were maidens, many to 40-year-old John Emburey, recalled for his
first Ashes Test in four years. The veteran off-spinner played Warne,
again operating for long periods around the wicket, in unique style,
mainly with his bat raised high above his head and both pads square
on and locked together like a shield. So successful were his unorthodox tactics that he shared in England's only century stand of the
match, with the impressive left-hander Graham Thorpe, who made
60. Thorpe's dismissal, brilliantly stumped down the leg-side by Ian
Healy, turned the match.

In another of Warne's most satisfying moments of a fairytale tour,
England's batting lynchpin Graham Gooch was bowled around his
legs, having batted three hours in the second innings. The night
before, Warne had discussed bowling fuller and outside leg stump to
Gooch in the hope that a leg-break could spin sharply enough and
bypass his pads, which like Emburey, he'd been using as a second
defence. Early on the fourth day, Warne's leg-break, pitching on a full
length, spun at least 50 centimetres, behind Gooch's outstretched left
leg, and struck his middle and leg stumps. Gooch was incredulous and

the Australians jubilant when the plan worked. His dismissal triggered a mid-innings collapse and set up Australia's fourth win in five Tests.

Having misread three consecutive wrong'uns, Robin Smith was adjudged lbw to a flipper, the fourth time he'd fallen to Warne for the summer. He was to be left out of the sixth Test, ironically for Graeme Hick, who'd been dropped after the opening two Tests having succumbed to the speed of the intimidating Merv Hughes.

Almost emulating his Manchester marathon, Warne bowled 36 overs from the Press Box Stand end on the third and fourth days before being spelled. Coming on at 4.54 p.m. in the 17th over with England 0/40 in its second innings, he finally came off in mid-afternoon after the 87th over with England 6/176 and on the precipice. His figures: 36–19–50–4.

'I think he [Warne] is terrific. He is the best young leg spin bowler I have seen and the incredible thing about him is that he has so few technical problems at this early stage of his career.'

Legendary leg-spinner RICHIE BENAUD

'If we batted to Shane we would do so a bit differently. You don't see many English blokes running down the wicket to him. Our guys would try and get after him.'   Australian captain ALLAN BORDER

---

43. **Australia v Kent**, at St Lawrence Ground, Canterbury, 11, 12 & 13 August 1993.
SCORES
AUSTRALIA 391 for 4 wickets dec. (S. R. Waugh 123, D. R. Martyn 105 not out, M. A. Taylor 78) and 34 for no wicket dec.; KENT 114 for 2 wickets dec. and 222 (T. R. Ward 69, G. R. Cowdrey 51). **Australia won by 89 runs**.
S. K. WARNE
1st inns: 9–1–30–1. Dismissed: G. R. Cowdrey lbw 25.
2nd inns: 20–6–50–1. Dismissed: T. R. Ward c M. A. Taylor 69.

A low-key county game at the St Lawrence ground in Canterbury saw Mark Taylor take his first first-class wicket of the tour and win a $200 side-bet.

With 1/30 and 1/50, Warne claimed his 150th first-class wicket when he dismissed Graham Cowdrey on the second afternoon.

44/17. **Australia v England**, Sixth Test Match, at The Oval, London, 19, 20, 21, 22 & 23 August 1993.

SCORES

ENGLAND 380 (G. A. Hick 80, A. J. Stewart 76, G. A. Gooch 56, M. A. Atherton 50) and 313 (G. A. Gooch 79, M. R. Ramprakash 64); AUSTRALIA 303 (I. A. Healy 83 not out, M. A. Taylor 70; A. R. C. Fraser 5/87) and 229. **England won by 161 runs**.

TEST

S. K. WARNE

1st inns: 20–5–70–2. Dismissed: M. P. Maynard b 20; N. Hussain c M. A. Taylor 30.

2nd inns: 40–15–78–3. Dismissed: G. A. Gooch c I. A. Healy 79; S. L. Watkin lbw 4; P. M. Such lbw 10.

In his final game of the tour, the now combative and fiercely aggressive Warne extended his series haul to a record 34 wickets, to be named man of the series.

The Australians were beaten for the first time, by 161 runs, the series being decided 4–1.

Newcomer Matthew Maynard said the Australians had been very chatty, trying to unsettle him. In an interview with a local paper, he said, 'When Warne got me, he said to me, "Take that f&$#ing shot back to Wales".'

Warne took two wickets in the first innings and three in the second, giving him 75 wickets in 16 matches, a new postwar high for a visiting Australian leg-spinner and the best since 1938 when Bill O'Reilly amassed 104 wickets in 20 matches. He bowled, on average, 75 overs per Test or a total of 2639 balls, the most in Ashes history, surpassing Clarrie Grimmett's 2390 balls in five 1928–29 Tests. It was also the most balls bowled in any Test series, surpassing Alf Valentine's 2580 balls for the West Indies against India in 1952–53.

With 37 in Australia's second innings, Warne also made his highest Test score. He was the last man out, having hit 6 fours in an 83-minute stay.

SUMMARY, 1993 (ENGLAND)

	Mts	Overs	Mdn	Runs	Wicks	Ave	BB	5wI	10wM
All First-Class matches	16	765.5	281	1698	75	22.64	5/61	2	–
Test matches v England	6	439.5	178	877	34	25.79	5/82	1	–

'Wanting Warne to survive, to see more of him, we must hope that he is not only super bowler, but super body. Without wrapping himself in cotton wool, he needs to take care.'

Noted English cricket writer ROBIN MARLAR

1993–94

MELBURNIANS LOVE THEIR SPORT and their big-name sportsmen and when Warne and Merv Hughes had an impromptu kick-to-kick session during a motorcade preceding the 1993 Australian Football League Grand Final, 100 000 roared their approval, especially when Warne's long shot from 50 metres bounced through at the Punt Road goals. With receptions in Sydney and Melbourne, the Australian team was treated like returning war heroes, Warne's diary suddenly chock full. None of the Aussies, especially Warne, a first-time tourist, had imagined the impact their triumphant march through England had made back home. Everywhere he went, he was being asked about *that* ball. Having had such a mesmeric, hypnotising effect on the Englishmen, he'd become the most marketable sportsman in the country. His life was changing irrevocably.

IN AUSTRALIA

45. **Victoria v South Australia**, at Adelaide Oval, 27, 28, 29 & 30 October 1993.

SCORES

VICTORIA 357 for 9 wickets dec. (W. N. Phillips 60, D. J. Ramshaw 58,
M. T. G. Elliott 54, A. I. C. Dodemaide 52) and 198 (M. T. G. Elliott 99;
P. E. McIntyre 5 for 61, T. B. A. May 5/80); SOUTH AUSTRALIA 430
(P. C. Nobes 141, J. A. Brayshaw 134; S. H. Cook 5/114) and 127 for
1 wicket (P. C. Nobes 63 not out, J. A. Brayshaw 54 not out).
South Australia won by nine wickets.
S. K. WARNE
1st inns: 43–11–119–4. Dismissed: P. C. Nobes c D. S. Berry 141;
J. A. Brayshaw c & b 134; J. D. Siddons c A. I. C. Dodemaide 5;
D. S. Lehmann c D. J. Ramshaw 1.
2nd inns: 11–1–48–0.

Warne was immediately in form for Victoria's opening Shield fixture,
in Adelaide, taking 4/119, including the wickets of centurions, the
unorthodox Paul Nobes and James Brayshaw, during a mid-innings
spell of 3/6 from 35 balls. He was denied a fifth wicket when teenage debutant Brad Hodge, at mid-off, dropped SA tailender Brad
Wigney. Having collapsed in their second innings to expatriate Peter
McIntyre and Ashes hero Tim May, the Victorians were beaten by
nine wickets.

For the first time since 1976–77, Victoria included a second specialist leg-spinner in their XI, 19-year-old Craig Howard from Ringwood.

---

46. **Victoria v Western Australia**, at Melbourne Cricket Ground, 4, 5, 6 &
7 November 1993.

SCORES

WESTERN AUSTRALIA 322 (J. L. Langer 144; A. I. C. Dodemaide 5/85) and 185
(D. R. Martyn 89 not out; S. K. Warne 6/42); VICTORIA 230 (B. J. Hodge 95)
and 278 for 4 wickets (M. T. G. Elliott 175 not out). *Victoria won by six wickets.*
S. K. WARNE
1st inns: 36–9–92–3. Dismissed: M. R. J. Veletta c D. J. Ramshaw 2;
B. P. Julian b 27; J. Angel c D. M. Jones 0.
2nd inns: 29.4–12–42–6. Dismissed: T. M. Moody st D. S. Berry 37;
T. J. Zoehrer c M. T. G. Elliott 5; B. P. Julian c D. J. Ramshaw 9; D. J. Spencer
lbw 0; J. Angel c B. J. Hodge 1; W. K. Wishart c D. J. Ramshaw 0.

On the eve of the first Test against New Zealand, Warne returned a Shield-best 6/42 as part of a nine-wicket match haul which triggered Victoria's first outright win in almost two years.

In biting cold and wind in the WA first innings, he took 3/92, including Brendon Julian and Jo Angel in his 31st over.

Enjoying far more responsive conditions in the second, he started with seven consecutive maidens from the MCC members' end to Test pair Damien Martyn and Tom Moody. After his first 14 overs, he boasted the figures 14–10–10–1. He took six of the last seven wickets to fall as WA slumped from 3/103 to 185 all out. WA top scorer Damien Martyn, dropped at slip at 56 from Warne's bowling, finished on 89 not out.

'He's an absolute treasure. I've never seen anyone who can spin the ball as well. His control is the freakish thing.'

Australian coach BOB SIMPSON

47/18. Australia v New Zealand, First Test Match, at WACA Ground, Perth, 12, 13, 14, 15 & 16 November 1993.
SCORES
AUSTRALIA 398 (I. A. Healy 113 not out, M. A. Taylor 64, P. R. Reiffel 51) and 323 for 1 wicket dec. (M. A. Taylor 142 not out, M. J. Slater 99, D. C. Boon 67 not out); NEW ZEALAND 419 for 9 wickets dec. (A. H. Jones 143, C. L. Cairns 78) and 166 for 4 wickets. ***Drawn***.

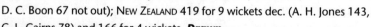

S. K. WARNE
1st inns: 37.1–6–90–1. Dismissed: C. L. Cairns b 78.
2nd inns: 13–6–23–0.

TEST

Having lost their first three games, including an embarrassing reverse to the Australian Cricket Academy in Adelaide, New Zealand was at long odds to wrest the Trans-Tasman trophy at the start of the three-Test series. However, the Kiwis, lifting for the occasion, started full of resolution and, replying to Australia's 398, established a slight lead thanks to the unconventional Andrew Jones who scored his seventh Test 100 and the feisty Chris Cairns, who made a whirlwind 78, including 11 fours and a towering six.

The Kiwis adopted the sweep shot against Warne at every opportunity, especially when he went around the wicket trying to exploit the foot-marks as he'd done so successfully in England.

Warne was into his 34th over and his fourth spell before he took his first wicket and extracted some revenge by bowling Cairns, who'd earlier dobbed him over long-off and into the Farley Stand. Warne's figures were an unflattering 1/90, but he could easily have had a second wicket, but for Ian Healy fumbling a stumping chance from man of the match Jones, who, on 113, was beaten by the extra angle created by Warne operating from around the wicket.

Later, Warne's coach Terry Jenner said Warne needed to consider changing his line from middle and leg to off and middle in Australian conditions. 'But Perth can be a nightmare for spinners,' he said. 'I can't remember any spinners doing really well there. That's nothing to be ashamed of.'

Paired with a young Glenn McGrath, in his maiden appearance, Craig McDermott took his 200th wicket in his 50th Test.

---

48. **Victoria v New South Wales**, at Melbourne Cricket Ground, 19, 20, 21 & 22 November 1993.

SCORES

NEW SOUTH WALES 227 (M. J. Slater 77, M. E. Waugh 58) and 268 for 7 wickets dec. (S. R. Waugh 122, M. A. Taylor 50; P. R. Reiffel 5/73); VICTORIA 233 (D. J. Ramshaw 85, B. J. Hodge 54; B. E. McNamara 6/43) and 263 for 9 wickets (B. J. Hodge 92, D. M. Jones 72). **Victoria won by one wicket**.

S. K. WARNE

1st inns: 31–9–72–4. Dismissed: M. J. Slater b 77; S. R. Waugh c P. R. Reiffel 1; M. G. Bevan c D. J. Ramshaw 0; W. J. Holdsworth c D. J. Ramshaw 23.

2nd inns: 29–1–103–2. Dismissed: M. E. Waugh b 24; M. G. Bevan b 9.

Seven Test players involved in the opening international with New Zealand figured in the Sheffield Shield clash between traditional rivals Victoria and New South Wales.

In another commanding performance, Warne took 4/72 and 2/103 as Victoria clinched a one-wicket win in bizarre circumstances. With just three balls remaining and the time past 7 p.m., Victoria needed only two runs and NSW just one wicket to win. Pace bowler Wayne Holdsworth thudded a delivery into Simon Cook's pads. There was a huge appeal, only for the bowler to turn away in disgust, umpire Steve Walpole having called no-ball. The two-run penalty was enough to give Victoria the game.

Highlighting his rapid improvement in just 12 months, Warne was introduced within the first hour, in the 11th over of New South Wales' first innings, and for the only time in his career dismissed Steve Waugh with his ninth delivery. He also snared the prestige scalps of Mark Waugh, Michael Slater and Michael Bevan (twice). He bowled 60 overs, more than one-third of Victoria's overs for the match.

49/19. **Australia v New Zealand**, Second Test Match, at Bellerive Oval, Hobart, 26, 27, 28 & 29 November 1993.

SCORES

AUSTRALIA 544 for 6 wickets dec. (M. J. Slater 168, M. E. Waugh 111, D. C. Boon 106, A. R. Border 60); NEW ZEALAND 161 (T. B. A. May 5/65) and 161 (K. R. Rutherford 55; S. K. Warne 6/31). *Australia won by an innings & 222 runs*.

TEST

S. K. WARNE

1st inns: 18–5–36–3. Dismissed: D. N. Patel c M. A. Taylor 18; M. L. Su'a c M. A. Taylor 6; S. B. Doull lbw 0.

2nd Inns: 19.5–9–31–6. Dismissed: B. A. Pocock st I. A. Healy 15; K. R. Rutherford b 55; T. E. Blain c & b 29; M. L. Su'a b 5; D. K. Morrison b 0; S. B. Doull c T. B. A. May 1.

Without injured captain Martin Crowe and leading all-rounder Chris Cairns, New Zealand's in-your-face resolve from Perth was but a memory, and Australia clinched victory by an innings in just over three days against a very dispirited opposition. While Mark Waugh was man of the match with 111, two key wickets and three catches, few would have objected if Warne had been chosen, given his nine wickets for the game, including 6/31 in NZ's second innings. Enjoying the south-westerly cross breeze, the reinstated Tim May also took seven wickets, prompting Richie Benaud to rate the Warne/May slow bowling combination Australia's best in 40 years. In seven Tests together, they'd taken 71 of Australia's 136 wickets.

Warne conceded under two runs per over, his most expensive being his fifth in the NZ second innings, which went for eight.

Once again he changed the direction of the game when he bowled NZ's stand-in captain and top scorer Ken Rutherford around his legs, on the third night. It took his calendar year haul to 59 in 14 Tests, surpassing the previous Australian spin bowling record of Arthur Mailey (1921) and Richie Benaud (1959), who each grossed 55 wickets.

Late in the game, NZ wicketkeeper Tony Blain withdrew from his stance so late at the point of a Warne delivery, that Warne continued with his action, the ball only narrowly missing the stumps.

'He gambles. I don't. I like hot curries. He likes plain food. He's a glamour. I'm not. He's young. I'm not. It goes on and on.'

TIM MAY discussing his spin partner, Shane Warne

50/20. **Australia v New Zealand**, Third Test Match, at Brisbane Cricket Ground, 3, 4, 5, 6 & 7 December 1993.

SCORES

NEW ZEALAND 233 (A. H. Jones 56) and 278 K. R. Rutherford 86,
B. A. Young 53); AUSTRALIA 607 for 6 wickets dec. (S. R. Waugh 147 not out,
A. R. Border 105, D. C. Boon 89, S. K. Warne 74 not out, M. E. Waugh 68,
M. A. Taylor 53). *Australia won by an innings & 96 runs*.

TEST

S. K. WARNE

1st inns: 28.3–12–66–4. Dismissed: A. H. Jones b 56; C. L. Cairns c & b 5;
D. K. Morrison c I. A. Healy 0; R. P. de Groen c A. R. Border 3.
2nd inns: 35–11–59–4. Dismissed: B. A. Young b 53; A. H. Jones
c A. R. Border 15; D. N. Patel b 3; S. B. Doull c M. A. Taylor 24. Man of the match.

Despite a strained spinning finger, the result of his incredible work-load which saw him in doubt on the eve of his first Test at the 'Gabba, Warne not only played, he took eight wickets and made a Test-best 74 not out. New Zealand slumped to another innings loss on a decidedly drier Brisbane wicket that favoured the Australian slow duo, Warne and Tim May.

A well-set Andrew Jones, NZ's senior batsman, was defeated by the wrong'un in the first innings and caught by Allan Border in the second.

Warne exchanged words with a pumped-up Chris Cairns – umpire Peter Parker stepping between them – before capturing his wicket, caught and bowled, in disputed circumstances, Cairns believing the return catch had ballooned directly from his pad.

NZ opener Bryan Young was the latest to be bowled around his legs by a savagely breaking leg-spinner.

Warne's 18-wicket haul in three Tests was a record by an Australian in Trans-Tasman Test history. He was also named man of the match and man of the series.

In Australia's huge score of 6/607 declared, Ian Healy became the first player in Australian Test cricket to be given out, run out, via third umpire Darrell Hair and a video replay. All five of NZ's frontline bowlers conceded 100 runs. Allan Border became the first to play 150 Tests.

---

51. **Victoria v New South Wales**, at Sydney Cricket Ground, 18, 19, 20 & 21 December 1993.

Scores

Victoria 264 (W. N. Phillips 57, B. J. Hodge 57) and 324 for 6 wickets dec.
(D. M. Jones 155, D. J. Ramshaw 80); New South Wales 283
(M. E. Waugh 119; S. K. Warne 5 for 77) and 275 for 9 wickets
(M. G. Bevan 81, R. Chee Quee 76). **Drawn.**

S. K. Warne

1st inns: 40–14–77–5. Dismissed: M. A. Taylor b 28; P. A. Emery lbw 31;
M. G. Bevan c D. M. Jones 2; R. Chee Quee c C. Howard 8; W. J. Holdsworth b 3.

2nd inns: 28–7–90–3. Dismissed: M. A. Taylor st D. S. Berry 14; M. E. Waugh
c D. W. Fleming 23; W. J. Holdsworth c P. R. Reiffel 21.

Having played his maiden one-day internationals on Australian soil, between first-class commitments, Warne was involved in one of his most memorable Shield matches, with his personal battle with Mark Waugh being the feature moment of the domestic summer.

New South Wales took first-innings points but was fortunate to avoid outright defeat. Coming into the game, Waugh had promised to take calculated risks to try and upset Warne's rhythm and while he made a superb 119, his only chance coming two balls before he was dismissed, Warne was also superb, claiming eight wickets on a typical Sydney turner. In the first innings, he took 3/13 from his first 12 overs and in a 21-over opening spell from the southern end, boasted the figures of 4/40.

From a precarious 5/89, NSW's fortunes revived as Waugh's innings blossomed after a quiet start. With Warne operating around the wicket, Waugh faced 19 balls before he could score a run. Often he used his pads to protect his stumps against balls pitching and spinning back from the footmarks.

It took him 65 balls to strike his first boundary against Warne, via a lifted drive to the mid-on fence. He struck 10 fours and 1 six and batted four-and-a-half hours for his 45th first-class century. A unanimous shout for caught behind against him at 21 was rejected by Darrell Hair, words being exchanged at the end of the over. Afterwards Warne said Waugh was clearly the best batsman in the world.

Ian Harvey, one of Victoria's two first-game players, was at mid-off throughout and marvelled at Warne's variety, length and line. 'For me to be at mid-off watching the best spinner in the world operating against one of the best batsmen was really something,' he said. 'Shane was turning them and doing all these different things I'd only seen on telly. I'd never seen anything like it before. Shane was superb – but so too was Mark. People said it was one of the best 100s ever at the SCG. It certainly was fantastic.'

The biggest crowd (4880) of the NSW domestic season, and second-best attendance of the Shield summer, attended the second day's play.

In 40 overs, Warne bowled 14 maidens and took 5/77, including Mark Taylor bowled by a conventional off-break, which he under-cut onto his stumps.

Warne was just as accurate in the second innings too, taking 2/9 from his first ten overs and 3/90 from 28. NSW tailender Wayne Holdsworth took 14 from his 27th over (4 . 6 . . 4).

'He is the best I have seen of any kind and undoubtedly the best bowler Australia has produced since Bill O'Reilly.'

Ex-Test opener COLIN MCDONALD

52/21. **Australia v South Africa**, First Test Match, at Melbourne Cricket Ground, 26, 27 (no play), 28, 29 & 30 December 1993.
SCORES
AUSTRALIA 342 for 7 wickets dec. (M. A. Taylor 179, M. E. Waugh 84);
SOUTH AFRICA 258 for 3 wickets (W. J. Cronje 71, A. C. Hudson 64 ret. hurt,
K. C. Wessels 63 not out). *Drawn*.
S. K. WARNE
Only inns: 31–8–63–1. Dismissed: W. J. Cronje c D. C. Boon 71.

TEST

The first Test between Australia and South Africa in 20 years was ruined by rain, only two hours being possible on Boxing Day and none at all on 27 December. Both days three and four were also interrupted.

Mark Taylor became the second batsman, after New Zealand's Martin Crowe, to score centuries against seven Test nations. Warne took 18 overs to take his only wicket, his 72nd of the calendar year. His run-out attempt while bowling to Andrew Hudson saw the South African retire hurt after he was struck on the forearm by an unnecessary return throw.

TEST

53/22. **Australia v South Africa**, Second Test Match, at Sydney Cricket Ground, 2, 3, 4, 5 & 6 January 1994.

SCORES

SOUTH AFRICA 169 (G. Kirsten 67; S. K. Warne 7/56) and 239 (J. N. Rhodes 76 not out; S. K. Warne 5/72); AUSTRALIA 292 (M. J. Slater 92, D. R. Martyn 59) and 111 (P. S. de Villiers 6/43).

South Africa won by five runs.

S. K. WARNE

1st inns: 27–8–56–7. Dismissed: G. Kirsten st I. A. Healy 67; D. J. Cullinan b 9; J. N. Rhodes lbw 4; K. C. Wessels c & b 3; D. J. Richardson c M. A. Taylor 4; P. L. Symcox b 7; C. R. Matthews c M. A. Taylor 0.

2nd inns: 42–17–72–5. Dismissed: K. C. Wessels b 18; D. J. Cullinan lbw 2; C. R. Matthews c M. E. Waugh 4; P. S. de Villiers lbw 2; A. A. Donald c I. A. Healy 10.

A remarkable finish overshadowed Warne's heroic solo and first-ever 10-wicket match return. Enjoying their finest moment in more than a century of international cricket, South Africa won by five runs after Australia capitulated for just 111 to revive the nightmares of Headingley, 1981.

In an extraordinary opening day, Warne overshadowed the new-ball bowlers Craig McDermott and Glenn McGrath to take 7/56 from 27 overs, the best figures by an Australian against South Africa.

Introduced at 11.50 a.m. to a most appreciative reception, Warne bowled ten wicketless overs in the first session, most to the defiant left-hander Gary Kirsten, before humbling the South African batsmen with 5/26 in nine overs between lunch and tea, his only blemish being the aggressive and unbecoming send-off of Daryll Cullinan after he'd knocked his off stump back with a flipper.

On a first-day wicket which turned, but not outrageously, Warne teased, taunted and tormented his opponents with wickets in seven of his final nine overs, including 6/19 from his final 67-ball spell. Highlights were the dismissals of top scorer Kirsten (stumped by Ian Healy from a googly which he misread) and wicketkeeper Dave Richardson, sensationally caught one-handed by Mark Taylor diving to his left at slip.

Capping off his two-hour blitz was the wicket of the talkative, combative Pat Symcox, bowled behind his legs by a massive leg-break, just moments after he'd declared: 'You won't get one through there, sonny!'

WIZARD BLAZES THROUGH S. AFRICANS, headlined the *Australian*. JOKER WARNE TRUMPS BATS said the Melbourne *Herald Sun*.

In the second innings, with South Africa desperate to build a fourth-innings target, Warne was again a bogyman, with 5/72 from 42 overs, including Cullinan again to the flipper, this time lbw, and injured captain Kepler Wessels bowled by a leg-break that hit his leg stump. He bowled his longest Test spell on Australian soil, 24 overs, taking 5/47.

His match haul of 12/128 was the best by an Australian leg-spinner in a Test in Sydney and best overall since C. T. B. 'Terror' Turner's 12/87 in 1887–88. All 12 wickets were taken from the southern, or Randwick, end.

'More than ever Warne resembles Toad from Toad Hall, a character continually seized by the joy of the moment, a character of excitement and excess capable of pinching a car and driving around with a beep and a toot.'   PETER ROEBUCK in the *Sydney Morning Herald*

54/23. **Australia v South Africa**, Third Test Match, at Adelaide Oval, 28, 29, 30, 31 January & 1 February 1994.

SCORES

AUSTRALIA 469 for 7 wickets dec. (S. R. Waugh 164, A. R. Border 84, M. A. Taylor 62, M. J. Slater 53, D. C. Boon 50) and 124 for 6 wickets dec.; SOUTH AFRICA 273 (A. C. Hudson 90, P. N. Kirsten 79) and 129.

TEST

Australia won by 191 runs.

S. K. WARNE

1st inns: 44.2–15–85–1. Dismissed: P. N. Kirsten c M. E. Waugh 79.

2nd inns: 30.5–15–31–4. Dismissed: G. Kirsten b 7; W. J. Cronje lbw 3; B. M. McMillan lbw 4; R. P. Snell c & b 1.

Having taken 22 wickets in nine matches in his first World Series, Warne had clinched the International Cricketer of the Year award even before the sixth and final Test of his finest summer.

However, his workload over a 12-month period had increased so dramatically that he'd developed tendonitis in his right shoulder and was having to limit his net time and rest more between games.

The deciding Test in Adelaide was dominated by Steve Waugh, with both bat and ball, but Warne again had a significant impact, dismissing top scorer Peter Kirsten in the first innings, taking his 100th wicket in his 23rd Test (Brian McMillan) and finishing the game with a caught and bowled (Richard Snell) in the second. The Australian record for the quickest 100 wickets is held jointly by C. T. B. Turner and Clarrie Grimmett, who each took 17 Tests.

It took Warne 43.3 overs in the first innings to claim Kirsten's wicket, yet bowling again on the fourth night after Allan Border's declaration, seven of his first nine overs were maidens and he'd taken 2/1. 'He's just a freak,' said Australian coach Bob Simpson. 'In 40 years of watching cricket I've never seen anything like him and the way he can spin the ball so far yet be so accurate.'

South Africa's brave fight to save the match virtually ended when McMillan, a charismatic and competitive all-rounder, played back to a flipper having made four in almost an hour. When Warne wasn't bowling he'd been baiting McMillan from gully, constantly calling him 'Gerard' after the leading French actor Gerard Depardieu.

He chided McMillan for not running a three and staying off strike. The message came back: 'Listen Warnie, people disappear every day in South Africa. One more won't make any difference!'

With 36 wickets for the summer, 18 against both New Zealand and South Africa, he'd given spin bowling a kiss of life and cricket a pleasurable new dimension.

SUMMARY, 1993–94 (Australia)

	Mts	Overs	Mdn	Runs	Wicks	Ave	BB	5wl	10wM
All First-Class matches	10	574.2	176	1255	63	19.92	7/56	5	1
Test matches v NZ	3	151.3	49	305	18	16.94	6/31	1	–
Test matches v South Africa	3	175.1	63	307	18	17.05	7/56	2	1
Sheffield Shield matches	4	247.4	64	643	27	23.81	6/42	2	–

Australia in South Africa

55. **Australia v Orange Free State**, at Springbok Park, Bloemfontein, 26, 27, 28 February & 1 March 1994.

Scores

Australia 450 for 8 wickets dec. (M. E. Waugh 154, S. R. Waugh 102, M. J. Slater 65) and 270 for 6 wickets dec. (M. J. Slater 105, M. A. Taylor 54; K. Venter 5/101); Orange Free State 264 (L. J. Wilkinson 53, J. M. Arthur 51; T. B. A. May 5/98) and 396 (W. J. Cronje 251).
Australia won by 60 runs.

S. K. Warne

1st inns: 23–5–73–3. Dismissed: J. M. Arthur b 51; B. T. Player lbw 10; N. Boje st I. A. Healy 7.
2nd inns: 28.2–6–70–2. Dismissed: N. Boje b 6; P. J. L. Radley lbw 4.

The South African tour was Australia's first since Kim Hughes' rebel tours in the mid-80s. Warne was rested for the opening two games and didn't bowl in the third, leading into the first leg of the limited-overs internationals.

From arrival at Johannesburg's Jan Smuts Airport, Warne had been in demand. Everyone wanted to see and talk to The Flipperman. Phone calls to the team's hotels weren't always screened and some mornings, he found himself being awoken by nuisance calls at 2 a.m. and 3 a.m.

The Warne/Tim May spin pairing was immediately under pressure from the Test-eve clash with Orange Free State in Bloemfontein. Hansie Cronje made 44 and 251 in an exhilarating double which allowed Free State to creep within 60 runs of their winning target of 457. Warne took five wickets and May six, but they were at heavy cost, Cronje striking 8 sixes for the game.

In the *Citizen* newspaper, Cronje claimed Warne wasn't so testing; patience was the key; just wait for the bad balls to hit.

As in the first-class tour openers in New Zealand and England, Warne deliberately masked his flipper and googly from Cronje, bowling only leg-breaks, often deliberately wide of leg stump. Cronje had been in brilliant form in the first four one-dayers, too, and in the second innings advanced to a career-best 251, the second-highest score by any South African against a first-class Australian team.

He denied his cavalier tactics against Warne were premeditated. 'I'm not going after him. I'm just trying to score at three an over,' he said. 'If he goes for more, that's my good fortune.'

56/24. Australia v South Africa, First Test Match, at Wanderers Stadium, Johannesburg, 4, 5, 6, 7 & 8 March 1994.

Scores

South Africa 251 (J. N. Rhodes 69) and 9/450 dec. (W. J. Cronje 122, A. C. Hudson 60, P. N. Kirsten 53, K. C. Wessels 50); Australia 248 and 256 (D. C. Boon 83). *South Africa won by 197 runs*.

TEST

S. K. Warne

1st inns: 14–4–42–1. Dismissed: D. J. Richardson lbw 31.

2nd inns: 44.5–14–86–4. Dismissed: A. C. Hudson b 60; K. C. Wessels c A. R. Border 50; B. M. McMillan b 24; D. J. Richardson c A. R. Border 20.

It had been 35 years since Australia had won at Wanderers, the stronghold of South African cricket. Spectators at the Bullring like to get involved, whether it's firing up their portable barbecues or barracking from the wide-open hill areas. The pitch invariably favours the seamers and the South Africans included four, 'White Lightning' Allan Donald, backed by Fanie de Villiers, Craig Matthews and Brian McMillan. However, the Australians, having enjoyed so much success with dual spin, preferred to keep spin twins Warne and May together and named only two fast bowlers, Craig McDermott and Merv Hughes.

In a game marred by sledging and unsavoury behaviour by fans, some of whom threw oranges and other missiles at Australian players fielding near the boundary, Hughes and Warne became too involved in the cut-and-thrust of the tensest of Tests and both verbally abused South African batsmen. Late in the game, under severe provocation, Hughes also brandished his bat at a spectator while walking back up the players' race. The backlash was immediate, with both Australians being reprimanded and then heavily fined for unbecoming conduct.

Warne admits he succumbed to all the hype, pressure and taunts. During the one-day series, the crowds would chant, WARNE'S A WANKER and as soon as the in-form Hansie Cronje emerged, would invariably call for Warne to bowl, believing easy runs would result. He initially laughed it all off, but Cronje's six sprees in the ODI series clouded his normally sunny attitude.

Inexplicably kept out of the attack until just after noon and the 44th over of South Africa's second innings, so pumped was Warne when he bowled opener Andrew Hudson from the Golf Course End, that he 'lost it' and twice told Hudson to 'F&*%-off' in the full hearing of umpires David Shepherd and Barry Lambson before being restrained by wicketkeeper Ian Healy.

It was uncharacteristic and unpalatable. Just weeks earlier, the Australian Cricket Board's chairman Alan Crompton had announced a crackdown on abusive behaviour, saying sledging was 'cowardly' and 'un-Australian' and erring players who acted outside the spirit of the game would be disciplined.

TEST UPROAR, headlined the Melbourne *Herald Sun*. WARNE, HUGHES FACE BANS FOR ABUSE said the *Age*. SEND THEM HOME said 3AW's David Hookes.

Initially both were fined only a percentage ($450) of their match fee by the International Cricket Council referee Donald Carr before the Australian Cricket Board added their own stiffer penalties, docking each their entire match wage of $4000.

Warne apologised to Hudson, the sunniest of opponents, saying there was nothing personal in the incident. He had allowed the constant taunting by a hostile crowd to affect his composure. Earlier in the day, he'd been struck in the back by an orange while fielding in the deep and his temper had bubbled out of control.

Warne also apologised to the umpires and Border and later to the Australian sporting public, saying he'd acted out of character and sincerely regretted his actions. 'I hope I don't get hung for it for the rest of my life because I stuffed up once,' he said. 'I've got a really short fuse at the moment and feel myself snapping. I'm letting everything get to me. I've never been reported before and I don't want to carry a bad-boy reputation for doing one stupid thing.'

His superb second-innings bowling, when he took 4/86 from almost 45 overs, paled into insignificance amidst the controversy and Australia's 197-run defeat.

Writing in his *South African Tour Diary*, Steve Waugh said the abuse from some sections of the crowd at Wanderers was as bad as he could remember in any game. 'There is a percentage of people who are there for the sole purpose of abusing us whenever they see fit,' he said. 'It is something you can endure, as long as it doesn't get too personal. But too often today it did.'

One of the few lighter moments came when Brian McMillan borrowed a security guard's rifle and marched into the Australian rooms saying, 'Right, that's it. I've had you blokes!' More than a few Aussies ducked for cover before seeing McMillan break out into a huge grin.

'I got a bit cocky and a bit arrogant. I did a couple of things in South Africa I am ashamed of when I sledged Andrew Hudson. I just couldn't believe I did that.'   SHANE WARNE

---

57. **Australia v Boland**, at Coetzenburg, Stellenbosch, 12, 13 & 14 March 1994.
SCORES
AUSTRALIA 254 for 7 wickets dec. (D. M. Jones 63, D. C. Boon 52) and 228 for 6 wickets dec. (M. A. Taylor 74, S. R. Waugh 71); BOLAND 155 and 132 for 5 wickets. **Drawn**.

S. K. WARNE

1st inns: 20.5–9–49–3. Dismissed: K. C. Jackson b 27; B. J. Drew
c S. R. Waugh 4; D. Smith lbw 3.
2nd inns: 15–7–24–1. Dismissed: J. S. Roos c P. R. Reiffel 9.

A drawn game at Coetzenburg in Stellenbosch saw Warne take four wickets. However, he was still smarting over the sledging controversy. Many of the Australians felt the Board's fines were excessive, and were disappointed Warne and Hughes were not asked for their side of the story.

In a brutally honest conversation with Australia's acting captain Mark Taylor, Taylor told Warne he wasn't acting 'like the Shane Warne we all know and love'.

He said high-profile sportsmen had a responsibility to be ambassadors for the game and the next generations of players. He said the Australian public would forgive and forget. Warne needed to put the past few weeks behind him, enjoy his cricket again and let his ability shine through.

There was a lighter moment when Boland's nominated 12th man, Robbie Dalrymple, who was allowed to bat after one of his teammates aggravated an injury, was struggling to put bat on ball against Warne. The Australians reminded him that maybe he wasn't up to scratch. 'Who did you bloody well expect?' he said. 'Don Bradman?!'

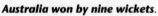

58/25. **Australia v South Africa**, Second Test Match, at Newlands, Cape Town, 17, 18, 19, 20 & 21 March 1994.

SCORES

SOUTH AFRICA 361 (A. C. Hudson 102, B. M. McMillan 74, P. N. Kirsten 70) and 164 (S. R. Waugh 5/28); AUSTRALIA 435 (D. C. Boon 96, S. R. Waugh 86, M. A. Taylor 70, I. A. Healy 61; C. R. Matthews 5/80) and 92 for 1 wicket.

Australia won by nine wickets.

S. K. WARNE

1st inns: 47–18–78–3. Dismissed: P. N. Kirsten lbw 70; B. M. McMillan b 74; P. S. de Villiers c M. A. Taylor 7.
2nd inns: 30–13–38–3. Dismissed: G. Kirsten lbw 10; P. N. Kirsten c M. A. Taylor 3; P. S. de Villiers lbw 0.

TEST

Australia's series-squaring victory at Newlands, the most arrestingly beautiful of all international venues and the happiest of hunting grounds for the Aussies, was again led by Steve Waugh, who made 86 and took a career-best 5/28 as the Proteas slumped from 1/69 to 164 all out in their second innings.

The reinstated Glenn McGrath, in only his fourth Test match, also made a telling four-wicket contribution.

With six wickets from almost 80 overs for the game, Warne regained his menacing form of the Australian season. After Taylor's heart-to-heart, he seemed more relaxed and showed much of his old zest. He'd also shaved off his machiavellian goatee beard.

Warne started South Africa's collapse by trapping Gary Kirsten lbw with his third delivery and for much of the time bowled with three and four close-in fieldsmen as the Australians went in for the kill.

59/26. **Australia v South Africa**, Third Test Match, at Kingsmead, Durban, 25, 26, 27, 28 & 29 March 1994.

SCORES

AUSTRALIA 269 (S. R. Waugh 64, I. A. Healy 55) and 297 for 4 wickets (M. E. Waugh 113 not out, M. J. Slater 95); SOUTH AFRICA 422 (B. M. McMillan 84, J. N. Rhodes 78, A. C. Hudson 65, D. J. Richardson 59). *Drawn*.

TEST

S. K. WARNE

Only inns: 55–20–92–4. Dismissed: W. J. Cronje c S. R. Waugh 26; J. N. Rhodes lbw 78; D. J. Richardson c P. R. Reiffel 59; C. R. Matthews lbw 1.

Allan Border's 156th and final Test ended in a tame draw, ensuring Australia a 1–1 series result, or 2–2 for the whole Test summer, home and away.

Warne again had several marathon spells and a record 55 overs in all during South Africa's elongated first innings which stretched from before lunch on day two to after lunch on day four. It took him 21 overs to secure his first wicket, Hansie Cronje, who was caught by Steve Waugh.

His second victim, Jonty Rhodes, was lbw to a flipper for 78. It was the seventh delivery of Warne's 36th over right on the tea interval. Rhodes had hit the previous delivery, a no-ball, for four. 'It was stupid,' Rhodes said. 'I was thinking we should be at tea because this is the seventh ball of the over. Shane bowled the flipper. I didn't pick it and I was gone.'

SUMMARY, 1993–94 (SOUTH AFRICA)

	Mts	Overs	Mdn	Runs	Wicks	Ave	BB	5wI	10wM
All First-Class matches	5	278	96	552	24	23.00	4/86	–	–
Test matches v South Africa	3	190.5	69	336	15	22.40	4/86	–	–

1994–95

WARNE'S METEORIC PROGRESS had seen him surpass acclaimed sub-continent spin wizards, Pakistan's Mushtaq Ahmed and India's Anil Kumble, as the game's No. 1 ranked slow bowler.

While some were not prepared to readily forgive his misdemeanour in Johannesburg, the majority treated it as an aberration, and he continued to be inundated by a flood of off-field opportunities from modelling and media work to endorsements and public speaking.

He'd been cleared of knee ligament damage after a fall during the Sharjah one-day tournament, his only wintertime commitment while en route to America an exhibition game at Highclere Castle in June, to celebrate the first appearance in 30 years of a South African team to England.

Leading into the springtime tour of Pakistan, the rest was a godsend for both his battle-weary bowling arm and spin finger, which had also been a growing concern. He may have been shoulder-strong and steel-wristed, but his workload had been Herculean. In just seven months he'd bowled 1017 overs, twice the workload of even the fittest spinners on the six-day-a-week English county circuit.

Ahead were tours of Sri Lanka, Pakistan, another Ashes campaign and the world championship showdown against the West Indies with the game's new batting hero Brian Lara.

For the first time in 16 years an Australian side departed without Allan Border. New captain Mark Taylor said only the fittest and most focused players could hope to survive and succeed in the months ahead, culminating in the world championship Tests against the West Indies on their own wickets.

Taylor told Warne he intended to use him purely in attacking roles, for shorter spells than he'd bowled under Border. By managing his workload, he thought Australian cricket would benefit for longer.

While Taylor was no expert on leg-spin theory, he knew that Warne had to rotate his shoulder differently when bowling his leg-break, compared with the googly and the flipper. Niggles were inevitable and overuse could only compound the problems.

AUSTRALIA IN PAKISTAN

60. **Australia v President's XI**, at Rawalpindi Cricket Stadium,
23, 24 & 25 September 1994.
SCORES
AUSTRALIA 338 (D. C. Boon 101, M. E. Waugh 57, S. R. Waugh 53 not out)
and 134 for 2 wickets dec. (M. G. Bevan 62 not out); PRESIDENT'S XI 145
and 270 for 9 wickets (Zahid Fazal 91, Shoaib Mohammad 55;
G. D. McGrath 6/49). **Drawn**.
S. K. WARNE
1st inns: 10–3–42–3. Dismissed: Ijaz Ahmed c D. C. Boon 38; Mohsin Kamal
c I. A. Healy 10; Ata-ur-Rehman c I. A. Healy 11.
2nd inns: 19–6–52–2. Dismissed: Ijaz Ahmed c S. R. Waugh 9; Manzoor
Akhtar lbw 11.

Monsoonal rains affected much of the Singer World Series tournament in Sri Lanka leading into the Pakistan tour, Australia's first since the ill-fated 1988–89 campaign when the team very nearly returned home early claiming Third World umpiring bias.

With only one first-class match available before the first Test, the Australians played a virtual Test team against the Pakistani Board XI at Rawalpindi, Warne showing encouraging early form with five wickets, including Ijaz Ahmed in both innings. He would have had a sixth but for Ian Healy fumbling a leg-side stumping against No. 11 batsman Ashfaq Ahmed in Warne's final over, the second-last of the drawn match.

61/27. **Australia v Pakistan**, First Test Match, at National Stadium, Karachi, 28, 29, 30 September, 1 & 2 October 1994.

SCORES

AUSTRALIA 337 (M. G. Bevan 82, S. R. Waugh 73, I. A. Healy 57) and 232 (D. C. Boon 114 not out; Wasim Akram 5/64); PAKISTAN 256 (Saeed Anwar 85) and 315 for 9 wickets (Saeed Anwar 77, Inzamam-ul-Haq 58 not out; S. K. Warne 5/89). *Pakistan won by one wicket.*

S. K. WARNE

1st inns: 27–10–61–3. Dismissed: Aamir Sohail c M. G. Bevan 36; Inzamam-ul-Haq c M. A. Taylor 9; Rashid Latif c M. A. Taylor 2.
2nd inns: 36.1–12–89–5. Dismissed: Zahid Fazal c D. C. Boon 3; Akram Raza lbw 2; Basit Ali lbw 12; Wasim Akram c & b 4; Waqar Younis c I. A. Healy 7. Man of the match.

TEST

Mark Taylor's pair in his maiden game as captain, David Boon's defiant five-hour century and a brave, matchwinning half-century 10th-wicket stand by Inzamam-ul-Haq and Mushtaq Ahmed highlighted the dramatic first Test in which Australia was denied a historic victory in Pakistan's largest city.

Set 314 to win, the Pakistans rallied from 7/184 to win by a single wicket to extend their proud record at Karachi's National Stadium to 30 matches without defeat, Inzamam sharing in three crucial partnerships: 52 for the eighth wicket with Rashid Latiff, 22 for the ninth with Waqar Younis and 57 in just 47 minutes for the last with Mushtaq.

The winning runs came via four byes from the first ball of the 107th over. Initially umpire Dickie Bird called leg-byes, but it was a genuine stumping chance which the normally sure Ian Healy failed to glove.

Instead of winning by two runs, the crestfallen Aussies lost by a single wicket, and Healy kicked the stumps in his disappointment. Later he took full blame for the defeat, saying it was the blackest moment of his career.

'Warnie bowled to a charging Inzamam and after it pitched the ball ran along the ground . . . and beat the bat, the stumps, the 'keeper, everything,' said Boon. 'Afterwards the dressing room was silent, much like it had been in Adelaide when we missed winning the Frank Worrell Trophy by two runs in 1992–93.'

Healy said he thought the ball was going to bowl big Inzi. 'But it just turned past the off-stump. That's what stuffed me,' he said.

Despite being on the losing side, Warne, with eight wickets, was named man of the match. His 5/89 in the second innings included three wickets in the first 75 minutes on the final morning, night-watchman Akram Raza and Basit Ali lbw and Wasim Akram caught and bowled. He bowled at one end virtually throughout the final day. Glenn McGrath strained a quadricep after bowling only six overs and Tim May was restricted by a ricked neck.

Months later cricket's greatest scandal since World Series became public knowledge. According to the *Sydney Morning Herald*'s Phil Wilkins, Pakistan's captain Saleem Malik had approached Warne and May on the penultimate night, offering them bribes to bowl badly to keep intact Pakistan's unbeaten record at Karachi. His offers were rejected out of hand, but the repercussions and the resultant ongoing controversy were to be a blight on the game and those central in the corruption for years, and would see Malik banned for life, in May 2000.

62/28. **Australia v Pakistan**, Second Test Match, at Rawalpindi Cricket Stadium, 5, 6, 7, 8 & 9 October 1994.
SCORES
AUSTRALIA 9/521 dec. (M. J. Slater 110, S. R. Waugh 98, M. G. Bevan 70, M. A. Taylor 69, M. E. Waugh 68, I. A. Healy 58) and 14 for 1 wicket;

TEST

PAKISTAN 260 (Aamir Sohail 80) and 537 (Saleem Malik 237, Saeed Anwar 75, Aamir Sohail 72, Aamir Malik 65). **Drawn.**

S. K. WARNE

1st inns: 21.4–8–58–1. Dismissed: Inzamam-ul-Haq lbw 14.

2nd inns: 25–6–56–0.

A marathon double century from Saleem Malik helped Pakistan scramble to a draw, deflating much of the Australian joy at first-game seamer Damien Fleming taking a hat-trick in the second innings with the fifth and sixth deliveries of his 23rd over and first of his 24th. It was a most distinguished trio, too: Aamir Malik, Inzamam-ul-Haq and Malik.

Asked to follow on, for only the second time at home since 1952, Pakistan batted for almost 11 hours, Malik's magnificent solo integral to the fightback. Dropped by Taylor at slip at 20, he made 237.

On a wicket more conducive to the faster bowlers, Warne took only one wicket from 47 overs for the match. His fifth over cost 14, courtesy of opener Aamir Sohail. He also dropped Sohail, at deep backward square leg, one of two particularly crucial catches turfed by the Australians.

Wasim Akram's spell to Steve Waugh with the second new ball after lunch on day two was the fastest Waugh had ever encountered. In one lightning three-over burst, Akram bowled 13 short-pitched deliveries. 'It was quick and short and nasty but that's okay, it's Test cricket,' said Waugh.

'Warne is a great bowler, but to pick him is not difficult. He can bowl only three different deliveries and has a completely different action for each one. The angle of his hand is different for each ball. I pick each one as it leaves his hand. I was confident and he knew that.'

Pakistan captain SALEEM MALIK

63/29. **Australia v Pakistan**, Third Test Match, at Gaddafi Stadium, Lahore, 1, 2, 3, 4 & 5 November 1994.

SCORES

PAKISTAN 373 (Moin Khan 115 not out, Saleem Malik 75, Inzamam-ul-Haq 66;

TEST

S. K. Warne 6/136) and 404 (Saleem Malik 143, Aamir Sohail 105);
AUSTRALIA 455 (M. G. Bevan 91, M. J. Slater 74, M. E. Waugh 71,
J. L. Langer 69). ***Drawn***.

S. K. WARNE

1st inns: 41.5–12–136–6. Dismissed: Saeed Anwar b 30; Ijaz Ahmed
c D. C. Boon 48; Basit Ali c M. E. Waugh 0; Akram Raza b 0; Aqib Javed
c M. E. Waugh 2; Mohsin Kamal lbw 4.
2nd inns: 30–2–104–3. Dismissed: Aamir Sohail st P. A. Emery 105;
Akram Raza lbw 32; Aqib Javed lbw 2.

Having won the Wills one-day trophy in between the second and
third Tests, a weakened Australian XI looked to square the Test series
in Lahore, but were once again thwarted. In a high-scoring draw the
resolute Pakistanis made 373 and 404, batting for 121 overs in the
first innings and 110 in the second. Four key catches were again
grassed, costing more than 150 runs.

Warne took nine wickets, including 6/136 from 41.5 overs in the
first innings when Pakistan batted into a fifth session. With a record-
equalling 18 wickets for the series, Warne had once again been the
lynchpin of the attack, Saleem the only one to master him. When
Warne went around the wicket, he'd move his guard wide of leg stump
and ignore the temptation to play the pull shot, instead keeping a
straight bat and relying on punch shots through the off side for his runs.

The casualties from the one-day series, injured pair Ian Healy and
Steve Waugh, were replaced by Phil Emery, who figured in six dismissals,
and Justin Langer, who made 69 in his maiden appearance on tour.

Other than a daily highlights package shown on Channel Nine,
there was virtually no coverage of the tour, on either free-to-air or
pay TV.

SUMMARY, 1994–95 (PAKISTAN)

	Mts	Overs	Mdn	Runs	Wicks	Ave	BB	5wl	10wM
All First-Class matches	4	210.4	59	598	23	26.00	6/136	2	–
Test matches v Pakistan	3	181.4	50	504	18	28.00	6/136	2	–

In Australia

64. **Victoria v Tasmania**, at Melbourne Cricket Ground, 17, 18,
19 & 20 November 1994.

Scores

Victoria 293 (D. M. Jones 126, G. B. Gardiner 64; S. Young 5/68) and 283
(D. M. Jones 76, M. T. G. Elliott 58, I. A. Wrigglesworth 58; S. Young 5/56);
Tasmania 302 for 7 wickets dec. (D. C. Boon 71; S. K. Warne 5/104) and 112
(T. F. Corbett 6/42). *Victoria won by 163 runs.*

S. K. Warne

1st inns: 38–10–104–5. Dismissed: D. F. Hills c G. J. Clarke 40; J. Cox
c S. H. Cook 27; M. J. Di Venuto c G. J. Clarke 31; D. C. Boon
c G. J. Clarke 71; R. J. Tucker c S. H. Cook 0.
2nd inns: 15.1–6–25–2. Dismissed: M. J. Di Venuto c I. A. Wrigglesworth 16;
S. Young c D. M. Jones 45.

Just days after returning via Bangkok to Melbourne and the new
Australian season, Warne was thrust into a controversy when he
declared his enthusiasm to play in the important Sheffield Shield
game against Queensland in Brisbane, only for the national selectors
to veto the move, saying he should rest with the Ashes series just a
fortnight away.

Instead, Warne and fellow Pakistani tourist Damien Fleming
played a week later, against Tasmania in Melbourne, Warne taking
seven wickets from 53.1 overs. In the first innings his return was
5/104, including four maidens in a row from overs 25 to 28. His 25th
over was a double wicket maiden, David Boon (71) and Rod Tucker
(0) falling in four balls. In the second, he took the final Tasmanian
wicket, top scorer Shaun Young (45), to end the match just minutes
before rain swept across the ground. 'We couldn't cover his bounce,'
said Tasmanian opener Jamie Cox.

Asked about a new mystery ball he claimed he'd developed on the
eve of the Ashes Tests, Warne said, 'It goes along the pitch and comes
back to me and spins up in the air.'

65/30. Australia v England, First Test Match, at Brisbane Cricket Ground, 25, 26, 27, 28 & 29 November 1994.

SCORES

AUSTRALIA 426 (M. J. Slater 176, M. E. Waugh 140, M. A. Taylor 59) and 248 for 8 wickets dec. (M. A. Taylor 58); ENGLAND 167 (M. A. Atherton 54; C. J. McDermott 6/53) and 323 (G. A. Hick 80, G. P. Thorpe 67, G. A. Gooch 56; S. K. Warne 8/71). *Australia won by 184 runs*.

TEST

S. K. WARNE

1st inns: 21.2–7–39–3. Dismissed: G. P. Thorpe c & b 28; P. A. J. DeFreitas c I. A. Healy 7; P. C. R. Tufnell c M. A. Taylor 0.

2nd inns: 50.2–22–71–8. Dismissed: M. A. Atherton lbw 23; A. J. Stewart b 33; G. A. Hick c I. A. Healy 80; G. P. Thorpe b 67; G. A. Gooch c I. A. Healy 56; P. A. J. DeFreitas b 11; D. Gough c M. E. Waugh 10; M. J. McCague lbw 0. Man of the match.

Unfazed by criticism from London and England's chairman of selectors Ray Illingworth that he was a negative bowler who concentrated too much on a leg stump line, Warne made a triumphant start to his Ashes campaign, triggering Australia's 184-run victory with three wickets in England's first innings and a career-best eight in the second.

He very nearly ended the game with a hat-trick when England's No. 11 Phil Tufnell played at a wrong'un and watched it curl between bat and pad and only just miss the top of his off stump. ENGLAND BEGUILED BY WIZARD, headlined the *Australian*. WARNE DEVASTATES ENGLAND, said the *Age*.

Set a massive 508 to win in two days, England was full of fight at 0/50 before Warne bowled Alec Stewart with a flipper and trapped Mike Atherton lbw with a full-length leg-break on his way to dismissing five of England's top six.

So dismayed were they by their failure to adjust to Warne's pace and spin variations that the pair borrowed binoculars and went up high into the back of the grandstand and sat on scaffolding with the Channel Nine cameramen to study their nemesis from behind his arm.

Using his flipper far more than in Pakistan where Saleem Malik had averaged 92 and played him with relative comfort on the slow and low turners of the subcontinent, Warne enjoyed the extra bounce available and again stamped his authority on the Englishmen, who played him with exaggerated care. Australia's 12th man for the match, Damien Fleming, said the English hardly dared venture outside their crease for fear of being stranded.

Warne conceded just seven runs from his first seven overs in the first innings and in the second, eight of his first nine overs were maidens. 'It was such a stark difference to the way the Pakistanis had played. They were forever looking to come down and take him on,' Fleming said.

After Stewart had hit a boundary, earlier in an over, he was made to look like an ungainly schoolboy as he positioned himself for a pull shot only to realise too late that it was the quicker, sliding flipper. It rushed through, scattering his stumps, his look of anguish reminding of Mike Gatting's pain at Old Trafford, 18 months previously.

The dismissal of Graham Gooch, who top-edged an attempted sweep shot, was equally satisfying. Responding to Warne's 'Well played Mr Gooch' after he'd reached 50, Gooch said, 'Thanks. You've got the others, but I'm damned if you're going to get me.' An over later, he too was out.

Having started the final day at a promising 2/211, the Englishmen were bowled out 40 minutes after lunch for 323. Warne, in irresistible form, took 6/27 from his final 25.2 overs, including for the first time three wickets in four balls (Gooch, Phil DeFreitas and Martin McCague).

Only one player, New Zealand's premier paceman Richard Hadlee (with 9/52 in 1985–86) had produced superior figures in a 'Gabba Test. And the only Australian to surpass his match haul of 11/110 was left-arm seamer Ernie Toshack, who took 11/31 against India in 1947–48.

For the first time in the world bowling ratings, Warne jumped ahead of West Indian Curtly Ambrose and Pakistani Waqar Younis as the No. 1 bowler in the game.

Mike Atherton said he was devastated to lose the game. 'Before the match, I said how important this match would be because in the last three series, the side which has won the first match has won the series. Warne is the best bowler from either side. If you go out there believing he is going to get you out, you will struggle.'

Three of Warne's 11 wickets for the match were caught behind by Ian Healy, who, with nine victims, equalled Gil Langley and Rod Marsh's Australian Test record.

---

66. Victoria v Western Australia, at WACA Ground, Perth, 16, 17, 18 & 19 December 1994.

SCORES

VICTORIA 342 (M. T. G. Elliott 171; J. Angel 5/87) and 161;
WESTERN AUSTRALIA 234 (T. M. Moody 55) and 241 (T. M. Moody 81).
Victoria won by 28 runs.

S. K. WARNE

1st inns: 28–8–72–2. Dismissed: D. R. Martyn c P. R. Reiffel 35;
T. M. Moody st D. S. Berry 55.
2nd inns: 36–15–64–4. Dismissed: M. P. Lavender b 48; M. W. Goodwin
c sub (G. J. Clarke) 3; A. C. Gilchrist b 5; J. Angel c B. J. Hodge 1.

Playing his second and final interstate match of the season, in the city where his only first-class wicket had cost 253 runs, Warne and fellow international Damien Fleming masterminded Victoria's 28-run outright win, both taking six wickets for the match. In Victoria's first innings, young opening batsman Matthew Elliott was last out, for 171, half of Victoria's sizeable 342. Warne bowled more than one third of Victoria's overs after Merv Hughes' breakdown in mid-match.

During his matchwinning, unbroken 30-over spell on the final day which saw Western Australia slump from an overnight 2/50 to 241 all out, Warne underlined his ability to spin his leg-break on even the glassiest of surfaces when he bowled rising left-hander Adam Gilchrist without playing a shot. Five of his first ten overs in the second innings were maidens.

'He's the sort of guy who, if we keep him fresh, will be a matchwinner for us for many years to come. He's only 25. We have to make sure the warning signs don't get too bad and force him out of the game before we can do something about it.'   Australian captain MARK TAYLOR

67/31. Australia v England, Second Test Match, at Melbourne Cricket Ground, 24, 26, 27, 28 & 29 December 1994.

SCORES

AUSTRALIA 279 (S. R. Waugh 94 not out, M. E. Waugh 71) and 320 for 7 wickets dec. (D. C. Boon 131); ENGLAND 212 (G. P. Thorpe 51; S. K. Warne 6/64) and 92 (C. J. McDermott 5/42). **Australia won by 295 runs**.

S. K. WARNE

1st inns: 27.4–8–64–6. Dismissed: M. A. Atherton lbw 44; A. J. Stewart c & b 16; G. P. Thorpe c M. E. Waugh 51; M. W. Gatting c S. R. Waugh 9; S. J. Rhodes c M. E. Waugh 0; P. A. J. DeFreitas st I. A. Healy 14. 2nd inns:13–6–16–3 (inc. hat-trick). Dismissed: P. A. J. DeFreitas lbw 0; D. Gough c I. A. Healy 0; D. E. Malcolm c D. C. Boon 0.

TEST

WARNE BOWLS INTO HISTORY, headlined the *Age*. It's a famous front page which adorns a wall of Warne's luxury seaside house in Melbourne.

Showing that his Brisbane mastery was no fluke, Warne claimed the first Ashes hat-trick in more than 90 years with the fourth, fifth and sixth deliveries of his 13th over.

Set 388 runs to win and square the series, the dispirited, crease-bound Englishmen were bowled out for 92, their lowest score against Australia since crumbling for 87 to Ian Meckiff and Co., also in Melbourne, in 1958–59.

With 6/64 and 3/16, Warne increased his series tally to 20 wickets in two matches, sparking speculation that he could break Jim Laker's Ashes record of 46. It also gave him 70 wickets for the calendar year. 'Suppose I'll wake up soon,' said a disbelieving Warne.

Reaching 50 wickets in eight Tests against England and 150 Test wickets in only his 31st match, Warne overshadowed the feats of Craig McDermott who took his 250th wicket, including 5/42 in the English second innings.

England had slumped to 4/79 on the penultimate night with hopes only of a draw. When Mike Gatting fell in the first minute on the fifth morning, an Australian win became inevitable. 'Sometimes you get the feeling sitting here, it's not Australia versus England, it's Warne versus England,' said the ABC's Neville Oliver.

Warne had bowled five maiden overs in a row from the southern end on the final morning, England's Steven Rhodes safely defending the ball away from David Boon at short leg and Mark Waugh, fielding in the kamikaze position, silly point. So in control seemed Rhodes that Mark Taylor considered a bowling change and second spinner Tim May began to warm up at mid-on.

Midway through Warne's 13th over, with Rhodes having fallen at the opposite end to McDermott, Warne trapped Phil DeFreitas lbw to a leg-break which skidded straight through and with his very next ball induced an edge behind from Darren Gough.

As Devon Malcolm, England's No. 10, ambled to the wicket, Alec Stewart, the non-striker, said to Warne, 'You'll never have a better chance of getting a hat-trick!'

He met Malcolm in mid-pitch and asked: 'What are you going to do then, Dev?'

'If it's up to me, I'll smack it,' said the big fast bowler.

'He might bowl you the flipper, the googly or just a leggie. Just block it,' said Stewart.

With a Test batting average of six, Malcolm was one of world cricket's ultimate bunnies. Having just missed a hat-trick with a wrong'un in Brisbane, all sorts of variations flashed through Warne's mind. His team-mates had plenty of suggestions, too.

Just as everyone was re-taking their positions, Damien Fleming walked past Warne and joked, 'Listen mate, do you really want to know how to get your hat-trick?'

'Yeah, how?'

'Well, I'd close my eyes and try to think of bowling the perfect yorker or the big outswinger . . . my wicket-taking balls,' said Fleming. 'When

I was going for my hat-trick [at Rawalpindi, just months earlier], I was thinking about bowling a bouncer, a slower ball or a yorker. I thought I'd stick with my stock delivery [the outswinger], because that is the ball which comes through for me eight times out of ten.'

Warne nodded, deep in thought, before producing an overspinning leg-break, which bounced and spun, caught Malcolm on the gloves and splayed to the right of short leg David Boon, who took a superb catch diving to his right. A delighted Warne charged across the wicket and picked Boon up in a bear hug. It was the first hat-trick of his life, even including the juniors at East Sandringham.

'It came out just as I wanted. I got lucky,' said the spin sultan.

The scorebook entry for his memorable 13th over read: 3 . . X X X.

England had capitulated, losing 6/13 in the final 56 minutes to be bowled out for 92 and prompt a fresh set of broadsides, aimed at virtually anybody connected with English cricket from the selectors to the captain Mike Atherton and the coach, Keith Fletcher. 'The worst touring side in memory . . . the most unimaginative captain . . . a coach out of his depth' were just some of the barbs from the dissatisfied English press contingent.

Graham Gooch, in his farewell Test series, said the Englishmen felt humiliated. They'd lost 13 and won just one of their previous 19 Tests against Australia, the most dismal sequence in Ashes history. A series loss of 5–0 was not out of the question.

'I did not like putting Australia in, knowing that Warne was around to bowl to us in the last innings.' England captain MIKE ATHERTON

68/32. **Australia v England**, Third Test Match, at Sydney Cricket Ground, 1, 2, 3, 4 & 5 January 1995.
SCORES
ENGLAND 309 (M. A. Atherton 88, J. P. Crawley 72, D. Gough 51; C. J. McDermott 5/101) and 255 for 2 wickets dec. (G. A. Hick 98 not out, M. A. Atherton 67); AUSTRALIA 116 (D. Gough 6/49) and 344 for 7 wickets

TEST

(M. A. Taylor 113, M. J. Slater 103; A. R. C. Fraser 5/73). **Drawn**.

S. K. WARNE

1st inns: 36–10–88–1. Dismissed: D. E. Malcolm b 29.

2nd inns: 16–2–48–0.

Approaching the Sydney Test, Warne had his customary net session with coach Terry Jenner who noted Warne wasn't extending through his action as well as he possibly could, or spinning his leg-break as violently as in the past.

'Gees, you're not bad are you?' said Warne. 'A fella gets 20 wickets in two Tests and you're still worried!'

Within days, however, he was making a reassessment. After taking just one wicket for 136 in more than 50 overs in a drawn game in Sydney, and being dobbed for 2 sixes by England's No. 11 Devon Malcolm in his 32nd and 34th overs, Warne conceded that Jenner just might have a point. His shoulder was starting to trouble him again and to compensate he hadn't been ripping his bowling arm through the action or across his body from right to left as previously.

He helped Australia save the Test on the final afternoon, however, by batting more than an hour, sharing an unbroken stand of 52 with Ian Healy. Set 449, the Aussies stumbled from 0/208 to 7/292 and were satisfied to settle for the draw, which ensured the retention of the Ashes.

Afterwards, Warne's former captain Allan Border echoed Jenner's concern, saying that Warne's action was not as energetic as it once was. 'Now and then he'll bubble up if something is on but there is no doubt he gets tired quicker,' he said. 'He is starting to look jaded and we will have to watch him very closely. Burnout is a very real threat.'

69/33. **Australia v England**, Fourth Test Match, at Adelaide Oval, 26, 27, 28, 29 & 30 January 1995.

SCORES

ENGLAND 353 (M. W. Gatting 117, M. A. Atherton 80) and 328 (P. A. J. DeFreitas 88, G. P. Thorpe 83, J. P. Crawley 71; M. E. Waugh 5/40); TEST

Australia 419 (G. S. Blewett 102 not out, M. A. Taylor 90, I. A. Healy 74, M. J. Slater 67) and 156 (I. A. Healy 51 not out). **England won by 106 runs**.

S. K. Warne

1st inns: 31–9–72–2. Dismissed: G. P. Thorpe c M. A. Taylor 26; J. P. Crawley b 28.

2nd inns: 30.5–9–82–2. Dismissed: S. J. Rhodes c D. W. Fleming 2; P. C. R. Tufnell lbw 0.

Mike Atherton's Englishmen were being billed as the worst-ever touring team to Australia, especially after their failure to make the finals of the World Series Cup ahead of either Australia or Australia 'A'. Most expected Australia to win the series 4–0.

However, by winning in Adelaide by 106 runs, the Englishmen earned new respect. Suddenly Australia led by only one Test with one to play.

Warne's four wickets for the match came from more than 60 overs. He bowled with far more flight than in Sydney and remarkably had virtually overnight improved the technical deficiencies coach Jenner had been noticing. 'One of Shane's greatest attributes has been to take what's said and immediately adapt it,' said Jenner. 'In this case his sheer workload had led to one or two slight flaws in his action. Once he was aware of them, he fixed them on the spot.'

Devon Malcolm again indulged in some big-hitting, one six soaring out of the ground. But Warne wasn't the only bowler to be treated so contemptuously. On the final morning, man of the match Phil DeFreitas smashed 22 from one of McDermott's overs (this equalled the record for the most runs conceded by an Australian in a six-ball over at Test level) as 85 runs came in the first hour in the most exhilarating run spree of the summer.

70/34. **Australia v England**, Fifth Test Match, at WACA Ground, Perth, 3, 4, 5, 6 & 7 February 1995.

Scores

Australia 402 (M. J. Slater 124, S. R. Waugh 99 not out, M. E. Waugh 88)

TEST

and 345 for 8 wickets dec. (G. S. Blewett 115, S. R. Waugh 80,
M. A. Taylor 52); ENGLAND 295 (G. P. Thorpe 123, M. R. Ramprakash 72) and
123 (C. J. McDermott 6/38). *Australia won by 329 runs*.
S. K. WARNE
1st inns: 23–8–58–2. Dismissed: G. P. Thorpe st I. A. Healy 123;
M. R. Ramprakash b 72.
2nd inns: 7–3–11–0.

Australia's massive 329-run victory ensured a 3–1 series win, with Warne dismissing England's two top-scorers Graham Thorpe (stumped) and Mark Ramprakash (bowled) mid-match to help swing the game.

Thorpe was beaten by the angle of a straight-spinner and Ramprakash played no shot to a leg-break which nipped between his legs and struck his leg stump.

From the third ball of the game when Graham Gooch dropped a sitter at third slip, England's fielding and catching was sub-standard. Five catches went down in Australia's first innings, again several from the bowling of the unfortunate Malcolm, who had 12 catches grassed in just four Tests.

English stalwarts Gooch, 41, and Mike Gatting, 37, both announced their retirements from representative cricket.

With 27 wickets for the summer, Warne was second only to player of the season Craig McDermott, with 32. He averaged 50 overs per Test and seemed fatigued.

There was great expectation, however, that his coming showdown with world No. 1 Brian Lara in the West Indies would be crucial in deciding the Frank Worrell Trophy.

First, the Aussies were involved in three one-day games in New Zealand to help celebrate the centenary of the New Zealand Cricket Council. At Dunedin, Warne was fined $500 after contravening International Cricket Council regulations by wearing a black wristband with a sponsor's name on it.

SUMMARY, 1994–95 (AUSTRALIA)

	Mts	Overs	Mdns	Runs	Wicks	Ave	BB	5wl	10wM
All First-Class matches	7	373.2	123	814	40	20.35	8/71	3	1
Test matches v England	5	256.1	84	549	27	20.33	8/71	2	1
Sheffield Shield matches	2	117.1	39	265	13	20.38	5/104	1	–

AUSTRALIA IN THE WEST INDIES

71. **Australia v Guyana**, at Bourda, Georgetown, Guyana, 20, 21 &
22 March 1995.
SCORES
GUYANA 105 (G. D. McGrath 5/47) and 207 (K. F. Semple 67;
B. P. Julian 5/54); AUSTRALIA 373 (G. S. Blewett 116, M. E. Waugh 75,
J. L. Langer 55). **Australia won by an innings & 61 runs**.
S. K. WARNE
1st inns: 11–6–21–3. Dismissed: K. F. Semple c I. A. Healy 6; S. Chanderpaul
c I. A. Healy 4; R. A. Harper c & b 2.
2nd inns: 15–5–42–3. Dismissed: S. Chanderpaul b 31; L. Joseph b 14;
K. A. Wong lbw 4.

Undeterred by their 4–1 loss in the one-day internationals, or their
call for replacements for injured frontline pacemen Craig McDermott
and Damien Fleming, the Australians remained convinced that their
best could finally be good enough to unseat the long-time world Test
champions.

In the opening first-class fixture of the tour, at Georgetown,
Guyana, the Australians took just two days and an hour of the third to
win by an innings. After proving expensive in the one-dayers, Warne
grabbed six wickets for the game, including 3/4 in 14 balls on the
opening day as Guyana was dismissed for 105 in three hours. His first
three overs were maidens.

Left-handed Test prospect Shivnarine Chanderpaul seemed out of
his depth. He struggled to pick Warne's variations before being bowled
by a leg-break.

72. Australia v President's XI, at Mindoo Phillip Park, Castries, St Lucia, 25 (no play), 26, 27 & 28 (no play) March 1995.

SCORES

AUSTRALIA 322 for 5 wickets dec. (M. J. Slater 90, S. R. Waugh 73 not out, M. E. Waugh 73); PRESIDENT'S XI 261 for 5 wickets (D. R. E. Joseph 83, K. L. T. Arthurton 75 not out). **Drawn.**

S. K. WARNE

Only inns: 14–0–84–2. Dismissed: R. I. C. Holder c & b 29; S. Chanderpaul c & b 2.

More than two days of the four-day Test trial at the idyllic holiday isle of St Lucia was washed out, yet Warne was lifted for 6 sixes, the heaviest punishment of his career. From 14 overs, he took 2/84.

Keith Arthurton hit 4 sixes and Dave Joseph 3 in a 142-run two-hour stand. Sixteen sixes were struck for the game. Sixteen runs came from Warne's seventh over, all to Arthurton. Switching ends, he conceded 11 from his ninth over and 13 from his last.

After advice from Australia's team physiotherapist Errol Alcott, Warne also threw the ball only underarm, to preserve his still-sore shoulder.

73/35. Australia v West Indies, First Test Match, at Kensington Oval, Bridgetown, Barbados, 31 March, 1 & 2 April 1995.

SCORES

WEST INDIES 195 (B. C. Lara 65, C. L. Hooper 60;) and 189 (G. D. McGrath 5/68); AUSTRALIA 346 (I. A. Healy 74 not out, S. R. Waugh 65, M. A. Taylor 55) and 39 for no wicket. **Australia won by ten wickets.**

TEST

S. K. WARNE

1st inns: 12–2–57–2. Dismissed: W. K. M. Benjamin c M. A. Taylor 14; C. A. Walsh c S. R. Waugh 1.
2nd inns: 26.3–5–64–3. Dismissed: S. L. Campbell c S. R. Waugh 6; J. R. Murray c S. R. Waugh 23; K. C. G. Benjamin b 5.

Few Test matches have started as dramatically as the opening international in Bridgetown, when the West Indies, electing to bat, lost 3/6 to the makeshift Australian new ball attack of Paul Reiffel and Brendon Julian.

Introduced in the 12th over of the morning from the Challenor Stand end, Warne's first two overs cost 23 to the joy of the cricket-crazy Bajans, among the most knowledgeable set of cricket fans in the world. When an aggressive Carl Hooper welcomed Warne, bowling around the wicket, with three consecutive leg-side fours, the fans erupted, dancing in the aisles, sounding horns and clanging cow bells. The atmosphere was intoxicating. As usual, Hooper hadn't worried about a thigh pad. He'd come to party.

Ex-Testman Keith Stackpole said by conceding 5 fours in his first 12 deliveries, Warne paid for his impetuosity and trying to bowl too many different deliveries, too early. 'It's obvious the West Indian batsmen are going to attack Warne at all costs and not allow him to dominate as he has done over the last couple of years,' he said.

On a bouncy Kensington Oval wicket, the Australians completed a ten-wicket win in just two and a half days, with Warne fighting back to take five wickets.

Glenn McGrath was the Australian hero with eight for the game. Not only did he dismiss Brian Lara with the delivery of his life, an off-cutter which seamed wickedly in the second innings, he bounced the West Indian tailenders in a rare show of venom. 'I figure I am going to be bounced so I might as well give it to them,' McGrath told pressmen.

'No bowler has ever arrived in the Caribbean with greater advance billing than the bouncy, blond leg-spinner. His encounter with the superstar batsman of the moment, Lara, was the stuff of which cricket lovers' dreams are made.'

West Indian writer and commentator TONY COZIER

74/36. **Australia v West Indies**, Second Test Match, at Recreation Ground, St John's, Antigua, 8, 9, 10, 12 & 13 April 1995.
SCORES
AUSTRALIA 216 (C. A. Walsh 6/54) and 300 for 7 wickets dec. (D. C. Boon 67,

TEST

S. R. Waugh 65 not out, M. E. Waugh 61); WEST INDIES 260 (B. C. Lara 88)
and 80 for 2 wickets. **Drawn**.
S. K. WARNE
1st inns: 28–9–83–3. Dismissed: S. C. Williams c D. C. Boon 16;
J. C. Adams lbw 22; K. L. T. Arthurton c M. A. Taylor 26.
2nd inns: 7–0–18–0.

Richie Richardson's stunning one-handed catch of the century, leap-
ing sideways at third slip to dismiss Michael Slater, was one of the
features of the drawn second Test, in which there were rain delays on
four of the five days.

With Chickie Baptiste's thumping disco blaring between overs, the
smell of grilled flying-fish wafting over the stands and limbo dancers
and cross-dressers parading at the breaks, at times the cricket almost
seemed an incidental.

Warne was in good rhythm and bowled 35 overs for the match,
despite being discomforted by his spin finger, for which he had previously had cortisone treatment. He dismissed left-handers Keith
Arthurton (caught at slip) and Jimmy Adams (lbw) as part of his 3/83
from 28 first-innings overs. Brian Lara's half century came from just
48 balls and included 3 fours from Warne in the first over after lunch
on the second day. Arthurton smashed Warne for 2 sixes, one into a
vacant schoolyard.

75/37. **Australia v West Indies**, Third Test Match, Queen's Park Oval,
Port-of-Spain, Trinidad, 21, 22 & 23 April 1995.
SCORES
AUSTRALIA 128 (S. R. Waugh 63 not out; C. E. L. Ambrose 5/45) and 105;
WEST INDIES 136 (G. D. McGrath 6/47) and 98 for 1 wicket. **West Indies
won by nine wickets**.
S. K. WARNE
1st inns: 12–5–16–1. Dismissed: W. K. M. Benjamin c M. J. Slater 7.
2nd inns: 3.5–0–26–0.

TEST

On an old-fashioned Port-of-Spain green-top in which the game was virtually decided by the toss, the West Indies squared the series in just three days, Steve Waugh made the best half-century of his life and the intimidating Curtly Ambrose all but lost his temper in an infamous mid-pitch confrontation with Waugh.

Warne bowled only 15.5 overs for the game and finished with a chipped right thumb after being struck two balls after lunch on the third day by a lifter from the scowling, pumped-up Ambrose.

'I was standing at the non-striker's end as Warnie faced Ambrose,' said Paul Reiffel in *Reiffel Inside Out*. 'I could hear him charging in, and as I looked around, it seemed his legs were about four metres long; it was if he was on stilts! I was thinking, "There's no way I'm going to take a run here. I'm not going anywhere."

'Then I realised that I would have to face Walsh anyway; frying pan at one end, fire at the other. Soon afterwards, Walsh bowled a short one to Warnie, which he nicked and I could see the relief written all over his face when the wicketkeeper caught it. Suddenly the umpire called out: "No-ball!" Then came Warnie's anguished reply: "Oh, no!".'

Sent in to bat on a wicket moist, soft and totally unsuitable for Test cricket, Australia could last only 47 overs in the first innings and 36.1 in the second. Waugh's double of 63 not out and 21 in a low-scoring game was one of the grittiest of his career.

76/38. Australia v West Indies, Fourth Test Match, at Sabina Park, Kingston, Jamaica, 29, 30 April, 1 & 3 May 1995.

SCORES

WEST INDIES 265 (R. B. Richardson 100, B. C. Lara 65) and 213 (W. K. M. Benjamin 51); AUSTRALIA 531 (S. R. Waugh 200, M. E. Waugh 126, G. S. Blewett 69). *Australia won by an innings & 53 runs*.

S. K. WARNE

1st inns: 25–6–72–2. Dismissed: B. C. Lara c I. A. Healy 65; C. O. Browne c D. C. Boon 1.

2nd inns: 23.4–8–70–4. Dismissed: K. L. T. Arthurton lbw 14; C. E. L. Ambrose st I. A. Healy 5; C. A. Walsh c G. S. Blewett 14; K. C. G. Benjamin c M. A. Taylor 6.

TEST

In the deciding Test on a browner and far more batsman-friendly wicket in Kingston, the Windies were thrashed by an innings in three-and-a-half days to forfeit the world championship.

Man of the series Steve Waugh's timely double century was one of the most outstanding in the annals of Test cricket and confirmed his standing as the No. 1 batsman in the world. 'Steve was our rock,' said wicketkeeper Ian Healy. 'We couldn't have won the series without him.'

It was the first time since 1958 the Windies had lost a Caribbean Test by such a comprehensive margin and first time since 1973 that they had been beaten by Australia in a home series.

Despite the inconvenience of his fractured thumb, Warne took his place in the XI and returned match figures of 6/142, including for the first time all series, the wicket of Brian Lara caught bat-pad after an acrobatic dive by Healy.

Healy kept wickets in a helmet with a full visor after lunch on the final day, Warne taking the three last wickets to finish with a tour-best 4/70 from 23.4 overs.

While the much-billed Lara–Warne contest was never central to the series fortunes, Warne claimed 15 wickets in four Tests, the best return for an Australian spinner since Peter Philpott (18) in 1964–65 and Richie Benaud (18) in 1954–55.

'I didn't get a big bag,' said Warne in the *Sunday Age*. 'But I was happy with my consistency. The pitches didn't suit me and as the quicks bowled so well, I didn't bowl as many overs as I normally do.'

The Australian victory celebrations spilled over into their three-match stopover in Bermuda where an official champagne victory dinner for players and their partners cost manager Jack Edwards upwards of $10 000 – and a stern 'please explain' from the Australian Cricket Board!

SUMMARY, 1994–95 (WEST INDIES)

	Mts	Overs	Mdn	Runs	Wicks	Ave	BB	5wI	10wM
All First-Class matches	6	178	46	553	23	24.04	4/70	–	–
Test matches v West Indies	4	138	35	406	15	27.06	4/70	–	–

'This is the biggest Test of our careers. Someone had to put their hand up and I was glad I was one of them.'   STEVE WAUGH

1995–96

CRICKET WAS AT ITS MOST fascinating with Warne in operation ripping the ball both ways and zipping his destructive flipper through the defences of even the most alert batsmen. His phenomenal success prompted a level of hero-worship enjoyed only by golfer Greg Norman and the reclusive AFL goalkicking champion Gary Ablett.

With 72 Test wickets in calendar year 1993 and 70 in 1994, Warne had set an extraordinary standard. Having being persuaded against accepting a rich English county offer from Northants, Warne travelled, worked out with weights and enjoyed the wintertime fortunes of his favourite football team, the St Kilda Saints. He also prepared for his marriage, in September, to his fiancée, Simone, whom he'd met at a Victorian cricket celebrity golf day in 1991.

In Darwin for Victoria's pre-season camp and matches against New Zealand and South Australia, Warne bowled mainly off-breaks, deliberately shielding his shoulder and over-worked spin finger. Rest was a priority with his 200 Test wickets milestone looming and the opportunity to be part of Australia's team for the '96 World Cup.

In Australia

77. **Victoria v Queensland**, at Brisbane Cricket Ground,
19, 20, 21 & 22 October 1995.

Scores

Queensland 361 for 8 wickets dec. (S. G. Law 89, J. P. Maher 88,
M. L. Hayden 64, W. A. Seccombe 54 not out) and 246 for 6 wickets
(A. R. Border 70 not out, S. G. Law 53); Victoria 482 (D. M. Jones 145,
M. T. G. Elliott 138, D. S. Berry 74). **Drawn**.

S. K. Warne

1st inns: 34–5–111–3. Dismissed: M. L. Hayden st D. S. Berry 64; J. P. Maher
c D. S. Berry 88; M. S. Kasprowicz lbw 9.
2nd inns: 27–4–62–1. Dismissed: W. A. Seccombe lbw 19.

Keen for the season to start to see if his sessions with Terry Jenner and
Bobby Simpson would result in him re-discovering the leg-break
which had propelled him to fame, Warne appeared in Victoria's first
two Sheffield Shield games of the new season.

Having viewed videos from the Caribbean which showed him lean-
ing over and bowling with a far higher action than when he was at his
best in England in 1993, Warne fine-tuned his action, concentrating
once again on imparting some of his signature 'rip' on the ball.

Named for the first time as Victoria's vice-captain, Warne started
with two maidens on his way to four wickets and more than 60 overs
in the opening game against reigning Sheffield Shield title-holders
Queensland.

Confronted by a farewelling Allan Border for only the second time
in his career, Warne had his third delivery smacked back over his head
for six as Border, one of his all-time heroes, reached 7000 first-class
runs for his adopted state.

Dean Jones made his 26th century for Victoria, equalling Bill Pons-
ford's 60-year-old record.

In mid-match, news came through from Pakistan that Judge
Fakharuddin Ebrahim had not only cleared Saleem Malik of any
wrongdoing in the 1994 bribery scandal, he had accused Warne, Tim

May and Mark Waugh of concocting the charges. His finding cleared the way for the controversial Saleem, known to the Australians as 'The Rat', to be named in Pakistan's touring team.

---

78. **Victoria v New South Wales**, at Melbourne Cricket Ground, 1, 2 & 3 November 1995.

SCORES
VICTORIA 158 (M. T. G. Elliott 53) and 241; NEW SOUTH WALES 344
(M. A. Taylor 126, S. R. Waugh 80; S. K. Warne 5/122) and 56 for 4 wickets.
New South Wales won by six wickets.

S. K. WARNE
1st inns: 45–9–122–5. Dismissed: M. J. Slater st D. S. Berry 29; P. A. Emery
c P. A. Broster 10; G. R. J. Matthews lbw 6; S. Lee lbw 20; G. D. McGrath
c J. R. Bakker 10.
2nd inns: 3.1–0–12–0.

Having been withdrawn from the Australian Cricket Board Chairman's XI for the opening match of Pakistan's tour at Lilac Hill, Warne took 5/122 from 45 overs in a three-day Shield match dominated by New South Wales in Melbourne. Introduced within half an hour of the match start in the 8th over, his spin finger again troubled him, despite continuing cortisone treatment. However, once he was warm, he dropped into his immaculate old line and started to vary his pace, enjoying the battle. Only once, in his 30th over, when NSW batsmen helped themselves to 11 runs, did his control wane.

'I could hear his fingers cracking at the non-striker's end, so that's a good sign,' NSW centurion Mark Taylor said. 'He bowled particularly well in his first spell (20 overs, 2/58) and kept it up all day with turn and bounce.'

On the opening night of the game, Warne was one of 210 first-class players to attend a dinner to commemorate 100 years of Victorian cricket and could be found in easy conversation with one of the guests-of-honour, 88-year-old Bodyline batsman Leo O'Brien, who'd always wanted to shake Warne's hand and thank him for rekindling much of his enjoyment in the game. 'Shane,' said O'Brien, with a toothy grin, 'you're a breath of fresh air.'

79/39. **Australia v Pakistan**, First Test Match, at Brisbane Cricket Ground, 9, 10, 11 & 13 November 1995.

Scores

Australia 463 (S. R. Waugh 112 not out, M. A. Taylor 69, M. E. Waugh 59, G. S. Blewett 57, D. C. Boon 54); Pakistan 97 (S. K. Warne 7/23) and 240 (Aamir Sohail 99, Inzamam-ul-Haq 62). *Australia won by an innings & 126 runs*.

TEST

S. K. Warne

1st inns: 16.1–9–23–7. Dismissed: Aamir Sohail st I. A. Healy 32; Rameez Raja c M. A. Taylor 8; Inzamam-ul-Haq c S. R. Waugh 5; Basit Ali c M. A. Taylor 1; Moin Khan c C. J. McDermott 4; Wasim Akram c D. C. Boon 1; Mohammad Akram c G. S. Blewett 1. 2nd inns: 27.5–10–54–4. Dismissed: Wasim Akram c M. J. Slater 6; Saleem Malik c C. J. McDermott 0; Waqar Younis lbw 0; Mohammad Akram lbw 0. Man of the match.

Stung by Pakistani talk that his variations were easy to read and he wasn't the menace of old, Warne's love affair with the 'Gabba continued when he destroyed Pakistan with 11 wickets. The first Test ended in just over three playing days, a rare rest day having been called for November 12, the day of the Australian Grand Prix.

With 7/23 in the first innings – including an astonishing burst of 6/10 from 56 balls – and 4/54 in the second, Warne produced the best match figures by an Australian in a Test against Pakistan and his second-best match tally in 39 Tests. He also moved into Australia's top 10 Test wicket-takers.

The Pakistanis surrendered meekly, many playing like carefree millionaires. Having made just one in 53 minutes, the much-vaunted Basit Ali succumbed to a death or glory swipe.

The long-awaited meeting with Saleem Malik lasted only several minutes before Saleem tamely spooned a full length leg-spinner to a diving Craig McDermott at mid-off. Warne was jubilant. 'It shows there is justice in the game,' he said. 'I don't know if he'll play next Test, but hopefully he'll get a duck in every innings he plays.'

Commenting on Pakistan's capitulation, Test fast bowling legend Jeff Thomson said the tourists had batted 'like a Z-grade pub team'.

80/40. Australia v Pakistan, Second Test Match, at Bellerive Oval, Hobart, 17, 18, 19 & 20 November 1995.

SCORES

AUSTRALIA 267 (M. E. Waugh 88; Mushtaq Ahmed 5/115) and 306 (M. A. Taylor 123, M. J. Slater 73); PAKISTAN 198 (Rameez Raja 59) and 220 (Aamir Sohail 57; G. D. McGrath 5/61). *Australia won by 155 runs.*

S. K. WARNE

1st inns: did not bowl.

2nd inns: did not bowl.

TEST

Having hit 3 sixes from the bowling of Mushtaq Ahmed on his way to a breezy 27 on the opening day, Warne was struck by an in-dipping express from Waqar Younis and cracked the big toe of his left foot. After finishing not out and fielding for nine overs on the first night, his toe started swelling as soon as he removed his shoes, a newly endorsed pair of Nike Air Flippers. He was unable to take any further part in the match.

81/41. Australia v Pakistan, Third Test Match, at Sydney Cricket Ground, 30 November, 1, 2, 3 & 4 December 1995.

SCORES

PAKISTAN 299 (Ijaz Ahmed 137) and 204 (Inzamam-ul-Haq 59; C. J. McDermott 5/49); AUSTRALIA 257 (M. E. Waugh 116; Mushtaq Ahmed 5/95) and 172 (M. A. Taylor 59). *Pakistan won by 74 runs.*

S. K. WARNE

1st inns: 34–20–55–4. Dismissed: Rameez Raja c M. J. Slater 33; Ijaz Ahmed c G. D. McGrath 137; Inzamam-ul-Haq c I. A. Healy 39; Mushtaq Ahmed c C. J. McDermott 0.

2nd inns: 37–13–66–4. Dismissed: Rameez Raja c M. E. Waugh 39; Ijaz Ahmed lbw 15; Basit Ali b 14; Rashid Latif lbw 3.

TEST

Despite a break of less than a fortnight, Warne surprised by taking his place for the Sydney Test. To help ease the pressure on his injured toe, Warne cut a hole in his new shoes.

Losing the toss, the Australians had to bowl first and while in some initial discomfort, Warne produced some memorable deliveries in several lengthy, high-class spells. Introduced at 12.15 p.m., 16 of his first 27 overs were maidens. In all he bowled 34 overs and took 4/55, his duel with Saleem Malik (36) one of the series highlights. He followed with 4/66 from 37 overs in the Pakistani second innings, the dismissal of Basit Ali a classic case of gamesmanship.

Before delivering the last ball of the third evening to Basit, Warne deliberately delayed proceedings, calling Ian Healy out from behind the stumps for a mid-pitch conversation. Rather than a tactical talk, it was more about where they were going to go for dinner that night! When play finally resumed, an unsettled Basit was bowled between his legs to a big-spinning leg-break delivered from around the wicket.

Set less than 250 to win, Australia started well only to tumble from 2/117 to 172 all out, presenting Pakistan with their first Test win in Australia since 1981–82.

82/42. **Australia v Sri Lanka**, First Test Match, at WACA Ground, Perth, 8, 9, 10 & 11 December 1995.

SCORES

SRI LANKA 251 (R. S. Kaluwitharana 50) and 330 (H. P. Tillekeratne 119); AUSTRALIA 617 for 5 wickets dec. (M. J. Slater 219, M. E. Waugh 111, M. A. Taylor 96, R. T. Ponting 96, S. G. Law 54 not out). **Australia won by an innings & 36 runs.**

TEST

S. K. WARNE

1st inns: 27–7–75–3. Dismissed: P. A. de Silva c & b 10; R. S. Kaluwitharana c M. A. Taylor 50; W. P. U. J. C. Vaas c I. A. Healy 4.

2nd inns: 29.4–6–96–3. Dismissed: P. A. de Silva c R. T. Ponting 20; H. P. Tillekeratne c R. T. Ponting 119; W. P. U. J. C. Vaas c I. A. Healy 4.

Granted their first-ever three-Test series in Australia, Sri Lanka's campaign started with an innings loss in Perth. Michael Slater's powerful straight hitting was a highlight of his career-best 219. So ferocious was his driving that Hashan Tillekeratne, fearing injury, asked to be moved from short cover.

After claiming 3/75 in the first innings, Warne took 3/96 in the second, including his 200th Test wicket in his 42nd Test when Chaminda Vaas, one of his six match victims, was caught behind attempting an on-side loft. Sri Lanka's No. 1 player Aravinda de Silva fell to Warne in both innings, for 10 and 20. Only the left-handed strokemaker Tillekeratne, who made 6 and 119, played him with authority.

Having been told on the eve of the game that the logos on their cricket shirts were too prominent, the Sri Lankans were accused of ball tampering early on day one while the action of their champion spinner Muttiah Muralitharan was also questioned, beginning a controversial, three-month tour in which relations between the two teams plummeted.

Warne was the ninth Australian to 200 wickets. Only two, Clarrie Grimmett (36 Tests) and Dennis Lillee (38) had achieved the milestone in fewer matches. Warne had averaged a wicket every 62 balls and completed his double century in record time: three years and 341 days.

'There is no doubt that Australia are the world leaders in verbal provocation. This can take the guise of overt hostility – "You can't effing bat, you bastard" – or the honeytrap methods of Shane Warne who might teasingly say to opposing batsmen, "Why aren't you trying to hit me over the top? Don't you think you're good enough?"'

Sri Lanka's leading batsman, ARAVINDA DE SILVA

83/43. **Australia v Sri Lanka**, Second Test Match, at Melbourne Cricket Ground, 26, 27, 28, 29 & 30 December 1995.
SCORES
AUSTRALIA 500 for 6 wickets dec. (S. R. Waugh 131 not out, D. C. Boon 110, R. T. Ponting 71, M. J. Slater 62, M. E. Waugh 61) and

TEST

41 for no wicket; Sri Lanka 233 (A. Ranatunga 51, R. S. Kaluwitharana 50; G. D. McGrath 5/40) and 307 (A. P. Gurusinha 143). **Australia won by ten wickets**.

S. K. Warne
1st inns: 18–5–49–1. Dismissed: H. P. Tillekeratne c M. A. Taylor 14.
2nd inns: 37–10–71–4. Dismissed: U. C. Hathurusinghe lbw 39;
R. S. Kaluwitharana st I. A. Healy 2; G. P. Wickremasinghe st I. A. Healy 17;
M. Muralitharan c M. A. Taylor 0.

In the most dramatic of Boxing Day Test matches in which Sri Lanka's prime bowler, finger-spinner Muttiah Muralitharan, was no-balled for throwing seven times in three overs by umpire Darrell Hair, David Boon made his 21st and final Test century and Mark Taylor claimed his 100th catch. Warne became the first bowler to tally 50 Test wickets in three consecutive calendar years.

Five dropped catches and a missed stumping allowed the Australians to again score 500, with only a six-hour innings of monumental concentration from Asanka Gurusinha forcing play into a fifth day. His 143 included one 6, high over mid-on into the Great Southern Stand.

'Let's see you do that again,' said Warne.

'I will if you pitch it in the same spot,' said Gurusinha.

Sparingly used in the first innings, Warne was again Australia's major attacker in the second, with 4/71 from 37 overs. He regularly bowled his wrong'un to the left-handers. At one stage, irritated by Arjuna Ranatunga's delaying tactics, he bowled when the Sri Lankan captain was only just looking up, prompting Keith Stackpole in the ABC commentary box to brand Warne's action 'arrogant'.

He was on a hat-trick after dismissing Pramodya Wickremasinghe and Muralitharan in successive balls, but overpitched his hat-trick delivery to last man Jayanatha Silva, playing his maiden Test.

The Sri Lankans were incensed at the treatment of Murali, who had toured all over the world without being called for throwing. Senior players went as far as saying it was a conspiracy, not only against Murali, but against Sri Lanka, which had shown in the lead-up to the tour with victories in Pakistan that its team was rapidly becoming world class.

84/44. **Australia v Sri Lanka**, Third Test Match, at Adelaide Oval, 25, 26, 27, 28 & 29 January 1996.

SCORES

AUSTRALIA 502 for 9 wickets dec. (S. R. Waugh 170, I. A. Healy 70, P. R. Reiffel 56) and 215 for 6 wickets dec. (S. R. Waugh 61 not out); SRI LANKA 317 (H. P. Tillekeratne 65, S. Ranatunga 60; P. R. Reiffel 5/39) and 252 (S. T. Jayasuriya 112, S. Ranatunga 65). *Australia won by 148 runs*.

S. K. WARNE

1st inns: 26–4–74–0.

2nd inns: 27–11–68–1. Dismissed: G. P. Wickremasinghe b 6.

TEST

Having helped Australia retain the World Series Cup with five wickets in the finals and 15 for the one-day summer, Warne declared himself a doubtful starter for the World Cup tour on the subcontinent for security reasons. Under a headline of I FEAR FOR MY LIFE, Warne said, 'I live and die for cricket but to go on a tour where there is a chance of maybe not coming back, that's a big thing to do.'

Several of the Australian players had received death threats from the subcontinent. News of a bomb blast in the heart of Colombo which killed five people and injured dozens of others added to their concern. The hotel in which they were due to stay was only minutes away. They were going into a war zone.

Had the Board not acted first and withdrawn the team, it is likely several members, if not the entire team, would have pulled out. Australia had been a big brother to Sri Lankan cricket ever since leading the push for the island country's elevation to Test status, but despite assurances of all-encompassing security, Australian officials were not prepared to imperil the safety of the team.

Not surprisingly, the Adelaide Test, David Boon's last, was overshadowed by the ruckus, Australia taking until the final session to complete a clean sweep.

Warne made 33 from just 39 balls in Australia's first innings, his highest Test score in 12 months. He took only one wicket for the game and was becomingly increasingly concerned by ongoing soreness to his stressed spinning finger which was not allowing him to 'rip' his leg-break as far as normal.

Having seen a leg-break flat-batted into the crowd by centurion Sanath Jayasuriya, he indulged in some gamesmanship.

'Okay,' he said, 'the next six are all going to be flighted. Let's see how many can go over [the fence]!'

Jayasuriya's partner, Asanka Gurusinha, immediately warned his mate not to lose his focus. 'Shane did flight them, but they were all varied deliveries and pitching well outside off-stump. Sanath just blocked them back.'

---

85. **Victoria v Queensland**, at Melbourne Cricket Ground, 23, 24, 25 & 26 March 1996.
SCORES
QUEENSLAND 142 (D. J. Saker 7/32) and 338 (M. L. Love 88; A. I. C. Dodemaide 5/70); VICTORIA 255 (D. M. Jones 69, W. G. Ayres 68; M. S. Kasprowicz 5/74) and 226 for 5 wickets (W. G. Ayres 100, M. T. G. Elliott 54; M. S. Kasprowicz 5/74). *Victoria won by five wickets*.
S. K. WARNE
1st inns: 15–5–25–2. Dismissed: J. P. Maher c M. T. G. Elliott 28; A. R. Border c D. M. Jones 4.
2nd inns: 46–13–94–0.

Having returned from the World Cup where his spinning finger and overworked shoulder affected his performance, Warne figured in a one-dayer against a World XI in Melbourne – bowling a bouncer first ball to team-mate Dean Jones – before playing in Victoria's final Sheffield Shield match of the summer, against Queensland in Melbourne.

Thirty-two of the 35 wickets fell to pacemen. Warne took two wickets in the Queensland first innings, including Allan Border in his last match for the only time in his career. In the second he went wicket-less, despite bowling 46 overs.

Of his rapidly deteriorating finger, he said in the *Sunday Age*, 'I am worried about it mainly because I want to get back to bowling my main delivery, the big leg-break. That is the ball I've built my bowling game around, but it is also the ball that seems to have done some damage to the finger. The sooner it is fixed the better.'

SUMMARY, 1995–96 (AUSTRALIA)

	Mts	Overs	Mdn	Runs	Wicks	Ave	BB	5wI	10wM
All First-Class matches	9	449.5	131	1057	42	25.16	7/23	2	1
Test matches v Pakistan	3	115	52	198	19	10.42	7/23	1	1
Test matches v Sri Lanka	3	164.4	43	433	12	36.08	4/71	–	–
Sheffield Shield matches	3	170.1	36	426	11	38.72	5/122	1	–

1996–97

WITH TWO YEARS of almost continuous cricket looming, Warne, 26, believed he had no choice during the winter break but to have surgery on his injured spinning finger. Cortisone injections directly into the knuckle to deaden the pain in his finger had become increasingly ineffective. He'd had three in the previous 12 months and feared the side effects.

On the eve of Australia's World Cup quarter-final game against New Zealand in cricket-mad Madras, the finger had all but collapsed. No longer could Warne bowl his signature leg-break at will. It was the delivery which spun the most – and also was the most physically demanding to bowl.

He was heavier, too, and noticeably more irritable, even with those closest to him. Having enjoyed such prolonged success, Warne found it difficult to accept that he might never again bowl with the same zip as in 1993 and 1994. He may have been wiser and more seasoned, but his big leg-break was central to his game. Unable to produce it as consistently, cricket was suddenly not as much fun as it used to be.

Many old spinners Warne consulted advised against finger surgery, saying the finger might become stiff and not allow him ever again to release the ball with the same ferocity. Others believed his troublesome shoulder was a more important priority to address.

An American specialist recommended rest for the finger and an operation for the shoulder. However, Warne believed his shoulder condition was manageable, whereas his sore finger needed immediate attention. He believed it would be a big enough battle rehabilitating from one operation, let alone two.

The healing process was to take months and at one stage Warne went public with his concerns, declaring he might not be able to bowl again. 'Right now I can't even shake hands, let alone bowl,' he said.

He missed the Super Eights one-day tournament in Kuala Lumpur, the one-off Test in India, was hammered in his comeback into club ranks with St Kilda and performed well below his best in his first game as Victoria's new captain in a one-day game against South Australia.

Such was his focus and commitment, however, to losing some excess weight and regaining his old form, no one was prepared to declare his career finished. And within weeks, he was to show why . . .

IN AUSTRALIA

86. **Victoria v New South Wales**, at Sydney Cricket Ground, 8, 9, 10 & 11 November 1996.
SCORES
NEW SOUTH WALES 264 (M. G. Bevan 79) and 353 for 8 wickets dec.
(M. G. Bevan 150 not out, M. J. Slater 69); VICTORIA 161 (W. G. Ayres 55; A. M. Stuart 5/63) and 398 (M. T. G. Elliott 187, D. S. Berry 148).
New South Wales won by 58 runs.
S. K. WARNE (capt.)
1st inns: 20–8–40–2. Dismissed: A. M. Stuart st D. S. Berry 0; S. C. G. MacGill lbw 4.
2nd inns: 25–5–75–0.

After two one-day games for Victoria, Warne captained the Bushrangers for the first time at Sheffield Shield level. His only two wickets were tailenders, but the flipper which trapped NSW No. 11, first-gamer Stuart MacGill, in front of his stumps was a confidence-booster.

Eight kilograms lighter than he'd finished the World Cup, Warne was satisfied to bowl 45 overs for the game after such a long lay-off. He bowled at third change in both innings.

Other than a shoulder-high full toss to Shane Lee in the first innings and two 10-run overs in the second, he bowled with com-mendable accuracy and growing confidence.

The game was most notable for a 290-run sixth-wicket stand on the final day by Matthew Elliott and wicketkeeper Darren Berry. Set 457 for victory they both made big hundreds as the Victorians were gallant in defeat.

---

87. **Victoria v South Australia**, at Melbourne Cricket Ground, 15, 16, 17 & 18 November 1996.

SCORES

VICTORIA 345 for 9 wickets dec. (D. M. Jones 152, I. J. Harvey 70) and 38 for 1 wicket; SOUTH AUSTRALIA 84 and 298 (G. R. Parker 112, B. A. Johnson 52; I. J. Harvey 7/44). *Victoria won by nine wickets*.

S. K. WARNE (capt.)

1st inns: 12–3–25–3. Dismissed: J. C. Scuderi c B. A. Williams 34; P. E. McIntyre st D. S. Berry 1; S. P. George c D. M. Jones 2.

2nd inns: 40–15–61–0.

Just a week before the long-awaited first Test against the West Indies, Warne showed he was ready to play at the highest level once again, with 61 overs for the game. He had planned to bowl only 20 in each innings, but felt so good he carried on.

Others were more important in Victoria's win, Warne's only victory in nine matches as state captain, but he captured three first-innings wickets, including South Australia's top scorer Joe Scuderi. From 40 second innings overs, he took 0/61. In mid-innings, he bowled seven maidens in a stretch of ten overs.

'The more I watch Shane Warne, the more I am convinced he will make a wonderful Australian captain.'   ALLAN BORDER

88/45. Australia v West Indies, First Test Match, at Brisbane Cricket Ground, 22, 23, 24, 25 & 26 November 1996.

SCORES

AUSTRALIA 479 (I. A. Healy 161 not out, R. T. Ponting 88, S. R. Waugh 66) and 217 for 6 wickets dec. (M. E. Waugh 57); WEST INDIES 277 (C. L. Hooper 102, S. Chanderpaul 82) and 296 (S. L. Campbell 113). **Australia won by 123 runs**.

TEST

S. K. WARNE

1st inns: 27–3–88–2. Dismissed: I. R. Bishop lbw 0; K. C. G. Benjamin lbw 9.
2nd inns: 41–16–92–2. Dismissed: R. G. Samuels c M. A. Taylor 29;
J. C. Adams lbw 2.

Having returned to the Australian XI after missing the one-off Test in India, Warne was the most used bowler in the match, sending down 68 overs on a discouragingly slow 'Gabba wicket. Accurate and economical without producing all of his old fizz, three of his four wickets were lbw (two to no shots).

Shortly after lunch on the final day, Warne, bowling from around the wicket from the Stanley Street end, ripped a wide leg-break to the left-handed Shivnarine Chanderpaul which bounced over his off-stump, one of his few big-spinning leg-breaks of the game. On the final day, he sent down 31 overs, 13 in the opening session, 12 in the second and six in the last. The West Indies, set 420 to win, were dismissed for 296.

In the Australian first innings, Warne (24) pulled Courtney Walsh for a four and a six during his 61-run eighth-wicket stand with man of the match Ian Healy.

89/46. Australia v West Indies, Second Test Match, at Sydney Cricket Ground, 29, 30 November, 1, 2 & 3 December 1996.

SCORES

AUSTRALIA 331 (G. S. Blewett 69; C. A. Walsh 5/98) and 312 for 4 wickets dec.

TEST

(M. T. G. Elliott 78 ret. hurt, M. E. Waugh 67, M. G. Bevan 52);
West Indies 304 (S. L. Campbell 77) and 215 (S. Chanderpaul 71,
C. L. Hooper 57). *Australia won by 124 runs*.

S. K. Warne

1st inns: 35.2–13–65–3. Dismissed: C. L. Hooper lbw 27; S. Chanderpaul
c & b 48; I. R. Bishop c M. T. G. Elliott 48.
2nd inns: 27.4–5–95–4. Dismissed: R. G. Samuels b 16; S. Chanderpaul
b 71; K. C. G. Benjamin c M. A. Taylor 4; C. A. Walsh c G. D. McGrath 18.

Warne produced one of the most-remembered deliveries of his career
to bowl Shivnarine Chanderpaul on the last day, as Australia took a
2–0 lead. The feature wicket, in seven for the match, was the dismissal of the feisty Chanderpaul, bowled by a huge turning leg-break
delivered from around the wicket, which ripped from the bowler's
footmarks to hit his middle and leg stumps just two balls before the
luncheon interval. It spun almost a metre, Warne raising two fists and
holding them in front of his face in jubilation. 'I gave that one a huge
rip and it worked,' he said afterwards. 'It was as unplayable a ball as
you could get,' said 'keeper Ian Healy.

Set 340 runs to square the series, the West Indies had lost 3/35
before Chanderpaul's exhilarating counter-attack which saw 125 runs
scored in the session, including 69 in the hour before lunch. Four
early Warne overs cost 37 as Mark Taylor attacked the West Indian
middle order without any outriders. Taylor's catch to dismiss Carl
Hooper at slip in the second innings from Michael Bevan's bowling
was extraordinary; he flicked the ball up soccer style from his feet and
caught it in two hands while lying on his back!

Warne also dismissed Chanderpaul in the first innings, along with
Carl Hooper, lbw without playing a shot, and Ian Bishop caught on
the leg side hitting out at a wrong'un. It was the perfect reply after
West Indian coach Malcolm Marshall's Test-eve dismissal of Warne
as a potential matchwinner, despite the SCG's powdery, spin-friendly
surface. WIZARD WARNE BACK WITH BITE headlined the Brisbane *Cou-
rier Mail*.

'He's getting back to the Shane Warne I know,' said Taylor after the match. 'In Brisbane he was seven out of ten. Now he is 8.5 or nine.'

During the game Warne passed Clarrie Grimmett's 216 wickets to become Australia's sixth most successful bowler in Test history.

'He's back. With arguably the best ball of his career, Shane Warne yesterday convinced a doubting world he was ready to re-emerge as the most venomous strike force in Test cricket.'

Cricket writer ROBERT CRADDOCK

90/47. **Australia v West Indies**, Third Test Match, at Melbourne Cricket Ground, 26, 27 & 28 December 1996.
SCORES
AUSTRALIA 219 (G. S. Blewett 62, S. R. Waugh 58; C. E. L. Ambrose 5/55) and 122; WEST INDIES 255 (J. C. Adams 74 not out, S. Chanderpaul 58, J. R. Murray 53; G. D. McGrath 5/50) and 87 for 4 wickets. **West Indies won by six wickets**.

TEST

S. K. WARNE
1st inns: 28.1–3–72–3. Dismissed: R. G. Samuels c M. A. Taylor 17; C. E. L. Ambrose b 8; C. A. Walsh c M. E. Waugh 4.
2nd inns: 3–0–17–0.

In a match dominated by Curtly Ambrose and the West Indian pacemen from the opening morning when Australia lost 3/26 after winning the toss and batting, Warne couldn't repeat his heroics from his maiden Test against the Windies in Melbourne four years earlier.

However, he did take 3/72, including opener Robert Samuels brilliantly caught in two hands by Mark Taylor low to his left early on the second morning Warne's first nine overs in the first innings cost just 12 runs, and his sharp catch at fourth slip soon afterwards to dismiss Brian Lara for yet another low score showed his growing confidence as a quality 'slipper'.

Taylor said afterwards the MCG wicket had been too bouncy and inconsistent. The first day crowd was 72 891, the biggest in a Test match in Australia for more than 20 years.

91/48. **Australia v West Indies**, Fourth Test Match, at Adelaide Oval,
25, 26, 27 & 28 January 1997.

SCORES

WEST INDIES 130 and 204 (B. C. Lara 78; M. G. Bevan 6/82); AUSTRALIA 517
(M. L. Hayden 125, G. S. Blewett 99, M. G. Bevan 85 not out,
M. E. Waugh 82). *Australia won by an innings & 183 runs*.

S. K. WARNE

1st inns: 16–4–42–3. Dismissed: S. Chanderpaul c M. A. Taylor 20; B. C. Lara
c G. S. Blewett 9; J. C. Adams c & b 10.

2nd inns: 20–4–68–3. Dismissed: B. C. Lara c I. A. Healy 78; C. L. Hooper
lbw 45; I. R. Bishop c M. G. Bevan 0.

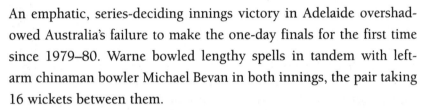

TEST

An emphatic, series-deciding innings victory in Adelaide overshadowed Australia's failure to make the one-day finals for the first time
since 1979–80. Warne bowled lengthy spells in tandem with left-
arm chinaman bowler Michael Bevan in both innings, the pair taking
16 wickets between them.

Five of Warne's six wickets were in the top order, including world
No. 1 Brian Lara in both innings. In Warne's first over of the match,
Lara lazily mishit an attempted lofted drive straight to mid-on Greg
Blewett. In the second, having made 78 including 60 in boundary
shots, he was caught at the wicket cutting at a faster, skidding delivery.

Warne bowled for long periods from the Bradman Stand end, with a
south-westerly wind over his shoulder, and while he didn't spin the
ball markedly, he impressed with his accuracy, change of pace and
variety.

Later, a forthright Curtly Ambrose blamed himself for the series
loss, saying had he not been forced to withdraw through injury, the
West Indies would have won.

92/49. **Australia v West Indies**, Fifth Test Match, at WACA Ground, Perth,
1, 2 & 3 February 1997.

SCORES

AUSTRALIA 243 (M. G. Bevan 87 not out, M. E. Waugh 79;

TEST

C. E. L. Ambrose 5/43) and 194 (C. A. Walsh 5/74); WEST INDIES 384
(B. C. Lara 132, R. G. Samuels 76, C. L. Hooper 57; P. R. Reiffel 5/73) and
57 for no wicket. ***West Indies won by ten wickets.***
S. K. WARNE
1st inns: 19–8–55–2. Dismissed: R. G. Samuels c M. E. Waugh 76;
B. C. Lara c I. A. Healy 132.
2nd inns: did not bowl.

Warne dismissed the two West Indian top scorers Brian Lara (132)
and Robert Samuels (76) in a heated, controversial game in which
umpires Peter Willey and Darrell Hair at one stage called rival cap-
tains Mark Taylor and Courtney Walsh together in mid-pitch and
ordered their teams to behave.

On the pace-friendly WACA wicket, Warne was used only sparingly – bowling only six of the first 61 overs. Michael Bevan, hero of
the Adelaide Test, hardly bowled at all.

In a stormy finale, Curtly Ambrose deliberately overstepped the
crease late in the Australian innings and peppered bouncers at Warne
and Andy Bichel, who shared a brave 55-run ninth-wicket stand, the
best of the innings. 'He [Ambrose] was trying to hurt Shane Warne,'
said ex-Testman Dean Jones. 'It was one of the worst things I've seen
on a cricket field.'

Operating around the wicket from the River end after tea with Australia almost down and out, Ambrose bowled a 15-ball over, including
nine no-balls, most where he had clearly overstepped by one or two feet.

'Watching Ambrose coming to Perth is like someone bowling with a
super ball,' said the ABC's Jim Maxwell.

In nine overs he bowled 19 no-balls as well as producing the
unplayable ball of the series when a high-pace delivery hit one of the
widening cracks and grubbed along the ground, catapulting into Greg
Blewett's off stump first ball.

With 22 wickets at an average of 27, Warne had made a notable
comeback after his off-season finger surgery. It was the perfect prelude
to another dip at the South Africans.

SUMMARY, 1996–97 (Australia)

	Mts	Overs	Mdn	Runs	Wicks	Ave	BB	5wI	10wM
All First-Class matches	7	314.1	87	795	27	29.44	4/95	–	–
Test matches v West Indies	5	217.1	56	594	22	27.00	4/95	–	–
Sheffield Shield matches	2	97	31	201	5	40.20	3/25	–	–

AUSTRALIA IN SOUTH AFRICA

93. Australia v Natal, at Kingsmead, Durban, 20, 21 & 22 February 1997.
SCORES
NATAL 335 (M. L. Bruyns 105, D. M. Benkenstein 103) and 112; AUSTRALIA 370
(M. E. Waugh 124, M. G. Bevan 52) and 81 for 2 wickets. **Australia won by
eight wickets**.
S. K. WARNE
1st inns: 20–5–89–0.
2nd inns: 13–6–25–2. Dismissed: D. J. Watson st I. A. Healy 9; M. L. Bruyns
c I. A. Healy 20.

Playing only the second of the two first-class lead-up games approaching the three-Test series against the South Africans, Warne was expensive in the first innings, with 0/89 from 20 overs, including 17 from
his ninth over (6 . 6 4 . 1) when Dale Benkenstein (103 from 130
balls) repeatedly lofted the ball to, or over, the on-side fence.

However, in Natal's second innings Warne took his 400th first-
class wicket, dismissing both openers Mark Bruyns and Doug Watson
before being withdrawn from the attack complaining of soreness in
his left knee.

The improving Michael Bevan then ran through the tail so impressively that Benkenstein, Natal's captain, afterwards rated him faster
and more difficult to combat than Warne.

Warne's cavalier 44 late on the second day came from just 33 balls
and included 5 fours and 3 sixes.

94/50. Australia v South Africa, First Test Match, at Wanderers Stadium,
Johannesburg, 28 February, 1, 2, 3 & 4 March 1997.
SCORES
SOUTH AFRICA 302 (W. J. Cronje 76, D. J. Richardson 72 not out) and 130;

TEST

AUSTRALIA 628 for 8 wickets dec. (G. S. Blewett 214, S. R. Waugh 160,
M. T. G. Elliott 85). ***Australia won by an innings & 196 runs***.
S. K. WARNE
1st inns: 27.4–9–68–2. Dismissed: W. J. Cronje c M. E. Waugh 76;
P. R. Adams lbw 15.
2nd inns: 28–15–43–4. Dismissed: G. Kirsten b 8; J. H. Kallis b 39;
D. J. Cullinan c I. A. Healy 0; J. N. Rhodes lbw 8.

Returning to Johannesburg and the scene of his most regretted moment in cricket, Warne, in his 50th Test match, was asked by team coach Geoff Marsh and captain Mark Taylor to address the players at their pre-Test dinner. He spoke of the rowdy crowd, the blood-curdling atmosphere and how intimidating it can be playing at Wanderers for the first time. He also said what a challenge the Australian side faced in continuing as Test cricket's world champion XI.

Taylor underlined the importance of breaking the South African spirit early and urged his players to remain close-knit and build pressure session by session.

With his key players all in form, Taylor's wishes were granted, Australia winning in virtually four days on a docile wicket. Warne again played a key role with six wickets for the match, including 4/43 as South Africa surrendered for just 130 in the second innings to plunge to their worst Test loss since 1949–50.

Used at first change behind Glenn McGrath and the fit-again Jason Gillespie, Warne's first 13-over spell on the opening day cost just 24 runs. The South Africans, particularly Daryll Cullinan, played him so cautiously they allowed even bad balls to escape punishment.

In the second innings, Warne bowled virtually unchanged from the 10th over right through until South Africa's innings was completed in the 69th after just one hour's play on the fifth morning. Having dismissed Gary Kirsten and Jacques Kallis from the Golf Course end in his first 15-over spell, Warne switched to the Corlett Drive end where he added fellow batting specialists Cullinan and Jonty Rhodes to his haul.

As Cullinan came to the wicket, Warne said to team-mate Mark Waugh, 'I'm going to have this bloke for breakfast.' He did, too. Cullinan made a 10th-ball duck.

'All I wanted this game was Daryll Cullinan,' Warne told journalists later. 'I wanted to make sure those old [psychological] scars don't heal too quick.'

Warne also thanked coach Terry Jenner, in Johannesburg with a supporters' group, for helping fine-tune his technique in mid-match. From bowling too many over-spinners, Warne was able to re-find his leg-break.

'He [Warne] probably didn't get it through as nicely as he would have wanted in the first innings,' said South African captain Hansie Cronje, 'but it was different in the second innings. One way of judging if he's bowling well or not is the pace of his flipper and it was certainly there this time around.'

The early highlight of the game was the mammoth 384-run fifth-wicket stand between Steve Waugh and Greg Blewett, the best by Australians in 60 Tests against South Africa. They were the tenth Test pair to bat through an uninterrupted day's play.

'The Australia media builds them up to be the best. Eventually you are seeing Shane Warne's googly spinning a metre. When you get down to play them, you realise they are good, but just another team.'

South African wicketkeeper DAVE RICHARDSON

---

95. **Australia v Border**, at Buffalo Park, East London, 7 & 8 March 1997.
SCORES
BORDER 117 (J. N. Gillespie 7/34) and 148 (P. C. Strydom 55);
AUSTRALIA 370 for 9 wickets dec. (G. S. Blewett 112, M. E. Waugh 62).
Australia won by an innings & 105 runs.
S. K. WARNE
1st inns: did not bowl.
2nd inns: 3–2–1–3. Dismissed: S. C. Pope lbw 26; D. Taljard lbw 0;
M. Ntini b 0.

After not bowling at all in the first innings of the match against an inexperienced, overawed opponent, Warne had only three overs in the second, his third over producing three wickets in four balls (. . X X . X) Having seen off the hat-trick, Border's teenage No. 11 Makhaya Ntini was out very next ball.

The game went only five full sessions. It was Australia's seventh touring win in a row.

96/51. Australia v South Africa, Second Test Match, at St George's Park, Port Elizabeth, 14, 15, 16 & 17 March 1997.

SCORES

SOUTH AFRICA 209 (B. M. McMillan 55; J. N. Gillespie 5/54) and 168; AUSTRALIA 108 and 271 for 8 wickets (M. E. Waugh 116). **Australia won by two wickets**.

TEST

S. K. WARNE

1st inns: 23.4–5–62–3. Dismissed: B. M. McMillan c S. R. Waugh 55; D. J. Richardson c G. D. McGrath 47; A. A. Donald c & b 9.
2nd inns: 17.4–7–20–2. Dismissed: S. M. Pollock lbw 17; P. R. Adams c M. A. Taylor 1.

In a famous match in which Mark Waugh produced the grittiest and most timely century of his career to help Australia win a cliffhanger on an under-prepared St George's Park wicket by two wickets, Warne, with five wickets, again outbowled the high-profile, cocky South African bosie bowler Paul Adams.

While all five were in the bottom order, they did include quality competitors, South Africa's top scorers Brian McMillan and wicket-keeper Dave Richardson in the first innings and the dangerous Shaun Pollock in the second.

The game was also notable for Ian Healy's winning slap over the square leg fence, ending one of the tensest days of Test cricket of the modern era. When Warne came to the wicket with Australia 7/258, still needing 12 to win, he said to Healy: 'I can't feel my legs.' He lifted one over the infield for three before falling lbw, adding to the drama.

In a remarkable comeback, the Australians took 10 South African wickets for just 81 runs on the third day to claw their way back into the match after being outplayed on the first two.

Warne was introduced in the 17th over of the game with South Africa 4/33. He went wicketless in his first 14-over spell, before taking 3/20 from 9.4 overs in his second.

Bowling into a gale in the second innings, the wicket still green and far from favourable for spinners, his first nine overs cost just ten runs, a remarkably accurate and pressure-packed spell in the conditions. His fifth and final wicket was No. 11 batsman Adams who was bowled after attempting an ungainly reverse sweep. Warne made quite a show of the dismissal, sending off Adams with mocking laughter, an over-reaction which his critics back in Australia were not prepared to over-look.

'Shane Warne was guilty of one of the most childish and embarrass-ing acts committed by an Australian Test cricketer,' said Melbourne-based sportswriter Patrick Smith in the *Age*. 'It says so much about the lack of temperament and maturity of Warne that he could not allow the dismissal to go without resorting to such puerile and demeaning behaviour. Under pressure he turns into a boor. The pleasant young man of television interviews is readily interchangeable with an imma-ture hothead.'

South African coach Bob Woolmer said Warne had unnecessarily mocked Adams, who was playing only his ninth Test.

'Not everyone will like you,' said Warne later. 'Some people just don't like the way you play. It doesn't worry me. I just go out and be myself. I'm an emotional cricketer.'

97/52. Australia v South Africa, Third Test Match, at Centurion Park, 21, 22, 23 & 24 March 1997.
Scores
Australia 227 (S. R. Waugh 67) and 185 (S. R. Waugh 60 not out; A. A. Donald 5/36); South Africa 384 (A. M. Bacher 96,

TEST

W. J. Cronje 79 not out, B. M. McMillan 55; G. D. McGrath 6/86) and 32 for
2 wickets. ***South Africa won by eight wickets***.
S. K. WARNE
1st inns: 36–11–89–0.
2nd inns: did not bowl.

Aiming for a tenth straight tour victory, the Australians finally
faltered, in only the second Test to be staged at Centurion Park,
formerly Verwoerdburg, near Pretoria. Warne went wicketless for
only the fifth time in 52 Tests.

After such a long campaign, with nine Tests and a one-day series in
five months, he was weary and well below the stellar standards of
1993–94. He even admitted that, without a break, his time in the game
could be limited.

Six of his first eight overs for the game were maidens but he didn't
pose the same menace as at Wanderers or St George's Park. South
Africa's batsmen were allowed to use their pads with impunity, fuelling
his frustrations.

Vice-captain Ian Healy was later suspended for two one-day games
after tossing his bat into the Australian dressing room upon a disputed
dismissal late on the fourth day. Replays showed that South African
umpire Cyril Mitchley had erred when he ruled Healy caught at the
wicket. It was one of several poor decisions the Australians claimed
had unfairly assisted South Africa to its eight-wicket win.

Warne's 11 wickets in three Tests was unspectacular, but he'd taken
some important wickets and continued to give the Australians the
variety of attack opponents envied.

SUMMARY, 1996–97 (SOUTH AFRICA)

	Mts	Overs	Mdn	Runs	Wicks	Ave	BB	5wI	10wM
All First-Class matches	5	169	60	397	16	24.81	4/43	–	–
Test matches v South Africa	3	133	47	282	11	25.63	4/43	–	–

1997

Having had less than three weeks back at home, Warne set out on his second tour of England without all of his normal focus, given that wife Simone was expecting their first child within weeks.

Australia in England

98. **Australia v Gloucestershire**, at County Ground, Bristol, 27, 28 & 29 May 1997.

Scores

Australia 249 (S. R. Waugh 92, M. E. Waugh 66) and 354 for 4 wickets (J. L. Langer 152 not out, M. T. G. Elliott 124); Gloucestershire 350 (N. J. Trainor 121, R. J. Cunliffe 61). **Drawn.**

S. K. Warne

Only inns: 35.2–10–97–4. Dismissed: R. P. Davis lbw 30; R. J. Cunliffe c M. S. Kasprowicz 61; R. C. Russell c M. G. Bevan 20; A. M. Smith c J. N. Gillespie 4.

A 40-overs-a-side friendly against a Rest of the World XI at the Kowloon Cricket Club in Hong Kong and several one-day warm-ups preceding the Texaco Cup one-day series saw Warne take only five wickets in six games. It was cold and he took to wearing a finger warmer for his spinning finger.

However, once the weather improved and the first-class section of the tour began at Bristol, a favourite old haunt, his fortunes immediately improved. In a drawn game against Gloucestershire, he took 1/60 in his 21-over first spell, before finishing with 4/97 from 35.2 overs. He was also elevated to No. 4 in the order in the Australian second innings but was out for an eighth-ball duck.

---

99. **Australia v Derbyshire**, at Racecourse Ground, Derby, 31 May, 1 & 2 June 1997.

SCORES

AUSTRALIA 362 for 6 wickets dec. (G. S. Blewett 121, M. T. G. Elliott 67, M. G. Bevan 56) and 265 for 4 wickets dec. (M. G. Bevan 104 not out, M. A. Taylor 63, B. P. Julian 62); DERBYSHIRE 257 for 9 wickets dec. (M. R. May 67) and 371 for 9 wickets (C. J. Adams 91, A. S. Rollins 66, D. M. Jones 57; S. K. Warne 7/103). *Derbyshire won by one wicket*.

S. K. WARNE

1st inns: 14–3–45–2. Dismissed: C. J. Adams lbw 7; D. M. Jones b 31.
2nd inns: 23–2–103–7. Dismissed: A. S. Rollins lbw 66; C. J. Adams c sub (G. D. McGrath) 91; I. D. Blackwell c & b 5; V. P. Clarke c B. P. Julian 28; K. M. Krikken c M. G. Bevan 21; P. A. J. DeFreitas c sub (M. E. Waugh) 26; A. J. Harris lbw 5.

On the eve of the first Test, the Australians lost their tour match to lowly Derbyshire, captained by ex-Australian batsman Dean Jones, by one wicket. Mark Taylor's return to form was courtesy of a fumble by Jones at first slip. Had he failed again, Taylor had determined to drop himself from the Tests.

With an English-best nine wickets for the game, including 7/103 in Derby's second innings, Warne fought back strongly after his first four overs went for 29 runs, courtesy of 14 runs in one over from big-hitting Chris Adams, who set up the win with 91 from just 76 balls.

In high winds, Warne bowled long stints in sunglasses and cap. The gusts forced the umpires to remove the bails.

'He spun a few to me and normally this track never turns,' Jones told pressmen. 'And to have control and strength in that wind was fantastic.' Discussing the first Test prospects, Jones rated Warne a perfect '10', saying he was the player the English feared most.

100/53. **Australia v England**, First Test Match, at Edgbaston, Birmingham, 5, 6, 7 & 8 June 1997.
Scores
Australia 118 (A. R. Caddick 5/50) and 477 (M. A. Taylor 129, G. S. Blewett 125, M. T. G. Elliott 66); England 478 for 9 wickets dec. (N. Hussain 207, G. P. Thorpe 138, M. A. Ealham 53 not out) and 119 for 1 wicket (M. A. Atherton 57 not out). *England won by nine wickets*.
S. K. Warne
1st inns: 35–8–110–1. Dismissed: N. Hussain c I. A. Healy 207.
2nd inns: 7.3–0–27–0.

TEST

Since becoming world champions, Australia's blueprint of success had been built around dominating and intimidating the opposition from the opening sessions of a series. For once the team plan backfired, the Australians starting their bid for a record fifth consecutive Ashes victory disastrously. In little more than two-and-a-half hours on a slow seamer at Edgbaston, home to the Warwickshire county cricket club, they were bowled out for just 118, Warne with 47 in 46 balls saving his team from the ignominy of a sub-100 score.

Despite gritty centuries in the second innings from Greg Blewett and Mark Taylor, who finally found some form after a horror run, the Australians lost by nine wickets, in extra time on the fourth night.

In his 100th first-class game, Warne's only victim in more than 40 overs was Nasser Hussain, whose Test-best 207 was pivotal in the match fortunes. Warne bowled mainly leg-breaks and hardly ripped a wrong'un all match, prompting increasing speculation that all was not well with his shoulder. When he dropped short, Hussain cut him with poise and power. In Warne's 27th over, Hussain hit 3 fours. Even Warne's flipper was ineffective.

Throughout the Test, he was criticised for bowling too flat, without his customary loop. On a dead wicket, there was little margin for error.

In his Test diary, *Ashes Summer*, Hussain admitted the ball from Warne which had dismissed him had been 'too good'. However, the Australians and particularly Warne had become testier the longer his innings went.

'When I was in the fifties, Shane bowled me a succession of good balls and, out of instinct, I nodded at him as if to acknowledge a good ball. But when I did it a third time I thought, "I shouldn't be doing this. He's going to think I'm taking the piss."

'Sure enough he let me have it, shouting "Stop &%$#ing nodding at me. I know it's a good ball. Who do you think you are?"

'Then later when I was well into a hundred he gave me some stick over the fact that I've got my name on my bat saying, in his best sarcastic voice, "I must get one of those Nasser Hussain sabres. Would you autograph it for me?"'

'There were two schools of thought on how best to negate the threat of Shane Warne. One involved sending a wheelbarrow of peperoni pizza to his room every night and the other was to make the pitches as unfriendly to spin as was acceptable within the bounds of good taste.'

English spin bowler PHIL TUFNELL

---

101. **Australia v Leicestershire**, at Grace Road, Leicester, 14, 15 & 16 June 1997.

SCORES

AUSTRALIA 220 for 8 wickets dec. (R. T. Ponting 64; J. Ormond 6/54) and 105 for 3 wickets dec. (M. A. Taylor 57); LEICESTERSHIRE 62 for 4 wickets dec. and 179 (S. K. Warne 5/42). **Australia won by 84 runs**.

S. K. WARNE

1st inns: 5–1–20–1. Dismissed: G. I. Macmillan c M. G. Bevan 34.

2nd inns: 16.4–2–42–5. Dismissed: J. J. Whitaker lbw 21; A. Habib c R. T. Ponting 13; P. A. Nixon st I. A. Healy 24; J. Ormond b 1; A. R. K. Pierson c J. L. Langer 0.

After a game off at Nottingham, Warne returned to something like his old form with six wickets against midlands county Leicestershire, including 5/42 in the second innings.

He drifted and looped his leg-spinners and in his 13th over, took two wickets, left-hander Paul Nixon and teenager James Ormond. Misty rain forced Warne to regularly wring the ball with a towel. Later he admitted he'd been having trouble holding the English Duke's ball with its hard lacquered seams. The expectations that he'd repeat his '93 successes, despite the green, seamer-friendly wickets, also weighed heavily.

'The problem is that everyone expects me to go out and bowl and get them drifting and turning and you can only do that if the wicket enables you to turn the ball,' he said.

He admitted his suspect shoulder was occasionally uncomfortable, especially before warming up. Asked by pressmen for reasons why he didn't appear as sharp as in his previous English visit in 1993, he said, 'About 10 000 overs and four years.'

102/54. **Australia v England**, Second Test Match, at Lord's, London, 19 (no play), 20, 21, 22 & 23 June 1997.

Scores

England 77 (G. D. McGrath 8/38) and 266 for 4 wickets dec. (M. A. Butcher 87, M. A. Atherton 77); Australia 213 for 7 wickets dec. (M. T. G. Elliott 112). TEST

Drawn.

S. K. Warne

1st inns: 2–0–9–0.

2nd inns: 19–4–47–2. Dismissed: M. A. Butcher b 87; N. Hussain c & b 0.

Rain on the first four days of the Test precluded a result, despite Glenn McGrath's awesome spell on the third morning in which he took 8/38 as England, sent in to bat, tumbled to 77 all out in just three hours.

Sent in at No. 5 to help accelerate the run-rate, Warne made a fourth-ball duck. He bowled only two overs in England's first innings and 19 in the second, bowling top scorer Mark Butcher and having first Test hero Nasser Hussain caught and bowled.

Significantly, however, he again failed to produce the spitting leg-breaks which had become his signature in '93. Former Test leg-spinner Kerry O'Keeffe claimed one of the reasons for the decline was the absence of the heavyweight Merv Hughes' footmarks for Warne to aim into at the opposite end.

Writing in the *Sunday Age*, Warne said, 'I felt before the tour that I would do something special during the series and I still believe that will happen.'

He denied his overworked right shoulder was a major concern and said he was seriously considering a further season in England in 1998. 'If any of it [the rumours] were true, I'd be running for cover, not looking to commit myself to a tough season in county cricket.'

'Around the team, the condition of Warne's shoulder is the most sensitive subject since Taylor's loss of form, that is, about as sensitive as the 1950s secrets of the hydrogen bomb.'

The *Herald Sun*'s BRUCE WILSON

---

103. **Australia v Hampshire**, at County Ground, Southampton, 28, 29 & 30 June 1997.
SCORES
HAMPSHIRE 156 and 176 (J. N. Gillespie 5/33); AUSTRALIA 465 for 8 wickets dec. (M. E. Waugh 173, M. A. Taylor 109, M. T. G. Elliott 61). **Australia won by an innings & 133 runs**.
S. K. WARNE
1st inns: 15–4–30–3. Dismissed: R. A. Smith c I. A. Healy 22; S. D. Udal c I. A. Healy 2; S. J. Renshaw lbw 4.
2nd inns: 19–3–26–1. Dismissed: S. D. Udal b 21.

The arrival of Warne's first child, a 4.2 kilogram baby girl, Brooke Victoria, back in Melbourne, prompted Australian coach Geoff Marsh to call 'a public holiday' as the Australians journeyed to Southampton after a wash-out in Oxford. Warne, the proudest of fathers, was pictured with a celebratory cigar, prompting a fresh wave of criticism from Australia, this time from the Anti-Cancer Council.

'It's such a shame that smoking is still deemed to be a symbol of success,' said spokesperson Judith Watt. 'Cigar smokers have a two-and-a-half times higher rate of lung cancer.'

In defeating Hants by an innings, the Australians began an imposing seven-week winning run, defying the record high rainfall.

With four wickets for the game, including 3/5 in 13 balls, Warne was satisfied with his input, especially his flipper, which landed consistently. Team-mate Jason Gillespie claimed seven high-speed wickets and later was described by Hampshire's coach Malcolm Marshall as one of the three fastest bowlers in the world.

104/55. **Australia v England**, Third Test Match, at Old Trafford, Manchester, 3, 4, 5, 6 & 7 July 1997.

SCORES

AUSTRALIA 235 (S. R. Waugh 108) and 395 for 8 wickets dec. (S. R. Waugh 116, M. E. Waugh 55, S. K. Warne 53); ENGLAND 162 (M. A. Butcher 51; S. K. Warne 6/48) and 200 (J. P. Crawley 83).

TEST

Australia won by 268 runs.

S. K. WARNE

1st inns: 30–14–48–6. Dismissed: A. J. Stewart c M. A. Taylor 30; N. Hussain c I. A. Healy 13; G. P. Thorpe c M. A. Taylor 3; J. P. Crawley c I. A. Healy 4; D. Gough lbw 1; A. R. Caddick c M. E. Waugh 15.
2nd inns: 30.4–8–63–3. Dismissed: A. J. Stewart b 1; G. P. Thorpe c I. A. Healy 7; A. R. Caddick c J. N. Gillespie 17.

In a triumphant return to Manchester and Old Trafford, where he'd produced *that* ball four years previously, Warne passed Richie Benaud's record 248 wickets for a leg-spinner as Australia squared the series with an emphatic 268-run win.

Dipping and curving the ball on a spinner's wicket, Warne produced his first Test 'five-for' in 18 months. Not only did he take nine wickets for the match, including 6/48 in the first innings, he made 53, his second Test half-century, to help change the course of the series. His partnership for the seventh wicket with Steve Waugh was worth 88.

With wickets in his 7th, 11th, 13th, 15th, 19th and 29th overs, Warne's cricket ability rather than off-field controversies was suddenly again cornering the front pages.

Other than an attempted flipper which veered high and fast past a retreating Andy Caddick, Warne's line was impeccable. His variations were on target and even included an off-spinner. In one 26-ball patch, he took 3/1.

After man of the match Waugh had made the second of two superb centuries for the match, England, set 469 to win, was bowled out a second time for 200. His confidence soaring, Warne enjoyed an uninterrupted spell of 30.4 overs to take 3/63. He was on in the 14th over at 3.10 p.m. with England 0/32 and bowled right through until England was bowled out at 12.31 p.m. on the final day, Warne's first 20 overs costing just 25.

On a bare, turning wicket which prompted wicketkeeper Ian Healy to don a full helmet and grille for only the second time in his career, Warne again bowled for long periods in tandem with Glenn McGrath, enjoying the hardened rough created by the Australian pacemen at the opposite end.

He claimed the wickets of top order pair Alec Stewart (his 250th Test wicket) and Graham Thorpe and wrapped up the match by having England's No.10 Caddick caught at mid-on.

On the balcony, Warne jigged up and down, swigged from a bottle of champagne and gave a one-fingered salute to the crowd, some of whom had been heckling him since the match started.

Some saw his hip-wiggling behaviour and finger gesture as uncouth and unnecessary. 'Had a footballer been spotted making a similar gesture he could be expected to be charged with bringing the game into disrepute,' said the London *Daily Mail*.

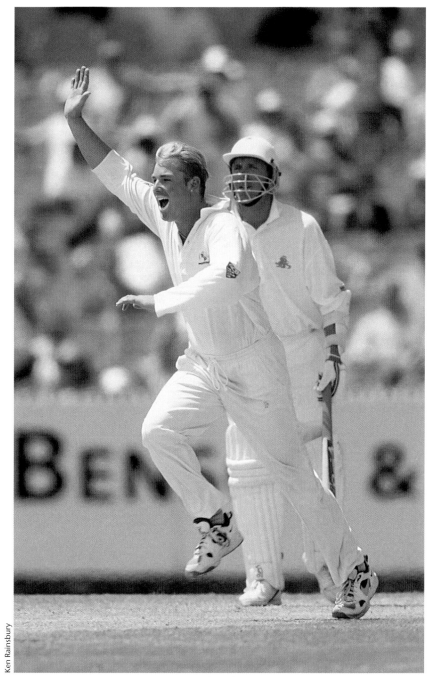

Warne's hat-trick, Melbourne, 1994–95 – the first of his career, even including his junior days with East Sandringham.

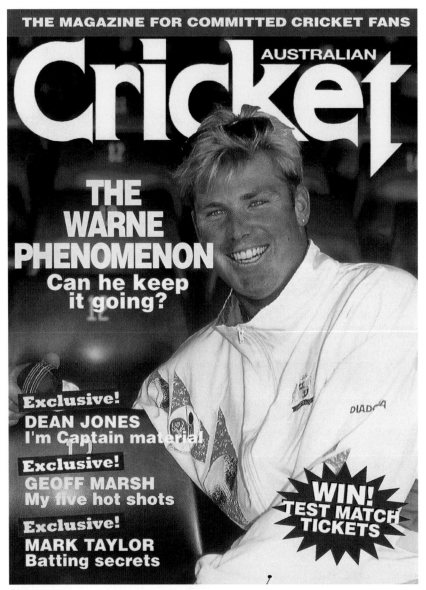

Warne's charismatic smile guaranteed him front-cover status in all the leading cricket magazines.

December 1995, shortly after taking the wicket of Sri Lanka's No. 1 batsman Aravinda de Silva at the WACA Ground in Perth.

Warne, along with Mark Taylor, was joint player of the finals in Australia's 1995–96 World Series win against Sri Lanka.

His comeback to cricket in 1996–97 after a finger operation saw him lose 4–5 kilograms in a rigorous pre-season training campaign, including the 'killer' fitness course at HMAS Cerberus in Hastings, Victoria.

A typically vociferous Warne appeal against the West Indies, fifth Test, Perth, 1996–97.

Warne the batsman is happiest playing shots. This pull-sweep against Pakistan's Saqlain Mushtaq disappeared over the midwicket boundary, Adelaide, 1996–97.

1997 tour of England: Warne celebrates one of his seven wickets in Australia's Ashes-clinching 264-run victory at Trent Bridge.

Mixing work with pleasure: another TV interview during the 1997 tour.

Playing up for the cameras, Texaco Cup, 1997.

Warne carried the controversy with him back to Australia for a lightning visit to see wife Simone and their just-born daughter – his time-off in mid-tour being yet another first for an Australian cricketer.

---

105. Australia v Middlesex, at Lord's, London, 19, 20 & 21 July 1997.
SCORES
MIDDLESEX 305 (M. W. Gatting 85, M. R. Ramprakash 76) and 201 for
6 wickets; AUSTRALIA 432 for 7 wickets dec. (M. E. Waugh 142 not out,
M. T. G. Elliott 83, S. R. Waugh 57). **Drawn.**
S. K. WARNE
1st inns: 23–4–76–1. Dismissed: O. A. Shah c M. E. Waugh 28.
2nd inns: 16–4–55–3. Dismissed: P. N. Weekes c & b 28; J. C. Pooley b 20;
M. R. Ramprakash c I. A. Healy 16.

Having bypassed the Irish and Welsh legs of the tour, Warne returned for the Middlesex game, preceding the fourth Test and along with team-mates, was presented to the Queen at Buckingham Palace.

With four wickets for the game, he was off-line early and bowled an accidental bean-ball at Mike Gatting before starting the second innings with 2/0 from his first seven deliveries and three wickets in his first seven overs.

106/56. Australia v England, Fourth Test Match, at Headingley, Leeds,
24, 25, 26, 27 & 28 July 1997.
SCORES
ENGLAND 172 (J. N. Gillespie 7/37) and 268 (N. Hussain 105,
J. P. Crawley 72; P. R. Reiffel 5/49); AUSTRALIA 501 for 9 wickets dec.
(M. T. G. Elliott 199, R. T. Ponting 127, P. R. Reiffel 54 not out;
D. Gough 5/149). **Australia won by an innings & 61 runs.**

TEST

S. K. WARNE
1st inns: 1–0–2–0.
2nd inns: 21–6–53–1. Dismissed: N. Hussain c J. N. Gillespie 105.

Rookie trio Jason Gillespie, Matthew Elliott and Ricky Ponting, making his series debut, were central in Australia's second consecutive victory, this time by an innings at Headingley.

Opposed by soon-to-be-forgotten players like Gloucestershire seam bowler Mike Smith, making his debut, the Australians scored 500-plus and bowled England out twice in 150 overs.

Warne had just one over in the first innings and 21 in the second. His only wicket was Nasser Hussain, deceived in flight and caught at mid-off, after he'd made his second century of the summer on a two-paced pitch which by late in the match was a health hazard.

'McGrath and Warne are easily the two noisiest bowlers in their side, while Steve Waugh says quite a bit on the field. They're the biggest sledgers.' England captain NASSER HUSSAIN

---

107. Australia v Somerset, at County Ground, Taunton, 1, 2, 3 (no play) & 4 (no play) August 1997.

SCORES

SOMERSET 284 (K. A. Parsons 71, R. J. Turner 58; S. K. Warne 5/57) and 147 for 3 wickets (R. J. Turner 65 not out); AUSTRALIA 323 (B. P. Julian 71, S. R. Waugh 62; A. R. Caddick 5/54). **Drawn.**

S. K. WARNE

1st inns: 18.3–7–57–5. Dismissed: S. C. Ecclestone lbw 12; M. N. Lathwell c M. E. Waugh 18; M. E. Trescothick b 8; A. R. Caddick c G. D. McGrath 16; P. S. Jones lbw 4.

2nd inns: 11–3–26–1. Dismissed: M. N. Lathwell st I. A. Healy 11.

In a bizarre twist to an otherwise innocuous county game at Taunton, Australia's acting captain Steve Waugh stopped play after the continued abuse of Warne by a section of rowdy spectators. Two men were escorted from the ground and others told to immediately quieten down or also face eviction.

Explaining that the barracking had become too personal, Waugh said the swearing was awful and detrimental to families attending first-class cricket. 'Shane can handle cries of "Fat boy". He's heard that a thousand times before. But it was a little bit more than that. I wouldn't have gone to the umpires if it wasn't,' he said. 'Shane is one of the best spin bowlers who has ever played the game and people should appreciate him for that fact. Come and watch him, instead of setting out to make fun and ridiculing him while he's bowling. It got beyond a joke today.'

With 5/57 and six wickets for the match, Warne was Australia's leading bowler. The game was also notable for the wayward bowling of Somerset's express, Dutchman Adrianus van Troost, who conceded 20 boundaries on his way to an analysis of 15.3–0–132–2.

108/57. **Australia v England**, Fifth Test Match, at Trent Bridge, Nottingham, 7, 8, 9 & 10 August 1997.

SCORES

AUSTRALIA 427 (M. A. Taylor 76, S. R. Waugh 75, M. T. G. Elliott 69, M. E. Waugh 68, G. S. Blewett 50) and 336 (I. A. Healy 63, G. S. Blewett 60); ENGLAND 313 (A. J. Stewart 87, G. P. Thorpe 53) and 186 (G. P. Thorpe 82 not out). *Australia won by 264 runs*.

S. K. WARNE

1st inns: 32–8–86–4. Dismissed: M. A. Atherton c I. A. Healy 27; A. J. Stewart c I. A. Healy 87; N. Hussain b 2; G. P. Thorpe c G. S. Blewett 53.

2nd inns: 16–4–43–3. Dismissed: B. C. Hollioake lbw 2; R. D. B. Croft c G. D. McGrath 6; A. R. Caddick lbw 0.

TEST

An overwhelming 264-run victory in just four days ensured the Ashes and extended Australia's series lead to 3–1, Warne instrumental yet again with seven wickets, including four of the top six in the English first innings.

From 0/106 chasing 427 shortly after tea on the second day, England lost four wickets in the final session, three in just 40 balls to Warne.

The dipping, looping leg-spinner which bowled Nasser Hussain was rated by wicketkeeper Ian Healy as unplayable 'and almost as good as the Mike Gatting ball'.

'We're a different team with and without Shane Warne,' Healy said. 'He gives us so much confidence. There's a set of footmarks way outside leg stump that only one spinner in the world uses at the moment. That makes it so difficult.'

England's top scorer in the game, Alec Stewart, said Warne was so formidable he could 'spin it on ice'.

Warne bowled almost 50 overs for the game and conceded just 129 runs. Other than two overs, his 31st and 32nd, which went for eight apiece, he conceded just over two runs an over, continuing his mastery over a rapidly fading band of crease-conscious batsmen.

Afterwards Mark Taylor said his team of '97 rated with the all-time best Australian XIs.

Heralding the victory by twirling his shirt and spraying champagne on the balcony afterwards, a cavorting Warne was once again accused of being boorish. 'It was just exuberance,' Taylor said later. 'I had no problem with it.'

'Shane Warne has made a goose of himself. Again. Swaying on the balcony outside the players' room, waving a stump high above his head. He then appeared to give the crowd the thumb as he left. His provocative and immature actions have sullied a fine victory.'

Melbourne *Age* columnist and long-time Warne critic, PATRICK SMITH

'The team's great performance, the relief I felt at winning the series and the effects of all the abuse I'd copped throughout the tour got to me and I went too far. I reacted emotionally and went over the top a bit.'

SHANE WARNE

109/58. **Australia v England**, Sixth Test Match, at The Oval, London, 21, 22 & 23 August 1997.
SCORES
ENGLAND 180 (G. D. McGrath 7/76) and 163 (G. P. Thorpe 62; M. S. Kasprowicz 7/36); AUSTRALIA 220 (P. C. R. Tufnell 7/66) and 104 (A. R. Caddick 5/42). *England won by 19 runs*.

TEST

S. K. WARNE
1st inns: 17–8–32–2. Dismissed: A. J. Hollioake b 0; P. C. R. Tufnell
c G. S. Blewett 1.
2nd inns: 26–9–57–2. Dismissed: N. Hussain c M. T. G. Elliott 2;
M. R. Ramprakash st I. A. Healy 48.

Weakened by injury and the unavailability of key players and again needing to bolster their squad with the inclusion of players from outside the original XVII, the Australians lost the last Test in three days on a dry, biscuit-coloured pitch at The Oval, despite seven wickets in the first innings from Glenn McGrath and seven in the second from Michael Kasprowicz.

Although sustaining a groin strain in mid-match and having to bat with a runner for the first time in his career, Warne took four wickets for the game. At times his turn was prodigious, reminiscent of Old Trafford '93.

With 24 wickets for the series, his aggregate was well down on his highs of '93 but still almost as good as Richie Benaud had achieved on three English tours combined.

For much of the summer, the English players, curators and administrators had been paranoid about him. The fans had given him a pasting, a not-so-nice reflection of the tall poppy syndrome. Having bowled 237 overs at an average of 40 overs per Test, the big question remained; how much longer could he continue without a major breakdown?

SUMMARY, 1997 (ENGLAND)

	Mts	Overs	Mdn	Runs	Wicks	Ave	BB	5wI	10wM
All First-Class matches	12	433.4	112	1154	57	20.24	7/103	4	–
Test matches v England	6	237.1	69	577	24	24.04	6/48	1	–

1997–98

AUSTRALIA'S EXHAUSTING SCHEDULE for the previous 12 months had included playing, training and travel commitments on 312 of 365 days. And there was just two months gap between the start of the sixth Test at The Oval and Victoria's opening Sheffield Shield game of the new season, at North Sydney.

With Tests scheduled against New Zealand and South Africa and autumn commitments in India and Sharjah, time-off was again going to be a rare commodity. Warne had been reappointed Victoria's captain, despite his only limited availability. He'd again seriously thought about, but ultimately rejected, the lure of a 14-week county season, wanting to spend more time with wife and daughter.

His decision was greeted with unanimous relief. The money, understood to be around $400 000, was only an incidental, given that he was already earning upwards of $1 million a year as the superstar of Australian cricket.

Australia needed its matchwinners as fit and rested as possible. By placing his national responsibilities first and not committing to county ranks, Warne was also inadvertently opening a national leadership door. Within weeks he'd been named as Steve Waugh's deputy for an Australian XI game against the Cricket Academy in Adelaide. Test captain Mark Taylor didn't make either side.

IN AUSTRALIA

110. **Victoria v New South Wales**, at North Sydney Oval,
22, 23, 24 & 25 October 1997.
SCORES
VICTORIA 509 for 6 wickets dec. (M. T. G. Elliott 187, L. D. Harper 160,
G. B. Gardiner 50 not out) and 279 for 8 wickets dec. (I. J. Harvey 109,
G. B. Gardiner 56); NEW SOUTH WALES 407 for 4 wickets dec.
(S. R. Waugh 202 not out, S. Lee 81 not out, M. E. Waugh 72) and 225 for
3 wickets (M. J. Slater 85, S. R. Waugh 60 not out, M. A. Taylor 50). **Drawn**.
S. K. WARNE (capt.)
1st inns: 33–3–117–1. Dismissed: M. G. Bevan c I. J. Harvey 13.
2nd inns: 25–6–78–2. Dismissed: M. A. Taylor c D. J. Saker 50;
M. E. Waugh b 2.

Playing one of only four early-season matches for Victoria leading into the new international season, Warne bowled almost 60 overs in the highest scoring match of the summer.

Amidst continuing talk of a players' strike from an increasingly militant Australian Cricketers' Association, more than 1400 runs were made during the four-day match, with four players making centuries.

While Warne's figures were an unflattering 1/117 and 2/78, the New South Wales team included ten internationals, plus a budding Testman in Stuart MacGill.

Warne revealed after the game he'd had saline and cortisone injections four weeks earlier to loosen his much talked about shoulder. 'I'm stiff and sore because I haven't been able to do any fitness work, but I feel a lot better injury-wise than in the last 12 to 18 months,' he said.

111. **Victoria v Queensland**, at Melbourne Cricket Ground, 31 October,
1, 2 & 3 November 1997.

SCORES

QUEENSLAND 231 (M. L. Hayden 53, J. P. Maher 50) and 313 for 9 wickets dec.
(J. P. Maher 77. M. L. Hayden 76); VICTORIA 318 for 9 wickets dec.
(D. M. Jones 151 not out, P. R. Reiffel 60) and 30 for 1 wicket. **Drawn.**

S. K. WARNE (capt.)

1st inns: 20–4–70–3. Dismissed: A. Symonds st D. S. Berry 19; G. I. Foley
c & b 14; I. A. Healy c D. J. Saker 7.

2nd inns: 34–8–106–1. Dismissed: M. P. Mott st D. S. Berry 44.

In a dramatic match in which Dean Jones made 151 not out in his
record-breaking 115th state game, Darren Berry claimed his 300th
Shield dismissal and Queenslander Geoff Foley was no-balled for
throwing, Warne took four wickets, but came in for some punishment from Bulls opener Matthew Hayden, who struck sixes in consecutive overs on the final day.

For the second time in as many matches, Warne was criticised for a
conservative declaration to the detriment of the match result. However, in bowling more than 50 overs and taking four wickets for the
match, he was approaching with confidence the first internationals of
the summer against the touring New Zealanders.

Foley's faster ball halfway through his fourth over was no-balled by
umpire Ross Emerson, who two years earlier had been one of three
umpires to call the Sri Lankan Muttiah Muralitharan.

112/59. **Australia v New Zealand**, First Test Match, at Brisbane Cricket
Ground, 7, 8, 9, 10 & 11 November 1997.

SCORES

AUSTRALIA 373 (M. A. Taylor 112, P. R. Reiffel 77, I. A. Healy 68) and 294 for
6 wickets dec. (G. S. Blewett 91, R. T. Ponting 73 not out); NEW ZEALAND 349
(S. P. Fleming 91, C. L. Cairns 64, B. A. Pocock 57, C. D. McMillan 54) and
132 (G. D. McGrath 5/32). **Australia won by 186 runs.**

S. K. WARNE

1st inns: 42–13–106–4. Dismissed: B. A. Pocock c M. A. Taylor 57;

TEST

C. D. McMillan lbw 54; A. C. Parore c M. A. Taylor 12; C. Z. Harris b 13.
2nd inns: 25–6–54–3. Dismissed: C. Z. Harris b 0; D. L. Vettori
c M. A. Taylor 0; G. I. Allott lbw 0.

Declaring on the eve of the first Test that it was more important to represent Australia than 'earn a few quick bucks playing county cricket' in England, Warne set after his season goal of 36 wickets in six Tests and 300 career wickets with zest and enthusiasm. 'I see myself playing the game for five years minimum,' he said in a media interview. 'As long as I'm enjoying myself and still feel competitive and not falling apart, I'll play as long as I can.'

No Test match in an Australian season had ever been scheduled as early as 7 November and Queensland administrators, mindful of disappointing crowds to previous 'Gabba Tests, worked hard in promotion and were rewarded with almost 30 000 attending, including 10 369 on the first day.

The young, underrated New Zealanders were competitive for four of the five days before Australia clinched a 186-run win midway through the last.

The Kiwis had a game plan to push forward to Warne at every opportunity, negate his flipper with a straight bat and wait for him to overpitch. Other than a six into the Clem Jones Stand by Craig McMillan to reach a fine Test 50 on debut, Warne rarely conceded more than two or three runs an over. He bowled into a stiff wind early in the match, his bowling featuring more drift than spin. Man of the match Mark Taylor snared a superb slips catch to dismiss Adam Parore from a genuine leg-break which bit and took a healthy edge. Initially unsighted, Taylor dived backwards and to his left and took a blinder in his outstretched left hand. Chris Harris was bowled soon afterwards, giving Warne a fourth wicket.

He added three more in the second innings on Remembrance Day: Harris, Daniel Vettori and Geoff Allott, all for ducks. He would have had Simon Doull, too, for no score, but for a dropped catch by Glenn

McGrath. Also notable in his unchanged 90-minute spell after lunch on the fifth day was a bouncer to Parore, whom the Australians had quickly identified as NZ's most combative cricketer along with the talkative all-rounder Chris Cairns.

The victory was Taylor's 20th in 34 matches, making him Australia's most successful captain since Don Bradman.

113/60. **Australia v New Zealand**, Second Test Match, at WACA Ground, Perth, 20, 21, 22 & 23 November 1997.

SCORES

NEW ZEALAND 217 (C. D. McMillan 54, C. L. Cairns 52) and 174 (A. C. Parore 63; S. H. Cook 5/39); AUSTRALIA 461 (S. R. Waugh 96, M. E. Waugh 86, I. A. Healy 85, P. R. Reiffel 54). *Australia won by an innings & 70 runs*.

TEST

S. K. WARNE

1st inns: 22.4–3–83–4. Dismissed: S. P. Fleming c G. S. Blewett 10; C. L. Cairns c M. E. Waugh 52; S. B. Doull c M. A. Taylor 8; G. I. Allott b 0.
2nd inns: 26–4–64–2. Dismissed: D. L. Vettori c M. A. Taylor 1; S. P. Fleming c G. S. Blewett 4.

Having bypassed Victoria's match against the New Zealanders, Warne, in his new role as treasurer and executive member of the Australian Cricketers' Association, was party to the militant action and a set of potential strike dates laid down by the ACA after a breakdown in their salary and welfare negotiations with the Australian Cricket Board.

The plan to boycott four one-day games became a national issue. A settlement was eventually agreed but not without casualties and much acrimony – the ACB furious at the threatened strike and the players aggrieved that previously confidential information, like the $400 000-plus ACB salaries of Warne and others had been leaked to major media outlets. The whole issue was fast becoming a public relations disaster and the second Test a mere sideshow as the fracas degenerated.

If the on-field focus of the players was a little clouded, it was totally understandable, yet they continued to perform admirably, the authoritative innings victory in Perth being achieved despite the absence of the injured Glenn McGrath.

Warne took six wickets and made 36 (from 25 balls) in another key contribution, NZ captain and specialist batsman Stephen Fleming twice dismissed cheaply bat-pad.

During his innings of 86, Mark Waugh lifted Daniel Vettori onto the roof of the Lillee–Marsh stand, an extraordinary six estimated at 130 metres, one of the biggest of all time.

The game was the first, at Test level, where play continued under artificial lighting, during the final session on the murky opening day.

114/61. **Australia v New Zealand**, Third Test Match, at Bellerive Oval, Hobart, 27, 28, 29, 30 November & 1 December 1997.

SCORES

AUSTRALIA 400 (M. T. G. Elliott 114, G. S. Blewett 99, M. E. Waugh 81) and 138 for 2 wickets dec. (M. A. Taylor 66 not out, G. S. Blewett 56); NEW ZEALAND 251 for 6 wickets dec. (M. J. Horne 133) and 223 for 9 wickets (S. K. Warne 5/88). **Drawn.**

TEST

S. K. WARNE

1st inns: 27–4–81–1. Dismissed: R. G. Twose lbw 2.

2nd inns: 28–6–88–5. Dismissed: C. L. Cairns st I. A. Healy 18; S. P. Fleming st I. A. Healy 0; C. D. McMillan c M. A. Taylor 41; B. A. Young c R. T. Ponting 10; A. C. Parore c M. T. G. Elliott 41.

Australia was denied a clean sweep of victories after leg-side boundary rider Simon Cook dropped a chance in the final half an hour, robbing Warne of a sixth wicket for the innings, seven for the match and 20 for the series.

With five for 88 on the last afternoon, Warne was at his menacing best, extracting biting turn from around the wicket. He bowled 17 overs unchanged after tea as the Kiwis desperately tried to hang on for a draw. In his final over, NZ No. 11 Shayne O'Connor had to combat five close-in fieldsmen.

Warne was also involved in some of the most action-packed batting of the game. After making 14, he was stumped from the bowling of Daniel Vettori, but not before he'd ploughed headlong into the stumps attempting to return to his crease.

His 19 wickets in three Tests broke his own Trans-Tasman record.

---

115. Victoria v Tasmania, at Bellerive Oval, Hobart,
19, 20, 21 & 22 December 1997.
SCORES
VICTORIA 180 for 9 wickets dec. and 348 (L. D. Harper 152, I. J. Harvey 83);
TASMANIA 130 and 401 for 3 wickets (D. F. Hills 205, J. Cox 95,
M. J. Di Venuto 53). ***Tasmania won by seven wickets***.
S. K. WARNE (capt.)
1st inns: 9–3–30–1. Dismissed: S. Young c D. S. Berry 19.
2nd inns: 20–4–87–0.

Never far from controversy, this time for a noticeable weight gain, which had caused old adversary Daryll Cullinan to call him 'a balloon' during the one-day series, Warne unleashed a salvo at journalists saying the interest in his weight was over the top, petty and nothing at all to do with the good cricket he was producing. Just days after walking out of a Melbourne function in which his weight was questioned, Warne said he was considering black-banning the media.

His mood was not improved after Tasmania achieved a rare victory at Bellerive chasing 399 on the last day and getting there with just three wickets lost.

Warne's match figures were an unflattering 1/117 and he complained of a stiff neck to go with his sore, overworked right shoulder.

In the second innings when he conceded more than four runs an over for the only time all season, his second over cost 16, courtesy of Dene Hills (4 4 4 . . 4) and 20th and final over, 15. He even resorted to bowling some seam-up deliveries in the swirly wind. The matchwinning opening stand between Hills and Jamie Cox was worth 297.

'Shane was at his peak from the ages of 24 to 26. Since then, he's had to adapt his thinking to a new set of standards and a new feeling when bowling his leg-break. He has to work a lot harder for his wickets now. If he was the same bowler from the point of view of whip and grip, you just can't consistently play that standard of bowling.'

Warne's coach, TERRY JENNER

116/62. Australia v South Africa, First Test Match, at Melbourne Cricket Ground, 26, 27, 28, 29 & 30 December 1997.

SCORES

AUSTRALIA 309 (R. T. Ponting 105, S. R. Waugh 96) and 257 (P. R. Reiffel 79 not out, M. A. Taylor 59; A. A. Donald 6/59); SOUTH AFRICA 186 (G. Kirsten 83) and 273 for 7 wickets (J. H. Kallis 101, W. J. Cronje 70). *Drawn*.

TEST

S. K. WARNE

1st inns: 42–15–64–3. Dismissed: W. J. Cronje c G. S. Blewett 0; S. M. Pollock lbw 7; L. Klusener lbw 11.

2nd inns: 44–11–97–3. Dismissed: A. M. Bacher c M. A. Taylor 39; D. J. Cullinan b 0; B. M. McMillan c M. A. Taylor 16.

Tipped as the key man in the long-awaited re-matches with South Africa, Warne took six wickets including his 500th first-class wicket but couldn't lift Australia to a first-up win after a match-saving six-hour century on the fifth day from Jacques Kallis.

As in the New Zealand series Warne bowled his flipper only sparingly, instead using a slider as his major variation. While he missed Daryll Cullinan in the first innings, he had him playing and missing twice in one over, and in the second bowled him for an eighth-ball duck, despite the wicket being slow and providing only occasional encouragement.

It was the tenth time Warne had dismissed Cullinan in international cricket, including the fourth time in seven Tests. 'If you're going to use gamesmanship, fine,' said Cullinan later, 'but if you're going to overstep that mark, it can be dangerous and it can get nasty. I respect him tremendously as a cricketer, but I don't know how much respect I have for him as a person.'

Warne also claimed South African captain Hansie Cronje for a duck, as he passed 50 wickets in his 10th Test against the South Africans.

Warne's marathon efforts – he bowled 86 overs for the match, including 35 on the last day – lifted him to 289 Test wickets, just 11 from becoming only the second Australian to a triple century of Test wickets.

Melbourne Cricket Club arenas manager Tony Ware doctored the wicket in mid-match, having deemed damaged footholes at the members' end dangerous to the bowlers.

'Warne fizzed them off the pitch, spun them out of footmarks, tortured the batsmen by bowling around the wicket and into the rough. Each ball was a Test in itself, a battle for survival. Warne wheeled down 42 overs for the innings and took 3/64, not spectacular figures. Yet his greatness was evident.'

Cricket writer MARTIN BLAKE of the Melbourne *Age*

117/63. **Australia v South Africa**, Second Test Match, at Sydney Cricket Ground, 2, 3, 4 & 5 January 1998.

SCORES

SOUTH AFRICA 287 (W. J. Cronje 88, H. H. Gibbs 54; S. K. Warne 5/75) and 113 (S. K. Warne 6/34); AUSTRALIA 421 (M. E. Waugh 100, S. R. Waugh 85, R. T. Ponting 62). **Australia won by an innings & 21 runs**.

TEST

S. K. WARNE

1st inns: 32.1–8–75–5. Dismissed: W. J. Cronje c M. A. Taylor 88; S. M. Pollock c M. A. Taylor 18; D. J. Richardson b 6; P. L. Symcox c I. A. Healy 29; P. R. Adams c S. R. Waugh 0.
2nd inns: 21–9–34–6. Dismissed: J. H. Kallis b 45; W. J. Cronje c R. T. Ponting 5; H. H. Gibbs c G. S. Blewett 1; B. M. McMillan b 11; S. M. Pollock c M. A. Taylor 4; D. J. Richardson c & b 0. Man of the match.

New Year celebrations extended long into the week as Steve Waugh became only the third Australian to reach 100 Tests and Warne triggered an innings victory with an extraordinary 11-wicket haul which gave him exactly 300 wickets from 63 Tests.

At 28, Warne was the second-youngest bowler behind India's Kapil Dev to 300. Only three others had achieved the milestone quicker: Dennis Lillee (in 56 Tests), Richard Hadlee (61) and Malcolm Marshall (61). And only one other spinner, West Indian Lance Gibbs, was a 300 club member.

'To be in that [elite] company is an honour and I'm very proud,' said Warne, who took 11/109 for the match, his third-best haul in Test cricket. 'I set myself the goal of reaching 300 Test wickets this season as I thought if I reached that, we would win both series. If this match wasn't my best effort, it's in the Grand Final.'

THE DAY MR MAGIC WEAVED HIS SPELL proclaimed the Melbourne *Herald Sun*. 300 NOT OUT. SHANE JOINS CRICKET'S TRUE GREATS headlined the Sydney *Daily Telegraph*.

Despite Sydney's reputation as a spinning haven, few had thought Warne could possibly reach his milestone before the final Test of the summer in Adelaide.

But from his opening overs shortly after midday on the opening day, he commanded an immediate respect and significantly, started catching the edges which had eluded him in Melbourne. The delivery which bowled Dave Richardson pitched outside leg stump and hit off.

He also dismissed South Africa's top scorer Hansie Cronje, who was slow-handclappped for batting four hours for 50 and almost six for 88. It was the first of five wickets in a row as the tourists forfeited a position of strength.

Trailing by 134, the South Africans were bowled out in extra time on the fourth night for just 113, Warne again central in the collapse with 6/34.

Kallis, the hero of Melbourne, was his 300th victim when he padded up and was bowled by a drifting topspinner which followed three consecutive leg-breaks. 'I think I know how to get batsmen out now,' said Warne. 'When I first started I had no idea.'

Despite Warne's heroics, he didn't deliver the ball of the match. That honour went to the high speed South African Allan Donald whose leg-cutter to Steve Waugh (85) pitched leg and hit off.

Afterwards Richie Benaud said a fully fit Warne had become such a master of his craft that he seemed capable of even doubling his 300. He told Warwick Hadfield of the *Australian*: 'If he goes on for as long as I did, he'll play for another six years, when he'll be 34. If you do your sums, in his case that's another 300 wickets, giving him 600.'

'I have seen a lot of people come out against him with a plan and when it doesn't work they are gone. The South Africans the other day were like kangaroos caught in the headlights. They didn't know what to do.
Australian wicketkeeper IAN HEALY

118/64. **Australia v South Africa**, Third Test Match, at Adelaide Oval, 30, 31 January, 1, 2 & 3 February 1998.
SCORES
SOUTH AFRICA 517 (B. M. McMillan 87 not out, G. Kirsten 77, W. J. Cronje 73, A. M. Bacher 64) and 193 for 6 wickets dec. (G. Kirsten 108 not out); AUSTRALIA 350 (M. A. Taylor 169 not out, M. E. Waugh 63; S. M. Pollock 7/87) and 227 for 7 wickets (M. E. Waugh 115 not out). **Drawn**.
S. K. WARNE
1st inns: 33–6–95–2. Dismissed: W. J. Cronje b 73;
D. J. Richardson c M. A. Taylor 15.
2nd inns: 15–2–52–1. Dismissed: A. M. Bacher c S. C. G. MacGill 41.

TEST

Having captained Australia for the first time during the one-day international series and reached his 300 wickets goal at the ground where it all started six years earlier, the final Test, Ian Healy's 100th, was somewhat of an anticlimax for Warne.

However, he took three wickets to bring his summer aggregate to 39, his best-ever season haul.

Temperatures reached a season-high 42°C on the third day of the game, umpires ordering two drink breaks per session.

Australia saved the game, but only just, thanks to Mark Waugh's unbeaten century when he batted through the entire fifth day's play for the first time in his career. He'd been dropped at 1 and again at 96, 107 and 108.

South African captain Hansie Cronje was so incensed when an appeal for hit wicket against Waugh was disallowed that he rammed a stump through the umpires' door as the players left the field, the drawn result allowing Australia to win the series 1–nil.

South Africa dropped ten chances for the match.

For the first time since the 1994–95 season, Australia named a second specialist leg-spinner to partner Warne, West Australian-born Stuart MacGill from New South Wales, who took five wickets on debut.

Citing shoulder soreness, Warne withdrew from a ten-day tour of New Zealand, captain Mark Taylor saying he needed a rest before the upcoming Indian tour. 'I don't think he turned the ball as far in this game as Stuart MacGill,' Taylor said. 'And that's just through tiredness. As captain of the Indian side I'd like him to have a rest.'

Warne delivered 357.5 overs in the six Tests, more than double any other Australian bowler, a workload he'd only previously shouldered once before, in 1993 during his triumphant tour of England. 'The amount of overs I bowl has made the shoulder a little bit sore after a game,' he said.

He was named man of the series against South Africa and, for the second time, the International Cricketer of the Year.

SUMMARY, 1997–98 (AUSTRALIA)

	Mts	Overs	Mdn	Runs	Wicks	Ave	BB	5wI	10wM
All First-Class matches	9	498.5	115	1381	47	29.38	6/34	3	1
Test matches v NZ	3	170.4	36	476	19	25.05	5/88	1	–
Test matches v South Africa	3	187.1	51	417	20	20.85	6/34	2	1
Sheffield Shield matches	3	141	28	488	8	61.00	3/70	–	–

'I would like to see Shane extend his career as much as he can. There will be a lot of cricket life for him after 30. Why not go for 500 Test wickets? Let's stamp the name Warne on the game for all time.'

Ex-captain and national cricket selector ALLAN BORDER

AUSTRALIA IN INDIA

119. **Australia v Mumbai**, at Brabourne Stadium, Mumbai
(formerly Bombay), 24, 25 & 26 February 1998.
SCORES
AUSTRALIA 305 for 8 wickets dec. (M. J. Slater 98, R. T. Ponting 53) and 135
(G. S. Blewett 50; N. M. Kulkarni 5/23); MUMBAI 410 for 6 wickets dec.
(S. R. Tendulkar 204 not out, A. A. Pagnis 50) and 31 for no wicket.
Mumbai won by ten wickets.
S. K. WARNE
1st inns: 16–1–111–0.
2nd inns: did not bowl.

Champion of the subcontinent, Sachin Tendulkar, previewed what was to come with a career-best 204 not out as Ranji Trophy champions Mumbai defeated the Australians comfortably in two-and-a-half days at Brabourne Stadium, India's one-time premier cricket ground. It was only the second time an Indian state team had defeated an international touring team (the other occasion being Karnataka's win against the West Indies in 1978–79).

First introduced in the 14th over and used in three different spells, Warne's first two overs cost 20, the next four 30, the next nine 45 and his last, 16. Never before had he conceded 100 runs without taking a wicket. And never before had his topspinning leg-breaks been rendered so innocuous.

From the second ball he faced from Warne, which he lofted imperiously for six, Tendulkar played superbly, his double century coming from just 192 balls and including 112 runs in boundary shots. 'I was determined to hang around and play my shots,' said Tendulkar. 'I don't underestimate anybody.'

It was an unceremonious entry for Warne, making his first-class debut in India, after missing the one-off Test in Delhi 18 months earlier.

Other than a solitary flipper and one googly, he'd deliberately with-held most of his variations to Tendulkar, continuing his early-tour practice of not allowing star opposition players to see his full reper-toire earlier than necessary.

Even Indian Under 19 captain Amit Pagnis punished him early with a succession of drives through extra cover. The only time Warne seemed to be in control was when he bowled a solitary maiden over to ex-Testman Sanjay Manjrekar, playing his last game.

'I'm not a great fan of Indian food and I've packed three jumbo-size jars of Vegemite to keep me going.'   SHANE WARNE

---

120. **Australia v Board President's XI**, at Municipal Stadium, Visakhapatnam, 1, 2 & 3 March 1998.
SCORES
BOARD PRESIDENT'S XI 329 for 4 wickets dec. (H. H. Kanitkar 102 not out, V. V. S. Laxman 65, V. Pratap 59 not out, S. Ramesh 58); AUSTRALIA 567 for 8 wickets (M. J. Slater 207, R. T. Ponting 155, G. S. Blewett 57, M. E. Waugh 52). **Drawn**.
S. K. WARNE
Only inns: 26–5–88–2. Dismissed: V. V. S. Laxman c R. T. Ponting 65; R. Dravid c & b 6.

The Indirapriyadarsini Stadium produced the flattest wicket of the tour and a mountain of runs, Warne the only Australian to take more than one wicket.

Bowling in sunglasses, he started the second day with a bouncer to Vanka Pratap. Both his wickets, V. V. S. Laxman and Rahul Dravid, were taken on the opening day.

121/65. **Australia v India**, First Test Match, at Chidambaram Stadium, Chennai (formerly Madras), 6, 7, 8, 9 & 10 March 1998.
SCORES
INDIA 257 (N. S. Sidhu 62, N. R. Mongia 58, R. Dravid 52) and 418 for

TEST

4 wickets dec. (S. R. Tendulkar 155 not out, N. S. Sidhu 64,
M. Azhharuddin 64, R. Dravid 56); AUSTRALIA 328 (I. A. Healy 90,
M. E. Waugh 66, G. R. Robertson 57) and 168. *India won by 179 runs*.
S. K. WARNE
1st inns: 35–11–85–4. Dismissed: R. Dravid c G. R. Robertson 52;
S. R. Tendulkar c M. A. Taylor 4; M. Azharuddin c P. R. Reiffel 26;
J. Srinath c M. A. Taylor 1.
2nd inns: 30–7–122–1. Dismissed: R. Dravid c I. A. Healy 56.

There are few more knowledgeable cricket crowds in the world than
those to be found in India's south-east shipping citadel, Chennai. When
Sachin Tendulkar crashed the first ball he faced slightly uppishly,
straight past Warne to the mid-off boundary, the heralding roar of
delight on the first afternoon was so prolonged it seemed likely to lift
the grandstand roof of the much-vaunted M. A. Chidambaram Stadium.

The expectation for Tendulkar to continue his awesome form from
the tour opener in Bombay was mountainous. Four balls later he was
out, caught by Mark Taylor at first slip, the silence deafening as he
trudged back to the pavilion.

It was the most prized of Warne's five wickets for the match, which
for the first three days was as intensely fought and competitive as any
under Mark Taylor's command.

The match and series fortunes changed dramatically in the final
session on the third day when 34-year-old Punjabi Navjot Sidhu, the
world's longest-serving Test cricketer, virtually ran at Warne in a full-
frontal, kamikaze attack Warne had never previously experienced.

After conceding just 10 runs from his first five overs and consistently beating the bat with big spinning leg-breaks, Warne's next three
overs cost 33 including 15 from his last (. N . 4 4 6 .) as Sidhu
freewheeled to an exhilarating half century in hot, humid and steamy
conditions. Thirty of his runs came in boundary shots, all against
Warne.

While Sidhu was out early on the fourth morning, the arrival of
Tendulkar continued the carnage. In a devastating retaliatory attack
after his first-innings failure, he made 155 not out and helped India to

declare at 4/418. He faced just 64 balls for his first 50 and 63 for his second, his power and placement superb. So fatigued were the Aussies that they were lucky to bat even two sessions and lost by 179, Warne's 35 top score.

In between overs on the fourth day, lynchpin Warne was often seen bent over, hands on knees and obviously distressed by the heat and his workload. With 1/122 from 30 overs he'd been collared and like the rest of Australia's attack, seemed powerless against the sure-footed, eagle-eyed Tendulkar. To the joy of the fans, his final over to Muhammad Azharuddin went for 18 (4 . 4 4 . 6), the most he'd ever conceded at Test level.

'It is now clear why Indian cricket stadiums are such fortress-like concrete structures,' wrote the award-winning Malcolm Conn in the *Australian*. 'Anything less would crumble like the walls of Jericho from the pandemonium such fine batting creates in this country.'

122/66. **Australia v India**, Second Test Match, at Eden Gardens, Calcutta, 18, 19, 20 & 21 March 1998.
Scores
Australia 233 (S. R. Waugh 80, R. T. Ponting 60) and 181 (A. Kumble 5/62); India 633 for 5 wickets dec. (M. Azharuddin 163 not out, N. S. Sidhu 97, V. V. S. Laxman 95, R. Dravid 86, S. R. Tendulkar 79, S. C. Ganguly 65).
India won by an innings & 219 runs.
S. K. Warne
Only inns: 42–4–147–0.

TEST

If Madras was only an aberration, someone forgot to tell Sachin Tendulkar and the man who'd replaced him as captain, Muhammad Azharuddin.

In the biggest thrashing of his career, Warne's 42 overs cost 147 without even one wicket and Australia's run of nine undefeated series came to an abrupt end.

Eden Gardens is wondrously large and the home to the Calcutta Cricket Club, the oldest cricket club outside the British Isles. To call cricket a religion in these parts is to understate its significance. More than 80 000 fans attended on each of the final two days as the Indians wrapped up the match and the series by an innings.

The Australians had never been beaten at Calcutta before, but from the first tumultuous over from Javagal Srinath when two wickets were lost, the world champions were humbled.

With 79 from just 86 balls, Tendulkar teed off like it was a one-day game. Azharuddin's classy unbeaten 163 was the ultimate knockout punch as India raced to its second-highest score in Test history and the highest against Australia in 60 years.

Warne had six different spells, the longest his third when he bowled 13 overs in a row. His 10th over to Sidhu (97) cost 10. He bowled six no-balls, most at the height of the carnage.

'Seldom in its cricketing history can Australia have received the sort of lathering it was getting after lunch today,' said Peter Roebuck in the *Sydney Morning Herald*.

THE MOTHER OF ALL THRASHINGS headlined the Melbourne *Herald Sun*. FROM BAD TO WORSE said the *Sunday Herald Sun*.

The fast, flint-like outfield saw 89 boundaries scored at the rate of one every two overs. The Australians were so depleted that an injured Paul Reiffel acted as a substitute fieldsman despite being able to throw only underarm. India's innings and 219-run victory was their biggest in history.

Warne was criticised for not bowling his stock leg-break enough, but his shoulder was fast fading. He was finding increasing difficulty throwing the ball in from the boundary edges, but was refusing to publicly concede that he was anything less than 100 per cent fit.

'Eventually he [Warne] will treasure this [thrashing]. Even the great bowlers have to have a bad series sometime and Shane hadn't really up to this point. This will make him think about things which work and things that don't.'

Ex-Indian captain and legendary left-arm spinner BISHEN BEDI

123/67. **Australia v India**, Third Test Match, at Chinnaswamy Stadium, Bangalore, 25, 26, 27 & 28 March 1998.

SCORES

INDIA 424 (S. R. Tendulkar 177, N. S. Sidhu 74) and 169 (M. S. Kasprowicz 5/28); AUSTRALIA 400 (M. E. Waugh 153 not out, M. J. Slater 91, D. S. Lehmann 52; A. Kumble 6/98) and 195 for 2 wickets (M. A. Taylor 102 not out). **Australia won by eight wickets.**

TEST

S. K. WARNE

1st inns: 35–9–106–3. Dismissed: N. S. Sidhu b 74; R. Dravid b 23; N. R. Mongia c R. T. Ponting 18.

2nd inns: 25–6–80–2. Dismissed: V. V. S. Laxman c R. T. Ponting 15; N. S. Sidhu c D. S. Lehmann 44.

Australia won its only Test of the tour, despite India batting into a fifth session on day two for 424. Sachin Tendulkar, with 177, again top-scored.

Despite a groin strain, Warne took 3/106 and 2/80 to pass Lance Gibbs' mark of 309 as the most successful spinner in Test history.

In the first innings, Warne struck in his 12th and 13th overs, Navjot Sidhu and Rahul Dravid being bowled, Dravid with a curving leg-break which pitched leg and hit off. He also dismissed Nayan Mongia in his 30th over.

In the second, he was introduced in the seventh over and immediately conceded 14 runs, all to Sidhu. His next 14 overs, however, cost just 29.

Overall, he'd produced only patches of his best form, the Indians confirming themselves as the finest players of spin bowling in the world. While he'd taken 10 wickets, they'd cost 54 runs apiece.

Tendulkar, the world's No. 1 batsman, amassed 446 runs at an average of 111.25. Later it was revealed he'd specifically been practising for his meetings with Warne by scuffing up marks outside his leg stump at training and having leg-spinners bowl from around the wicket for several hours in the hottest part of the day so he could replicate, as closely as possible, Test match conditions.

Warne's shoulder was a constant worry and while he remained on tour and played in the two one-day series, including Sharjah, a tumble during the Zimbabwe game left him clutching his shoulder in agony. Rather than an option, surgery was now a necessity.

SUMMARY, 1997–98 (INDIA)

	Mts	Overs	Mdn	Runs	Wicks	Ave	BB	5wI	10wM
All First-Class matches	5	209	43	739	12	61.58	4/85	–	–
Test matches v India	3	167	37	540	10	54.00	4/85	–	–

1998–99

THE AUSTRALIAN CRICKET BOARD'S long overdue appointment of a full-time fitness adviser was one positive from the chastening news from Shane Warne's surgeon that the most-discussed shoulder in Australian sport had deteriorated so much that the star's return for the new-season Ashes Tests couldn't be guaranteed.

Warne was among a growing group of bowlers who had paid the price for an ever-increasing workload. Those who had also succumbed to injury in the previous 12–18 months included Glenn McGrath, Paul Reiffel, Andy Bichel and Damien Fleming.

When operating on Warne's shoulder, specialists said had he played even one or two more games, his shoulder could have become so damaged that he would never have been able to bowl again. He had a torn labrum which lines the shoulder socket, a partial tear of the cuff tendon and widespread scarring – all the direct result of being the game's most overworked bowler for years. Less than three months later he had additional surgery, to soothe continuing stiffness.

Warne was ordered to keep his shoulder in a sling for six weeks and spend up to six months rehabilitating. He was to miss the

Commonwealth Games tournament and the triumphant tour of Pakistan as well as four of the five Ashes Tests. Having flirted with retirement, it was to be almost a year before he was able to bowl with anything like the same vigour, or results.

IN AUSTRALIA

124. **Victoria v Western Australia**, at WACA Ground, Perth,
13 (no play), 14, 15 & 16 November 1998.
SCORES
WESTERN AUSTRALIA 319 for 9 wickets dec. (S. M. Katich 120 not out,
M. E. Hussey 71, A. C. Gilchrist 55) and 140; VICTORIA 254 for 9 wickets dec.
(J. L. Arnberger 97) and 203. **Western Australia won by two runs**.
S. K. WARNE (capt.)
1st inns: 10–1–46–0.
2nd inns: 7–2–28–1. Dismissed: A. C. Gilchrist c G. R. Vimpani 7.

A rehabilitating Warne had to wait more than six months to play again. In his first match since 24 April, a one-dayer against New South Wales on a portable pitch at the Melbourne Cricket Ground, he made 24 and took 1/23 from eight overs, an encouraging start leading into his first-class comeback several days later in Perth.

With only a week before the first Ashes Test in Brisbane, Warne had reluctantly agreed that even he, with all his recuperative powers, couldn't go into a Test match with so little match practice.

Warne told friends that despite his enthusiasm to play as soon as possible for Australia, he might not be ready until the Christmas Test in Melbourne or even the New Year Test in Sydney.

A modest comeback saw him take just one wicket in 17 overs against Western Australia in Perth. After taking 0/46 from ten slow and indifferent overs in the first innings and being struck for a towering six by Adam Gilchrist down the ground, he'd conceded only ten runs from his first six in the second before Tom Moody, batting with a runner at No. 9 after re-injuring his knee, hit him for 18 runs from his final over (4 2 . 4 6 2).

The climactic and controversial ending was notable for Warne's run-out with Victoria within a boundary of a third consecutive outright win. Having made a breezy 38, he attempted a dare-devil single to Matthew Nicholson at mid-on and was run out by centimetres, via a direct hit from side-on.

Later, at the mandatory press conference, he slammed the standard of umpiring in the game, especially an lbw decision against Graeme Vimpani and was fined his entire match fee of $2400.

'I like bowling in tandem with Shane. We feed off the other's hard work until something "gives" with the batsman.'   GLENN MCGRATH

---

125. **Victoria v South Australia**, at Melbourne Cricket Ground, 26, 27, 28 & 29 November 1998.

SCORES

VICTORIA 373 for 5 wickets dec. (M. T. G. Elliott 161, J. L. Arnberger 80) and 300 for 7 wickets dec. (B. J. Hodge 90, M. T. G. Elliott 68);
SOUTH AUSTRALIA 350 (D. S. Lehmann 171, G. S. Blewett 51) and 324 for 3 wickets (G. S. Blewett 158, D. S. Lehmann 78 not out). **South Australia won by seven wickets**.

S. K. WARNE (capt.)

1st inns: 15.4–3–88–2. Dismissed: D. A. Fitzgerald c & b 9; B. N. Wigney c D. J. Saker 7.
2nd inns: 22–3–97–2. Dismissed: G. S. Blewett c D. J. Saker 158; D. A. Fitzgerald c P. R. Reiffel 30.

Warne's second comeback game was more successful than the first, but only just. He took four wickets from almost 40 overs, but was expensive, going for more than five runs an over in the first innings and four in the second. His captaincy was also condemned, especially when he failed to employ deep fields to free-scoring pair Darren Lehmann and Greg Blewett who shared an important stand of 139 early on the final day as South Australia, set 324 runs in 84 overs, won with eight balls to spare.

While Warne had Blewett (158) eventually caught at long-off, the team hierarchy believed he had attacked for too long and not been quick enough to employ boundary riders in run-saving positions. The South Australians took just 40.2 overs after tea to score the 220 runs required for a memorable seven-wicket win.

In SA's first innings, Lehmann made a blistering 171, including a century from 86 balls. Warne conceded 47 runs from his first eight overs, Lehmann striking 7 fours and 1 six. Later, Warne's 14th over cost ten as he continued to struggle to produce the same curve and fizz at anything like his old pace.

---

126. **Victoria v Queensland**, at Melbourne Cricket Ground, 11, 12, 13 & 14 December 1998.
SCORES
QUEENSLAND 354 for 9 wickets dec. (G. I. Foley 97, J. P. Maher 62, M. L. Hayden 50) and 152 for 3 wickets dec. (S. G. Law 77 not out, J. P. Maher 59); VICTORIA 206 (M. T. G. Elliott 67; A. C. Dale 7/40) and 292 for 9 wickets (B. J. Hodge 100, M. T. G. Elliott 50; P. W. Jackson 5/65). **Drawn**.
S. K. WARNE (capt.)
1st inns: 23–5–79–1. Dismissed: W. A. Seccombe c J. R. Bakker 3.
2nd inns: 7–0–39–0.

News that the Australian Cricket Board had secretly fined Warne and Mark Waugh almost four years earlier after they'd accepted money from an Indian bookmaker for pitch and weather information added spice to the continuing saga of cricket's woes over matchfixing and bribery allegations.

CRICKET STARS HUMILIATE NATIONAL GAME said the *Australian*. DAY OF SHAME headlined the *Herald Sun*. Looking sheepish, Warne and Waugh publicly admitted receiving secret payments from bookmakers. Warne had received $6000 and been heavily fined after an internal investigation headed by the ACB's then media manager Ian McDonald.

Warne flew back to Melbourne to prepare for the Queensland match amidst speculation that he might miss the entire Ashes summer.

Several in the packed press gallery at the Adelaide Oval questioned whether the latest revelations would once-and-all finish his run at the national captaincy.

While he was to have minimal influence on the game, with 1/79 and 0/39, he felt he was regaining some of his old rhythm. His shoulder, while still sore, was ever improving.

Only 773 attended on the first day and it was impossible to truly judge the people's reaction to news of Warne's latest impropriety. However, at nearby Jolimont Terrace, home of Victorian cricket, receptionists were fielding irate phone calls, several asking that Warne be sacked immediately as state captain. In heat-wave conditions in Adelaide, Waugh was booed walking to and from the wicket on day one of the Test.

---

127. **Victoria v New South Wales**, at Sydney Cricket Ground, 19, 20, 21 & 22 December 1998.

SCORES

NEW SOUTH WALES 360 (S. R. Waugh 116, M. E. Waugh 64, P. A. Emery 58) and 362 for 4 wickets (M. E. Waugh 126, S. Lee 71 not out); VICTORIA 438 for 9 wickets dec. (B. J. Hodge 120, M. P. Mott 105, I. J. Harvey 82). **Drawn**.

S. K. WARNE (capt.)

1st inns: 29.3–6–80–2. Dismissed: P. A. Emery c M. W. H. Inness 58; S. H. Cook c M. P. Mott 8.

2nd inns: 25–5–64–0.

The backlash from the bribery scandal raged for weeks, totally overshadowing Australia's record fifth consecutive defence of the Ashes. Sacked from his lucrative Sunday newspaper writing commitments and stung by the widespread condemnation of his actions by leading home-town feature writers such as the *Herald Sun*'s Ron Reed, who said he should never be allowed to hold a leadership role in Australian cricket, Warne used the Sheffield Shield match press conferences as a forum to clear the air. He said the latest bookmaking scandal, while not a petty issue, was entirely separate to the game-fixing allegations which had seen Pakistani Saleem Malik ostracised from the game. Others, not him, had decided to keep in-house the fines from four years earlier. The scandal was unsettling but he remained fully focused and determined to regain his Test place.

Warne's replacement, Stuart MacGill, had complained of a minor hamstring injury, raising speculation that Warne could return as early as the Christmas Test match in Melbourne, despite appearing well short of his best in the Test-eve Shield match against New South Wales in Sydney.

Importantly, however, he bowled more than 50 overs for the game, his longest stint since the Indian tour in March. His two wickets, Phil Emery and Simon Cook, were only tailenders, but he bowled economically and at times, extracted considerable spin.

As in Melbourne, when his first balls, a slow full toss in the first innings and a long hop in the second were both smashed for four, he conceded eight runs from his opening over and struggled, at least initially, to bowl his normal, impeccable line. When fully warmed-up, however, he bowled some excellent overs, without enjoying a great deal of luck.

On a lifeless wicket devoid of grass, Mark Taylor criticised Warne's lack of adventure in not declaring Victoria's innings closed earlier to help contrive an exciting finish. Clearly miffed, Taylor refused to end the game early on the final afternoon. Warne responded by using 10 bowlers, including wicketkeeper Darren Berry and batsman Graeme Vimpani, who'd never before bowled in a first-class match.

128/68. **Australia v England**, Fifth Test Match, at Sydney Cricket Ground, 2, 3, 4 & 5 January 1999.

SCORES

AUSTRALIA 322 (M. E. Waugh 121, S. R. Waugh 96) and 184 (M. J. Slater 123; P. M. Such 5/81); ENGLAND 220 (S. C. G. MacGill 5/57) and 188 (N. Hussain 53; S. C. G. MacGill 7/50). **Australia won by 98 runs**.

TEST

S. K. WARNE

1st inns: 20–4–67–1. Dismissed: M. A. Butcher lbw 36.

2nd inns: 19–3–43–1. Dismissed: M. A. Butcher st I. A. Healy 27.

Having told chairman of selectors Trevor Hohns that he was ready to resume at top level, Warne was named, alongside Stuart MacGill, in the Australian squad for the final Test of the summer in Sydney. His season figures for Victoria, eight wickets in four matches at 65 runs apiece, may have been only modest, but he'd been so good for so long, it was felt he'd automatically rise to the challenge of the centre stage. It had been 277 days since he'd last represented Australia in a Test and seven years since he'd first stepped onto the Sydney Cricket Ground as Australia's 350th Test cricketer.

'Everyone expected him to play,' said England's captain Alec Stewart in *A Captain's Diary*. 'After all, you don't pick someone with over 300 Test wickets just to carry the drinks.'

The roar which greeted Warne as he marked his approach for the first time was undeniable proof of his enduring popularity, despite the unwanted, lingering pre-Christmas publicity.

He claimed an immediate wicket, from his favourite Randwick end, when left-hand opener Mark Butcher was lbw fourth ball early on the second day. He'd lifted Warne's second ball over midwicket for four, only to play back to a leg-break which scooted through, with hardly any side-spin. Caught on his crease, it would have hit middle and off stumps. Warne, arm raised in jubilation, was so confident it was out he didn't even bother looking back at umpire Darrell Hair for confirmation.

'Love him or hate him you have to admire him for being able to do that [take a wicket first over],' said Stewart, 'and although I'd rather he didn't get any wickets against us, it's still good to see a fellow sportsman back at the highest level after career-threatening surgery.'

It was Warne's only success, however, in 20 overs. He bowled mainly overspun leg-breaks and tried only one flipper, late in the day to England tailender Dean Headley.

He dismissed Butcher in the second innings, too, stumped from the sixth ball of his first over. Overall, however, he was unconvincing, taking 2/110 for the match from 39 overs, without producing either the curve or expected side-spin. By comparison, MacGill spun the ball markedly and from his very first overs when he was introduced ahead of Warne.

However, Warne did have a share in Glenn McGrath's 200th wicket, when he took a juggled catch at third slip to dismiss Stewart on the second morning.

MacGill was the hero of the game with 12 wickets in a career-best return, increasing his series aggregate to 27 from just four Tests and guaranteeing his place for the autumn tour of the West Indies.

Having played in Sydney and throughout the one-day series, Warne, too, was an automatic selection. He again captained the one-day team, in 10 of 12 matches, substituting for the injured Steve Waugh.

SUMMARY, 1998–99 (AUSTRALIA)

	Mts	Overs	Mdns	Runs	Wicks	Ave	BB	5wI	10wM
All First-Class matches	5	178.1	32	631	10	63.10	2/80	–	–
Test match v England	1	39	7	110	2	55.00	1/43	–	–
Sheffield Shield matches	4	139.1	25	521	8	65.12	2/80	–	–

AUSTRALIA IN THE WEST INDIES

129. **Australia v West Indies Board XI**, at Recreation Ground, St John's, Antigua, 22, 23 & 24 February 1999.
SCORES
AUSTRALIA 156 (G. S. Blewett 52) and 209 for 4 wickets dec. (R. T. Ponting 61 not out, G. S. Blewett 58); WEST INDIES BOARD XI 55 (A. C. Dale 7/24) and 121 for 4 wickets. **Drawn**.
S. K. WARNE (capt.)
1st inns: did not bowl.
2nd inns: 12–3–20–1. Dismissed: R. J. J. McLean c A. J. Bichel 15.

Mark Taylor's abdication after five years and 50 Tests as captain gave a fit-again Steve Waugh his first opportunity to lead Australia on tour.

Warne, his deputy, led in the very first match of the Caribbean tour, at the Recreation Ground in St John's – the first time he'd captained Australia in a first-class fixture.

Rain caused lengthy delays on the first and third days and the game was drawn, Warne bowling only 12 of Australia's 89 overs for the match. At one stage, swing bowler Adam Dale had 6/3 from 9.3 overs as the Board XI collapsed for 55 in just over two hours on the second day.

---

130. **Australia v President's XI**, at Guaracara Park, Pointe-a-Pierre, Trinidad, 27, 28 February & 1 March 1999.
SCORES
PRESIDENT'S XI 177 (D. R. E. Joseph 64; S. C. G. MacGill 6/45) and 185 (S. Ragoonath 53; S. C. G. MacGill 7/29); AUSTRALIA 368 (M. E. Waugh 106, S. R. Waugh 57; R. D. King 5/75). **Australia won by an innings & six runs**.
S. K. WARNE
1st inns: 16–2–50–1. Dismissed: R. N. Lewis c G. D. McGrath 8.
2nd inns: 20–4–82–3. Dismissed: D. Rampersad c G. S. Blewett 0; W. Phillip lbw 3; N. A. M. McLean c M. J. Slater 14.

Leg-spinning apprentice Stuart MacGill continued to press for a Test place and out-perform the master with an extraordinary 13-wicket match haul against a West Indian President's XI, eight of whom had played, or were about to play, for the national team.

With Pointe-a-Pierre's huge oil refinery as a backdrop and on a wicket conducive to slow bowling, Warne took four wickets for the match but was totally overshadowed by MacGill who ripped the ball savagely, seven of his wickets either being caught or stumped by Ian Healy.

Healy, Australia's most senior player, told Malcolm Knox of the *Sydney Morning Herald* that despite their diverse form, both wrist-spinners were likely to play in the Tests. 'One will get wickets one day, the other the next,' he said. 'They'll interchange a bit. Warnie bowled well once he had the incentive of bowling to a Test batsman, Keith Arthurton. He got his rhythm and everything right. He's got more up his sleeve.'

131/69. **Australia v West Indies**, First Test Match, at Queen's Park Oval, Port-of-Spain, Trinidad, 5, 6, 7 & 8 March 1999.
SCORES
AUSTRALIA 269 (G. S. Blewett 58) and 261 (M. J. Slater 106); WEST INDIES 167 (B. C. Lara 62, D. R. E. Joseph 50; G. D. McGrath 5/50) and 51 (G. D. McGrath 5/28). **Australia won by 312 runs**.
S. K. WARNE
1st inns: 14–4–35–0.
2nd inns: did not bowl.

TEST

Despite a damning 5–0 defeat in South Africa, Brian Lara was re-appointed West Indian captain, but only for the first two Tests, rather than for the entire summer. RALLY AROUND THE WEST INDIES banners were erected in main streets around each of the islands as Test cricket fever again gripped the Caribbean.

The disappointment at another huge loss, this time by 312 runs, at Queen's Park saw many disputing Lara's right to lead for even one more game.

Inter-island jealousies are forever bubbling in the West Indies. Defeats are often blamed on the non-selection of a particular player and when the Windies collapsed horribly for just 51 in their second innings, Lara the leader was treated mercilessly.

Warne bowled only 14 overs in the first innings and wasn't even required in the second, Jason Gillespie and Glenn McGrath taking less than 20 overs to demolish the once-mighty world champions for their lowest-ever Test score.

132/70. **Australia v West Indies**, Second Test Match, at Sabina Park, Kingston, Jamaica, 13, 14, 15 & 16 March 1999.
SCORES
AUSTRALIA 256 (S. R. Waugh 100, M. E. Waugh 67) and 177 (N. O. Perry 5/70); WEST INDIES 431 (B. C. Lara 213, J. C. Adams 94; G. D. McGrath 5/93) and 3 for no wicket. **West Indies won by ten wickets**.
S. K. WARNE
1st inns: 30–8–94–1. Dismissed: R. D. Jacobs c J. N. Gillespie 25.
2nd inns: did not bowl.

TEST

The confident Aussies continued their dual spin tactics in Kingston, only to hit a rare brick wall with Brian Lara making a masterly double century to pilot a ten-wicket West Indian win. The West Indies did not lose a wicket on the second day as Lara and fellow left-hander Jimmy Adams shared a monumental triple-century stand.

Both Warne and MacGill were negated, Warne taking only one wicket from an unproductive 30 overs. However, he was given the senior spinner's role and bowled more overs than MacGill, despite MacGill's superior return (three wickets from 22.3 overs).

Introduced at first change in the 15th over, Warne's first five overs cost just two runs, but he rarely menaced the batsmen and bowled little more than his leg-break and slider, having lost confidence in his flipper and googly. The battalion of West Indian left-handers had clearly unsettled him.

'It's frustrating for Warnie, but that's understandable when you haven't taken wickets for a while,' said captain Steve Waugh to pressmen afterwards. 'I'm sure he can work through it. It hasn't helped that we haven't been able to bowl on fourth- or fifth-day wickets. Sabina Park didn't give the spinners much help at all on day two, but it was going to turn a lot if we'd been able to get through the match into a fifth day.'

---

133. **Australia v West Indies 'A'**, at Recreation Ground, St John's, Antigua, 20, 21, 22 & 23 March 1999.

SCORES

AUSTRALIA 303 (J. L. Langer 134; C. L. Hooper 5/53) and 263 for 8 wickets dec. (M. T. G. Elliott 115); WEST INDIES 'A' 102 and 310 (C. L. Hooper 102, S. C. Williams 50; A. C. Dale 6/67). **Australia won by 154 runs.**

S. K. WARNE

1st inns: 14–7–26–3. Dismissed: S. C. Williams lbw 24; M. G. Sinclair c J. L. Langer 1; N. C. McGarrell c I. A. Healy 0.

2nd inns: 17–3–63–1. Dismissed: R. J. J. McLean lbw 40.

For the fourth consecutive game on tour, Warne was outbowled by MacGill, raising speculation that he might be dropped for the crucial third Test the following week in Barbados.

Opposed by an inexperienced West Indian 'A' team, with few Test players, other than captain Carl Hooper and opening batsman Stuart Williams, Warne was again largely ineffective and, on the last day, was struck out of the ground and into neighbouring Independence Drive by Hooper, who made 102 to earn a Test recall.

While Warne claimed 3/26 in the first innings, he took just 1/63 in the second and conceded almost four runs an over. Hooper said afterwards Warne was not at the top of his game. His body language portrayed a fragility Hooper had never seen before.

At Wanderers, on the eve of the third Test, Warne hardly bowled a ball at training, instead having just a dozen deliveries to wicketkeeper Ian Healy in the centre after everyone had finished.

134/71. Australia v West Indies, Third Test Match, at Kensington Oval, Bridgetown, Barbados, 26, 27, 28, 29 & 30 March 1999.

TEST

SCORES

AUSTRALIA 490 (S. R. Waugh 199, R. T. Ponting 104, J. L. Langer 51) and 146 (C. A. Walsh 5/39); WEST INDIES 329 (S. L. Campbell 105, R. D. Jacobs 68) and 311 for 9 wickets (B. C. Lara 153 not out; G. D. McGrath 5/92).

West Indies won by one wicket.

S. K. WARNE

1st inns: 15.5–2–70–1. Dismissed: C. A. Walsh c M. J. Slater 12.
2nd inns: 24–4–69–0.

In the most memorable Test match since the Centenary Test and one of the finest games of them all, the West Indies defied the odds and won by a single wicket with a record fourth-innings chase led by Brian Lara who made an imperious 153 not out.

Warne's woes were so considerable that on the third morning, even before the Australian warm-up, he enlisted coach Terry Jenner for a most-public on-ground tutorial, the pair working for more than half an hour, concentrating on Warne's shoulder turn.

Warne took only one wicket in the first innings, when West Indian No. 11 Courtney Walsh holed out to deep mid-off. He and Curtly

Ambrose had toyed with Warne while adding 38 for the 10th wicket. Warne bowled with little variety or spark. MacGill, coming to the end of his longest-ever season, was also below his best.

Australia's stunning second-innings collapse saw the West Indies set 308 runs to win in four full sessions, a target they reached in a fairytale finish via a thudding cover-driven boundary by man of the match Lara. With the Australian field up, the ball disappeared into the crowd which had already jumped the fence to herald the win.

Introduced ahead of MacGill after just half an hour, Warne had three spells, but went wicketless in 24 overs. To the joy of the Bajans who'd been dancing in the aisles from the opening delivery, anticipating a win, Lara took 11 from Warne's 15th over (. . 6 . 4 1) and he was immediately spelled.

The Australians bowled another 50 overs before Warne was reintroduced, but after five overs which cost 28, he was withdrawn again.

Never before had Warne bowled with six and seven men dotted around the boundaries as occurred shortly after tea with Lara already past 100 and the Windies within 50 runs of victory. The only fieldsmen not on the fence were first slip and cover.

Lara hit MacGill so hard straight back at him that the ball cannoned into his wrist and broke his watchband.

Warne bowled only variations of his leg-break and used his slider to defend himself. Unhappy with his flipper and believing Lara too easily picked his googly, he bowled neither.

Significantly at his press conference immediately afterwards, Steve Waugh said no player had an automatic right to a place in the XI. With Australia having to win the last Test to hold the Frank Worrell Trophy, changes were certain.

And Warne, in the most controversial of omissions, was to be one of the casualties. As the Australians clinched a comfortable win in four-and-a-half days, MacGill being given the second new ball on the final day, Warne did nothing more serious than to casually hit a few late-afternoon tennis shots with another out-of-favour Victorian,

Matthew Elliott, in front of the player dressing rooms during the tea intervals.

SUMMARY, 1998–99 (WEST INDIES)

	Mts	Overs	Mdns	Runs	Wicks	Ave	BB	5wI	10wM
All First-Class matches	6	162.5	37	509	11	46.27	3/26	–	–
Test matches v West Indies	3	83.5	18	268	2	134.00	1/70	–	–

'The head had to rule over the heart. Geoff and I both had the gut feeling that Stuart was the right man for this time. Shane did tell us that he was ready and fired up for a big one and of course we believe him. But Stuart would probably say the same thing too.' STEVE WAUGH

'I have to have a serious think about what I want to do in the future.'

SHANE WARNE

'To drop Shane Warne from the Test side was the toughest decision I've ever had to make.' Australian coach GEOFF MARSH

1999–2000

SITTING ON THE SIDELINES in Antigua, his ego bruised and badly missing his family, Shane Warne's immediate reaction was to retire. In a rare selection veto, his own captain Steve Waugh and coach Geoff Marsh had voted against his inclusion at St John's. They wanted Stuart MacGill. Warne was outnumbered 2–1.

Having taken just four wickets in four comeback Tests, Warne's confidence was at an all-time low. He knew he hadn't been getting enough action on the ball. For the first time since his roller-coaster start in Test cricket, he seriously wondered if he could ever again extract the gigantic turn that had rocketed him to fame.

Most importantly, he felt betrayed by those closest to him. Never before had he been as sensitive to criticism. At the nets at Club Antigua, a veritable paradise where players freely mingled with Aussie supporters and enjoyed news from home, Warne was stern-faced and surly. He couldn't wait to retreat to the team's minibus.

Normally affable and bubbly, he found it impossible to mask his disappointment.

Having fast-tracked his comeback to try and match the spectacular feats of leg spinning replacement MacGill, for the first time in his career his form had deserted him. Physically he was okay. But mentally, he was still scarred from his shoulder operation 10 months earlier. The harder he tried the less effective his leg-break seemed to be.

Never before in Australian cricket had such a big-name player been axed. Don Bradman was, but he was 20 at the time and had played only one Test. Much-loved Keith Miller was controversially omitted from the postwar tour of South Africa, but ended up going anyway, his best years still to come. Warne was 29 and soon to be acknowledged as one of the five outstanding cricketers of the century by the cricketing bible, *Wisden*. His near-record 317 wickets were a monument to his long-running success.

His wife, Simone, said he didn't have anything more to prove. And even after some encouraging efforts during the one-day series in the Caribbean, Warne remained undecided. The controversies were wearing him down and with a young family his priorities rapidly changing. No longer was cricket his all-consuming passion.

Having been subjected to some cavalier treatment by India's Robin Singh and Zimbabwe left-hander Neil Johnson midway through the World Cup campaign, so disheartened was he that he told team-mates he was retiring.

It had now been a year since his shoulder operation, yet he was still struggling to bowl at a standard he found personally acceptable.

He walked with Steve Waugh in a park, talking of the constant pressure and happenings which had made his life a soap opera. Waugh suggested he play through the tournament, go home and talk it over with his family. There was no need to make such a momentous decision so far from home.

'It was do or die time,' Warne said in a Channel Nine interview. 'I had to know, under pressure, whether I could do it or not.'

The turning point came on 15 June, in match 40, the World Cup second semi-final against South Africa at Edgbaston. He took 4/29 to inspire a magnificent comeback with some big-spinning leg-breaks reminding of his halcyon years in 1993 and 1994. By forcing a tie in the most memorable one-day game of them all, Australia advanced. Five days later, in the final against Pakistan in front of a sellout 30 000 crowd at Lord's, the Australians won easily and with another 'four-for', Warne was again man of the match. The King was back . . . and keen to reign a little longer.

'He [Warne] is the only guy I've watched since I retired to cause the hair to stand up on the back of my neck.'

Australian pace bowling great DENNIS LILLEE

AUSTRALIA IN SRI LANKA

135. **Australia v Sri Lanka Board XI**, at P. Saravanamuttu Stadium, Colombo, 3, 4, 5 & 6 September 1999.

SCORES
SRI LANKA BOARD XI 228 (S. I. de Saram 67, R. P. Arnold 63) and 271 (R. P. Arnold 79, L. P. C. de Silva 70; C. R. Miller 6/57); AUSTRALIA 179 and 321 for 6 wickets (G. S. Blewett 148, J. L. Langer 52, M. J. Slater 51).
Australia won by four wickets.

S. K. WARNE
1st inns: 19–4–37–2. Dismissed: P. R. Hewage st I. A. Healy 17; I. S. Gallage lbw 1.
2nd inns: 16.1–5–74–3. Dismissed: T. M. Dilshan c M. J. Slater 23; L. P. C. de Silva c M. J. Slater 70; S. I. de Saram c I. A. Healy 0.

There was only a two-month break between the World Cup victory and the first of Australia's extended new-season commitments which were to take in 13 Tests and 24 one-day internationals in four different countries.

It had been yet another tumultuous winter for Warne. He may have re-ignited his career late in the World Cup campaign, but he'd been fined $2000 and given a suspended two-match suspension after a scathing attack on Sri Lankan captain Arjuna Ranatunga in his column in the *Times*. Back in Australia, he'd also forfeited his Victorian captaincy, one of his most cherished honours.

However, his wife Simone had given birth to their second child, Jack, and plans to build a dream house on a huge, very private block in Sandringham's best street, just a few stone throws from where he'd played as a junior, were getting underway.

Warne had used his weeks off to holiday and strengthen his shoulder and started his season buoyantly in Australia's opening first-class fixture in Colombo, the only major lead-up match before the long-awaited three-Test series with Sri Lanka. Dipping and spinning the ball with confidence, the mental scars from his shoulder surgery and personal self-doubts having finally disappeared, he took five wickets, including a wicket with his fifth ball of the game. He took two wickets in the first innings and three in the second. His 12th over also cost 17 runs, courtesy of youngsters Nimesh Perera and Chamara Silva (1 3 1 4 4). On his 22nd birthday the left-handed Perera smashed three boundaries in a row.

'I think nothing of bowling 30 or 40 overs, but ask me to run 8 kilometres and I struggle.'

SHANE WARNE

136/72. **Australia v Sri Lanka**, First Test Match, at Asgiriya Stadium, Kandy, 9, 10 & 11 September 1999.

SCORES

AUSTRALIA 188 (R. T. Ponting 96) and 140 (R. T. Ponting 51); SRI LANKA 234 (P. A. de Silva 78; S. K. Warne 5/52) and 95 for 4 wickets. *Sri Lanka won by six wickets*.

TEST

S. K. WARNE

1st inns: 16–4–52–5. Dismissed: P. A. de Silva c R. T. Ponting 78; D. P. M. de S. Jayawardene c R. T. Ponting 46; A. Ranatunga c I. A. Healy 4; U. D. U. Chandana c sub (M. L. Hayden) 12; D. N. T. Zoysa c C. R. Miller 7. 2nd inns: 6.5–3–18–0.

Sri Lanka's historic six-wicket victory on the redeveloped and picturesque playing fields of Kandy's Trinity College was overshadowed by the sickening collision between Australian captain Steve Waugh and fast bowler Jason Gillespie after they ran into each other attempting an outfield catch. Forced to bat two short in their second innings, the Australians lost in three days, Ricky Ponting's 96 and 51 representing almost half of Australia's runs for the match.

Thrust into leading the Australian team in the most unfortunate circumstances, with Waugh and Gillespie both being airlifted by military helicopter to Colombo, Warne was superb, claiming his 15th five-wicket Test haul. Significantly it was his first in 20 months.

From a freewheeling 3/177, Sri Lanka's lead was restricted to just 46, Warne taking 2/4 in five balls before lunch and 3/25 from 6.5 overs afterwards.

The wicket of provocative former Sri Lankan captain Arjuna Ranatunga right on lunch was greeted with all of Warne's old enthusiasm. Ranatunga lofted the second ball he faced high to the mid-off boundary before two balls later being brilliantly caught by Ian Healy, cutting at a faster one.

By stumps on the second day, Australia, at 6/89, had virtually forfeited the match, the top order collapsing to the off-spinning power of local hero Muttiah Muralitharan.

---

137. **Australia v Sri Lanka Board XI**, at Colombo Cricket Club Ground, 17, 18 & 19 September 1999.
SCORES
AUSTRALIA 226 (K. R. Pushpakumara 5/37) and 296 for 5 wickets dec.
(M. J. Slater 119); SRI LANKA BOARD XI 185 (L. P. C. de Silva 66;
S. A. Muller 5/64) and 90. **Australia won by 247 runs**.
S. K. WARNE (capt.)
1st inns: 9–2–43–1. Dismissed: N. R. G. Perera c C. R. Miller 1.
2nd inns: 2.3–0–3–1. Dismissed: H. P. W. Jayawardene b 40.

Amidst news of his signing with Hampshire for a season of English county cricket in 2000 (in a five-month playing, promotion and writing deal worth more than A$1 million), Warne, having just turned 30, again captained Australia in place of the injured Steve Waugh. In a match dominated by Damien Fleming and fast bowling replacement

Scott Muller, who each took seven wickets, Warne allowed himself less than a dozen overs. He took two wickets.

When the Board XI's Chamara Silva disputed a gully catch by Michael Slater and stood his ground, Warne and Slater approached him, said it was a clean catch and advised him to walk. The umpires, on discussion, gave the Sri Lankan out. Suresh Perera had earlier hit Warne for 3 sixes, two in consecutive balls.

138/73. **Australia v Sri Lanka**, Second Test Match, at Galle International Stadium, 22, 23, 24, 25 (no play) & 26 September 1999.

SCORES

SRI LANKA 296 (P. A. de Silva 64, R. P. Arnold 50) and 55 for no wicket;
AUSTRALIA 228 (M. J. Slater 96, G. S. Blewett 62; M. Muralitharan 5/71).
Drawn.

TEST

S. K. WARNE

1st inns: 25–11–29–3. Dismissed: M. S. Atapattu c I. A. Healy 29;
D. P. M. de S. Jayawardene c G. S. Blewett 46; A. Ranatunga c C. R. Miller 10.
2nd inns: 3.2–1–5–0.

Monsoonal rains washed away Australia's chance of a series-squaring victory, three of the scheduled five days being affected. Steve Waugh took his place despite four broken bones in his nose and was dismayed to see the Australians surrender a strong early position with more inept batting against the world-class Muttiah Muralitharan.

Warne was again a danger, bowling 25 overs for 3/29, all three being top-order players, including Marvan Atapattu caught behind to a big-spinning leg-break which really ripped like old times.

139/74. **Australia v Sri Lanka**, Third Test Match, at Sinhalese Sports Club Ground, Colombo, 29, 30 September, 1, 2 & 3 (no play) October 1999.

SCORES

AUSTRALIA 342 (R. T. Ponting 105 not out, G. S. Blewett 70, M. J. Slater 59);
SRI LANKA 61 for 4 wickets. *Drawn*.

TEST

S. K. WARNE

Only inns: 5–1–11–0.

More rain ruined the third and final Test at the Sinhalese Sports Club Ground, the centre for Sri Lankan cricket and the very ground where Warne's career had turned around so dramatically seven years previously. The draw gave Sri Lanka a historic 1–0 series victory.

Other than five overs, Warne's major contribution all match was to coach young Sri Lankan spinners Upul Chandana and Rangana Herath for 15 minutes on the soggy opening morning.

With eight wickets at an average of under 15, Warne had bounced back to top the Australian averages. He and player of the series Ricky Ponting had been consistently outstanding.

Geoff Marsh coached the Australian team for the final time before handing over to Allan Border for the short tour of Zimbabwe.

SUMMARY, 1999–2000 (SRI LANKA)

	Mts	Overs	Mdns	Runs	Wicks	Ave	BB	5wI	10wM
All First-Class matches	5	102.5	31	272	15	18.13	5/52	1	–
Test matches v Sri Lanka	3	56.1	20	115	8	14.37	5/52	1	–

AUSTRALIA IN ZIMBABWE

140. **Australia v Zimbabwe President's XI**, at Queen's Sports Club, Bulawayo, 9, 10 & 11 October 1999.

SCORES

AUSTRALIA 335 for 7 wickets dec. (J. L. Langer 148, M. E. Waugh 63) and 304 for 5 wickets dec. (S. R. Waugh 161, M. E. Waugh 116); ZIMBABWE PRESIDENT'S XI 219 (T. R. Gripper 59, T. R. Madondo 59; G. D. McGrath 5/36) and 176 (J. A. Rennie 50). **Australia won by 244 runs.**

S. K. WARNE

1st inns: 22–7–51–1. Dismissed: E. A. Brandes c D. W. Fleming 30.
2nd inns: 17–7–50–3. Dismissed: G. Lamb c G. S. Blewett 47;
B. D. Moore-Gordon b 5; E. A. Brandes c M. E. Waugh 6.

Having averaged 7.25 in another disastrous Test tour of Sri Lanka, Mark Waugh hit back in the opening match of the short tour of Zimbabwe, with 63 and 116. He and brother Steve added 254 for the third wicket in Australia's second innings.

One of the few Australians to have previously played a first-class match in Bulawayo, Warne continued his imposing form with four wickets for the match, including 3/50 in an unchanged 17-over spell in the second innings. He claimed wickets in his 6th, 7th and 12th overs.

141/75. **Australia v Zimbabwe**, Inaugural Test Match, at Harare Sports Ground, 14, 15, 16 & 17 October 1999.

SCORES

ZIMBABWE 194 (N. C. Johnson 75) and 232 (M. W. Goodwin 91, T. R. Gripper 60); AUSTRALIA 422 (S. R. Waugh 151 not out, M. E. Waugh 90, D. W. Fleming 65) and 5 for no wicket. **Australia won by ten wickets**.

S. K. WARNE

1st inns: 23–2–69–3. Dismissed: T. R. Gripper lbw 4; H. H. Streak c M. E. Waugh 3; G. J. Whittall c I. A. Healy 27.

2nd inns: 30.1–11–68–3. Dismissed: M. W. Goodwin c S. R. Waugh 91; G. J. Whittall c M. E. Waugh 2; H. H. Streak lbw 0.

TEST

Victory in the inaugural one-off Test against Test minnows Zimbabwe in Harare was the first in a record run for the Australians which was to extend through their tour of New Zealand six months later.

The Waugh twins were again dominant, as were Damien Fleming who reached his highest Test score and Glenn McGrath who took six wickets.

Warne also claimed six wickets for the game, his biggest Test haul since January 1998. Included was Zimbabwe debutant Trevor Gripper lbw to the flipper, having batted 48 minutes for 4. Later in the innings in his 23rd over, Warne conceded 15 runs including 10 in two balls to top scorer Neil Johnson.

In the second innings, he bowled 30.1 overs in three spells, 13, 5 and 12.1, dismissing top scorer Murray Goodwin for 91. He seemed unaffected by the Zimbabwe strategy of including four left-handers in their top six and bowled more googlies than at any other time in his career. In their second innings, Zimbabwe tumbled from 2/200 to 232 all out in just 25 overs.

After the game, in-fighting within the Zimbabwe team bubbled into the public arena, Goodwin criticising his captain Alistair Campbell for batting first on a lively pitch. Campbell said the last thing Zimbabwe needed to do was bat fourth late in the match on a wearing wicket against Shane Warne.

'We backed ourselves to play out the seamers, but we didn't know it would move around as much as it did. It was tremendous fast bowling, especially by Glenn McGrath,' he said.

SUMMARY, 1999–2000 (Zimbabwe)

	Mts	Overs	Mdns	Runs	Wicks	Ave	BB	5wI	10wM
All First-Class matches	2	92.1	27	238	10	23.80	3/50	–	–
Test match v Zimbabwe	1	53.1	13	137	6	22.83	3/68	–	–

In Australia

142/76. **Australia v Pakistan**, First Test Match, at Brisbane Cricket Ground, 5, 6, 7, 8 & 9 November 1999.

Scores

Pakistan 367 (Yousuf Youhana 95, Inzamam-ul-Haq 88, Saeed Anwar 61, Moin Khan 61) and 281 (Saeed Anwar 119, Yousuf Youhana 75; D. W. Fleming 5/59); Australia 575 (M. J. Slater 169, M. E. Waugh 100, G. S. Blewett 89, S. K. Warne 86, A. C. Gilchrist 81) and 74 for no wicket.

Australia won by ten wickets.

S. K. Warne

1st inns: 28.1–11–73–1. Dismissed: Saeed Anwar c M. E. Waugh 61.
2nd inns: 25–8–80–2. Dismissed: Abdur Razzaq c R. T. Ponting 2; Azhar Mahmood st A. C. Gilchrist 0.

TEST

For only the second time in his Test career, Warne went into a Test without wicketkeeping ally Ian Healy. The Queensland veteran's request for a farewell Test in front of his home-town crowd had been rejected. His replacement, Adam Gilchrist, may have lacked Healy's flair standing up to the stumps but was at least well practised against Warne, having played more than 75 one-day internationals.

Having been beaten in each of their three lead-up games, Pakistan were far more competitive in the first of the three Tests, especially early when they outplayed the Australians for all but the final hour on day one.

Warne's only first-innings wicket was the dangerous Saeed Anwar, for 61. He bowled virtually unchanged between lunch and tea and could have had a second wicket, but for Mark Waugh grassing a chance at slip when the impressive Yousuf Youhana had made just 23.

The Australians built a 208-run lead on the first innings, thanks to a debut 81 from Gilchrist and a belligerent Test-best 86 from Warne. He hit 9 fours and 4 sixes, all from the bowling of fellow leg-spinner Mushtaq Ahmed. One of Mushtaq's overs cost 19. Having bowled Pakistan out a second time for 281, Australia completed a ten-wicket victory.

Warne dismissed all-rounders Abdur Razzaq with a rank full toss and Azhar Mahmood with one which drifted and spun, creating an easy stumping chance for Gilchrist. Warne had bowled flat and fast at Mahmood and to the very first one given more air, Mahmood tried to attack and was beaten by the curve and spin to be left stranded.

With Taylor's retirement, Warne stood as a full-time first slipsman for the first time in a Test in Australia. The game was John Buchanan's first as Australia's new national coach.

143/77. **Australia v Pakistan**, Second Test Match, at Bellerive Oval, Hobart, 18, 19, 20, 21 & 22 November 1999.

SCORES

PAKISTAN 222 (Mohammad Wasim 91) and 392 (Inzamam-ul-Haq 118, Ijaz Ahmed 82, Saeed Anwar 78; S. K. Warne 5/110); AUSTRALIA 246 (M. J. Slater 97, J. L. Langer 59; Saqlain Mushtaq 6/46) and 369 for 6 wickets (A. C. Gilchrist 149 not out, J. L. Langer 127). *Australia won by four wickets*.

TEST

S. K. WARNE

1st inns: 16–5–45–3. Dismissed: Azhar Mahmood b 27; Wasim Akram c A. C. Gilchrist 29; Saqlain Mushtaq lbw 3.

2nd inns: 45.4–11–110–5. Dismissed: Saeed Anwar b 78; Saqlain Mushtaq lbw 8; Inzamam-ul-Haq c M. E. Waugh 118; Azhar Mahmood lbw 28; Wasim Akram c G. S. Blewett 31.

After the first of just two one-day appearances for the entire season for Victoria, Warne had a major role in one of the most memorable Australian wins of the decade at picturesque Bellerive Oval, Australia's most southern Test stronghold.

Set 369 runs to win, a tough ask on even one of the plumbest batting wickets in the country, the Australians won by four wickets, thanks to left-handers Justin Langer and Adam Gilchrist who both made centuries.

Taking eight wickets for the game, Warne recovered from an early onslaught by Muhammad Wasim when his first four overs cost 26 to finish with 3/45 from 16 overs.

In the second innings, he took 5/110 and at one stage bowled 37 consecutive overs into the breeze.

His mid-match marathon yielded three wickets, including top-scorer Inzamam-ul-Haq (118), miraculously caught at slip by the gifted Mark Waugh. Going for a full-blooded cut shot, Inzamam top-edged the ball high and wide of Waugh's right. He flung out his hand and the ball stuck. It was easily the feature catch of the season.

Saeed Anwar, bowled out of the rough, was also an important wicket as he was threatening to take the game away from Australia. Shaping a cut shot at Warne, who'd just changed to around the wicket, he lost his leg stump.

144/78. Australia v Pakistan, Third Test Match, at WACA Ground, Perth, 26, 27 & 28 November 1999.

SCORES

PAKISTAN 155 and 276 (Ijaz Ahmed 115, Wasim Akram 52); AUSTRALIA 451 (R. T. Ponting 197, J. L. Langer 144; Mohammad Akram 5/138).

Australia won by an innings & 20 runs.

S. K. WARNE

1st inns: 2–0–6–0.

2nd inns: 13–1–56–1. Dismissed: Azhar Mahmood b 17.

TEST

Demoralised by their defeat in Hobart, Pakistan crumbled in only three days at the WACA Ground in Perth, pace trio Glenn McGrath,

Damien Fleming and the recalled Michael Kasprowicz taking 19 of the 20 wickets to fall.

Warne was required to bowl only two overs in the first innings and 13 in the second.

He dismissed Azhar Mahmood for the fourth time in six innings.

It was only the third time Australia had made a clean sweep of a three-Test series, following their success against Pakistan in 1972–73 and Sri Lanka in 1995–96.

With 12 wickets, Warne had increased his Test tally to 343, just 12 short of Dennis Lillee's Australian record of 355.

145/79. **Australia v India**, First Test Match, at Adelaide Oval, 10, 11, 12, 13 & 14 December 1999.

SCORES

AUSTRALIA 441 (S. R. Waugh 150, R. T. Ponting 125, S. K. Warne 86) and 239 for 8 wickets dec. (G. S. Blewett 88); INDIA 285 (S. R. Tendulkar 61, S. C. Ganguly 60) and 110 (D. W. Fleming 5/30). *Australia won by 285 runs*.

TEST

S. K. WARNE

1st inns: 42–12–92–4. Dismissed: R. Dravid c J. L. Langer 35, S. R. Tendulkar c J. L. Langer 61; S. C. Ganguly st A. C. Gilchrist 60; M. S. K. Prasad b 14.
2nd inns: 10–6–21–2. Dismissed: S. Ramesh lbw 28; R. Dravid c A. C. Gilchrist 6.

Having been catapulted into more controversy between Tests, this time with new Australian team-mate Scott Muller, after it was alleged, incorrectly, that Warne had made disparaging on-field remarks about Muller's ability, Warne's re-matches with Sachin Tendulkar and the Indians were keenly anticipated.

Warne's 11 wickets in five previous Tests against the Indians had cost almost 70 apiece. He'd been pummelled by Tendulkar in India and despite his re-emergence in the Tests against Pakistan, some still believed he was fortunate to be playing ahead of MacGill, one of the stars of the 1998–99 Ashes summer.

Lifting for the occasion at the prettiest of all Australian Test venues, adjacent to the magnificent St Peter's Cathedral, Warne bowled his finest spell of the calendar year, having repeated his big-hitting from Brisbane with another 86, an innings full of his inside-out lifts over cover point and big shots to the midwicket fence.

Having lost rookie openers Devang Gandhi and Sandagoppan Ramesh in the opening overs, the Indians were building a substantial reply when Warne ran through the middle order, dismissing India's big three, Rahul Dravid, Tendulkar and Saurav Ganguly, all when well set.

Tendulkar's dismissal, caught at bad-pad, was debatable, but a charging Ganguly was stranded by a googly, delivered wider and from around the wicket – a brilliant piece of strategy.

When wicketkeeper Mannava Prasad was bowled around his legs by an extraordinary back-break, Warne was so excited he pumped his arm three times like the immortal Elvis Presley at his pulsating best. It was a genuine show of emotion from Australia's king of spin. The ball spun back more than 30 centimetres, a reminder that Warne still had some fire in his arsenal. 'It was a ripper,' said Warne afterwards. 'I was very happy with that one.'

SPIN DOCTOR BACK IN BUSINESS proclaimed the *Australian*. WARNIE BACK TO BAFFLING BEST said the *Herald Sun*.

Warne bowled 22 overs in a row and 42 for the innings to take 4/92. So well was he bowling that he was even given the second new ball, in combination with Glenn McGrath. 'His bowling was the best since his shoulder surgery,' said McGrath. 'He really gave the ball a rip.'

In the second innings, his accuracy and reputation resulted in two of the Indian top order, Ramesh and Dravid, treating his leg-breaks with the utmost suspicion. Both were dismissed without playing a shot, Ramesh falling lbw to a straight one and Dravid caught at the wicket after an overspinning leg-break flicked his glove. Six of Warne's 10 overs were maidens. He took 2/21.

But at least some of his pleasure was diluted near the end of Pakistan's innings when he dropped Anil Kumble, first ball at slip, with

Damien Fleming on a hat-trick. The straightforward catch flew at easy pace, at eye level just to his right. Warne was inconsolable afterwards. 'He's taken some great catches for me this summer,' said Fleming. 'He's allowed to drop one every now and again.'

146/80. **Australia v India**, Second Test Match, at Melbourne Cricket Ground, 26, 27, 28, 29 & 30 December 1999.

SCORES

AUSTRALIA 405 (M. J. Slater 91, A. C. Gilchrist 78, R. T. Ponting 67) and 208 for 5 wickets dec. (A. C. Gilchrist 55, M. E. Waugh 51 not out); INDIA 238 (S. R. Tendulkar 116; B. Lee 5/47) and 195 (S. R. Tendulkar 52). *Australia won by 180 runs*.

S. K. WARNE

1st inns: 24–5–77–1. Dismissed: H. H. Kanitkar lbw 11.
2nd inns: 26–7–63–1. Dismissed: S. R. Tendulkar lbw 52.

TEST

Having hosted a Christmas Eve party for the team, family and friends including Merv Hughes, Rex Hunt and Sam Newman, who provided some team motivation, Warne's focus switched back to the business of taking the six wickets he needed to equal Dennis Lillee's 355. Most expected Warne to reach the record in Melbourne, a venue where he'd taken 32 wickets in six previous MCG Tests.

However, Brett Lee, an athletic fast bowler from Wollongong, south of Sydney, momentarily wrested the spotlight from Warne. By taking seven wickets on debut, Lee bowled almost as fast as Pakistan's Shoaib Akhtar, who earlier in the summer, in Hobart, had delivered a bean-ball at Justin Langer at 154.3 km/h.

India again crumbled, despite a masterly first-innings century from Sachin Tendulkar.

Warne claimed only two wickets for the game, left-hander Hrishikesh Kanitkar becoming his 350th victim in the first innings and Tendulkar his 351st in the second. Both were out padding up.

Tendulkar's dismissal, lbw, was as much to do with the Indian captain's concern at continuing poor team performances, as Warne cornering his prey. Having seen opener Sandagoppan Ramesh retire hurt during the opening over and No. 3 Rahul Dravid fall victim to Lee's express pace, Tendulkar concentrated on trying to force a draw and save the series, rather than playing his natural, aggressive game.

He lasted more than two-and-a half hours for 52 after earlier padding up to Warne and being fortunate to be given not out. So defensive did he become that Warne enjoyed the rare luxury of employing three close-in fieldsmen against the Little Master: a slip, silly point and short leg.

Warne wasn't as outwardly aggressive against Tendulkar as he was against the other Indian top-order specialists, especially Saurav Ganguly, whom the Australians were always looking to intimidate, believing his focus and concentration could become affected. When Ganguly was out right on lunch, to part-timer Greg Blewett and Tendulkar lbw, having misjudged Warne's drift soon afterwards, India caved in. The Australians comfortably clinched a sixth consecutive Test victory with a day to spare.

147/81. **Australia v India**, Third Test Match, at Sydney Cricket Ground, 2, 3 & 4 January 2000.

SCORES

INDIA 150 (G. D. McGrath 5/48) and 261 (V. V. S. Laxman 167; G. D. McGrath 5/55); AUSTRALIA 552 for 5 wickets dec. (J. L. Langer 223, R. T. Ponting 141 not out, S. R. Waugh 57). **Australia won by an innings & 141 runs**.

TEST

S. K. WARNE
1st inns: 12–4–22–0.
2nd inns: 13–1–60–0.

Most of Warne's family were in Sydney for what loomed as the record-breaking Test. With four to tie Dennis Lillee and five to pass him, bookmakers were punting on the day and time that the famous record would change hands.

But again Warne was overshadowed by Glenn McGrath and Brett

Lee, who took 16 wickets as India lost by an innings despite an astonishing late-match counter-attack by opener V. V. S. Laxman.

The Indians lasted less than 70 overs in the first innings and just 58 in the second, Warne's share 25 overs, 12 in the first innings and 13 in the second. Other than a confident lbw shout against Laxman, Warne rarely troubled the Indians. Later he conceded he may have been trying too hard, instead of working on his line and gradually introducing his variations, rather than chasing wickets and looking to bowl six different deliveries per over, as if he were back at the Keysborough playing fields representing Mentone Grammar.

No one had expected him to go wicketless, especially as Sydney was one of his all-time favourite and most successful venues.

With 127 overs in the three Tests, Warne had bowled more overs than anyone else. However, his return of eight wickets at 41.88 was below his normal standard. In Melbourne and Sydney, Steve Waugh had preferred to use the fast bowlers to clean up the tail, when once it was Warne's exclusive province.

Of consolation was his inclusion in Australia's Team of the Century and his award on Allan Border Medal night as Australia's One-Day Cricketer of the Year. For the Test summer he took 20 wickets, behind Glenn McGrath, 32 and Damien Fleming, 30.

SUMMARY, 1999–2000 (AUSTRALIA)

	Mts	Overs	Mdns	Runs	Wicks	Ave	BB	5wI	10wM
All First-Class matches	6	256.5	71	705	20	35.25	5/110	1	–
Test matches v Pakistan	3	129.5	36	370	12	30.83	5/110	1	–
Test matches v India	3	127	35	335	8	41.87	4/92	–	–

AUSTRALIA IN NEW ZEALAND

148. **Australia v Northern Districts**, at Westpac Trust Park (formerly Seddon Park), Hamilton, 5, 6, 7 & 8 March 2000.

SCORES

AUSTRALIA 383 for 4 wickets dec. (J. L. Langer 155, D. R. Martyn 109, M. L. Hayden 67 not out) and 198 for 5 (G. S. Blewett 83 not out);

NORTHERN DISTRICTS 300 (J. A. H. Marshall 64) and 280
(G. E. Bradburn 63, H. J. H. Marshall 50). *Australia won by five wickets*.
S. K. WARNE (capt.)
1st inns:14–2–53–2. Dismissed: J. A. H. Marshall c D. W. Fleming 64;
M. D. Bailey c G. D. McGrath 32.
2nd inns: 15–3–52–0.

With Steve Waugh resting a minor ankle problem after Australia's 4–1 victory in the ODIs, Warne led Australia for the fourth time and maintained his unbeaten run as stand-in captain.

In his first, light-hearted spell, he conceded almost five runs an over. One delivery went for five wides. However, he did dismiss Northern Districts' opener and top scorer James Marshall and No. 3 batsman Mark Bailey.

When Australia batted a second time, needing less than 200 to win, Warne virtually reversed the order, coming in at No. 4 himself and promoting Brett Lee to 5, Colin Miller 6 and Glenn McGrath 7. It was Australia's only first-class fixture leading into the National Bank three-Test series.

149/82. **Australia v New Zealand**. First Test Match, at Eden Park, Auckland, 11, 12, 13, 14 (no play) & 15 March 2000.
SCORES
AUSTRALIA 214 (M. E. Waugh 72 not out, D. L. Vettori 5/62) and 229 (A. C. Gilchrist 59, D. L. Vettori 7/87); NEW ZEALAND 163 (G. D. McGrath 4/33) and 218 (C. D. McMillan 78, C. R. Miller 5/55).
Australia won by 62 runs.
S. K. WARNE
1st inns: 22–4–68–3. Dismissed: M. S. Sinclair lbw 8; N. J. Astle, c M. E. Waugh 31; C. D. McMillan lbw 6.
2nd inns: 20.3–4–80–2: Dismissed: N. J. Astle b 35; P. J. Wiseman, c A. C. Gilchrist 9.

TEST

With wife Simone and family, parents Keith and Brigitte and brother Jason having flown in to lend support for his continuing record-breaking bid, it took Warne until the very last play of the tensest of

Test matches to surpass Dennis Lillee as Australia's most successful bowler.

On a spin-conducive Eden Park wicket on which Daniel Vettori gathered 12 wickets and 36-year-old Colin Miller seven, Warne was nervous and erratic, bowling more short deliveries in one Test than he did for the entire 1993 NZ tour.

He took three first-innings wickets, including Nathan Astle for the first of five times for the summer and the Australian-born Kiwi No. 3 Mathew Sinclair, who was lbw on the first night, one of 14 wickets to fall on the spectacular opening day.

Warne sent down 22 overs unchanged from just before stumps on the opening day to after lunch on the second and while he bowled some superb deliveries, it again took him time to settle. In his first over on day two, NZ captain Stephen Fleming stroked him for 2 fours in four balls from over-pitched deliveries.

In the second innings, the conditions were cold and chilly and initially difficult for the spinners to grip the ball with confidence. Warne had taken some heavy punishment from Craig McMillan and old adversary Chris Cairns on the final days – his first 13 overs in the second innings cost 51 runs, including 31 from his first five.

Warne was upstaged by Miller and Glenn McGrath before bowling Astle around his legs with a leg-spinner, to equal Lillee. And when it seemed he'd have to wait until a further Test in Wellington, he claimed the final Black Cap wicket – No. 10 batsman Paul Wiseman caught at the wicket by Gilchrist attempting a sweep, giving Warne the record and Australia another emphatic win.

Warne raised his left arm in triumph and was engulfed by team-mates. After weeks of playing under increasing pressure and expectation, he was delighted and relieved to finally achieve the milestone. Wiseman threw his head back in the air in exasperation, initially thinking the ball had ballooned from his forearm, rather than his glove.

Steve Waugh's game-plan had seen him mix his bowlers, according to who was in. For left-handers such as Fleming he favoured Miller's off-spin breaking towards the slips. For the right-handers such as Astle and Craig McMillan, Warne's leg-breaks were invariably employed. Sometimes bowling strategies revolved around who happened to be on strike at the start of a new over.

When Warne was withdrawn and Miller immediate dismissed left-handed No. 9 Vettori, it seemed Warne would be denied further opportunity. However, when Miller couldn't deliver the killer blow against right-handers Wiseman or last man Simon Doull, Waugh recalled Warne. After conceding a boundary to the midwicket fence early in the over, he finally struck with a leg-break, Wiseman being beaten by the spin and the bounce and gloving the ball straight into the air. Umpire Srinivas Venkataraghavan was in no doubt and immediately raised his finger.

'I probably tried too hard through the whole Test match,' Warne told pressmen later. 'In these sorts of games your own expectations are up, too.'

Lillee sent a message of congratulation from Perth: 'I was very honoured to have achieved the record in my time but I'm just as pleased that a bowler and a bloke as great as Shane Warne has overtaken my record. It makes me smile that I took the record from one of the greatest leg-spinners in Richie Benaud and now possibly the greatest leg-spinner has repeated the dose on me.'

The Australian team formed a guard of honour for Warne leading into the dressing rooms. Gilchrist presented him with the ball.

'Shane has been great for cricket in Australia. He has turned the game around. People have come back to the cricket, particularly the young kids. You're born with that talent and you've got to harness it and then have the cricket brain to go with it. He's got the whole package which very few players have.' Australian captain STEVE WAUGH

150/83. **Australia v New Zealand**. Second Test Match, at Basin Reserve, Wellington, 24, 25, 26 & 27 March 2000.

SCORES

NEW ZEALAND 298 (N. J. Astle 61, C. L. Cairns 109, S. K. Warne 4/68) and 294 (S. P. Fleming 60, C. L. Cairns 69); AUSTRALIA 419 (M. J. Slater 143, S. R. Waugh 151 not out, D. R. Martyn 78) and 177 for 4 (J. L. Langer 57).

Australia won by six wickets.

S. K. WARNE

1st inns: 14.5–1–68–4. Dismissed: S. P. Fleming c C. R. Miller 16; N. J. Astle c M. E. Waugh 61; D. L. Vettori c J. L. Langer 27; S. B. Doull c M. J. Slater 12.

2nd inns: 27–7–92–3. Dismissed: N. J. Astle b 14; C. D. McMillan, c M. E. Waugh 0; S. B. Doull, c S. R. Waugh 40.

TEST

Amidst talk that his powers were waning and no longer was he the force he once was, Warne gathered seven wickets for the game as Australia won its ninth Test in succession, breaking the 79-year-old mark of eight wins in a row by Warwick Armstrong's famous 1920–21 teams.

While Warne claimed a wicket with his fifth ball of the game and first to captain Stephen Fleming, he was also punished severely by Chris Cairns, who hit 2 sixes in three balls including a monster wind-assisted straight drive 30–40 metres back into the R. A. Vance Grandstand. Soon afterwards, when brought back with the wind, Warne conceded 14 from an over, again to the belligerent Cairns who crashed 7 fours and 2 sixes in his first 50 on his way to 109 from just 123 balls. Warne was again withdrawn before two tail-end wickets improved his figures.

It was noticeable that Waugh kept Warne away from Cairns as much as possible for the remainder of the series. In the second innings, Cairns careered to 61 not out at stumps on day three, hitting 5 sixes in the space of 17 balls from Warne, Greg Blewett and Brett Lee. Warne had earlier skittled Nathan Astle with a magnificent flipper, his best of the tour, before dismissing Craig McMillan first ball.

Along with Cairns' Botham-like smiting, an early highlight was Colin Miller's opening over of the game in which he bowled five off-breaks from his short run to left-hander Fleming before reverting to his longer run when the strike turned over. With his very first ball to the right-handed Mathew Sinclair, he trapped him lbw with a medium-paced delivery which held its line. Even the great and versatile Gary Sobers would have especially enjoyed that.

Used as a nightwatchman on the first night after NZ had been dismissed for 298, Warne fell lbw to Daniel Vettori's arm ball during the final over.

151/84. **Australia v New Zealand**. Third Test Match, at Westpac Trust Park, Hamilton, 31 March, 1, 2 & 3 April 2000.

SCORES

NEW ZEALAND 232 (C. D. McMillan 79, G. D. McGrath 4/58) and 229 (C. L. Cairns 71); AUSTRALIA 252 (A. C. Gilchrist 75, D. R. Martyn 89 not out) and 212 for 4 (J. L. Langer 122 not out). *Australia won by six wickets*.

S. K. WARNE

1st inns: 20–5–45–1. Dismissed: P. J. Wiseman b 1.

2nd inns: 25–11–61–2. Dismissed: N. J. Astle c A. C. Gilchrist 26; C. D. McMillan, c M. E. Waugh 30.

TEST

Australia's third four-day Test in a row ended early thanks to Justin Langer's continuing brilliance. He made his fourth century of the extended international season, including his first 50 from a record 42 balls and 100 from 103.

While Warne took only three wickets for the game and looked less menacing than in his prime, he still finished with 15 wickets for the three Tests, second only to the Wollongong Express Brett Lee with 18.

Batsmen may have been beneficiaries to more half-trackers and wide ones, but he was still taking wickets at a reasonably rapid rate of 80 balls per dismissal, the majority in the top six. His length and line occasionally erred, his flipper was no longer the most destructive ball on the international stage and the vicious side-spin of '93 was but a memory, but so high a standard had he set, there was bound to be criticism at any fall-off.

Used sparingly in NZ's first innings, Warne had initial six-over spells before being withdrawn for a two-hour period when player of the season Chris Cairns was at his most threatening. His only wicket was Paul Wiseman, again sweeping.

In the second innings, Warne helped turn the game with the dismissal of an in-form Craig McMillan, who was given out caught at slip from the last delivery before lunch on the third day. Coming around the wicket for the final delivery, Warne pitched a leg-break just outside McMillan's leg stump. It spun across the face of his bat and caught him on the back pad before being taken by Mark Waugh, who threw the ball into the air speculatively rather than with his normal conviction. The appeal was confident, even 'furious' according to the *Sydney Morning Herald*'s man-on-the-spot Phil Wilkins, and umpire Steve Dunne gave McMillan out. The Kiwi expressed his anger by lingering at the wicket and watching a replay on the big screen while the Australians were marching off.

There were at least nine contentious decisions in the game, but none more important to the fortunes than this one. Having batted an hour-and-a half to score 30, McMillan was looking to be a major danger in pushing NZ's score towards 300, which would have added degrees of difficulty to Australia's fourth-innings chase.

Waugh was proud his team had been able to recover from 5/29 on the second morning to win on the fourth by six wickets. Ominously, he warned that the best was yet to come.

SUMMARY, 1999–2000 (NEW ZEALAND)

	Mts	Overs	Mdns	Runs	Wicks	Ave	BB	5wI	10wM
All First-Class matches	4	158.2	36	519	17	30.05	4/68	–	–
Test matches v NZ	3	129.2	32	414	15	27.66	4/68	–	–

'Two things made him exceptional: his control and the amount of action he gets on the ball, giving him more drift in the air than any other spinner I have played against.'

Ex-England captain MIKE ATHERTON

PART TWO

ONE-DAY CRICKET

1991–92

Australia B in Zimbabwe

1. Australia B v Zimbabwe, at Harare Sports Club, 8 September 1991.
Scores
Australia B 173 (49.1 overs) (A. J. Traicos 4/20); Zimbabwe 176 for 4 wickets
(44.3 overs) (K. J. Arnott 85). *Zimbabwe won by six wickets.*
S. K. Warne
10–2–33–0.

On his Australian representative debut, Warne was hit for 5 fours by
top scorer, 30-year-old Zimbabwe opener Kevin Arnott.

2. Australia B v Zimbabwe, at Bulawayo Athletic Club,
15 September 1991.
Scores
Australia B 244 for 7 wickets (50 overs) (S. R. Waugh 116 not out,
S. G. Law 53; M. P. Jarvis 4/46); Zimbabwe 209 (48.4 overs) (K. J. Arnott 61;
R. J. Tucker 4/41). *Australia B won by 35 runs.*
S. K. Warne
10–1–37–1. Dismissed: K. J. Arnott c T. J. Nielsen 61.

3. **Australia B v Zimbabwe**, at Harare Sports Club, 22 September 1991.

SCORES

AUSTRALIA B 248 for 8 wickets (50 overs) (S. R. Waugh 116, M. G. Bevan 55); ZIMBABWE 240 (49.5 overs) (A. J. Pycroft 104; R. J. Tucker 4/41). *Australia B won by eight runs*.

S. K. WARNE

6–0–32–1. Dismissed: D. L. Houghton b 24.

Leg-spinners Warne and Peter McIntyre conceded 82 runs from just 15 overs.

SUMMARY, 1991–92 (ZIMBABWE)

	Mts	Overs	Mdns	Runs	Wicks	Ave	BB	4w	RpO
All limited-overs matches	3	26	3	102	2	51.00	1/32	–	3.92

IN AUSTRALIA

4. **Prime Minister's XI v India**, at Manuka Oval, Canberra, 17 December 1991.

SCORES

PRIME MINISTER'S XI 244 for 7 wickets (G. S. Blewett 65, M. G. Bevan 60, D. R. Martyn 50); INDIANS 169 (44 overs) (G. J. Rowell 6/27). *Prime Minister's XI won by 75 runs*.

S. K. WARNE

10–0–47–1. Dismissed: P. K. Amre c T. J. Zoehrer 0.

Warne was among four ex-Cricket Academy scholars invited to play for Prime Minister Bob Hawke's XI, the last PM's game in his eight-year reign as Australia's Prime Minister. Greg Blewett and Damien Martyn, fellow members of the '90 intake, were also selected, along with Michael Bevan from the '89 squad.

5. **Victoria v India**, at Gardens Oval, Benalla, 9 February 1992.
SCORES
VICTORIA 204 for 9 wickets (50 overs) (D. S. Lehmann 71); INDIA 171
(42.5 overs) (S. R. Tendulkar 59). *Victoria won by 33 runs*.
S. K. WARNE
10–0–37–2. Dismissed: S. R. Tendulkar st D. S. Berry 59; P. K. Amre
c & b 31.

Warne's dismissal of teenage starlet Sachin Tendulkar helped turn the match, a warm-up game for India before its '92 World Cup campaign. Earlier, the gifted right-hander had taken 17 runs from all-rounder Tony Dodemaide's sixth over.

SUMMARY, 1991–92 (AUSTRALIA)

	Mts	Overs	Mdns	Runs	Wicks	Ave	BB	4w	RpO
All limited-overs matches	2	20	0	84	3	28.00	2/37	–	4.20

1992–93

IN AUSTRALIA

6. **Victoria v Tasmania**, at Devonport Oval, 13 December 1992.
SCORES
VICTORIA 222 (49 overs) (D. S. Lehmann 76, P. C. Nobes 52;
N. C. P. Courtney 4/19); TASMANIA 164 (46.5 overs). **Victoria won
by 58 runs**.
S. K. WARNE
5.5–0–31–3. Dismissed: R. J. Tucker c D. S. Berry 10; M. G. Farrell lbw 5;
C. D. Matthews c D. W. Fleming 10.

On his Victorian domestic one-day debut, Warne had an involvement
in four of the last five dismissals, running out Shaun Young and taking three wickets himself. Earlier, he made 26, the third-top score,
batting at No. 7.

SUMMARY, 1992–93 (AUSTRALIA)

	Mts	Overs	Mdns	Runs	Wicks	Ave	BB	4w	RpO
Mercantile Mutual Cup	1	5.5	0	31	3	10.33	3/31	–	5.31

Australia in New Zealand

7. Australia v New Zealand President's XI, at Trafalgar Park, Nelson, 22 February 1993.

SCORES

AUSTRALIA 222 for 8 wickets (50 overs) (D. C. Boon 75, M. E. Waugh 56); NEW ZEALAND PRESIDENT'S XI 223 for 7 wickets (48.4 overs) (K. R. Rutherford 97, B. A. Young 57). *New Zealand President's XI won by three wickets*.

S. K. WARNE

8–2–35–0.

8/1. Australia v New Zealand (3rd One-Day International), at Basin Reserve, Wellington, 24 March 1993.

SCORES

NEW ZEALAND 214 (50 overs) (M. D. Crowe 91); AUSTRALIA 126 (37.2 overs) (M. A. Taylor 50). *New Zealand won by 98 runs*.

S. K. WARNE

10–0–40–2. Dismissed: A. H. Jones st I. A. Healy 29; J. W. Wilson c S. R. Waugh 15.

After being Australia's 12th man in the first two one-day internationals, Warne displaced Tim May and batted at No. 11 in his maiden ODI, being last man out, bowled by Otago all-rounder Jeff Wilson.

Earlier, introduced in the 18th over, Warne's first over in ODI cricket, was just five balls. It was his only match in the five-game Bank of New Zealand trophy series, won by Australia 3–2.

SUMMARY, 1992–93 (NEW ZEALAND)

	Mts	Overs	Mdns	Runs	Wicks	Ave	BB	4w	RpO
All limited-overs matches	2	18	2	75	2	37.50	2/40	–	4.16
One-Day International	1	10	0	40	2	20.00	2/40	–	4.00

1993–94

In Australia

9. Victoria v Queensland, at Melbourne Cricket Ground, 17 October 1993.

Scores

Victoria 224 for 4 wickets (50 overs) (D. J. Ramshaw 82, D. M. Jones 68);
Queensland 225 for 3 wickets (46.3 overs) (S. G. Law 107 not out,
D. M. Wellham 70). *Queensland won by seven wickets*.

S. K. Warne

10–0–60–0.

In making 107 from 105 balls, Stuart Law was particularly aggressive
in Warne's early overs, Warne going for a run a ball. A high full toss
to Dirk Wellham saw the Queenslander stumped by Darren Berry
only for umpire Bill Sheahan, at square leg, to call no-ball.

10. Victoria v South Australia, at Adelaide Oval, 31 October 1993.

Scores

South Australia 226 for 4 wickets (50 overs) (J. D. Siddons 90 not out);
Victoria 227 for 3 wickets (46.4 overs) (D. M. Jones 95 not out).
Victoria won by seven wickets.

S. K. WARNE
10–1–24–0.

11/2. **Australia v South Africa** (WSC 1st match), at Melbourne Cricket
Ground, 9 December 1993 (day/night).
SCORES
AUSTRALIA 189 (45.5 overs) (M. J. Slater 73); SOUTH AFRICA 190 for 3 wickets
(48.4 overs) (W. J. Cronje 91 not out, K. C. Wessels 70). *South Africa
won by seven wickets.*
S. K. WARNE
10–0–43–1. Dismissed: D. J. Cullinan b 0.

Brought on fourth change from the 25th over to a generous Melbourne
reception, Warne, making his Australian ODI debut, bowled Daryll
Cullinan for a fourth-ball duck, beginning a rare mastery over the
Proteas' renowned top-order batsman. Another debutant, Michael
Slater, raced to 50 from 46 balls, including a huge six over extra cover
from Hansie Cronje's third delivery of the innings.

12/3. **Australia v New Zealand** (WSC 3rd match), at Adelaide Oval,
12 December 1993.
SCORES
NEW ZEALAND 135 (48.2 overs) (S. K. Warne 4/25, G. D. McGrath 4/32);
AUSTRALIA 136 for 2 wickets (38.5 overs) (D. C. Boon 51 not out,
M. L. Hayden 50 not out). *Australia won by eight wickets.*
S. K. WARNE
10–1–25–4. Dismissed: M. J. Greatbatch lbw 28; C. L. Cairns c A. R. Border
31; C. Z. Harris c & b 4; G. R. Larsen c P. R. Reiffel 8. Man of the match.

Warne was again used sixth and from the 30th over. Mark Greatbatch
succumbed to a flipper.

13/4. **Australia v South Africa** (WSC 4th match), at Sydney Cricket
Ground, 14 December 1993 (day/night).
SCORES
AUSTRALIA 172 for 9 wickets (50 overs) (C. R. Matthews 3/23,
P. S. de Villiers 3/37); SOUTH AFRICA 69 (28 overs) (P. R. Reiffel 4/13).
Australia won by 103 runs.

S. K. WARNE
Did not bowl.

Not wanting to overly expose Warne to the South Africans leading into the soon-to-start Test series, Allan Border was keen to re-include a fit-again Tim May, but was overruled. On a grassy, two-paced wicket, South Africa slumped to its lowest ODI score, Warne not being required to bowl.

14/5. Australia v New Zealand (WSC 5th match), at Melbourne Cricket Ground, 16 December 1993 (day/night).
SCORES
AUSTRALIA 202 for 5 wickets (50 overs) (M. A. Taylor 81, M. E. Waugh 53); NEW ZEALAND 199 for 9 wickets (50 overs) (S. K. Warne 4/19). **Australia won by three runs.**
S. K. WARNE
10–1–19–4. Dismissed: R. T. Latham st I. A. Healy 39; M. J. Greatbatch lbw 41; C. L. Cairns c I. A. Healy 5; T. E. Blain c A. R. Border 1.
Man of the match.

Helping to swing the game, Warne cemented his ODI place once and for all, three of his four wickets being in the NZ top order. Again he was held back until the halfway mark of the innings. The turning point in the run-chase came when Mark Greatbatch was controversially given out lbw, when well set. The Kiwis charged after needing 46 runs from five overs. With one ball to go they needed six to win, but could score only two.

15/6. Australia v New Zealand (WSC 9th match), at Sydney Cricket Ground, 11 January 1994 (day/night).
SCORES
NEW ZEALAND 198 for 9 wickets (50 overs) (K. R. Rutherford 65, M. J. Greatbatch 50); AUSTRALIA 185 (48.3 overs) (D. C. Boon 67; C. Pringle 4/40). **New Zealand won by 13 runs.**
S. K. WARNE
10–1–27–2. Dismissed: M. J. Greatbatch lbw 50; S. A. Thomson st I. A. Healy 1.

Mark Greatbatch was out lbw Warne for the third time in consecutive matches.

16/7. **Australia v South Africa** (WSC 11th match), at WACA Ground, Perth, 16 January 1994.
SCORES
SOUTH AFRICA 208 for 7 wickets (50 overs) (G. Kirsten 55); AUSTRALIA 126 (41 overs). *South Africa won by 82 runs.*
S. K. WARNE
10–0–36–2. Dismissed: D. J. Callaghan lbw 26; C. R. Matthews st T. J. Zoehrer 0.

The South Africans maintained their hopes of qualifying for the finals with a runaway victory. Opening batsman Peter Kirsten was, however, a casualty when he suffered a depressed fracture of the cheekbone when struck on the helmet and grille by first-season paceman Glenn McGrath. The Australians were led by Mark Taylor, Allan Border being rested and acting as 12th man. Warne flippered Dave Callaghan while Craig Matthews was so far down the wicket when he was stumped that umpire Terry Prue wasn't even required to give a decision.

17/8. **Australia v New Zealand** (WSC 12th match), at Melbourne Cricket Ground, 19 January 1994 (day/night).
SCORES
AUSTRALIA 217 for 3 wickets (50 overs) (D. M. Jones 82, D. C. Boon 65); NEW ZEALAND 166 (47.5 overs). *Australia won by 51 runs.*
S. K. WARNE
10–1–28–3. Dismissed: B. A. Young b 43; M. J. Greatbatch c P. R. Reiffel 13; T. E. Blain c M. L. Hayden 4.

After Warne had taken 3/28 in another polished performance, captain Allan Border said: 'Superstar Hollywood, he's just unbelievable. He's bowling so well.' At one stage, Warne had 2/9 from his first five overs. He was named player of the preliminary series, receiving a gold-handled crystal champagne bucket on a plinth.

18/9. Australia v South Africa (WSC 1st Final), at Melbourne Cricket
Ground, 21 January 1994 (day/night).
SCORES
SOUTH AFRICA 230 for 5 wickets (50 overs) (G. Kirsten 112 not out);
AUSTRALIA 202 (48.5 overs) (R. P. Snell 5/40). *South Africa won
by 28 runs.*
S. K. WARNE
10–1–45–1. Dismissed: W. J. Cronje c D. M. Jones 40.

Almost 70 000 attended, the biggest crowd of the summer and the
biggest Warne had ever played in front of. He started with a wide,
the ball pitching on off stump and being taken by Ian Healy wide of
the return crease!

19/10. Australia v South Africa (WSC 2nd Final), at Sydney Cricket
Ground, 23 January 1994 (day/night).
SCORES
AUSTRALIA 247 for 6 wickets (50 overs) (M. E. Waugh 107, D. M. Jones 79;
A. A. Donald 4/40); SOUTH AFRICA 178 (45.5 overs) (J. N. Rhodes 52).
Australia won by 69 runs.
S. K. WARNE
10–0–42–3. Dismissed: W. J. Cronje st I. A. Healy 28; D. J. Cullinan
c S. R. Waugh 3; B. M. McMillan lbw 0.

Warne took 3/4 from 15 balls in mid-innings, including Daryll Cullinan
caught on the square leg boundary in a juggling effort by Steve Waugh.

20/11. Australia v South Africa (WSC 3rd Final), at Sydney Cricket
Ground, 25 January 1994 (day/night).
SCORES
AUSTRALIA 223 for 8 wickets (50 overs) (D. C. Boon 64, M. E. Waugh 60);
SOUTH AFRICA 188 for 9 wickets (50 overs). *Australia won by 35 runs.*
S. K. WARNE
10–0–36–2. Dismissed: J. N. Rhodes c I. A. Healy 43; E. L. R. Stewart b 13.

The toss was all-important in the decider, runs on the board a clear
factor in Australia's 2–1 win. Warne was used at first change, an
indication of his advancing status within the team. Allan Border made
his farewell representative appearance in Australia.

SUMMARY, 1993–94 (AUSTRALIA)

	Mts	Overs	Mdns	Runs	Wicks	Ave	BB	4w	RpO
All limited-overs matches	12	110	6	385	22	17.50	4/19	2	3.50
One-Day Internationals	10	90	5	301	22	13.68	4/19	2	3.34
Mercantile Mutual Cup	2	20	1	84	0	–	–	–	4.20

AUSTRALIA IN SOUTH AFRICA

21. Australia v Board President's XI, at Witrand Cricket Field, Potchefstroom, 17 February 1994.

SCORES
AUSTRALIA 142 for 5 wickets (35 overs) (M. E. Waugh 55); BOARD PRESIDENT'S XI did not bat. **No result**.

S. K. WARNE
Did not bowl.

22/12. Australia v South Africa (1st One-Day International), at Wanderers Stadium, Johannesburg, 19 February 1994.

SCORES
SOUTH AFRICA 232 for 3 wickets (50 overs) (W. J. Cronje 112); AUSTRALIA 227 for 5 wickets (50 overs) (D. C. Boon 58). **South Africa won by five runs**.

S. K. WARNE
10–0–56–0.

Warne's figures were easily his most expensive at ODI level to that time. Hansie Cronje hit him for 2 sixes in three balls on his way to his maiden limited-overs ton.

23/13. Australia v South Africa (2nd One-Day International), at Centurion Park, Verwoerdburg, 20 February 1994.

SCORES
SOUTH AFRICA 265 for 5 wickets (50 overs) (W. J. Cronje 97); AUSTRALIA 209 (42.4 overs) (S. R. Waugh 86). **South Africa won by 56 runs**.

S. K. WARNE
8–1–41–1. Dismissed: J. N. Rhodes lbw 44.

All three of Hansie Cronje's sixes came from Warne's bowling. He also played a reverse sweep against Warne which went for four. Craig McDermott's last over cost 26.

24/14. Australia v South Africa (3rd One-Day International),
at St George's Park, Port Elizabeth, 22 February 1994.
SCORES
AUSTRALIA 281 for 6 wickets (50 overs) (D. C. Boon 76, D. M. Jones 67,
M. E. Waugh 60); SOUTH AFRICA 193 (43 overs) (S. K. Warne 4/36).
Australia won by 88 runs.
S. K. WARNE
10–0–36–4. Dismissed: P. N. Kirsten c G. D. McGrath 27; P. L. Symcox
c D. C. Boon 4; C. R. Matthews b 0; P. S. de Villiers b 4.

Warne's most significant contribution in the series, included one spell
of 3/3 in 15 balls.

25/15. Australia v South Africa (4th One-Day International),
at Kingsmead, Durban, 24 February 1994.
SCORES
AUSTRALIA 154 (43.2 overs) (A. R. Border 69 not out; C. R. Matthews 4/10);
SOUTH AFRICA 157 for 3 wickets (45 overs) (W. J. Cronje 50 not out).
South Africa won by seven wickets.
S. K. WARNE
8–2–32–1. Dismissed: J. N. Rhodes c M. E. Waugh 3.

Warne's 23 was third-top score and his 38-run eighth-wicket stand
with Allan Border the second-best of the innings.

26/16. Australia v South Africa (5th One-Day International),
at Buffalo Park, East London, 2 April 1994 (day/night).
SCORES
SOUTH AFRICA 158 (49.5 overs) (P. N. Kirsten 53); AUSTRALIA 159 for 3 wickets
(40 overs) (S. R. Waugh 67 not out). *Australia won by seven wickets.*
S. K. WARNE
10–0–34–1. Dismissed: P. N. Kirsten c M. E. Waugh 53.

27/17. Australia v South Africa (6th One-Day International),
at St George's Park, Port Elizabeth, 4 April 1993 (day/night).
SCORES
SOUTH AFRICA 227 for 6 wickets (50 overs) (J. N. Rhodes 66,

A. C. Hudson 63); AUSTRALIA 201 (49.1 overs) (P. R. Reiffel 58,
S. K. Warne 55). *South Africa won by 26 runs*.
S. K. WARNE
3–0–18–0.

The Warne/Paul Reiffel stand of 119 in 117 balls was a new world ODI record for the eighth wicket, Warne run out attempting a second run. His ODI-best 55 came from 58 balls and included 8 fours. Together they lifted the Australian score from 7/77 to 8/196.

28/18. **Australia v South Africa** (7th One-Day International),
at Newlands, Cape Town, 6 April 1994 (day/night).
SCORES
AUSTRALIA 242 for 6 wickets (50 overs) (M. E. Waugh 71, M. A. Taylor 63;
C. R. Matthews 4/47); SOUTH AFRICA 206 for 5 wickets (50 overs)
(A. C. Hudson 62). *Australia won by 36 runs*.
S. K. WARNE
10–0–31–3. Dismissed: A. C. Hudson lbw 62; W. J. Cronje
c M. A. Taylor 37; J. N. Rhodes st I. A. Healy 35.

On a Newlands spin-top, Warne dismissed three of the top four Proteas, including top scorer Andrew Hudson.

29/19. **Australia v South Africa** (8th One-Day International),
at Springbok Park, Bloemfontein, 8 April 1994 (day/night).
SCORES
AUSTRALIA 203 for 6 wickets (50 overs); SOUTH AFRICA 202 for 8 wickets
(50 overs) (A. C. Hudson 84). *Australia won by one run*.
S. K. WARNE
10–0–37–1. Dismissed: A. P. Kuiper c M. E. Waugh 6.

Australia tied the Benson & Hedges one-day series 4–4 after a thrilling finish in which Dave Richardson was run out from the very last ball, leaving Australia one-run winners. The game was Allan Border's 273rd and final ODI.

SUMMARY, 1993–94 (SOUTH AFRICA)

	Mts	Overs	Mdns	Runs	Wicks	Ave	BB	4w	RpO
All limited-overs matches	9	69	3	285	11	25.90	4/36	1	4.13
One-Day Internationals	8	69	3	285	11	25.90	4/36	1	4.13

AUSTRALIA IN SHARJAH, UNITED ARAB EMIRATES

30/20. **Australia v Sri Lanka** (Austral–Asia Cup 2nd match),
at Sharjah C. A. Stadium, 14 April 1994.
SCORES
SRI LANKA 154 (49.3 overs) (H. P. Tillekeratne 64); AUSTRALIA 158 for 1 wicket
(36.5 overs) (M. A. Taylor 68 not out, M. E. Waugh 64 not out). **Australia
won by nine wickets**.
S. K. WARNE
10–1–29–3. Dismissed: R. S. Kalpage c M. G. Bevan 4;
P. B. Dassanayake lbw 7; C. P. H. Ramanayake lbw 2.

Justin Langer made his maiden appearance as Australia's wicketkeeper. Roshan Mahanama captained Sri Lanka for the first time
after the controversial omission of Aravinda de Silva on fitness
grounds.

31/21. **Australia v New Zealand** (Austral–Asia Cup 4th match),
at Sharjah C. A. Stadium, 16 April 1994.
SCORES
NEW ZEALAND 207 for 9 wickets (50 overs) (B. A. Young 63;
S. K. Warne 4/34); AUSTRALIA 208 for 3 wickets (47.5 overs)
(D. C. Boon 68, M. L. Hayden 67). **Australia won by seven wickets**.
S. K. WARNE
10–0–34–4. Dismissed: B. R. Hartland lbw 23; M. W. Douglas lbw 0;
A. C. Parore c & b 12; C. Z. Harris lbw 14. Man of the match.

32/22. **Australia v India** (Austral–Asia Cup 1st Semi-Final),
at Sharjah C. A. Stadium, 19 April 1994.

SCORES

AUSTRALIA 244 for 9 wickets (50 overs) (S. R. Waugh 53); INDIA 245 for
3 wickets (45.4 overs) (A. Jadeja 87, N. S. Sidhu 80). **India won
by seven wickets.**

S. K. WARNE

9–0–40–2. Dismissed: A. Jadeja c D. C. Boon 87; N. S. Sidhu
st J. L. Langer 80.

Warne's first eight overs cost 18 before his ninth, eight-ball, over
went for a record 22, courtesy of 2 sixes and 2 fours by left-hander
Vinod Kambli. The loss excluded Australia from the Austral–Asia
Cup final.

SUMMARY, 1993–94 (SHARJAH, UAE)

	Mts	Overs	Mdns	Runs	Wicks	Ave	BB	4w	RpO
One-Day Internationals	3	29	1	103	9	11.44	4/34	1	3.55

1994–95

Australia in Sri Lanka

33/23. **Australia v Pakistan** (Singer World Series 2nd match),
at Sinhalese Sports Club Ground, Colombo, 7 September 1994.
Scores
Australia 179 for 7 wickets (50 overs); Pakistan 151 for 9 wickets
(50 overs). *Australia won by 28 runs*.
S. K. Warne
10–1–29–3. Dismissed: Inzamam-ul-Haq st I. A. Healy 29; Basit Ali c & b 0;
Waqar Younis c M. J. Slater 2. Man of the match.

An unusual aspect of Warne's 40-ball 30 was that none of his scoring
shots were boundaries.

34/24. **Australia v India** (Singer World Series 3rd match),
at R. Premadasa Stadium, Colombo, 9 September 1994 (day/night).
Scores
India 246 for 8 wickets (50 overs) (S. R. Tendulkar 110); Australia 215

(47.4 overs) (M. E. Waugh 61). *India won by 31 runs*.
S. K. WARNE
10–0–53–2. Dismissed: M. Prabhakar c M. J. Slater 20; N. R. Mongia
c I. A. Healy 3.

Play started 15 minutes late to allow an Indian satellite television link
to be established.

35/25. **Australia v Sri Lanka** (Singer World Series 5th match),
at P. Saravanamuttu Stadium, Colombo, 13 September 1994.
SCORES
AUSTRALIA 225 for 6 wickets (50 overs); SRI LANKA 164 for 4 wickets
(34.4 overs) (A. Ranatunga 59). *Sri Lanka won on faster run-rate*.
S. K. WARNE
8–0–27–2. Dismissed: R. S. Mahanama b 20; P. A. de Silva st I. A. Healy 33.

Warne took his 50th ODI wicket when Roshan Mahanama was
bowled.

SUMMARY, 1994–95 (SRI LANKA)

	Mts	Overs	Mdns	Runs	Wicks	Ave	BB	4w	RpO
One-Day Internationals	3	28	1	109	7	15.57	3/29	–	3.89

AUSTRALIA IN PAKISTAN

36/26. **Australia v South Africa** (Wills Series 1st match),
at Gaddafi Stadium, Lahore, 12 October 1994.
SCORES
AUSTRALIA 207 for 6 wickets (50 overs) (M. A. Taylor 56, S. R. Waugh 56);
SOUTH AFRICA 201 for 8 wickets (50 overs) (W. J. Cronje 98 not out). *Australia
won by six runs*.
S. K. WARNE
10–0–39–0.

The first triangular tournament in Pakistan saw the players dressed in
normal whites and using a red ball.

37/27. Australia v Pakistan (Wills Series 2nd match),
at Qasim Bagh Stadium, Multan, 14 October 1994.
SCORES
PAKISTAN 200 for 8 wickets (50 overs) (Inzamam-ul-Haq 59;
D. W. Fleming 4/49); AUSTRALIA 201 for 3 wickets (46 overs)
(D. C. Boon 84 not out, S. R. Waugh 59 not out). *Australia won by seven wickets*.
S. K. WARNE
10–1–29–1. Dismissed: Saleem Malik c I. A. Healy 32.

38/28. Australia v South Africa (Wills Series 4th match),
at Iqbal Stadium, Faisalabad, 18 October 1994.
SCORES
AUSTRALIA 208 for 6 wickets (50 overs); SOUTH AFRICA 186 (48.2 overs)
(W. J. Cronje 64; S. K. Warne 4/40). *Australia won by 22 runs*.
S. K. WARNE
9.2–0–40–4. Dismissed: E. O. Simons st I. A. Healy 11; M. W. Pringle
lbw 0; C. E. Eksteen st I. A. Healy 0; P. S. de Villiers st I. A. Healy 0.

Warne took 4/1 in six balls in his eighth and ninth overs. Three were stumped by Ian Healy.

39/29. Australia v Pakistan (Wills Series 6th match),
at Rawalpindi Cricket Stadium, 22 October 1994.
SCORES
AUSTRALIA 250 for 6 wickets (50 overs) (M. E. Waugh 121 not out); PAKISTAN
251 for 1 wicket (39 overs) (Saeed Anwar 104 not out, Inzamam-ul-Haq
91 not out). *Pakistan won by nine wickets*.
S. K. WARNE
9–1–47–0.

Warne was taken to hospital after being hit on the toe by a high-speed yorker from Waqar Younis. He was cleared of any bone damage.

40/30. Australia v South Africa (Wills Series 7th match), at Arbab Niaz
Stadium, Peshawar, 24 October 1994.

SCORES

SOUTH AFRICA 251 for 6 wickets (50 overs) (W. J. Cronje 100 not out);
AUSTRALIA 252 for 7 wickets (49.4 overs) (M. J. Slater 54). **Australia won by three wickets.**

S. K. WARNE

10–0–51–1. Dismissed: D. J. Cullinan b 36.

41/31. **Australia v Pakistan** (Wills Series Final), at Gaddafi Stadium, Lahore, 30 October 1994.

SCORES

AUSTRALIA 269 for 5 wickets (50 overs) (M. J. Slater 66, M. A. Taylor 56, M. G. Bevan 53 not out); PAKISTAN 204 (46.5 overs) (Basit Ali 63; G. D. McGrath 5/52). **Australia won by 65 runs.**

S. K. WARNE

10–2–32–0.

After a semi-serious exhibition game at a water-laden Jinnah Stadium in Gujranwala in which Warne's 1.5 overs cost 37, the Aussies won the Wills Series trophy by 65 runs, their third ODI title of the summer.

SUMMARY, 1994–95 (PAKISTAN)

	Mts	Overs	Mdns	Runs	Wicks	Ave	BB	4w	RpO
One-Day Internationals	6	58.2	4	238	6	39.33	4/40	1	4.08

IN AUSTRALIA

42/32. **Australia v Zimbabwe** (World Series 1st match), at WACA Ground, Perth, 2 December 1994 (day/night).

SCORES

ZIMBABWE 166 for 9 wickets (50 overs); AUSTRALIA 167 for 8 wickets (47.2 overs). **Australia won by two wickets.**

S. K. WARNE

10–1–27–2. Dismissed: A. D. R. Campbell hit wkt 22; H. H. Streak c D. W. Fleming 7. Man of the match.

In a low-scoring match in which Mark Taylor's 45 was top score, Warne took two key wickets and bowled economically, restricting Zimbabwe's score. He also took an important catch. It was Zimbabwe's first international in Australia, after having been granted full membership status of the International Cricket Council only two years previously.

43/33. Australia v England (World Series 3rd match),
at Sydney Cricket Ground, 6 December 1994 (day/night).
SCORES
AUSTRALIA 224 for 4 wickets (50 overs) (D. C. Boon 64 not out,
M. A. Taylor 57, M. J. Slater 50); ENGLAND 196 (48.3 overs)
(M. A. Atherton 60). *Australia won by 28 runs.*
S. K. WARNE
10–0–46–1. Dismissed: G. A. Gooch c C. J. McDermott 21.

Warne's only wicket came with his last delivery of his 10th over.

44/34. Australia v Zimbabwe (World Series 4th match),
at Bellerive Oval, Hobart, 8 December 1994.
SCORES
AUSTRALIA 254 for 3 wickets (50 overs) (S. G. Law 110, D. C. Boon
98 not out); ZIMBABWE 170 for 8 wickets (50 overs). *Australia won
by 84 runs.*
S. K. WARNE
9–0–23–1. Dismissed: W. R. James c I. A. Healy 15.

Promoted to open the innings, Stuart Law hit a six to go from 94 to 100 and his maiden century.

---

45. Australia v Australia 'A' (World Series 6th match),
at Adelaide Oval, 11 December 1994.
SCORES
AUSTRALIA 202 (48.3 overs) (M. J. Slater 64); AUSTRALIA 'A' 196 (47.4 overs)
(G. D. McGrath 4/43). *Australia won by six runs.*
S. K. WARNE
10–1–40–3. Dismissed: D. R. Martyn b 37; J. L. Langer c S. G. Law 1;
R. T. Ponting c M. G. Bevan 42.

Many in the sell-out Adelaide Oval crowd supported the underdogs Australia 'A', much to Australian captain Mark Taylor's frustration. There was a mid-pitch confrontation between Glenn McGrath and Matthew Hayden, Taylor saying afterwards he was not a supporter of the involvement of Australia 'A' at such an elite level, especially if it led to his players being booed.

46/35. **Australia v England** (World Series 11th match),
at Melbourne Cricket Ground, 10 January 1995 (day/night).
SCORES
ENGLAND 225 for 8 wickets (50 overs) (G. A. Hick 91; G. D. McGrath 4/25);
AUSTRALIA 188 (48 overs) (I. A. Healy 56; A. R. C. Fraser 4/22). *England won by 37 runs*.
S. K. WARNE
10–0–37–2. Dismissed: G. A. Hick c D. W. Fleming 91; N. H. Fairbrother c I. A. Healy 35.

The hoodoo against teams batting second in Melbourne continued when Australia was beaten by 37 runs. Top scorer Graeme Hick was dropped by a diving Michael Slater from the bowling of Warne at 58.¯

47. **Australia v Australia 'A'** (World Series 1st Final),
at Sydney Cricket Ground, 15 January 1995 (day/night).
SCORES
AUSTRALIA 'A' 209 for 8 wickets (50 overs) (M. G. Bevan 73,
M. L. Hayden 50; C. J. McDermott 4/25); AUSTRALIA 213 for 5 wickets
(50 overs) (M. J. Slater 92). *Australia won by five wickets*.
S. K. WARNE
10–2–37–1. Dismissed: D. R. Martyn c M. A. Taylor 20.

Ian Healy won the match on the very last ball with a sliced off-side four from Greg Rowell to break the tie.

48. **Australia v Australia 'A'** (World Series 2nd Final),
at Melbourne Cricket Ground, 17 January 1995 (day/night).
SCORES
AUSTRALIA 'A' 226 (49.4 overs) (G. S. Blewett 64, D. R. Martyn 58;
D. W. Fleming 4/28); AUSTRALIA 229 for 4 wickets (49 overs) (S. R. Waugh
56 not out, M. J. Slater 56, M. A. Taylor 50). **Australia won by**
six wickets.
S. K. WARNE
10–0–55–1. Dismissed: D. R. Martyn lbw 58.

Having dropped a catch in front of his home-town crowd, Warne received a bronx cheer when he fielded cleanly soon afterwards. Making a face before bowling the first ball after drinks to Damien Martyn, who'd made 58 from 39 balls, he trapped his close friend lbw, his only wicket of an eventful innings.

49. **Victoria v South Australia**, at Adelaide Oval, 11 February 1995.
SCORES
VICTORIA 236 for 7 wickets (50 overs); SOUTH AUSTRALIA 157 (48.1 overs)
(J. C. Scuderi 51). **Victoria won by 79 runs**.
S. K. WARNE
10–2–34–2. Dismissed: J. D. Siddons c T. F. Corbett 33; J. C. Scuderi
c R. P. Larkin 51.

Warne shared in a 61-run seventh-wicket stand with Paul Reiffel before taking the key wickets of SA's top scorers Joe Scuderi and Jamie Siddons. He did, however, drop a catch at slip, before Darren Lehmann (13) had scored.

SUMMARY, 1994–95 (AUSTRALIA)

	Mts	Overs	Mdns	Runs	Wicks	Ave	BB	4w	RpO
All limited-overs matches	8	79	6	299	13	23.00	3/40	–	3.78
One-Day Internationals	4	39	1	133	6	22.16	2/27	–	3.41
Australia v Australia 'A'	3	30	3	132	5	26.40	3/40	–	4.40
Mercantile Mutual Cup	1	10	2	34	2	17.00	2/34	–	3.40

AUSTRALIA IN NEW ZEALAND

50/36. **Australia v South Africa** (Centenary Cup 1st match),
at Basin Reserve, Wellington, 15 February 1995.
SCORES
SOUTH AFRICA 123 (46.2 overs) (P. R. Reiffel 4/27); AUSTRALIA 124 for
7 wickets (43.2 overs). *Australia won by three wickets*.
S. K. WARNE
10–3–18–2. Dismissed: D. J. Cullinan st I. A. Healy 0; D. J. Callaghan
c S. R. Waugh 1.

Before going to the West Indies for the world Test championship,
Australia visited New Zealand as part of NZ cricket's centenary celebrations. Warne's 2/18 was one of his finest efforts at ODI level. 'Shane's
first four overs were as good as he can bowl,' said captain Mark Taylor.

51/37. **Australia v New Zealand** (Centenary Cup 4th match), at Eden
Park, Auckland, 19 February 1995.
SCORES
AUSTRALIA 254 for 5 wickets (50 overs) (M. A. Taylor 97, M. E. Waugh 74);
NEW ZEALAND 227 for 9 wickets (50 overs) (M. J. Greatbatch 74,
S. P. Fleming 53). *Australia won by 27 runs*.
S. K. WARNE
10–1–40–1. Dismissed: K. R. Rutherford st I. A. Healy 7.

52/38. **Australia v India** (Centenary Cup 5th match),
at Carisbrook, Dunedin, 22 February 1995.
SCORES
AUSTRALIA 250 for 6 wickets (50 overs) (R. T. Ponting 62); INDIA 252
for 5 wickets (47.5 overs) (N. S. Sidhu 54, V. G. Kambli 51 not out,
M. Prabhakar 50). *India won by five wickets*.
S. K. WARNE
10–0–61–0.

Warne's first over went for 19 (4 3 4 1 3 4) courtesy of Indian
openers Manoj Prabhakar and Sachin Tendulkar. Afterwards he
was fined $500 for wearing a Nike wristband.

53/39. **Australia v New Zealand** (Centenary Cup Final),
at Eden Park, Auckland, 26 February 1995.
Scores
New Zealand 137 for 9 wickets (50 overs); Australia 138 for 4 wickets
(31.1 overs). *Australia won by six wickets*.
S. K. Warne
10–2–21–2. Dismissed: S. A. Thomson c & b 9; A. C. Parore
c M. A. Taylor 2.

SUMMARY, 1994–95 (New Zealand)

	Mts	Overs	Mdns	Runs	Wicks	Ave	BB	4w	RpO
One-Day Internationals	4	40	6	140	5	28.00	2/18	–	3.50

Australia in West Indies

54/40. **Australia v West Indies** (1st One-Day International),
at Kensington Oval, Bridgetown, Barbados, 8 March 1995.
Scores
West Indies 257 (49.4 overs) (C. L. Hooper 84, B. C. Lara 55); Australia 251
for 6 wickets (50 overs) (D. C. Boon 85 not out). *West Indies won by
six runs*.
S. K. Warne
10–0–56–1. Dismissed: P. V. Simmons c M. A. Taylor 37.

55/41. **Australia v West Indies** (2nd One-Day International),
at Queen's Park Oval, Port-of-Spain, Trinidad, 11 March 1995.
Scores
Australia 260 for 8 wickets (50 overs) (S. R. Waugh 58, M. J. Slater 55,
I. A. Healy 51); West Indies 234 (47.5 overs) (B. C. Lara 62,
C. L. Hooper 55). *Australia won by 26 runs*.
S. K. Warne
10–0–63–1. Dismissed: C. L. Hooper c G. S. Blewett 55.

Warne's first two overs cost 18 on his way to his most expensive
analysis (to that time) in ODIs.

56/42. **Australia v West Indies** (3rd One-Day International),
at Queen's Park Oval, Port-of-Spain, Trinidad, 12 March 1995.
Scores
West Indies 282 for 5 wickets (50 overs) (B. C. Lara 139, J. C. Adams
51 not out); Australia 149 (34.5 overs) (P. V. Simmons 4/18).
West Indies won by 133 runs.
S. K. Warne
10–1–52–0.

57/43. **Australia v West Indies** (4th One-Day International),
at Arnos Vale, Kingstown, St Vincent, 15 March 1995.
Scores
Australia 210 for 9 wickets (M. J. Slater 68); West Indies 208 for 3 wickets
(43.1 overs) (P. V. Simmons 86, C. L. Hooper 60 not out). *West Indies
won on faster run-rate.*
S. K. Warne
9.1–3–33–2. Dismissed: P. V. Simmons c I. A. Healy 86; S. L. Campbell
st I. A. Healy 20.

After this match, Warne and David Boon were rested from the fifth
and final ODI, in Guyana, where the Windies clinched a 4–1 series
win.

SUMMARY, 1994–95 (West Indies)

	Mts	Overs	Mdns	Runs	Wicks	Ave	BB	4w	RpO
One-Day Internationals	4	39.1	4	204	4	51.00	2/33	–	5.20

1995–96

In Australia

58. **Victoria v Queensland**, at Brisbane Cricket Ground,
8 October 1995.
Scores
Queensland 173 for 4 wickets (33.2 overs) (S. G. Law 77,
M. L. Hayden 62 not out); Victoria did not bat. *No result*.
S. K. Warne
9–1–36–1. Dismissed: M. L. Love c D. M. Jones 1.

Rain reduced the game to 45 overs a side, then washed out the game
completely before Queensland's innings was completed.

59. **Victoria v New South Wales**, at Melbourne Cricket Ground,
5 November 1995.
Scores
Victoria 106 (38 overs) (N. D. Maxwell 4/15); New South Wales 91 for
3 wickets (26.2 overs). *New South Wales won on faster run-rate*.
S. K. Warne
3–0–17–0.

Five Victorians failed to score.

60/44. **Australia v West Indies** (World Series 2nd match),
at Adelaide Oval, 17 December 1995.
SCORES
AUSTRALIA 242 for 6 wickets (47 overs) (M. E. Waugh 53;
R. A. Harper 4/46); WEST INDIES 121 for 6 wickets (47 overs).
Australia won by 121 runs.
S. K. WARNE
7–1–22–0.

61/45. **Australia v West Indies** (World Series 3rd match),
at Melbourne Cricket Ground, 19 December 1995 (day/night).
SCORES
AUSTRALIA 249 for 6 wickets (50 overs) (S. G. Law 74, M. A. Taylor 63);
WEST INDIES 225 (49.1 overs) (S. Chanderpaul 73). *Australia won
by 24 runs.*
S. K. WARNE
9.1–1–41–2. Dismissed: R. A. Harper st I. A. Healy 15; C. A. Walsh
c I. A. Healy 1.

62/46. **Australia v Sri Lanka** (World Series 4th match),
at Sydney Cricket Ground, 21 December 1995 (day/night).
SCORES
SRI LANKA 255 for 9 wickets (50 overs) (P. A. de Silva 75, H. P. Tillekeratne
62); AUSTRALIA 257 for 5 wickets (49.4 overs) (M. A. Taylor 90,
R. T. Ponting 56, M. E. Waugh 55). *Australia won by five wickets.*
S. K. WARNE
10–1–53–0.

63/47. **Australia v West Indies** (World Series 5th match),
at Sydney Cricket Ground, 1 January 1996 (day/night).
SCORES
WEST INDIES 172 for 9 wickets (43 overs) (C. L. Hooper 93 not out;
P. R. Reiffel 4/29); AUSTRALIA 173 for 9 wickets (43 overs) (M. G. Bevan
78 not out). *Australia won by one wicket.*
S. K. WARNE
9–2–30–3. Dismissed: S. L. Campbell lbw 15; J. C. Adams c M. E. Waugh 0;
C. E. L. Ambrose b 0.

Warne took two wickets in three balls among his 3/30 from nine overs. The match hero was Michael Bevan who hit a boundary down the ground on the very last ball of the night to give Australia a one-wicket win in one of the most-remembered one-day finishes of all.

64/48. **Australia v Sri Lanka** (World Series 9th match),
at Melbourne Cricket Ground, 9 January 1996 (day/night).
SCORES
AUSTRALIA 213 for 5 wickets (50 overs) (R. T. Ponting 123, M. G. Bevan
65 not out); SRI LANKA 214 for 7 wickets (47.3 overs) (R. S. Kaluwitharana 77,
R. S. Mahanama 51). *Sri Lanka won by three wickets*.
S. K. WARNE
10–1–37–1. Dismissed: R. S. Kalpage b 1.

65/49. **Australia v Sri Lanka** (World Series 10th match),
at WACA Ground, Perth, 12 January 1996 (day/night).
SCORES
AUSTRALIA 266 for 6 wickets (50 overs) (M. E. Waugh 130, M. A. Taylor 85);
SRI LANKA 183 for 9 wickets (50 overs) (H. P. Tillekeratne 58 not out).
Australia won by 83 runs.
S. K. WARNE
10–0–45–1. Dismissed: W. P. U. J. C. Vaas st I. A. Healy 10.

66/50. **Australia v Sri Lanka** (World Series 12th match),
at Melbourne Cricket Ground, 16 January 1996 (day/night).
SCORES
AUSTRALIA 242 for 4 wickets (50 overs) (S. R. Waugh 102 not out);
SRI LANKA 246 for 7 wickets (49.4 overs) (R. S. Kaluwitharana 74).
Sri Lanka won by three wickets.
S. K. WARNE
10–0–40–3. Dismissed: R. S. Kaluwitharana c M. E. Waugh 74;
H. P. Tillekeratne c I. A. Healy 0; R. S. Mahanama b 31.

Sri Lankan fans at the MCG heckled umpire Darrell Hair as he walked onto the ground, in reaction to his no-balling of Muttiah Muralitharan just weeks previously during the Christmas Test.

67/51. **Australia v Sri Lanka** (World Series 1st Final),
at Melbourne Cricket Ground, 18 January 1996 (day/night).
SCORES
AUSTRALIA 201 for 7 wickets (50 overs) (M. G. Bevan 59, R. T. Ponting 51,
I. A. Healy 50 not out); SRI LANKA 183 (48.1 overs). *Australia won
by 18 runs.*
S. K. WARNE
10–1–29–2. Dismissed: P. A. de Silva c M. A. Taylor 34; H. P. Tillekeratne
c I. A. Healy 1.

Warne changed the game with the dismissal of Aravinda de Silva and
Hashan Tillekeratne in mid-spell.

68/52. **Australia v Sri Lanka** (World Series 2nd Final),
at Sydney Cricket Ground, 20 January 1996 (day/night).
SCORES
AUSTRALIA 273 for 5 wickets (50 overs) (M. A. Taylor 82, M. E. Waugh 73);
SRI LANKA 159 for 8 wickets (25 overs). *Australia won on faster run-rate.*
S. K. WARNE
5–0–20–3. Dismissed: S. T. Jayasuriya c G. D. McGrath 30; A. Ranatunga
c S. G. Law 41; H. D. P. K. Dharmasena c S. R. Waugh 7. Player of the
Finals (shared with M. A. Taylor).

The rain-affected second final didn't finish until almost 11 p.m.,
believed to be the latest-ever finish for an ODI in Australia.

69. **Victoria v Western Australia**, at Melbourne Cricket Ground,
2 February 1996 (day/night).
SCORES
VICTORIA 180 (49.2 overs); WESTERN AUSTRALIA 181 for 5 wickets (45.4 overs)
(M. P. Lavender 72, J. L. Langer 58). *Western Australia won by five wickets.*
S. K. WARNE
10–0–51–0.

SUMMARY, 1995–96 (AUSTRALIA)

	Mts	Overs	Mdns	Runs	Wicks	Ave	BB	4w	RpO
All limited-overs matches	12	102.1	8	421	16	26.31	3/20	–	4.12
One-Day Internationals	9	80.1	7	317	15	21.13	3/20	–	3.95
Mercantile Mutual Cup	3	22	1	104	1	104.00	1/36	–	4.72

AUSTRALIA IN INDIA & PAKISTAN – 1996 WORLD CUP

70/53. Australia v Kenya (World Cup 12th match),
at Indira Priyadarshani Stadium, Visakhapatnam, 23 February 1996.
SCORES
AUSTRALIA 304 for 7 wickets (50 overs) (M. E. Waugh 130, S. R. Waugh 82);
KENYA 207 for 7 wickets (50 overs) (K. Otieno 85, M. Odumbe 50).
Australia won by 97 runs.
S. K. WARNE
10–0–25–1. Dismissed: T. Odoyo st I. A. Healy 10.

Having forfeited their opening game of the 1996 World Cup, scheduled for strife-torn Colombo, the Australians began an assault on the
title with the first of three consecutive wins, Warne the most economical of seven bowlers used.

71/54. Australia v India (World Cup 19th match), at Wankhede
Stadium, Bombay, 27 February 1996 (day/night).
SCORES
AUSTRALIA 258 (50 overs) (M. E. Waugh 126, M. A. Taylor 59); INDIA 242
(48 overs) (S. R. Tendulkar 90, S. V. Manjrekar 62; D. W. Fleming 5/36).
Australia won by 16 runs.
S. K. WARNE
10–1–28–1. Dismissed: N. R. Mongia c M. A. Taylor 27.

Four Australian wickets fell in the 50th over, including Warne for a
first-ball duck.

72/55. Australia v Zimbabwe (World Cup 22nd match),
at Vidarbha C. A. Stadium, Nagpur, 1 March 1996.
SCORES
ZIMBABWE 154 (A. C. Waller 67; S. K. Warne 4/34); AUSTRALIA 158 for
2 wickets (36 overs) (M. E. Waugh 76 not out). *Australia won by
eight wickets.*
S. K. WARNE
9.3–1–34–4. Dismissed: A. Flower st I. A. Healy 7; C. N. Evans c I. A. Healy
18; S. G. Peall c I. A. Healy 0; A. C. I. Lock b 5. Man of the match.

73/56. **Australia v West Indies** (World Cup 26th match),
at Sawai Mansingh Stadium, Jaipur, 4 March 1996.
SCORES
AUSTRALIA 229 for 6 wickets (50 overs) (R. T. Ponting 102, S. R. Waugh 57);
WEST INDIES 232 for 6 wickets (48.5 overs) (R. B. Richardson 93 not out,
B. C. Lara 60). *West Indies won by four wickets*.
S. K. WARNE
10–1–30–0.

74/57. **Australia v New Zealand** (World Cup, 4th Quarter-Final),
at M. A. Chidambaram Stadium, Madras, 11 March 1996 (day/night).
SCORES
NEW ZEALAND 286 for 9 wickets (50 overs) (C. Z. Harris 130, L. K. Germon 89);
AUSTRALIA 289 for 4 wickets (47.5 overs) (M. E. Waugh 110, S. R. Waugh
59 not out). *Australia won by six wickets*.
S. K. WARNE
10–0–52–2. Dismissed: C. Z. Harris c P. R. Reiffel 130; A. C. Parore lbw 11.

Australia registered their highest ever total batting second to win an
epic quarter-final clash. Used as a pinch-hitter at No. 4, Warne scored
24 from just 15 balls with 1 four and 2 sixes. He showed great
courage to even play after his troublesome finger virtually collapsed
at practice 24 hours before the game. 'The veins started popping out
through the knuckle,' he said in *My Own Story*.

75/58. **Australia v West Indies** (World Cup, 2nd Semi-Final),
at Punjab C. A. Ground, Mohali, 14 March 1996 (day/night).
SCORES
AUSTRALIA 207 for 8 wickets (50 overs) (S. G. Law 72, M. G. Bevan 69);
WEST INDIES 202 (S. Chanderpaul 80; S. K. Warne 4/36). *Australia won
by five runs*.
S. K. WARNE
9–0–36–4. Dismissed: C. O. Browne c & b 10; O. D. Gibson c I. A. Healy 1;
J. C. Adams lbw 2; I. R. Bishop lbw 3. Man of the match.

Mark Taylor described Australia's titanic semi-final victory as the 'most unbelievable match' he'd ever played in. With 4/36, Warne was instrumental in a startling West Indian collapse which saw the Windies lose by five runs after crumbling from 2/165 to 202 all out.

76/59. Australia v Sri Lanka (World Cup Final),
at Gaddafi Stadium, Lahore, 17 March 1996 (day/night).
SCORES
AUSTRALIA 241 for 7 wickets (50 overs) (M. A. Taylor 74); SRI LANKA 245 for 3 wickets (46.2 overs) (P. A. de Silva 107 not out, A. P. Gurusinha 65).
Sri Lanka won by seven wickets.
S. K. WARNE
10–0–58–0.

In one of the upsets of the tournament, the international minnows motored to an extraordinary win, the biggest in Sri Lanka's history. Struggling to hold the ball in the Lahore humidity, Warne's 10 overs cost 58, including 11 from his first. Arjuna Ranatunga stuck his tongue out at Warne after hitting him for a six.

'When I first came into the side, a lot of cricketing nations used to treat us like babies,' Ranatunga said later. 'They thought we were good cricketers but they automatically felt they were better. When I took over as captain I felt I'd had enough of those [barbs] and that we should do something about it.'

The Sri Lankans had started the tournament as 16/1 outsiders. Ranatunga said they would have been happy to make the semi-finals. To make the final and score an against-the-odds victory against the powerful Australians, just weeks after their humbling tour in 1995–96, had been beyond even his expectations

SUMMARY, 1996 (WORLD CUP IN INDIA & PAKISTAN)

	Mts	Overs	Mdns	Runs	Wickets	Ave	BB	4w	RpO
One-Day Internationals	7	68.4	3	263	12	21.91	4/34	2	3.83

In Australia

77. Australia v World XI, at Melbourne Cricket Ground,
21 March 1996 (day/night).
Scores
World XI 210 for 9 wickets (50 overs) (D. M. Jones 103); Australia 211 for
5 wickets (49 overs) (M. A. Taylor 78, M. E. Waugh 56 not out). **Australia
won by five wickets**.
S. K. Warne
10–0–57–0.

Warne bowled a bouncer first ball at Dean Jones, who made his maiden international 100 at the MCG – but it was 20-year-old Jason Gillespie who announced his arrival as a bowler of genuine pace by skittling West Indian Richie Richardson for three. Sri Lanka's World Cup hero Aravinda de Silva also played in the game, as did Sanath Jayasuriya, Martin Crowe, Jonty Rhodes, Shaun Pollock and Heath Streak. Six weeks later, Warne had an operation to repair his overworked, damaged spinning finger.

SUMMARY, 1996 (Australia)

	Mts	Overs	Mdns	Runs	Wicks	Ave	BB	4w	RpO
Australia v World XI	1	10	0	57	0	–	–	–	5.70

1996–97

In Australia

---

78. Victoria v South Australia, at Adelaide Oval, 12 October 1996.

Scores

Victoria 238 for 4 wickets (50 overs) (D. M. Jones 93 not out,
B. J. Hodge 50); South Australia 208 for 9 wickets (50 overs)
(G. S. Blewett 61). *Victoria won by 30 runs*.

S. K. Warne (capt.)

10–0–55–2. Dismissed: J. D. Siddons st D. S. Berry 21; B. E. Young
c M. T. G. Elliott 16.

Rating the fitness of his spinning finger at only 70 per cent after
wintertime surgery, Warne took 2/55 from his 10 overs. Batting No. 6
he made 12 not out from as many balls coming in with just minutes
to play.

---

79. Victoria v Tasmania, at Carlton Cricket Ground (Optus Oval),
27 October 1996.

Scores

Victoria 250 for 4 wickets (50 overs) (D. M. Jones 100 not out,

M. T. G. Elliott 59); TASMANIA 192 (45.4 overs) (D. C. Boon 52;
S. K. Warne 5/35). *Victoria won by 58 runs*.
S. K. WARNE (capt.)
10–1–35–5. Dismissed: D. F. Hills st D. S. Berry 39; D. C. Boon
c D. S. Berry 52; C. R. Miller c M. R. Foster 0; S. Young c & b 13;
M. N. Atkinson b 6.

In his most successful one-day game at state level, Warne's mid-innings spell of 5/18 clinched the game.

80/60. Australia v West Indies (World Series 1st match),
at Melbourne Cricket Ground, 6 December 1996 (day/night).
SCORES
WEST INDIES 172 (49.2 overs) (S. Chanderpaul 54); AUSTRALIA 5 for 173
(48.4 overs) (G. S. Blewett 57 not out). *Australia won by five wickets*.
S. K. WARNE
10–0–34–2. Dismissed: J. R. Murray c G. S. Blewett 24;
K. C. G. Benjamin b 8.

Used from the 30th over, Warne took his 100th ODI wicket when Junior Murray lofted a full toss straight to mid-on.

81/61. Australia v West Indies (World Series 2nd match),
at Sydney Cricket Ground, 8 December 1996 (day/night).
SCORES
WEST INDIES 161 (48.3 overs) (S. K. Warne 5/33); AUSTRALIA 162 for 2 wickets
(42 overs) (M. E. Waugh 83 not out). *Australia won by eight wickets*.
S. K. WARNE
9.3–1–33–5. Dismissed: R. I. C. Holder b 7; J. R. Murray c M. G. Bevan 8;
N. A. M. McLean c G. S. Blewett 0; K. C. G. Benjamin lbw 3;
C. A. Walsh b 0. Man of the match.

Warne took 5/4 from 15 balls in his second spell, twice being on a hat-trick as he returned his career-best ODI figures. Umpire Terry Prue rejected a concerted appeal for lbw against Ken Benjamin on the first hat-trick ball. The second, a waist-high flipper to Courtney Walsh, was blocked.

82/62. **Australia v Pakistan** (World Series 3rd match), at Adelaide Oval, 15 December 1996.

SCORES

PAKISTAN 223 (49.5 overs) (Aamir Sohail 67; S. K. Warne 4/52);
AUSTRALIA 211 (47.5 overs) (S. R. Waugh 57; Saqlain Mushtaq 5/29).
Pakistan won by 12 runs.

S. K. WARNE

9.5–1–52–4. Dismissed: Wasim Akram st I. A. Healy 7; Moin Khan st I. A. Healy 7; Saqlain Mushtaq c M. E. Waugh 3; Waqar Younis b 2.

Warne took four of the last six Pakistani wickets to fall, including Saqlain Mushtaq and Waqar Younis with his final two deliveries.

83/63. **Australia v Pakistan** (World Series 5th match),
at Sydney Cricket Ground, 1 January 1997 (day/night).

SCORES

AUSTRALIA 199 (47.1 overs); PAKISTAN 203 for 6 wickets (45.3 overs)
(Ijaz Ahmed 58, Aamir Sohail 52; S. K. Warne 4/37). *Pakistan won by four wickets.*

S. K. WARNE

10–1–37–4. Dismissed: Aamir Sohail lbw 52; Shahid Afridi c G. S. Blewett 34; Zahoor Elahi c & b 0; Inzamam-ul-Haq b 8. Man of the match.

Showing he was back in the form of 1993 and 1994, Warne claimed another four wickets, including Inzamam-ul-Haq to a leg-break which pitched on leg stump and flattened off.

84/64. **Australia v West Indies** (World Series 7th match), at Brisbane Cricket Ground, 5 January 1997 (day/night).

SCORES

AUSTRALIA 281 for 4 wickets (50 overs) (M. E. Waugh 102, S. G. Law 93);
WEST INDIES 284 for 3 wickets (48.5 overs) (C. L. Hooper 110 not out, B. C. Lara 102). *West Indies won by seven wickets.*

S. K. WARNE

9–0–51–0.

Centurion Carl Hooper lifted Michael Bevan (0/46 from 10 overs) into the top tier of the new stand at the Vulture Street end . . . one of the biggest sixes seen at the 'Gabba. The hit was estimated at 115 metres. Warne was also expensive, conceding almost six runs an over, including 13 from his ninth. It was the Windies' sixth consecutive win against Australia in Brisbane.

85/65. **Australia v Pakistan** (World Series 8th match),
at Bellerive Oval, Hobart, 7 January 1997.
SCORES
PAKISTAN 149 (45.2 overs) (Mohammad Wasim 54); AUSTRALIA 120
(41.3 overs). *Pakistan won by 29 runs*.
S. K. WARNE
7.2–0–35–2. Dismissed: Mohammad Wasim c M. A. Taylor 54;
Wasim Akram st I. A. Healy 1.

86/66. **Australia v West Indies** (World Series 10th match),
at WACA Ground, Perth, 12 January 1997.
SCORES
AUSTRALIA 267 for 7 wickets (50 overs) (M. E. Waugh 92); WEST INDIES 269
for 6 wickets (49.2 overs) (B. C. Lara 90, J. R. Murray 56). *West Indies
won by four wickets*.
S. K. WARNE
10–1–46–2. Dismissed: S. L. Campbell c M. A. Taylor 15; B. C. Lara
c S. G. Law 90.

Warne was on in the sixth over, the earliest in his ODI career. After bowling eight overs for 18, his last two overs cost 28. It was Australia's fifth consecutive loss of the one-day summer and effectively ended its hopes of making the World Series finals for the first time since the inaugural summer in 1979–80.

87/67. **Australia v Pakistan** (World Series 12th match), at Melbourne
Cricket Ground, 16 January 1997 (day/night).
SCORES
PAKISTAN 181 for 9 wickets (50 overs) (Inzamam-ul-Haq 64;
A. M. Stuart 5/26 inc. hat-trick); AUSTRALIA 182 for 7 wickets (49.3 overs)
(M. G. Bevan 79 not out; Wasim Akram 4/25). *Australia won
by three wickets*.
S. K. WARNE
10–2–37–0.

Warne argued with umpire Peter Parker in mid-pitch after a delivery
was called wide despite it striking the pads of one of the Pakistanis
and veering to backward square leg for a leg-bye.

---

88. **Victoria v Western Australia**, at WACA Ground, Perth,
17 January 1997 (day/night).
SCORES
VICTORIA 143 (43.5 overs) (R. P. Larkin 61); WESTERN AUSTRALIA 146 for
5 wickets (43.1 overs). *Western Australia won by five wickets*.
S. K. WARNE (capt.)
10–2–17–2. Dismissed: M. E. Hussey st D. S. Berry 9; J. L. Langer
c D. S. Berry 20.

Lifting himself up the list to No. 3, Warne was out for a second-ball
duck before a commanding spell in which he conceded under two
runs an over, the stumping of Mike Hussey by the recalled Darren
Berry particularly brilliant.

SUMMARY, 1996–97 (AUSTRALIA)

	Mts	Overs	Mdns	Runs	Wicks	Ave	BB	4w	RpO
All limited-overs matches	11	105.4	9	432	28	15.42	5/33	4	4.08
One-Day Internationals	8	75.4	6	325	19	17.10	5/33	3	4.29
Mercantile Mutual Cup	3	30	3	107	9	11.88	5/35	1	3.56

AUSTRALIA IN SOUTH AFRICA

89. Australia v Boland, at Boland Bank Park, Paarl,
18 February 1997 (day/night).
SCORES
AUSTRALIA 319 for 3 wickets (50 overs) (M. E. Waugh 101, M. G. Bevan
80 not out, J. L. Langer 57, M. A. Taylor 56); BOLAND 269 (47.2 overs).
Australia won by 50 runs.
S. K. WARNE
10–0–62–2. Dismissed: E. J. Ferreira b 38; A. P. Kuiper c M. L. Hayden 48.

In his first match for a month, Warne came off second-best against
noted big-hitter Adrian Kuiper who hit two of his 3 sixes from
Warne's bowling. Later, Warne said he was so rusty he'd forgotten his
run-up.

90. Australia v Eastern Province Invitation XI,
at Dan Qeqe Stadium, Zwide, 11 March 1997.
SCORES
AUSTRALIA 243 for 4 wickets (45 overs) (M. L. Hayden 68, M. G. Bevan
57 not out, J. L. Langer 56); EASTERN PROVINCE INVITATION XI 228 for 8 wickets
(45 overs) (L. J. Koen 78). *Australia won by 15 runs.*
S. K. WARNE
9–0–32–2. Dismissed: L. Masikazana lbw 0; Q. Ferreira c S. R. Waugh 2.

Warne (15 not out) shared a 53-run stand with Michael Bevan,
having been elevated in the final overs to No. 6.

91/68. Australia v South Africa (1st One-Day International),
at Buffalo Park, East London, 29 March 1997.
SCORES
AUSTRALIA 223 for 9 wickets (50 overs) (M. G. Bevan 51 not out,
S. G. Law 50, S. R. Waugh 50); SOUTH AFRICA 227 for 4 wickets (47 overs)
(D. J. Cullinan 85 not out, J. H. Kallis 63). *South Africa won by six wickets.*
S. K. WARNE
10–0–36–2. Dismissed: J. H. Kallis st A. C. Gilchrist 63; L. Klusener b 0.

92/69. Australia v South Africa (2nd One-Day International),
at St George's Park, Port Elizabeth, on 31 March 1997.
SCORES
SOUTH AFRICA 221 for 8 wickets (50 overs) (J. H. Kallis 82, J. N. Rhodes 57);
AUSTRALIA 222 for 3 wickets (45 overs) (M. E. Waugh 115 not out,
S. R. Waugh 50 not out). *Australia won by seven wickets*.
S. K. WARNE
6–0–39–1. Dismissed: S. M. Pollock c A. C. Dale 9.

Elevated to No. 4, Warne was out for a first-ball duck to 36-year-old
veteran Pat Symcox.

93/70. Australia v South Africa (3rd One-Day International),
at Newlands, Cape Town, 2 April 1997 (day/night).
SCORES
SOUTH AFRICA 245 for 8 wickets (J. N. Rhodes 83 not out); AUSTRALIA 199
(44.5 overs) (M. G. Bevan 82). *South Africa won by 46 runs*.
S. K. WARNE
10–0–64–2. Dismissed: J. H. Kallis b 23; S. M. Pollock lbw 21.

Warne conceded more than a run per ball for one of the few times in
his ODI career. A reverse sweep to the backward point boundary by
Jonty Rhodes was classic improvisation.

94/71. Australia v South Africa (4th One-Day International),
Kingsmead, Durban, 5 April 1997 (day/night).
SCORES
AUSTRALIA 211 for 9 wickets (50 overs) (A. C. Gilchrist 77, G. S. Blewett 53;
S. M. Pollock 4/33); SOUTH AFRICA 196 (48.1 overs). *Australia won
by 15 runs*.
S. K. WARNE
8.1–1–36–2. Dismissed: A. M. Bacher lbw 45; D. J. Cullinan c & b 38.

95/72. **Australia v South Africa** (5th One-Day International),
Wanderers Stadium, Johannesburg, 8 April 1997 (day/night).
SCORES
AUSTRALIA 258 for 7 wickets (50 overs) (M. J. Di Venuto 89);
SOUTH AFRICA 250 for 8 wickets (50 overs) (J. H. Kallis 55, D. J. Cullinan 53).
Australia won by eight runs.
S. K. WARNE
10–0–45–1. Dismissed: S. M. Pollock c S. G. Law 40.

With South Africa needing 14 runs from the 50th over to take a 3–2
lead, Warne restricted Hansie Cronje and Rudi Bryson to just five
singles in a masterly final over.

96/73. **Australia v South Africa** (6th One-Day International),
Centurion Park, 10 April 1997 (day/night).
SCORES
SOUTH AFRICA 284 for 7 wickets (50 overs) (D. J. Cullinan 89,
W. J. Cronje 80); AUSTRALIA 287 for 5 wickets (49 overs)
(M. G. Bevan 103, S. R. Waugh 89). *Australia won by five wickets*.
S. K. WARNE
10–1–52–2. Dismissed: D. J. Cullinan c M. E. Waugh 89; J. H. Kallis
st I. A. Healy 3.

Warne dismissed Daryll Cullinan and Jacques Kallis with consecutive
deliveries in the 44th over.

SUMMARY, 1996–97 (SOUTH AFRICA)

	Mts	Overs	Mdns	Runs	Wicks	Ave	BB	4w	RpO
All limited-overs matches	8	73.1	2	366	14	26.14	2/36	–	5.00
One-Day Internationals	6	54.1	2	272	10	27.20	2/36	–	5.02

1997

AUSTRALIA IN ENGLAND

97. Australia v Northamptonshire, at County Ground, Northampton, 17 May 1997.

SCORES

AUSTRALIA 232 (47.4 overs) (M. A. Taylor 76); NORTHAMPTONSHIRE 134 for 5 wickets (35 overs) (M. B. Loye 65 not out). *Australia won by 17 runs (Duckworth–Lewis method).*

S. K. WARNE

6–0–21–2. Dismissed: A. L. Penberthy c M. E. Waugh 19; T. C. Walton st A. C. Gilchrist 2.

---

98. Australia v Worcestershire, at New Road, Worcester, 18 May 1997.

SCORES

AUSTRALIA 121 (35 overs) (D. A. Leatherdale 5/10, G. R. Haynes 4/40); WORCESTERSHIRE 123 for 5 wickets (38.5 overs). *Worcestershire won by five wickets.*

S. K. WARNE

10–1–36–2. Dismissed: W. P. C. Weston c B. P. Julian 12; V. S. Solanki c A. C. Gilchrist 6.

99/74. **Australia v England** (Texaco Trophy 1st match),
at Headingley, Leeds, 22 May 1997.
Scores
Australia 170 for 8 wickets (50 overs); England 175 for 4 wickets
(40.1 overs) (G. P. Thorpe 75 not out, A. J. Hollioake 66 not out).
England won by six wickets.
S. K. Warne
10–0–46–0.

Warne was wicketless in his first ODI in England.

100/75. **Australia v England** (Texaco Trophy 2nd match),
at The Oval, London, 24 May 1997.
Scores
Australia 249 for 6 wickets (50 overs) (M. G. Bevan 108 not out,
A. C. Gilchrist 53); England 253 for 4 wickets (48.2 overs)
M. A. Atherton 113 not out, A. J. Hollioake 53 not out).
England won by six wickets.
S. K. Warne
10–0–39–1. Dismissed: A. J. Stewart b 40.

101/76. **Australia v England** (Texaco Trophy 3rd match),
at Lord's, London, 25 May 1997.
Scores
Australia 269 (49.2 overs) (M. E. Waugh 95; D. Gough 5/44);
England 270 for 4 wickets (49 overs) (A. J. Stewart 79, B. C. Hollioake 63,
J. P. Crawley 52). *England won by six wickets.*
S. K. Warne
9–0–44–0.

SUMMARY, 1997 (England)

	Mts	Overs	Mdns	Runs	Wicks	Ave	BB	4w	RpO
All limited-overs matches	5	45	1	186	5	37.20	2/21	–	4.13
One-Day Internationals	3	29	0	129	1	129.00	1/39	–	4.44

1997–98

IN AUSTRALIA

102. **Victoria v New South Wales**, at North Sydney Oval,
26 October 1997.
SCORES
NEW SOUTH WALES 275 for 9 wickets (M. J. Slater 68, M. G. Bevan 62
not out, M. E. Waugh 57); VICTORIA 238 (44.4 overs) (D. S. Berry 64 not out,
B. J. Hodge 53). *New South Wales won by 37 runs*.
S. K. WARNE (capt.)
8–1–43–3. Dismissed: M. J. Slater c D. M. Jones 68, M. E. Waugh
c L. D. Harper 57, S. Lee b 0.

Warne took 3/1 in nine balls.

103/77. **Australia v South Africa** (World Series 1st match),
at Sydney Cricket Ground, 4 December 1997 (day/night).
SCORES
SOUTH AFRICA 200 (50 overs); AUSTRALIA 133 (38 overs) (P. L. Symcox 4/28).
South Africa won by 67 runs.
S. K. WARNE
10–0–33–0.

240

Warne was dismissed lbw by Daryll Cullinan, enjoying a rare stint at the crease. Earlier, Warne struck Pat Symcox for the only six of the match. Wicketkeeper Adam Gilchrist made his ODI debut on Australian soil.

104/78. Australia v New Zealand (World Series 3rd match), at Adelaide Oval, 7 December 1997 (day/night).

SCORES

NEW ZEALAND 260 for 7 wickets (N. J. Astle 66, S. P. Fleming 61); AUSTRALIA 263 for 7 wickets (49.4 overs) (M. E. Waugh 104, M. J. Di Venuto 77). *Australia won by three wickets.*

S. K. WARNE

10–0–48–3. Dismissed: M. J. Horne lbw 31; C. D. McMillan c I. J. Harvey 43; R. G. Twose c M. G. Bevan 26.

Warne's tenth over, the 50th of the innings, went for ten.

105/79. Australia v South Africa (World Series 4th match), at Melbourne Cricket Ground, 9 December 1997 (day/night).

SCORES

SOUTH AFRICA 170 for 8 wickets (50 overs); AUSTRALIA 125 (39.1 overs) (L. Klusener 5/24). *South Africa won by 45 runs.*

S. K. WARNE

10–0–36–0.

---

106. Australia v Australia 'A', at Sydney Cricket Ground, 14 December 1997 (day/night).

SCORES

AUSTRALIA 'A' 203 for 9 wickets (50 overs) (D. S. Lehmann 84 not out); AUSTRALIA 206 for 7 wickets (49 overs) (R. T. Ponting 79 not out). *Australia won by three wickets.*

S. K. WARNE

10–2–36–2. Dismissed: A. M. Stuart c M. L. Hayden 3; S. H. Cook c A. J. Bichel 1.

107/80. Australia v New Zealand (World Series 6th match), at Melbourne Cricket Ground, 17 December 1997 (day/night).

SCORES

NEW ZEALAND 141 (49.3 overs) (C. Z. Harris 62 not out); AUSTRALIA 142 for 4 wickets (38.5 overs) (R. T. Ponting 60 not out; C. L. Cairns 4/40). *Australia won by six wickets.*

S. K. WARNE

10–0–25–1. Dismissed: C. D. McMillan c I. J. Harvey 9.

108/81. Australia v South Africa (World Series 8th match), at Brisbane Cricket Ground, 11 January 1998 (day/night).

SCORES

AUSTRALIA 235 for 8 wickets (50 overs); SOUTH AFRICA 236 for 5 wickets (47.3 overs) (G. Kirsten 89, W. J. Cronje 59 not out). *South Africa won by five wickets.*

S. K. WARNE

10–0–47–0.

109/82. Australia v New Zealand (World Series 9th match), at Sydney Cricket Ground, 14 January 1998 (day/night).

SCORES

AUSTRALIA 250 (47.5 overs) (R. T. Ponting 84, D. S. Lehmann 52; S. B. O'Connor 4/51); NEW ZEALAND 119 (33.1 overs). *Australia won by 131 runs.*

S. K. WARNE (capt.)

6.1–0–19–2. Dismissed: D. J. Nash b 5; D. L. Vettori c M. G. Bevan 4.

Warne was stand-in captain for the first time, replacing Steve Waugh, who'd hurt his hip while bowling in the previous ODI in Brisbane.

110/83. Australia v New Zealand (World Series 12th match), at Melbourne Cricket Ground, 21 January 1998 (day/night).

SCORES

AUSTRALIA 251 for 4 wickets (50 overs) (R. T. Ponting 100); NEW ZEALAND 253 for 6 wickets (49.1 overs) (S. P. Fleming 116 not out). *New Zealand won by four wickets.*

S. K. WARNE
8.1–0–50–1. Dismissed: C. D. McMillan lbw 26.

Chris Harris hit the winning runs, a four through midwicket, from the bowling of Warne at the start of the final over.

111/84. Australia v South Africa (World Series 1st Final),
at Melbourne Cricket Ground, 23 January 1998 (day/night).
SCORES
SOUTH AFRICA 241 for 9 wickets (50 overs) (G. Kirsten 70);
AUSTRALIA 235 (49.5 overs) (M. G. Bevan 57, S. R. Waugh 53).
South Africa won by six runs.
S. K. WARNE
10–1–52–3. Dismissed: D. J. Cullinan st A. C. Gilchrist 26;
S. M. Pollock c M. G. Bevan 36; B. M. McMillan lbw 2.

Warne again dismissed Daryll Cullinan in an extraordinary opening over, the eighth of the match. The scorebook entry read: 2 4 . W 2 X . , Cullinan, in death-or-glory tactics, being stranded by Warne's offside slider, after hitting eight runs from Warne's first four legal deliveries.

Warne also dismissed Shaun Pollock but not before he'd flat-batted him over the mid-on fence for the only six of the game. Brian McMillan was given out to a flipper which he'd snicked onto his pad.

112/85. Australia v South Africa (World Series 2nd Final),
at Sydney Cricket Ground, 26 January 1998 (day/night).
SCORES
SOUTH AFRICA 228 for 6 wickets (50 overs) (J. N. Rhodes 82 not out,
W. J. Cronje 73); AUSTRALIA 229 for 3 wickets (41.5 overs)
(A. C. Gilchrist 100). *Australia won by seven wickets.*
S. K. WARNE
10–0–52–1. Dismissed: W. J. Cronje c M. G. Bevan 73.

The second final was delayed for 24 hours because of rain. Steve Waugh opened Australia's bowling with brother Mark. Hansie Cronje lifted Warne over square leg onto the roof of the Bill O'Reilly Stand.

113/86. Australia v South Africa (World Series 3rd Final),
at Sydney Cricket Ground, 27 January 1998 (day/night).
SCORES
AUSTRALIA 247 for 7 wickets (50 overs) (R. T. Ponting 76, S. R. Waugh 71);
SOUTH AFRICA 233 (48.1 overs). *Australia won by 14 runs*.
S. K. WARNE
9.1–0–43–1. Dismissed: W. J. Cronje st A. C. Gilchrist 5.

Protea No. 11 Paul Adams took 14 runs from Warne's ninth over, the
Australians winning the final series 2–1, despite being outplayed for
much of the qualifying period.

SUMMARY, 1997–98 (AUSTRALIA)

	Mts	Overs	Mdns	Runs	Wicks	Ave	BB	4w	RpO
All limited-overs matches	12	111.3	6	484	17	28.46	3/43	–	4.34
One-Day Internationals	10	93.3	3	405	12	33.75	3/48	–	4.33
Australia v Australia 'A'	1	10	2	36	2	18.00	2/36	–	3.60
Mercantile Mutual Cup	1	8	1	43	3	14.33	3/43	–	5.37

AUSTRALIA IN INDIA

114/87. Australia v India (Pepsi Cup 1st match),
at Jawaharlal Nehru Stadium, Cochin, 1 April 1998.
SCORES
INDIA 309 for 5 wickets (50 overs) (A. Jadeja 105 not out,
M. Azharuddin 82, H. H. Kanitkar 57); AUSTRALIA 268 (45.5 overs)
(M. G. Bevan 65, A. C. Gilchrist 61; S. R. Tendulkar 5/32). *India won
by 41 runs*.
S. K. WARNE
10–0–42–0.

The 40°C heat and accompanying humidity in Cochin resulted in
numerous Australian casualties. Scorer Mike Walsh said the conditions were so oppressive he couldn't even hold a pencil!

115/88. Australia v Zimbabwe (Pepsi Cup 2nd match),
at Sardar Patel Stadium, Motera, Ahmedabad, 3 April 1998.

SCORES

AUSTRALIA 252 for 7 wickets (50 overs) (M. G. Bevan 65, R. T. Ponting 53);
ZIMBABWE 239 (49.5 overs) (A. D. R. Campbell 102, M. W. Goodwin 55).
Australia won by 13 runs.

S. K. WARNE

10–0–45–2. Dismissed: G. W. Flower c M. G. Bevan 35; M. W. Goodwin b 55.

In 43°C heat, Warne triggered a collapse when he bowled Murray
Goodwin around his legs, Zimbabwe losing 9/96 after seeming well
placed at 1/143 chasing 253 to win.

116/89. Australia v India (Pepsi Cup 4th match),
at Green Park, Kanpur, 7 April 1998.

SCORES

AUSTRALIA 222 for 9 wickets (50 overs) (R. T. Ponting 84;
A. B. Agarkar 4/46); INDIA 223 for 4 wickets (44.3 overs)
(S. R. Tendulkar 100, S. C. Ganguly 72). ***India won by six wickets***.

S. K. WARNE

9–0–43–1. Dismissed: S. R. Tendulkar c sub (D. R. Martyn) 100.

Sachin Tendulkar struck 7 sixes in a rare display, his century coming
from just 88 balls. He and the gifted Saurav Ganguly added 175 for
the first wicket.

117/90. Australia v Zimbabwe (Pepsi Cup 6th match),
at Feroz Shah Kotla Ground, Delhi, 11 April 1998.

SCORES

AUSTRALIA 294 for 3 wickets (50 overs) (R. T. Ponting 145, M. E. Waugh 87);
ZIMBABWE 278 for 9 wickets (G. W. Flower 89, A. Flower 73). ***Australia
won by 16 runs***.

S. K. WARNE

10–0–54–1. Dismissed: G. W. Flower b 89.

Before bowling top scorer Grant Flower with a flipper, Warne
threatened to run him out 'Mankad' style. With 1/54, he was
expensive and his battle-weary shoulder was becoming a genuine
concern.

118/91. **Australia v India** (Pepsi Cup Final),
at Feroz Shah Kotla Ground, Delhi, 14 April 1998.
SCORES
INDIA 227 (49.3 overs); AUSTRALIA 231 for 6 wickets (48.4 overs)
(M. G. Bevan 75 not out, S. R. Waugh 57). *Australia won by four wickets*.
S. K. WARNE
10–0–35–1. Dismissed: A. B. Agarkar c S. R. Waugh 4.

Batting at No. 5, Warne was bowled by a waist-high full toss by
Venkat Prasad, the ball just flicking his off bail after he'd made 14
from 14 balls in typically flamboyant fashion.

SUMMARY, 1997–98 (INDIA)

	Mts	Overs	Mdns	Runs	Wicks	Ave	BB	4w	RpO
One-Day Internationals	5	49	0	219	5	43.80	2/45	–	4.46

AUSTRALIA IN SHARJAH, UNITED ARAB EMIRATES

119/92. **Australia v New Zealand** (Coca-Cola Cup 2nd match),
at Sharjah C. A. Stadium, 18 April 1998 (day/night).
SCORES
NEW ZEALAND 159 (48.4 overs) (S. P. Fleming 59; D. W. Fleming 4/28);
AUSTRALIA 160 for 4 wickets (A. C. Gilchrist 57, R. T. Ponting 52).
Australia won by six wickets.
S. K. WARNE
10–1–28–2. Dismissed: M. J. Horne c T. M. Moody 14;
C. D. McMillan c D. S. Lehmann 1.

Ignoring advice to return to Australia for shoulder surgery, Warne
took his place for the final leg of the tour, the Coca-Cola Cup in
Sharjah and, in Game 1, produced his most economical figures of the
extended campaign.

120/93. **Australia v India** (Coca-Cola Cup 3rd match),
at Sharjah C. A. Stadium, 19 April 1998 (day/night).
SCORES
AUSTRALIA 264 for 9 wickets (50 overs) (M. G. Bevan 58);
INDIA 206 (44 overs) (S. R. Tendulkar 80; S. R. Waugh 4/40).
Australia won by 58 runs.
S. K. WARNE
8–1–37–1. Dismissed: A. Jadeja st A. C. Gilchrist 14.

Warne's 32-run late-innings stand with Damien Martyn (30) came in just 13 minutes. He injured his shoulder during the game and could only throw underarm.

121/94. **Australia v New Zealand** (Coca-Cola Cup 5th match),
at Sharjah C. A. Stadium, 21 April 1998 (day/night).
SCORES
NEW ZEALAND 259 for 5 wickets (50 overs) (N. J. Astle 78, C. L. Cairns 56);
AUSTRALIA 261 for 5 wickets (47.5 overs) (T. M. Moody 63,
M. G. Bevan 57). ***Australia won by five wickets.***
S. K. WARNE
10–0–56–1. Dismissed: C. L. Cairns st A. C. Gilchrist 56.

122/95. **Australia v India** (Coca-Cola Cup 6th match),
at Sharjah C. A. Stadium, 22 April 1998 (day/night).
SCORES
AUSTRALIA 284 for 7 wickets (50 overs) (M. G. Bevan 101 not out,
M. E. Waugh 81); INDIA 250 for 5 wickets (46 overs)
(S. R. Tendulkar 143). ***Australia won by 26 runs.***
S. K. WARNE
9–0–39–0.

India's original target of 285 was revised to 276 from 46 overs after a sandstorm stopped play. Sachin Tendulkar's 143 included 5 sixes and 9 fours. He faced just 131 balls.

123/96. **Australia v India** (Coca-Cola Cup Final),
at Sharjah C. A. Stadium, 24 April 1998 (day/night).
SCORES
AUSTRALIA 272 for 9 wickets (50 overs) (S. R. Waugh 70, D. S. Lehmann 70);
INDIA 275 for 4 wickets (48.3 overs) (S. R. Tendulkar 134,
M. Azharuddin 58). *India won by six wickets*.
S. K. WARNE
10–0–61–0.

In his final match for six months, Warne's ten overs cost 61 as India won the final, Sachin Tendulkar again awesome. On his 25th birthday, the Mumbai Master made his 15th ODI century at a run a ball and was named batsman of the series. Within a week Warne was back in Melbourne for the operation he'd been putting off for years.

SUMMARY, 1997–98 (SHARJAH, UAE)

	Mts	Overs	Mdns	Runs	Wicks	Ave	BB	4w	RpO
One-Day Internationals	5	47	2	221	4	55.25	2/28	–	4.70

1998–99

124. Victoria v New South Wales, at Melbourne Cricket Ground,
8 November 1998.
SCORES
VICTORIA 163 (50 overs) (M. P. Mott 53; S. C. G. MacGill 4/29); NEW SOUTH
WALES 134 (43.4 overs) (G. C. Rummans 75). *Victoria won by 29 runs*.
S. K. WARNE (capt.)
8–1–23–1. Dismissed: S. M. Thompson c M. P. Mott 5.

After his wintertime shoulder surgery, Warne bowled only eight overs
in his first return game. Batting at No. 4, his 24 was third-top score.

125/97. Australia v England (C&U Series 1st match),
at Brisbane Cricket Ground, 10 January 1999 (day/night).
SCORES
ENGLAND 178 for 8 wickets (50 overs); AUSTRALIA 145 for 9 wickets
(36 overs) (M. G. Bevan 56 not out; A. D. Mullally 4/18).
England won on faster run-rate.
S. K. WARNE (capt.)
10–0–42–0.

249

Having missed the Commonwealth Games tournament in Kuala Lumpur and the Wills International Cup on the subcontinent, Warne was impatient to return and re-establish himself ahead of fellow leg-spinner Stuart MacGill. Far from his best in his comeback Test, he was also rusty at the start of the one-day series, conceding more than four an over at the 'Gabba. He captained the team in the absence of Steve Waugh (injured hamstring).

126/98. **Australia v Sri Lanka** (C&U Series 3rd match), at Sydney Cricket Ground, 13 January 1999 (day/night).
SCORES
SRI LANKA 259 for 9 wickets (50 overs) (H. P. Tillekeratne 73, S. T. Jayasuriya 65); AUSTRALIA 260 for 2 wickets (46.1 overs) (A. C. Gilchrist 131, M. E. Waugh 63). **Australia won by eight wickets**.
S. K. WARNE (capt.)
10–1–44–2 Dismissed: R. S. Kaluwitharana b 32; M. S. Atapattu c M. E. Waugh 18.

The wicket of Romesh Kaluwitharana, bowled around his legs, was a confidence booster. After having Marvan Atapattu caught, Warne would have had a third wicket, too, but for a caught behind appeal from the faintest of edges from Hashan Tillekeratne being disallowed.

127/99. **Australia v England** (C&U Series 4th match), at Melbourne Cricket Ground, 15 January 1999 (day/night).
SCORES
ENGLAND 178 (43.2 overs) (G. D. McGrath 4/54); AUSTRALIA 182 for 1 wicket (39.2 overs) (M. E. Waugh 83 not out, R. T. Ponting 75 not out).
Australia won by nine wickets.
S. K. WARNE (capt.)
10–0–44–1. Dismissed: N. V. Knight c M. E. Waugh 27.

The fifth-largest MCG cricketing crowd on record, 82 299, saw for the first time at Australian level Warne captain in front of his home-town crowd.

128/100. **Australia v England** (C&U Series 5th match),
at Sydney Cricket Ground, 17 January 1999 (day/night).
SCORES
ENGLAND 282 for 4 wickets (50 overs) (G. A. Hick 108, N. Hussain 93);
AUSTRALIA 275 for 6 wickets (50 overs) (M. E. Waugh 85,
D. S. Lehmann 76). *England won by seven runs*.
S. K. WARNE
10–0–57–0.

One of centurion Graeme Hick's leg-side hits saw Warne lifted onto the top of the Bill O'Reilly Stand during his 100th appearance at ODI level.

129/101. **Australia v Sri Lanka** (C&U Series 7th match),
at Bellerive Oval, Hobart, 21 January 1999.
SCORES
AUSTRALIA 210 for 9 wickets (50 overs) (M. E. Waugh 65,
D. S. Lehmann 51); SRI LANKA 211 for 7 wickets (49.3 overs)
(M. S. Atapattu 82, R. S. Kaluwitharana 54). *Sri Lanka won by three wickets*.
S. K. WARNE
10–0–45–3. Dismissed: U. D. U. Chandana c A. C. Dale 8; H. P. Tillekeratne
c sub (D. R. Martyn) 3; R. S. Mahanama b 4.

Warne's first four overs cost 22 before he swapped ends and immediately improved.

130/102. **Australia v Sri Lanka** (C&U Series 9th match),
at Adelaide Oval, 24 January 1999 (day/night).
SCORES
AUSTRALIA 270 (50 overs) (M. E. Waugh 57); SRI LANKA 190 (41.4 overs)
(R. S. Mahanama 55; G. D. McGrath 5/40). *Australia won by 80 runs*.
S. K. WARNE (capt.)
9–0–53–0.

Warne bowled nothing but leg-breaks, but struggled to impart his renowned side-spin on the ball.

131/103. Australia v England (C&U Series 10th match),
at Adelaide Oval, 26 January 1999 (day/night).
SCORES
AUSTRALIA 239 for 8 wickets (50 overs) (M. E. Waugh 65, D. R. Martyn
59 not out, D. S. Lehmann 51); ENGLAND 223 (48.3 overs) (G. A. Hick 109).
Australia won by 16 runs.
S. K. WARNE (capt.)
10–0–39–3. Dismissed: N. V. Knight c & b 43; M. A. Ealham
c & b 4; D. Gough c A. C. Dale 2.

Warne's best performance of the summer, in which he concentrated
on rotating his shoulder through the whole action. Coming back in
the 44th over, he ensured Australia a narrow victory.

132/104. Australia v Sri Lanka (C&U Series 12th match),
at WACA Ground, Perth, 31 January 1999 (day/night).
SCORES
AUSTRALIA 274 for 7 wickets (50 overs) (M. G. Bevan 72 not out); SRI LANKA
229 (46.3 overs) (S. T. Jayasuriya 50 ret. hurt). *Australia won by 45 runs.*
S. K. WARNE (capt.)
10–0–53–3. Dismissed: H. P. Tillekeratne c R. T. Ponting 30;
W. P. U. J. C. Vaas c R. T. Ponting 20; D. P. M. Jayawardene
c A. C. Dale 36.

133/105. Australia v England (C&U Series 14th match),
at Sydney Cricket Ground, 5 February 1999 (day/night).
SCORES
ENGLAND 210 for 8 wickets (50 overs); AUSTRALIA 211 for 6 wickets
(47 overs). *Australia won by four wickets.*
S. K. WARNE (capt.)
10–0–48–1. Dismissed: M. A. Ealham c M. G. Bevan 33.

134/106. Australia v Sri Lanka (C&U Series 15th match),
at Melbourne Cricket Ground, 7 February 1999.
SCORES
AUSTRALIA 310 for 8 wickets (50 overs) (A. C. Gilchrist 154,

R. T. Ponting 61); SRI LANKA 267 (47.1 overs) (A. Gunewardene 75,
R. S. Kaluwitharana 68; S. Lee 5/33). *Australia won by 43 runs*.
S. K. WARNE (capt.)
8–1–51–1. Dismissed: R. S. Kaluwitharana c D. R. Martyn 68.

On a roped-off MCG, one of Warne's overs went for 19 courtesy of the 'Pocket Rocket', Romesh Kaluwitharana.

135/107. **Australia v England** (C&U Series 1st Final),
at Sydney Cricket Ground, 10 February 1999 (day/night).
SCORES
AUSTRALIA 232 for 8 wickets (50 overs) (M. G. Bevan 69 not out);
ENGLAND 222 (49.2 overs) (N. Hussain 58; G. D. McGrath 4/45).
Australia won by ten runs.
S. K. Warne (capt.)
10–0–40–2. Dismissed: N. Hussain st A. C. Gilchrist 58; A. J. Hollioake lbw 0.

Warne's dismissal of Nasser Hussain stumped and Adam Hollioake lbw in consecutive deliveries changed the match fortunes.

136/108. **Australia v England** (C&U Series 2nd Final),
at Melbourne Cricket Ground, 13 February 1999 (day/night).
SCORES
AUSTRALIA 272 for 5 wickets (50 overs) (D. S. Lehmann 71, D. R. Martyn 57,
A. C. Gilchrist 52); ENGLAND 110 (31.5 overs). *Australia won by 162 runs*.
S. K. Warne (capt.)
5.5–0–16–3. Dismissed: V. J. Wells b 23; M. A. Ealham b 12;
A. D. Mullally lbw 9.

Australia won the title and its seventh match in a row under Warne's captaincy. He finished the match with his best ball of the summer, a flipper which caught England's No. 11 Alan Mullally lbw.

SUMMARY, 1998–99 (AUSTRALIA)

	Mts	Overs	Mdns	Runs	Wicks	Ave	BB	4w	RpO
All limited-overs matches	13	120.5	3	555	20	27.75	3/16	–	4.59
One-Day Internationals	12	112.5	2	532	19	28.00	3/16	–	4.71
Mercantile Mutual Cup	1	8	1	23	1	23.00	1/23	–	2.87

AUSTRALIA IN WEST INDIES

137/109. Australia v West Indies (1st One-Day International),
at Arnos Vale, Kingstown, St Vincent, 11 April 1999.
SCORES
WEST INDIES 209 (48.1 overs) (S. L. Campbell 62); AUSTRALIA 165
(41.5 overs) (H. R. Bryan 4/24). *West Indies won by 44 runs*.
S. K. WARNE
10–3–30–2. Dismissed: K. L. T. Arthurton st A. C. Gilchrist 10;
H. R. Bryan lbw 0.

Playing his first game after his controversial axing from the Test team
in Antigua, Warne's final three overs were maidens.

138/110. Australia v West Indies (2nd One-Day International),
at Queen's Park, St George's, Grenada, 14 April 1999.
SCORES
AUSTRALIA 288 for 4 wickets (50 overs) (D. S. Lehmann 110 not out,
M. G. Bevan 72 not out); WEST INDIES 242 (47.3 overs). *Australia won
by 48 runs*.
S. K. WARNE
10–2–39–3. Dismissed: J. C. Adams b 40; S. C. Williams c sub
(T. M. Moody) 25; H. R. Bryan lbw 6.

West Indies newcomer Hendy Bryan joined the growing list of batsmen to be trapped by Warne's flipper.

139/111. Australia v West Indies (3rd One-Day International),
at Queen's Park Oval, Port-of-Spain, Trinidad, 17 April 1999.
SCORES
AUSTRALIA 242 for 7 wickets (50 overs) (M. E. Waugh 74);
WEST INDIES 244 for 5 wickets (49 overs) (J. C. Adams 82,
S. L. Campbell 64, C. L. Hooper 56). *West Indies won by five wickets*.
S. K. WARNE
9–0–59–0.

140/112. **Australia v West Indies** (4th One-Day International),
at Queen's Park Oval, Port-of-Spain, Trinidad, 18 April 1999.
SCORES
AUSTRALIA 189 for 8 wickets (50 overs) (M. G. Bevan 59 not out;
M. Dillon 4/20); WEST INDIES 169 (46.2 overs). *Australia won by 20 runs*.
S. K. WARNE
10–1–35–3. Dismissed: B. C. Lara b 6; S. C. Williams b 0;
C. E. L. Ambrose lbw 4.

Continuing his improvement with the bat, Warne made 29 and shared a match-winning 77-run stand from 127 balls, with Michael Bevan, for the ninth wicket.

141/113. **Australia v West Indies** (5th One-Day International),
at Bourda, Georgetown, Guyana, 21 April 1999.
SCORES
WEST INDIES 173 for 5 wickets (30 overs); AUSTRALIA 173 for 7 wickets
(30 overs) (S. R. Waugh 72 not out). *Tied*.
S. K. WARNE
6–0–35–2. Dismissed: J. C. Adams b 7; C. L. Hooper st A. C. Gilchrist 8.

A 54-run stand for the eighth wicket with Steve Waugh helped force a controversial tie.

142/114. **Australia v West Indies** (6th One-Day International),
at Kensington Oval, Bridgetown, Barbados, 24 April 1999.
SCORES
WEST INDIES 249 for 8 wickets (50 overs) (R. D. Jacobs 68);
AUSTRALIA 253 for 6 wickets (48.3 overs) (A. C. Gilchrist 64).
Australia won by four wickets.
S. K. WARNE
10–1–28–3. Dismissed: S. L. Campbell c A. C. Gilchrist 24;
R. D. Jacobs c B. P. Julian 68; S. C. Williams st A. C. Gilchrist 9.

Warne bowled at first change.

143/115. **Australia v West Indies** (7th One-Day International),
at Kensington Oval, Bridgetown, Barbados, 25 April 1999.
SCORES
AUSTRALIA 252 for 9 wickets (50 overs) (T. M. Moody 50 not out);
WEST INDIES 197 for 2 wickets (37 overs) (S. L. Campbell 62,
R. D. Jacobs 54). *West Indies won on faster run-rate*.
S. K. WARNE
8–3–28–0.

Warne made 20 and shared a 50-run ninth-wicket stand with Tom
Moody. Crowd misbehaviour, however, overshadowed the on-field
action. Hundreds of bottles were thrown onto the field in an angry
protest against local hero Sherwin Campbell's run-out after a mid-
pitch collision with Brendon Julian. Leading his players from the
ground into the safety of the Challenor Stand, one bottle missed Steve
Waugh's head by only centimetres. Waugh recalled Campbell and the
game finished without further incident.

SUMMARY, 1998–99 (WEST INDIES)

	Mts	Overs	Mdns	Runs	Wicks	Ave	BB	4w	RpO
One-Day Internationals	7	63	10	254	13	19.53	3/28	–	4.03

1999

AUSTRALIA IN ENGLAND – WORLD CUP

144. Australia v Glamorgan, at Sophia Gardens, Cardiff, 8 May 1999.

SCORES

GLAMORGAN 21 for 2 wickets (10 overs); AUSTRALIA did not bat. **No result**.

S. K. WARNE

Did not bowl.

---

145. **Australia v Worcestershire**, at New Road, Worcester, 10 May 1999.

SCORES

WORCESTERSHIRE 162 for 7 wickets (44 overs); AUSTRALIA 181 for 4 wickets (34.1 overs) (A. C. Gilchrist 86, M. E. Waugh 64). **Australia won by six wickets (Duckworth–Lewis method)**.

S. K. WARNE

10–2–27–2. Dismissed: P. R. Pollard lbw 14; K. R. Spiring st A. C. Gilchrist 19.

Warne took a wicket with his third ball to finish with 2/27 from a full ten overs. Worcestershire's 7/162 from 44 overs was adjusted up to a revised target of 178 from 44 overs, the match referee ruling that

Worcestershire had been denied several overs of slogging by a rain interruption in the middle of its innings.

---

146. **Australia v Somerset**, at County Ground, Taunton, 12 May 1999.

SCORES

AUSTRALIANS 243 for 5 wickets (50 overs) (M. G. Bevan 68 not out); SOMERSET 208 (45.2 overs). *Australia won by 32 runs (Duckworth–Lewis method).*

S. K. WARNE

10–3–35–3. Dismissed: M. Burns lbw 38; P. C. L. Holloway c M. E. Waugh 40; R. J. Turner c & b 13.

147/116. **Australia v Scotland** (World Cup 4th match), at New Road, Worcester, 16 May 1999.

SCORES

SCOTLAND 181 for 7 wickets (50 overs); AUSTRALIA 182 for 4 wickets (46.5 overs) (M. E. Waugh 67). *Australia won by six wickets.*

S. K. WARNE

10–0–39–3. Dismissed: M. J. de G. Alingham st A. C. Gilchrist 3; G. M. Hamilton b 33; J. E. Brinkley b 33.

Began his second World Cup in impressive style. Scotland's English professional, left-hander Gavin Hamilton, twice played the reverse sweep on his way to top score.

148/117. **Australia v New Zealand** (World Cup 11th match), at Sophia Gardens, Cardiff, 20 May 1999.

SCORES

AUSTRALIA 213 for 8 wickets (50 overs) (D. S. Lehmann 76; G. I. Allott 4/37); NEW ZEALAND 214 for 5 wickets (45.2 overs) (R. G. Twose 80 not out, C. L. Cairns 60). *New Zealand won by five wickets.*

S. K. WARNE

10–1–44–1. Dismissed: C. D. McMillan c D. W. Fleming 29.

Was expensive in his second spell.

149/118. **Australia v Pakistan** (World Cup 15th match),
at Headingley, Leeds, 23 May 1999.
SCORES
PAKISTAN 275 for 8 wickets (50 overs) (Inzamam-ul-Haq 81,
Abdur Razzak 60); AUSTRALIA 265 (49.5 overs) (M. G. Bevan 61;
Wasim Akram 4/40). *Pakistan won by ten runs*.
S. K. WARNE
10–0–50–1. Dismissed: Abdur Razzaq c D. W. Fleming 60.

Pakistan scored 108 runs in happy hour as Australia lost its second
one-day game in a row.

150/119. **Australia v Bangladesh** (World Cup 22nd match),
at Riverside Ground, Chester-le-Street, 27 May 1999.
SCORES
BANGLADESH 178 for 7 wickets (50 overs) (Minhazul Abedin 53 not out);
AUSTRALIA 181 for 3 wickets (19.5 overs) (A. C. Gilchrist 63,
T. M. Moody 56 not out). *Australia won by seven wickets*.
S. K. WARNE
10–2–18–1. Dismissed: Akram Khan lbw 0.

Conceded fewer than 20 runs from his ten overs for only the fourth
time in 119 ODIs.

151/120. **Australia v West Indies** (World Cup 27th match),
at Old Trafford, Manchester, 30 May 1999.
SCORES
WEST INDIES 110 (46.4 overs) (G. D. McGrath 5/14); AUSTRALIA 111 for
4 wickets (40.4 overs). *Australia won by six wickets*.
S. K. WARNE
10–4–11–3. Dismissed: S. Chanderpaul b 16; C. E. L. Ambrose lbw 1;
R. D. King lbw 1.

Used at third change, Warne produced one of his finest-ever one-day
efforts. Economy-wise, it was second only to one Australian, Mick
Malone's 2/9 against the West Indies in Melbourne in 1981–82.

152/121. **Australia v India** (World Cup 31st match),
at The Oval, London, 4 June 1999.
SCORES
AUSTRALIA 282 for 6 wickets (50 overs) (M. E. Waugh 83); INDIA 205
(48.2 overs) (A. Jadeja 100 not out, R. R. Singh 75). **Australia won
by 77 runs**.
S. K. WARNE
6.2–0–49–0.

His sixth over cost 21 runs, including 3 sixes, two by Robin Singh
and another by Ajay Jadeja.

153/122. **Australia v Zimbabwe** (World Cup 35th match),
at Lord's, London, 9 June 1999.
SCORES
AUSTRALIA 303 for 4 wickets (50 overs) (M. E. Waugh 104, S. R. Waugh 62);
ZIMBABWE 259 for 6 wickets (50 overs) (N. C. Johnson 132). **Australia won
by 44 runs**.
S. K. WARNE
9–0–55–1. Dismissed: D. P. Viljoen st A. C. Gilchrist 5.

Zimbabwe left-hander Neil Johnson hit Warne for 4 fours in an over,
all to big drives. Unhappy with his form roller-coaster, Warne seriously contemplated retirement.

154/123. **Australia v South Africa** (World Cup 39th match),
at Headingley, Leeds, 13 June 1999.
SCORES
SOUTH AFRICA 271 for 7 wickets (50 overs) (H. H. Gibbs 101,
D. J. Cullinan 50); AUSTRALIA 272 for 5 wickets (49.4 overs)
(S. R. Waugh 120 not out, R. T. Ponting 69). **Australia won by five wickets**.
S. K. WARNE
10–1–33–2. Dismissed: D. J. Cullinan b 50; W. J. Cronje lbw 0.

Australia's sudden-death victory was set up by Steve Waugh's counter-
punching 120 not out, having been bizarrely dropped at 56 by
Herschelle Gibbs at forward square leg. Gibbs was in the process of

tossing the ball skyward in celebration when it slipped from his grasp, the umpires ruling that he had not controlled the ball at any stage. At the end of the over, Waugh, ever poker-faced, said to Gibbs: 'Do you realise you've just cost your team the game?'

Later Waugh explained that the pair had staged a running battle that day. 'He had his say and I had my say. It was going back and forth. We both got hundreds so we both had pretty good days. In the end he lost out because he had the chance to have a victory over myself and the team, and threw it away – literally.'

155/124. **Australia v South Africa** (World Cup 2nd Semi-Final), at Edgbaston, Birmingham, 17 June 1999.

Scores

Australia 213 (49.2 overs) (M. G. Bevan 65, S. R. Waugh 56; S. M. Pollock 5/36); South Africa 213 (49.4 overs) (J. H. Kallis 53; S. K. Warne 4/29). *Tied*.

S. K. Warne

10–4–29–4. Dismissed: G. Kirsten b 18; H. H. Gibbs b 30; W. J. Cronje c M. E. Waugh 0; J. H. Kallis c S. R. Waugh 53. Man of the match.

The first tie in 200 World Cup matches was triggered by a marvellous spell from a re-energised Warne. Coming on in the 13th over with South Africa 0/48, Warne changed the face of the game by bowling openers Gary Kirsten and Herschelle Gibbs with big-spinning legbreaks before also dismissing captain Hansie Cronje and top-scorer Jacques Kallis.

The run-out of South African No. 11 Allan Donald, via Mark Waugh to Damien Fleming to Adam Gilchrist, lifted Australia into the World Cup final, thanks to its slightly superior run-rate.

In a match captain Steve Waugh claimed was the most exciting of his career, Warne was man of the match in a remarkable solo.

156/125. **Australia v Pakistan** (World Cup Final), at Lord's, London, 20 June 1999.

SCORES

PAKISTAN 132 (39 overs) (**S. K. WARNE** 4/33); AUSTRALIA 133 for 2 wickets (20.1 overs) (A. C. Gilchrist 54). **Australia won by eight wickets.**

S. K. WARNE

9–1–33–4. Dismissed: Ijaz Ahmed b 22; Moin Khan c A. C. Gilchrist 6; Shahid Afridi lbw 13; Wasim Akram c S. R. Waugh 8. Man of the match.

On a hard and bouncy Lord's wicket, Warne again revelled in a strike role, taking four cheap wickets and again being man of the match as Australia won its second World Cup with almost 30 overs to spare.

With 20 wickets for the tournament, at under four runs per over, Warne had created a new Australian record, surpassing Craig McDermott's 18 wickets in the 1987 World Cup. 'I just went out and enjoyed myself,' he said of his dramatic form swing-around.

SUMMARY, 1999 (WORLD CUP IN ENGLAND)

	Mts	Overs	Mdns	Runs	Wicks	Ave	BB	4w	RpO
All limited-overs matches	13	114.2	18	413	25	16.52	4/29	2	3.61
One-Day Internationals	10	94.2	13	361	20	18.05	4/29	2	3.82

By 1997, Warne's hair may not have been as blond, but the ready smile and affable manner told of a young man contented with life as never before.

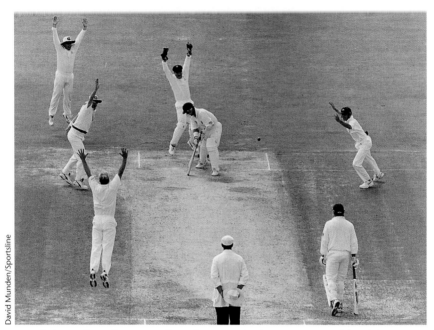

One of Warne's all-time favourite wickets: Alec Stewart bowled by the zoota, a front-of-the-hand floater which died on pitching and went straight through Stewart's defences, Old Trafford, 1997.

With man of the match Ian Healy, Trent Bridge, 1997.

Sergio Dionisio

At times Warne's action has developed little imperfections, but the full shoulder turn and follow-through here are more akin to a fast bowler's finish.

Ken Rainsbury

Warne's coach, Terry Jenner, says Warne's appetite for training has been one of the least-recognised elements of his success.

Patrick Eagar

The victorious Australians, 3–1 winners of the Ashes, 1998–99. Warne, front row at the extreme right, played only the final Test after wintertime shoulder surgery.

Patrick Eagar

Sharing in the World Cup spoils, Lord's 1999. Warne was man of the match in both the semi-final and final.

One of the moments of the 1999 World Cup. Pumped-up and emotional, Warne has just bowled
South Africa's Herschelle Gibbs at Edgbaston on his way to a match-swinging 4/29.

Record-breaking wicket No. 356: umpire Srini Venkataraghavan rules New Zealander Paul Wiseman caught behind by Adam Gilchrist at Eden Park, Auckland, 15 March 2000.

The proudest of moments: Warne leads the Australians from Eden Park, having broken Dennis Lillee's all-time Australian record.

A time for celebrating: Warne with his brother Jason and father Keith after taking wicket No. 356.

1999–2000

AUSTRALIA IN SRI LANKA

157/126. **Australia v Sri Lanka** (Aiwa Cup 1st match),
at Galle International Stadium, 22 August 1999.
SCORES
AUSTRALIA 205 for 9 wickets (43 overs) (S. T. Jayasuriya 5/28);
SRI LANKA 160 (37.4 overs). *Australia won by 51 runs*
(Duckworth–Lewis method).
S. K. WARNE
9–1–39–2. Dismissed: A. S. A. Perera c M. G. Bevan 26; D. N. T. Zoysa
c D. S. Lehmann 4.

The Australians wore black armbands in memory of former West
Australian batsman Mark McPhee, killed in a car crash outside Perth.

158/127. **Australia v India** (Aiwa Cup 2nd match),
at Galle International Stadium, 23 August 1999.
SCORES
INDIA 151 for 7 wickets (38 overs); AUSTRALIA 159 for 2 wickets (29.1 overs)
(A. Symonds 68 not out, A. C. Gilchrist 68). *Australia won by*
eight wickets (Duckworth–Lewis method).

S. K. WARNE
7–0–36–2. Dismissed: A. Jadeja c D. W. Fleming 30; M. S. K. Prasad b 4.

Warne might have conceded almost a run per ball, but the faster delivery which castled Mannava Prasad was a gem.

159/128. **Australia v Sri Lanka** (Aiwa Cup 4th match), at R. Premadasa Stadium, Colombo, 26 August 1999 (day/night).
SCORES
AUSTRALIA 241 for 9 wickets (50 overs) (M. E. Waugh 84);
SRI LANKA 214 (47.1 overs) (L. P. C. Silva 54). *Australia won by 27 runs*.
S. K. WARNE
9–0–51–2. Dismissed: L. P. C. Silva st A. C. Gilchrist 54; A. S. A. Perera
st A. C. Gilchrist 6.

Australia extended its record to ten matches without defeat and guaranteed a place in the Aiwa Cup final.

160/129. **Australia v India** (Aiwa Cup 5th match),
at Sinhalese Sports Club Ground, Colombo, 28 August 1999.
SCORES
AUSTRALIA 252 for 8 wickets (50 overs) (A. C. Gilchrist 77); INDIA 211
(48.3 overs) (R. R. Singh 75, S. Ramesh 71; J. N. Gillespie 4/26).
Australia won by 41 runs.
S. K. WARNE
7–0–41–0.

161/130. **Australia v Sri Lanka** (Aiwa Cup Final), at R. Premadasa Stadium, Colombo, 31 August 1999 (day/night).
SCORES
AUSTRALIA 202 (50 overs); SRI LANKA 208 for 2 wickets (39.3 overs)
(R. S. Kaluwitharana 95 not out). *Sri Lanka won by eight wickets*.
S. K. WARNE
8–0–46–0.

Captain Steve Waugh played his record-equalling 273rd one-day international as the Aussies' unbeaten run ended.

SUMMARY, 1999–2000 (Sri Lanka)

	Mts	Overs	Mdns	Runs	Wicks	Ave	BB	4w	RpO
One-Day Internationals	5	40	1	213	6	35.50	2/36	–	5.32

Australia in Zimbabwe

162/131. **Australia v Zimbabwe** (1st One-Day International),
at Queen's Sports Club, Bulawayo, 21 October 1999.
Scores
Australia 303 for 6 wickets (50 overs) (M. E. Waugh 106, R. T. Ponting 67,
D. R. Martyn 57 not out); Zimbabwe 220 (43.4 overs) (N. C. Johnson 110).
Australia won by 83 runs.
S. K. Warne
9–1–40–2. Dismissed: A. Flower st A. C. Gilchrist 11; A. R. Whittall
c M. E. Waugh 2.

Warne took a wicket in his very first over, when Andy Flower was
stumped.

163/132. **Australia v Zimbabwe** (2nd One-Day International),
at Harare Sports Ground, 23 October 1999.
Scores
Zimbabwe 116 (37.3 overs); Australia 117 for 1 wicket (28.3 overs)
(M. E. Waugh 54 not out). *Australia won by nine wickets.*
S. K. Warne
Did not bowl.

164/133. **Australia v Zimbabwe** (3rd One-Day International),
at Harare Sports Ground, 24 October 1999.
Scores
Zimbabwe 200 for 9 wickets (50 overs) (A. Flower 99 not out);
Australia 201 for 1 wicket (39 overs) (R. T. Ponting 87 not out,
M. G. Bevan 77 not out). *Australia won by nine wickets.*
S. K. Warne
10–0–42–2. Dismissed: M. W. Goodwin c A. Symonds 14; A. M. Blignaut
c M. G. Bevan 1.

Murray Goodwin and Andy Blignaut were both out on the drive, caught at cover and at point respectively.

SUMMARY, 1999–2000 (ZIMBABWE)

	Mts	Overs	Mdns	Runs	Wicks	Ave	BB	4w	RpO
One-Day Internationals	3	19	1	82	4	20.50	2/40	–	4.31

IN AUSTRALIA

---

165. **Victoria v Australian Capital Territory**,
at Richmond Cricket Ground, Melbourne, 13 November 1999.
SCORES
VICTORIA 259 for 8 wickets (50 overs) (B. J. Hodge 110);
AUSTRALIAN CAPITAL TERRITORY 241 (48.4 overs) (G. T. Cunningham 72,
A. D. McQuire 58; I. J. Harvey 5/34). *Victoria won by 18 runs*.
S. K. WARNE
10–0–31–2. Dismissed: A. D. McQuire b 58; J. J. Swift lbw 0.

---

166. **Victoria v Queensland**, at Brisbane Cricket Ground,
22 December 1999 (day/night).
SCORES
VICTORIA 193 (48.2 overs); QUEENSLAND 194 for 2 wickets (31.3 overs)
(M. L. Hayden 78 not out, S. G. Law 60). *Queensland won by
eight wickets*.
S. K. WARNE
6–0–43–1. Dismissed: S. G. Law c G. R. Vimpani 60.

After being booed for much of the game, a reaction to the 'Can't bowl, can't throw' Scott Muller controversy, Warne said the Queensland crowd was only being parochial and supporting one of its own. His six overs in greasy, wet conditions, went for 43.

167/134. Australia v Pakistan (C&U Series 1st match),
at Brisbane Cricket Ground, 9 January 2000 (day/night).
SCORES
PAKISTAN 184 for 8 wickets (50 overs); AUSTRALIA 139 (39 overs)
(Abdur Razzaq 4/23). *Pakistan won by 55 runs.*
S. K. WARNE
10–0–52–2. Dismissed: Inzamam-ul-Haq lbw 12; Moin Khan
c M. E. Waugh 33.

Moin Khan hit Warne for six over extra cover as his first five overs
cost 32 runs (for two wickets). Late in his spell he injured a rib mus-
cle in his side (a common occurrence for faster bowlers) and didn't
play again until the end of the month.

168/135. Australia v India (C&U Series 12th match),
at WACA Ground, Perth, 30 January 2000.
SCORES
INDIA 226 for 6 wickets (50 overs) (R. Dravid 65); AUSTRALIA 230 for
6 wickets (49.3 overs) (M. G. Bevan 71). *Australia won by four wickets.*
S. K. WARNE
9–0–57–1. Dismissed: D. J. Gandhi c D. R. Martyn 13.

169/136. Australia v Pakistan (C&U Series 1st Final),
at Melbourne Cricket Ground, 2 February 2000 (day/night).
SCORES
PAKISTAN 154 (47.2 overs); AUSTRALIA 155 for 4 wickets (42.4 overs)
(M. G. Bevan 54, R. T. Ponting 50). *Australia won by six wickets.*
S. K. WARNE
10–2–33–1. Dismissed: Moin Khan c D. R. Martyn 47.

Warne's last over cost nine.

170/137. Australia v Pakistan (C&U Series 2nd Final),
at Sydney Cricket Ground, 4 February 2000 (day/night).
SCORES
AUSTRALIA 337 for 7 wickets (50 overs) (R. T. Ponting 78, M. E. Waugh 53,

A C. Gilchrist 51); PAKISTAN 185 (36.3 overs) (G. D. McGrath 5/49).
Australia won by 152 runs.
S. K. WARNE
7–2–28–0.

SUMMARY, 1999–2000 (AUSTRALIA)

	Mts	Overs	Mdns	Runs	Wicks	Ave	BB	4w	RpO
All limited-overs matches	6	52	4	244	7	34.85	2/31	–	4.69
One-Day Internationals	4	36	4	170	4	42.50	2/52	–	4.72
Mercantile Mutual Cup	2	16	0	74	3	24.66	2/31	–	4.62

AUSTRALIA IN NEW ZEALAND

171/138. **Australia v New Zealand** (1st One-Day International),
at Westpac Trust Stadium (formerly Basin Reserve), Wellington,
17 February 2000 (day/night).
SCORES
AUSTRALIA 119 for 1 wicket (23 overs) (M. L. Hayden 64 not out);
NEW ZEALAND did not bat. **No result**.
S. K. WARNE
Did not bowl.

Even in a rained-out game in which little play was available, Warne found himself embroiled in controversy when an amateur photographer snapped him smoking a cigarette at smoke-free Westpac Trust Stadium. Wanting to avoid publicity which could result in authorities imposing a NZ$20 000 fine, Warne asked for the camera from 15-year-old Daniel Bassett and when he refused, Warne impounded a bag and returned it only after police intervention. 'If there is any misunderstanding, I do apologise,' Warne said later. He denied he'd sworn at Bassett or his friend, fellow schoolboy Shannon Nightingale.

172/139. **Australia v New Zealand** (2nd One-Day International),
at Eden Park, Auckland, 19 February 2000 (day/night).
SCORES
NEW ZEALAND 122 (30.1 overs); AUSTRALIA 123 for 5 wickets (24.4 overs)

(M. L. Hayden 50). *Australia won by five wickets*.
S. K. WARNE
10–0–35–2. Dismissed: R. G. Twose b 25; S. B. Styris c M. E. Waugh 1.

173/140. **Australia v New Zealand** (3rd One-Day International),
at Carisbrook, Dunedin, 23 February 2000 (day/night).
SCORES
AUSTRALIA 310 for 4 wickets (50 overs) (A. C. Gilchrist 77, M. E. Waugh 75,
M. G. Bevan 52); NEW ZEALAND 260 (45 overs) (N. J. Astle 81,
R. G. Twose 62). *Australia won by 50 runs*.
S. K. WARNE
10–1–50–2. Dismissed: N. J. Astle b 81; C. D. McMillan c sub (I. J. Harvey) 1.

Warne conceded 38 runs from his first five overs, noticeably using his wrong'un only very sparingly, even against the left-handers. He captained the side after Steve Waugh (twisted ankle) left the field early in NZ's innings.

174/141. **Australia v New Zealand** (4th One-Day International),
at Jade Stadium (formerly Lancaster Park), Christchurch, 26 February 2000
(day/night).
SCORES
AUSTRALIA 349 for 6 wickets (50 overs) (A. C. Gilchrist 128, M. E. Waugh 70,
S. R. Waugh 54); NEW ZEALAND 301 for 9 wickets (50 overs)
(S. P. Fleming 82, C. Z. Harris 59 not out). *Australia won by 48 runs*.
S. K. WARNE
9–0–50–3. Dismissed: N. J. Astle lbw 45; S. P. Fleming c S. R. Waugh 82;
D. L. Vettori b 3.

Bowled some important overs to help restrict New Zealand's run-rate after they'd made a helter-skelter start after Australia's record ODI score.

175/142. **Australia v New Zealand** (5th One-Day International),
at McLean Park, Napier, 1 March 2000 (day/night).
SCORES
NEW ZEALAND 243 for 9 wickets (50 overs) (N. J. Astle 104;

D, W, Fleminq 4/41); Australia 245 for 4 wickets (45.4 overs)
(M. G. Bevan 107, M. L. Hayden 57). *Australia won by five wickets*.
S. K. WARNE
10–2–34–1. Dismissed: C. J. Nevin c D. R. Martyn 11.

Batted at No. 5, scoring 12 from 10 balls in a pinch-hitting role as Australia extended its record to 14 games in a row without defeat.

176/143. **Australia v New Zealand** (6th One-Day International),
at Eden Park, Auckland, 3 March 2000 (day/night).
SCORES
Australia 191 (46.2 overs) (D. R. Martyn 116 not out);
New Zealand 194 for 3 wickets (41 overs) (C. J. Nevin 74,
S. P. Fleming 60 not out). *New Zealand won by seven wickets*.
S. K. WARNE
10–1–25–1. Dismissed: M. S. Sinclair c S. Lee 19.

On in the eighth over of the match, Warne had Kiwi rookie Matthew Sinclair caught at second slip from the Sandringham Road end. Warne and the Australians went out of their way to make Australian-born Sinclair unwelcome.

SUMMARY, 1999–2000 (NEW ZEALAND)

	Mts	Overs	Mdns	Runs	Wicks	Ave	BB	4w	RpO
One-Day Internationals	6	49	4	194	9	21.55	3/50	–	4.72

AUSTRALIA IN SOUTH AFRICA

177/144. **South Africa v Australia** (1st One-Day International),
at Kingsmead, Durban, 12 April 2000 (day/night).
SCORES
Australia 240 for 9 (50 overs) (A. C. Gilchrist 51, D. R. Martyn 74,
M. Ntini 4/56); South Africa 241 for 4 wickets (48 overs) (G. Kirsten 97,
J. H. Kallis 61). *South Africa won by six wickets*.
S. K. WARNE
8–0–47–0

Stunning revelations of Hansie Cronje's involvement with an Indian bookmaker totally overshadowed the South African leg of six one-day internationals scheduled between the two countries, in April and August, indoors at Melbourne's Colonial Stadium.

Australian captain Steve Waugh said the game's history had been tainted. The disgraced Cronje withdraw from the series after having initially proclaimed his innocence.

Having only just arrived in the country, the jet-lagged Australians were comfortably beaten. Warne made a duck and struggled to grip the ball in Kingsmead's early-evening dew. He bowled several rank, head-high full tosses and rarely spun it, going for almost a run a ball.

178/145. **South Africa v Australia** (2nd One-Day International),
at Newlands, Cape Town, 14 April 2000 (day/night).
SCORES
SOUTH AFRICA 144 for 9 (50 overs); AUSTRALIA 145 for 5 wickets (24.3 overs)
(D. R. Martyn 50). *Australia won by five wickets*.
S. K. WARNE
10–1–21–1. Dismissed: D. J. Callaghan c Gilchrist 15.

Warne played a part in Adam Gilchrist's new ODI world record of six catches, when Proteas middle-order batsman Dave Callaghan, replacing ex-captain Cronje, was caught behind from a sharply spun leg-break.

Bowling his first seven-over spell with the wind over his right shoulder, Warne bowled beautifully, a flipper which rushed on and cut back at Neil McKenzie only just being kept out. Opposing Lance Klusener, one of the most respected of the South Africans, Warne sent down his full repertoire, prompting a Klusener quip: 'Got anything else mate?'

Warne's 1/21 from 10 overs was his most economical figures in a ODI in South Africa. He suffered a slight calf strain late in the innings.

179/146. South Africa v Australia (3rd One-Day International),
at New Wanderers, Johannesburg, 16 April 2000.
SCORES
AUSTRALIA 205 (49.5 overs) (S. R. Waugh 51, S. M. Pollock 4/37);
SOUTH AFRICA 209 for 6 (47.5 overs) (M. V. Boucher 55 not out,
L. Klusener 52 not out). **South Africa won by four wickets.**
S. K. WARNE
10–2–30–2. Dismissed: A. J. Hall c Symonds 46; J. N. Rhodes,
c sub (Hayden) 4.

Warne's 43-minute half-century stand with fellow Victorian Ian
Harvey helped the Australians set a competitive target after another
top-order collapse at the Bullring. He broke one of his new County
bats during his 32, shortly having lifted Makhaya Ntini over the
square leg fence. It was his second-highest score in an ODI and came
in front of a hostile, capacity crowd of 31 500, who targeted him from
the time he walked out to bat. Warne was the fifth bowler used, in the
16th over, and his first over cost 12 runs, courtesy of 3 fours in a row
from Jacques Kallis. His second went for 7 before his final eight cost
just 11. After bowling a perfectly pitched googly which was carefully
defended by the left-handed Lance Klusener, he indulged in some
banter with the star South African, asking if he'd 'picked that one'.

His economical spell maintained the pressure while express bowler
Brett Lee charged in from the opposite end, one of his deliveries from
the Golf Course end being timed at 156.1 km/h, the fastest in 20
years. It was Warne's 38th match for the Australians in five different
countries during the exhausting, extended eight-month season.
Within 24 hours, Warne and family, who had been enjoying time at
luxurious Sun City, took a flight to London as Warne continued his
non-stop cricket diet with an inaugural season of county cricket in
England with Hampshire.

SUMMARY, 1999–2000 (SOUTH AFRICA)

	Mts	Overs	Mdns	Runs	Wicks	Ave	BB	4w	RpO
One-Day Internationals	3	28	3	98	3	32.66	2/30	–	3.50

PART THREE

MISCELLANEOUS MATCHES

1990–91 (IN AUSTRALIA)

1. Australian Cricket Academy v England XI, at St Peter's College, Adelaide, 29 November 1990.

SCORES

AUSTRALIAN CRICKET ACADEMY 95 (42 overs); ENGLAND XI 96 for 5 wickets (32.2 overs). England XI won by five wickets.

S. K. WARNE

4–2–9–0.

2. Australian Cricket Academy v England XI, at St Peter's College, Adelaide, 30 November 1990.

SCORES

ENGLAND XI 237 for 6 wickets (45 overs) (J. E. Morris 63); AUSTRALIAN CRICKET ACADEMY 87 (32.2 overs) (M. P. Bicknell 4/30). **England won by 150 runs**.

S. K. WARNE

6–0–42–1. Dismissed: R. A. Smith c B. Ruddell 37.

For the second time in two days the Academy team failed to make 100. Warne was the only player to score double figures in both games held at one of Adelaide's premier schools, St Peter's. He made 11 from No. 8 in both fixtures and, in the second match, began what was to be quite a mastery over England's Robin Smith.

3. Victoria 2nd XI v Western Australia 2nd XI, at Albert Ground, Melbourne, 12, 13 & 14 December 1990.

SCORES

WESTERN AUSTRALIA 2nd XI 252 (J. L. Langer 85; L. N. Herbert 6/61) and 333 for 6 wickets dec. (D. R. Martyn 116, J. L. Langer 60, M. P. Lavender 50); VICTORIA 2nd XI 256 for 6 wickets dec. (S. S. Prescott 112, G. R. Parker 79) and 310 for 9 wickets (D. A. Harris 140). **Drawn**.

S. K. WARNE

1st inns: 17–3–60–1. Dismissed: J. Stewart c D. A. Harris 7.
2nd inns: 14.5–2–78–3. Dismissed: J. L. Langer c C. White 60; J. A. Brayshaw c C. E. Bradley 0; R. S. Russell c G. R. Parker 49.

4. **Victoria 2nd XI v South Australia 2nd XI**, at Adelaide Oval,
4, 5 & 6 February 1991.

SCORES

SOUTH AUSTRALIA 2nd XI 527 for 9 wickets dec. (T. J. Nielsen 252,
J. A. Bolton 65, C. J. Williamson 58, G. H. Armstrong 56); and 93 for
1 wicket dec. (G. H. Armstrong 51); VICTORIA 2nd XI 325
(C. White 69, G. J. Allardice 58; P. W. Gladigau 5/65) and 122 for
3 wickets (D. J. Ramshaw 56 not out). **Drawn**.

S. K. WARNE

1st inns: 43.4–9–161–4. Dismissed: J. A. Bolton c D. J. Ramshaw 65;
T. J. Nielsen c sub (M. P. O'Keefe) 252; P. W. Gladigau c N. R. Strong 8;
D. A. Clarke c G. J. Clarke 15.
2nd inns: 3.1–0–19–1. Dismissed: G. H. Armstrong c S. S. Prescott 51.

Tim Nielsen's 252 in heatwave conditions was the biggest-ever individual score against a team with Warne as a member until West Indian Brian Lara's massive 277 in Sydney two years later. The young Victorians didn't arrive until the morning of the match and fielded for the best part of two days.

1991–92 (AUSTRALIANS IN ZIMBABWE)

5. **Australians v Zimbabwe 'B'**, at Mutare Sports Club,
10, 11 & 12, September 1991.

SCORES

ZIMBABWE 'B' 220 (I. P. Butchart 60) and 164 (N. P. Hough 53);
AUSTRALIANS 291 (T. J. Nielsen 79, S. R. Waugh 59; H. Hira 5/74) and
94 for 4 wickets. **Australians won by six wickets**.

S. K. WARNE

1st inns: 17–2–41–1. Dismissed: I. P. Butchart b 60.
2nd inns: 13–4–36–1. Dismissed: C. N. Evans lbw 9.

1993 (AUSTRALIANS IN ENGLAND)

6. **Australians v England Amateur XI**, at Radlett, 30 April 1993.

SCORES

AUSTRALIANS 292 for 3 wickets (55 overs) (M. L. Hayden 151,

M. A. Taylor 53); ENGLAND AMATEUR XI 198 (45.2 overs).
Australians won by 94 runs.
S. K. WARNE
9.2–1–41–2. Dismissed: K. A. Arnold c W. J. Holdsworth 5; N. P. Hackett b 1.

---

7. **Australians v Lavinia, Duchess of Norfolk's XI**, at Arundel Castle,
2 May 1993.
SCORES
AUSTRALIANS 203 for 9 wickets (50 overs) (S. R. Waugh 59;
D. W. Headley 5/51); LAVINIA, DUCHESS OF NORFOLK'S XI 196
(49.5 overs) (P. W. G. Parker 77; M. E. Waugh 5/32).
Australians won by 7 runs.
S. K. WARNE
10–1–26–0.

---

8. **Australians v Minor Counties**, at Lichfield Road, Stone,
8 July 1993.
SCORES
AUSTRALIANS 230 (54.3 overs) (M. A. Taylor 53, P. R. Reiffel 50 not out);
MINOR COUNTIES 172 (48.3 overs) (I. Cockbain 70; P. R. Reiffel 5/28).
Australians won by 58 runs.
S. K. WARNE
11–5–22–1. Dismissed: J. Derrick st T. J. Zoehrer 16.

1994 (IN ENGLAND)

9. **Earl of Carnarvon's XI v South Africans**, at Highclere Castle,
23 June 1994.
SCORES
EARL OF CARNARVON'S XI 223 (48.2 overs) (G. I. Macmillan 78);
SOUTH AFRICANS 224 for 3 (47.2 overs) (K. C. Wessels 68 not out,
J. N. Rhodes 111). **South Africans won by seven wickets.**
S. K. WARNE
10–0–57–0

To commemorate South Africa's first official game in England for
29 years, a charity match was held into which six Test players,

including Warne and West Indians Courtney Walsh and Carl Hooper, were co-opted.

Warne's 22 helped to set a target of 224. He and Hooper (37) added 49 for the eighth wicket, the second-best partnership of the innings. Warne went wicketless as South Africa made the runs with 22 balls to spare, 72 of Jonty Rhodes' 111 coming in boundary hits. Queen Elizabeth and the Duke of Edinburgh were introduced to the teams as part of the festivities.

1994–95 (Australians in Bermuda)

10. **Australians v St George's**, at Wellington Oval, St George,
11 May 1995.
Scores
Australians 235 (48 overs); St George's 182 for 9 wickets (50 overs).
Australians won by 53 runs.
S. K. Warne
8–3–31–0.

11. **Australians v Bermuda**, at Somerset Cricket Club,
14 May 1995.
Scores
Australians 225 (46.2 overs) (M. A. Taylor 58, R. T. Ponting 56;
C. Trott 4/66); Bermuda 207 for 9 wickets (50 overs). *Australians won by 18 runs.*
S. K. Warne
10–5–11–3. Dismissed: A. Steede b 32; B. Perinchief c M. A. Taylor 9;
C. Trott st I. A. Healy 0.

1995–96 (In Australia)

12. **Victoria v South Australia**, at Fred's Pass, Darwin,
17 September 1995.
Scores
Victoria 208 (49.2 overs) (D. M. Jones 95, P. Wilson 4/22);

SOUTH AUSTRALIA 209 for 6 wickets (48.4 overs) (D. S. Lehmann 76).
South Australia won by four wickets.
S. K. WARNE
10–0–46–2. Dismissed: P. C. Nobes c D. J. Saker 40, D. S. Lehmann
c J. R. Bakker 76.

---

13. **Victoria v New Zealand**, at Tracy Village Oval, Darwin,
18 September 1995.
Scores
NEW ZEALAND 215 for 8 wickets (50 overs) (B. A. Young 72); VICTORIA 206
(49.4 overs) (P. A. Broster 117; M. N. Hart 6/58, G. I. Allott 4/31).
New Zealand won by nine runs.
S. K. WARNE
9–0–40–1. Dismissed: M. N. Hart st. D. S. Berry 0.

---

14. **Victoria v South Australia**, at Tracy Village Oval, Darwin,
21 September 1995.
Scores
SOUTH AUSTRALIA 210 (50 overs) (D. S. Lehmann 67, I. J. Harvey 5/22);
VICTORIA 210 (50 overs) (D. S. Berry 54, L. D. Harper 53). *Tied*.
S. K. WARNE
10–0–28–1. Dismissed: P. Wilson st D. S. Berry 1.

---

15. **Victoria v New Zealand**, at Marrara Oval, 22 September 1995.
Scores
VICTORIA 161 for 8 wickets (50 overs); NEW ZEALAND 162 for 7 wickets
(46.2 overs) (M. J. Greatbatch 68, A. C. Parore 51, I. J. Harvey 4/12).
New Zealand won by three wickets.
S. K. WARNE
10–1–40–0.

Billed as 'The Feast of Cricket' and played at the conclusion of the
1995 Northern Territory 'summer', the full-strength New Zealand
team competed, along with South Australia, Victoria and a Northern
Territory XI. Warne played in four of Victoria's five games. He didn't
play against the NT.

1997 (AUSTRALIANS IN HONG KONG)

16. Australians v Rest of the World, at Kowloon Cricket Club,
11 May 1997.
SCORES
REST OF THE WORLD 245 for 8 wickets (40 overs) (S. V. Manjrekar 80,
R. S. Gavaskar 51 not out); AUSTRALIANS 248 for 6 wickets (28.4 overs)
(M. E. Waugh 116). *Australians won by four wickets*.
S. K. WARNE
8–1–33–0.

This was the only match of Warne's representative career to be played
on synthetic turf. Sunil Gavaskar's son, Rohan, made an unbeaten 51
from only 30 balls, before conceding 43 runs (for two wickets) from
just 3.4 overs.

1997–98 (IN AUSTRALIA)

17. Australians v Australian Cricket Academy, at Adelaide Oval,
28 October 1997.
SCORES
AUSTRALIAN CRICKET ACADEMY 277 for 9 wickets (50 overs) (M. J. Slater 56,
R. T. Ponting 51 not out);
AUSTRALIANS 277 for nine (50 overs) (M. G. Bevan 130). *Tied*.
S. K. WARNE
7–1–40–2. Dismissed M. J. Slater, c A. C. Dale 56; A. C. Gilchrist,
c D. S. Lehmann 45.

A boundary by Adam Dale from the final delivery of Australia's
innings saw the scores tied in a high-standard exhibition match to
celebrate 10 years of the AIS Cricket Academy's highly successful
operation. Steve Waugh captained Australia ahead of Mark Taylor,
who was not named. Six members of Waugh's side had attended the
Academy: Warne, Michael Di Venuto, Michael Bevan, Shane Lee, Ian
Harvey and Glenn McGrath.

1999–2000 (AUSTRALIA IN SRI LANKA)

18. Australian XIII v Sri Lanka Board President's XI,
at Sinhalese Sports Club Ground, Colombo, 19 August 1999.
SCORES
SRI LANKAN BOARD PRESIDENT'S XI 208 for 5 wickets (50 overs)
(S. I Fernando 67); AUSTRALIAN XIII 212 for 4 wickets (45.1 overs)
(R. T. Ponting 60 retired not out). ***Australian XIII won by six wickets***.
S. K. WARNE
9–1–41–1. Dismissed: U. Fernando c S. R. Waugh 23.

1999–2000 (IN AUSTRALIA)

19. Ian Healy's XII v Steve Waugh's XII, Allan Border Field,
Albion, Queensland, 15 August 1999.
SCORES
IAN HEALY'S XII 213 for 7 (50 overs) (M. J. Slater 104);
STEVE WAUGH'S XII 214 for 6 (49.3 overs) (M. G. Bevan 53 not out).
Steve Waugh's XII won by four wickets.
S. K. WARNE
9–0–35–2. Dismissed: D. R. Martin c R. T. Ponting 14; A. Symonds
c D. S. Lehmann 24.

Played prior to the Australian ODI team's departure for Sri Lanka, the
match involved all 24 of the ACB-contracted players and was played
to Australian DOD rules with only 11 batting per side. Tom Moody
caused confusion among the crowd of 3000 by batting in a shirt
marked McGRATH.

PART FOUR

THE RECORDS

(all records up to and including Australia's tour of South Africa, April 2000)

SHANE WARNE'S CAREER

TEAMS

Brighton, St Kilda, Glenelg, Australian Cricket Academy, Victoria, Australia 'B', Australia.

TOURS

Zimbabwe (Australia 'B') 1991–92; Sri Lanka 1992–93; New Zealand 1992–93; England 1993; South Africa & UAE † 1993–94; Sri Lanka † & Pakistan 1994–95; New Zealand † 1994–95; West Indies 1994–95; World Cup † (India & Pakistan) 1995–96; South Africa 1996–97; England 1997, India 1997–98, Sharjah † 1997–98, West Indies 1998–99, World Cup † (England) 1999, Sri Lanka & Zimbabwe 1999, New Zealand 1999–2000, South Africa † 1999–2000.
† denotes one-day internationals only

MAJOR HONOURS

International Cricketer of the Year 1993–94 & 1997–98; Victorian captain 1996–97, 1997–98 & 1998–99; Australian ODI captain (substituting for Steve Waugh) 1997–98 (one game), 1998–99 (10); Australia's one-day Cricketer of the Year 1999–2000; selected in the Australian Team of the Century; and named one of Five Wisden Cricketers of the Century (along with Sir Donald Bradman, Sir Garfield Sobers, Sir Vivian Richards and Sir Jack Hobbs).

SHANE WARNE AS CAPTAIN

Test cricket: Nil
Australia in one-day internationals: Games: 11, Won: 10, Lost: 1
Other Australian matches: Games: 4, Won: 3, Lost: 0, Drawn: 1
Victoria in Sheffield Shield: Games: 9, Won: 1, Lost: 4, Drawn: 4
Victoria in Mercantile Mutual Cup: Games: 5, Won: 3, Lost: 2
SUMMARY
Games: 29, wins: 17, losses: 7, draws: 5

TEST CRICKET

Debut: 1991–92 Australia v India, Sydney
Honours: Australia's all-time highest Test wickets record-holder; Australia's Test vice-captain 1999 to 2000; hat-trick v England 1994–95.

BATTING & FIELDING

RECORD SERIES BY SERIES

	Mts	Inns	NO	Runs	HS	Ave	50s	Ct
1991–92 v Ind (A)	2	4	1	28	20	9.33	–	1
1992–93 v SL (SL)	2	3	0	66	35	22.00	–	1
1992–93 v WI (A)	4	7	0	42	14	6.00	–	3
1992–93 v NZ (NZ)	3	4	2	49	22*	24.50	–	1
1993 v Eng (E)	6	5	2	113	37	37.66	–	4
1993–94 v NZ (A)	3	2	1	85	74*	85.00	1	4
1993–94 v SA (A)	3	4	1	16	11	5.33	–	2
1993–94 v SA (SA)	3	5	0	41	15	8.20	–	0
1994–95 v Pak (P)	3	4	0	69	33	17.25	–	2
1994–95 v Eng (A)	5	10	1	60	36*	6.66	–	5
1994–95 v WI (WI)	4	5	0	28	11	5.60	–	2
1995–96 v Pak (A)	3	4	1	39	27*	13.00	–	0
1995–96 v SL (A)	3	1	0	33	33	33.00	–	5
1996–97 v WI (A)	5	7	0	128	30	18.28	–	6
1996–97 v SA (SA)	3	5	0	42	18	8.40	–	3
1997 v Eng (E)	6	10	0	188	53	18.80	1	2
1997–98 v NZ (NZ)	3	3	0	71	36	23.66	–	0
1997–98 v SA (A)	3	5	1	27	12	6.75	–	5
1997–98 v Ind (I)	3	5	0	105	35	21.00	–	0
1998–99 v Eng (A)	1	2	1	10	8	10.00	–	2
1998–99 v WI (WI)	3	6	0	138	32	23.00	–	3
1999–2000 v SL (SL)	3	4	0	6	6	1.50	–	2
1999–2000 v Zim (Z)	1	1	0	6	6	6.00	–	0
1999–2000 v Pak (A)	3	4	1	99	86	33.00	1	4
1999–2000 v Ind (A)	3	3	0	88	86	29.33	1	3
1999–2000 v NZ (NZ)	3	4	0	36	12	9.00	–	4
Total	84	117	12	1613	86	15.36	4	64

RECORD AGAINST INDIVIDUAL COUNTRIES

Opponent	Mts	Inns	NO	Runs	HS	Ave	50s	Ct
England	18	27	4	371	53	16.13	1	13
India	8	12	1	221	86	20.09	1	4
New Zealand	12	13	3	241	74*	24.10	1	9
Pakistan	9	12	2	207	86	20.70	1	6
South Africa	12	19	2	126	18	7.41	–	10

RECORD AGAINST INDIVIDUAL COUNTRIES continued

Opponent	Mts	Inns	NO	Runs	HS	Ave	50s	Ct
Sri Lanka	8	8	0	105	35	13.12	–	8
West Indies	16	25	0	336	32	13.44	–	14
Zimbabwe	1	1	0	6	6	6.00	–	0
Total	84	117	12	1613	86	15.36	4	64

HIGHEST SCORES

86	v Pakistan, first Test, Brisbane, 1999–2000
86	v India, first Test, Adelaide, 1999–2000
74 not out	v New Zealand, third Test, Brisbane, 1993–94
53	v England, third Test, Manchester, 1997

HIGHEST PARTNERSHIPS

142	7th wicket, with Steve Waugh, v New Zealand (1), third Test, Brisbane, 1993–94
108	7th wicket, with Steve Waugh, v India (1), first Test, Adelaide, 1999–2000
88	7th wicket, with Steve Waugh, v England (2), third Test, Old Trafford, Manchester, 1997
86	10th wicket, with Scott Muller, v Pakistan (1), first Test, Brisbane, 1999–2000 (Muller made 6 not out)

BOWLING

RECORD SERIES BY SERIES

	Mts	Overs	Mdns	Runs	Wkts	Ave	Best	5w	10wM
1991–92 v Ind (A)	2	68	9	228	1	228.00	1/150	–	–
1992–93 v SL (SL)	2	38.1	8	158	3	52.66	3/11	–	–
1992–93 v WI (A)	4	108.2	23	313	10	31.30	7/52	1	–
1992–93 v NZ (NZ)	3	159	73	256	17	15.05	4/8	–	–
1993 v Eng (E)	6	439.5	178	877	34	25.79	5/82	1	–
1993–94 v NZ (A)	3	151.3	49	305	18	16.94	6/31	1	–
1993–94 v SA (A)	3	175.1	63	307	18	17.05	7/56	2	1
1993–94 v SA (SA)	3	190.5	69	336	15	22.40	4/86	–	–
1993–94 v Pak (P)	3	181.4	50	504	18	28.00	6/136	2	–
1994–95 v Eng (A)	5	256.1	84	549	27	20.33	8/71	2	1
1994–95 v WI (WI)	4	138	35	406	15	27.06	4/70	–	–
1995–96 v Pak (A)	3	115	52	198	19	10.42	7/23	1	1
1995–96 v SL (A)	3	164.4	43	433	12	36.08	4/71	–	–
1996–97 v WI (A)	5	217.1	56	594	22	27.00	4/95	–	–
1996–97 v SA (SA)	3	133	47	282	11	25.63	4/43	–	–

RECORD SERIES BY SERIES continued

	Mts	Overs	Mdns	Runs	Wkts	Ave	Best	5wI	10wM
1997 v Eng (E)	6	237.1	69	577	24	24.04	6/48	1	–
1997–98 v NZ (A)	3	170.4	36	476	19	25.05	5/88	1	–
1997–98 v SA (A)	3	187.1	51	417	20	20.85	6/34	2	1
1997–98 v Ind (I)	3	167	37	540	10	54.00	4/85	–	–
1998–99 v Eng (A)	1	39	7	110	2	55.00	1/43	–	–
1998–99 v WI (WI)	3	83.5	18	268	2	134.00	1/70	–	–
1999–2000 v SL (SL)	3	56.1	20	115	8	14.37	5/52	1	–
1999–2000 v Zim (Z)	1	53.1	13	137	6	22.83	3/68	–	–
1999–2000 v Pak (A)	3	129.5	36	370	12	30.83	5/110	1	–
1999–2000 v Ind (A)	3	127	35	335	8	41.87	4/92	–	–
1999–2000 v NZ (NZ)	3	129.2	32	414	15	27.60	4/68	–	–
Total	84	3916.5	1193	9505	366	25.96	8/71	16	4

RECORD AGAINST INDIVIDUAL COUNTRIES

	Mt	Overs	Mdns	Runs	Wkts	Ave	Best	5wI	10wM
v England	18	972.1	338	2113	87	24.28	8/71	4	1
v India	8	362	81	1103	19	58.05	4/85	–	–
v New Zealand	12	610.3	190	1451	69	21.02	6/31	2	–
v Pakistan	9	426.3	138	1072	49	21.87	7/23	4	1
v South Africa	12	686.1	230	1342	64	20.96	7/56	4	2
v Sri Lanka	8	259	71	706	23	30.69	5/52	1	–
v West Indies	16	547.2	132	1581	49	32.26	7/52	1	–
v Zimbabwe	1	53.1	13	137	6	22.83	3/68	–	–
Total	84	3916.5	1193	9505	366	25.96	8/71	16	4

RECORD BY VENUE

	Mts	Overs	Mdns	Runs	Wkts	Ave	Best	5wI	10wM
In Australia:									
Adelaide	8	357	101	889	26	34.19	4/31	–	–
Brisbane	6	367.2	128	805	44	18.29	8/71	2	2
Hobart	4	154.3	40	391	23	17.00	6/31	3	–
Melbourne	7	341.1	93	770	34	22.64	7/52	2	–
Perth	7	231.3	52	668	18	37.11	4/83	–	–
Sydney	9	458.1	130	1112	43	25.86	7/56	4	2
Total in Australia	41	1909.4	544	4635	188	24.65	8/71	11	4

RECORD BY VENUE continued

	Mts	Overs	Mdns	Runs	Wkts	Ave	Best	5wI	10wM
In England:									
Birmingham	2	112.3	38	282	7	40.28	5/82	1	–
Leeds	2	85	31	161	2	80.50	1/43	–	–
Lord's	2	104.5	33	215	10	21.50	4/57	–	–
Manchester	2	133.4	58	248	17	14.58	6/48	1	–
Nottingham	2	138	50	311	13	23.92	4/86	–	–
The Oval	2	103	37	237	9	26.33	3/78	–	–
Total in England	12	677	247	1454	58	25.06	6/48	2	–
In India:									
Bangalore	1	60	15	186	5	37.20	3/106	–	–
Calcutta	1	42	4	147	0	–	–	–	–
Chennai	1	65	18	207	5	41.40	4/85	–	–
Total in India	3	167	37	540	10	54.00	4/85	–	–
In New Zealand:									
Auckland	2	84.3	28	210	11	19.09	4/8	–	–
Christchurch	1	48	19	86	7	12.28	4/63	–	–
Hamilton	1	45	16	106	3	35.33	2/61	–	–
Wellington	2	110.5	42	268	11	24.36	4/68	–	–
Total in New Zealand	6	288.2	105	670	32	20.93	4/8	–	–
In Pakistan:									
Karachi	1	63.1	22	150	8	18.75	5/89	1	–
Lahore	1	71.5	14	240	9	26.66	6/136	2	–
Rawalpindi	1	46.4	14	114	1	114.00	1/58	–	–
Total in Pakistan	3	181.4	50	504	18	28.00	6/136	2	–
In South Africa:									
Cape Town	1	77	31	116	6	19.33	3/38	–	–
Centurion	1	36	11	89	0	–	–	–	–
Durban	2	110.4	44	203	10	20.30	4/43	–	–

RECORD BY VENUE continued

	Mts	Overs	Mdns	Runs	Wkts	Ave	Best	5wl	10wM
Johannesburg	1	58.5	18	128	5	25.60	4/86	–	–
Port Elizabeth	1	41.2	12	82	5	16.40	3/62	–	–
Total in South Africa	6	323.5	116	618	26	23.76	4/43	–	–
In Sri Lanka:									
Colombo (SSC)	2	32.1	6	129	3	43.00	3/11	–	–
Galle	1	28.2	12	34	3	11.33	3/29	–	–
Kandy	1	22.5	7	70	5	14.00	5/52	1	–
Moratuwa	1	11	3	40	0	–	–	–	–
Total in Sri Lanka	5	94.2	28	273	11	24.81	5/52	1	–
In West Indies:									
Bridgetown	2	78.2	13	260	6	43.33	3/64	–	–
Kingston	2	78.4	22	236	7	33.71	4/70	–	–
Port-of-Spain	2	29.5	9	77	1	77.00	1/16	–	–
St John's	1	35	9	101	3	33.66	3/83	–	–
Total in West Indies	7	221.5	53	674	17	39.64	4/70	–	–
In Zimbabwe:									
Harare	1	53.1	13	137	6	22.83	3/68	–	–
Total in Australia	41	1909.4	544	4635	188	24.65	8/71	13	4
Overseas	43	2007.1	651	4870	178	27.35	6/48	5	–
Total	84	3916.5	1193	9505	366	25.96	8/71	16	4

RECORD IN FIRST AND SECOND INNINGS

	Overs	Mdns	Runs	Wkts	Ave	Best	5wl
First Innings:							
In Australia	1045.4	283	2612	91	28.70	7/23	4
Overseas:							
England	280	98	645	28	23.03	6/48	1
India	112	24	338	7	48.28	4/85	–
New Zealand	122.5	43	271	17	15.94	4/8	–
Pakistan	90.3	30	255	10	25.50	6/136	1

RECORD IN FIRST AND SECOND INNINGS continued

	Overs	Mdns	Runs	Wkts	Ave	Best	5wl
South Africa	203.2	67	431	13	33.15	4/92	–
Sri Lanka	79	21	239	8	29.87	5/52	1
West Indies	136.5	36	427	10	42.70	3/83	–
Zimbabwe	23	2	69	3	23.00	3/69	–
Total Overseas	1047.3	321	2675	96	27.86	6/48	3
Total	2093.1	604	5287	187	28.27	7/23	7

Second Innings:

	Overs	Mdns	Runs	Wkts	Ave	Best	5wl
In Australia	864	261	2023	97	20.85	8/71	7
Overseas:							
England	397	149	809	30	26.96	5/82	1
India	55	13	202	3	67.33	2/80	–
New Zealand	165.3	60	399	15	26.60	4/63	–
Pakistan	91.1	20	249	8	31.12	5/89	1
South Africa	120.3	49	187	13	14.38	4/43	–
Sri Lanka	15.2	7	34	3	11.33	3/11	–
West Indies	85	17	247	7	35.28	4/70	–
Zimbabwe	30.1	11	68	3	22.66	3/68	–
Total Overseas	959.4	328	2195	82	26.76	5/82	2
Total	1823.4	589	4218	179	23.56	8/71	9

CALENDAR YEAR RECORD

	Mts	Overs	Mdns	Runs	Wkts	Ave	Best	5wl	10wM
1992	5	153.3	32	503	12	41.91	7/52	1	–
1993	16	842.2	316	1697	72	23.56	6/31	2	–
1994	10	629	217	1274	70	18.20	8/71	6	2
1995	12	508.3	156	1254	52	24.11	7/23	1	1
1996	4	215.1	55	571	15	38.06	4/95	–	–
1997	15	681.5	194	1661	68	24.42	6/48	2	–
1998	5	268.1	62	796	24	33.16	6/34	2	1
1999	13	464	124	1253	38	32.97	5/52	2	–
2000	4	154.2	37	496	15	33.06	4/68	–	–
Total	84	3916.5	1193	9505	366	25.96	8/71	16	4

TEST BOWLING, BEFORE AND AFTER HIS FINGER OPERATION (May 1996)

	Seasons	Games	Wkts	Runs	Ave	BB	5wl	10wM
Before	5	44	207	4870	23.52	8/71	10	3
After	4	40	159	4635	29.15	6/34	6	1

TEST BOWLING, BEFORE AND AFTER HIS SHOULDER OPERATION (April 1998)

	Seasons	Games	Wkts	Runs	Ave	BB	5wl	10wM
Before	7	67	313	7756	24.77	8/71	14	4
After	2	17	53	1749	33.00	5/52	2	–

FIRST & LAST 10 TESTS

	Wkts	Runs	Ave	BB	5wl	10wM
First 10	25	893	35.72	7/52	1	–
Last 10	41	1256	30.63	5/110	1	–

TEN WICKETS IN A MATCH (4)

12/128 (7/56 & 5/72)   v South Africa, 2nd Test (Sydney) 1993–94.
11/77 (7/23 & 4/54)   v Pakistan, 1st Test (Brisbane) 1995–96.
11/109 (5/75 & 6/34)   v South Africa, 2nd Test (Sydney) 1997–98.
11/110 (3/39 & 8/71)   v England, 1st Test (Brisbane) 1994–95.

FIVE WICKETS IN AN INNINGS (16)

8/71   v England, 1st Test (Brisbane) 1994–95
7/23   v Pakistan, 1st Test (Brisbane) 1995–96
7/52   v West Indies, 2nd Test (Melbourne) 1992–93
7/56   v South Africa, 2nd Test (Sydney) 1993–94
6/31   v New Zealand, 2nd Test (Hobart) 1993–94
6/34   v South Africa, 2nd Test (Sydney) 1997–98
6/48   v England, 3rd Test (Manchester) 1997
6/64   v England, 2nd Test (Melbourne) 1994–95
6/136   v Pakistan, 3rd Test (Lahore) 1994–95
5/52   v Sri Lanka, 1st Test (Kandy) 1999–2000
5/72   v South Africa, 2nd Test (Sydney) 1993–94
5/75   v South Africa, 2nd Test (Sydney) 1997–98
5/82   v England, 5th Test (Birmingham) 1993
5/88   v New Zealand, 3rd Test (Hobart) 1997–98
5/89   v Pakistan, 1st Test (Karachi) 1994–95
5/110   v Pakistan, 2nd Test (Hobart) 1999–2000

HAT-TRICK (1)

v England, second Test, Melbourne, 29 December 1994
 – Phil DeFreitas, Darren Gough, Devon Malcolm
It was the first hat-trick in Melbourne since Hugh Trumble,
v England, in 1903–04.

THREE WICKETS IN FOUR BALLS (1)

v England, first Test, Brisbane, 29 November 1994
 – Graham Gooch, Phil DeFreitas (second ball), Martin McCague (first)

MOST WICKETS IN A SESSION

Six

v West Indies, Melbourne, 30 December 1992 (day five, session two)
v Pakistan, Brisbane, 11 November 1995 (day three, session one)

Five

v South Africa, Sydney, 2 January 1994 (day one, session two)
v South Africa, Sydney, 3 January 1998 (day two, session one)

Four

v New Zealand, Hobart, 29 November 1993 (day four, session one)
v England, Brisbane, 29 November 1994 (day five, session two)
v Pakistan, Brisbane, 13 November 1995 (day four, session one)
v South Africa, Sydney, 5 January 1998 (day four, session two)

IMPORTANT MILESTONES

1st wicket	Ravi Shastri (India), third Test, Sydney, 1991–92 (Warne's 1st match)
50th	Nasser Hussain (England), third Test, Trent Bridge, Nottingham, 1993 (14th match)
100th	Brian McMillan (South Africa), third Test, Adelaide, 1993–94 (23rd)
150th	Steven Rhodes (England), second Test, Melbourne, 1994–95 (31st)
200th	Chaminda Vaas (Sri Lanka), first Test, Perth, 1995–96 (42nd)
250th	Alec Stewart (England), third Test, Old Trafford, Manchester, 1997 (55th)
300th	Jacques Kallis (South Africa), second Test, Sydney, 1997–98 (63rd)
350th	Hrishikesh Kanitkar (India), second Test, Melbourne, 1999–2000 (80th)
356th	Paul Wiseman (New Zealand), first Test, Auckland, 1999–2000 (82nd)

MAN OF THE MATCH AWARDS
1992–93 v West Indies, first Test (Melbourne)
1992–93 v New Zealand, first Test (Christchurch)
1993 v England, first Test (Manchester)
1993–94 v New Zealand, third Test (Brisbane)
1994–95 v Pakistan, first Test (Karachi)
1994–95 v England, first Test (Brisbane)
1995–96 v Pakistan, first Test (Brisbane)
1997–98 v South Africa, second Test (Sydney)

MAN OF THE SERIES
1992–93 New Zealand (three-Test series)
1993 England (six)
1994–95 Pakistan (three)
1995–96 Pakistan (three)
1997–98 South Africa (three)

MOST OVERS IN AN INNINGS
55   v South Africa (only inns), third Test, Kingsmead, Durban, 1993–94
50.2   v England (2), first Test, 'Gabba, Brisbane, 1994–95
50   v England (2), third Test, Trent Bridge, Nottingham, 1993
49   v England (2), first Test, Old Trafford, Manchester, 1993
49   v England (2), fifth Test, Edgbaston, Birmingham, 1993
48.5   v England (2), second Test, Lord's, 1993
47   v South Africa (1), second Test, Newlands, Cape Town, 1993–94
45.4   v Pakistan (2), second Test, Bellerive Oval, Hobart, 1999–2000

MOST OVERS IN A MATCH
90   v England, third Test, Trent Bridge, Nottingham, 1993
86   v South Africa, first Test, Melbourne, 1997–98
83.5   v England, second Test, Lord's, 1993
77   v South Africa, second Test, Newlands, Cape Town, 1993–94
75.1   v South Africa, third Test, Adelaide, 1993–94

LONGEST SPELLS
41 overs   v England, first Test, Old Trafford, Manchester,
            6 & 7 June 1993
37   v Pakistan, second Test, Bellerive Oval, Hobart,
            20 November 1999
36   v England, fifth Test, Edgbaston, Birmingham,
            8 & 9 August 1993

30.4	v England, third Test, Old Trafford, Manchester, 6 & 7 July 1997
26	v New Zealand, first Test, Lancaster Park, Christchurch, 28 February 1993
24	v South Africa, second Test, Sydney, 5 January 1994
22	v England, third Test, Trent Bridge, Nottingham, 5 & 6 July 1993
22	v India, first Test, Adelaide, 12 December 1999
22	v New Zealand, first Test, Lancaster Park, Christchurch, 27 February 1993
22	v New Zealand, first Test, Eden Park, Auckland, 11 & 12 March 2000

MOST MAIDENS IN A ROW

7	v New Zealand, first Test, Lancaster Park, Christchurch, 26 February 1993
6	v New Zealand, second Test, Basin Reserve, Wellington, 8 March 1993
6	v South Africa, third Test, Adelaide, 1 February 1994

THE DISMISSALS

Warne has dismissed 141 different batsmen in Tests:

9 times: A. J. Stewart (E); G. P. Thorpe (E).

8 times: W. J. Cronje (SA); N. Hussain (E); D. J. Richardson (SA).

7 times: M. A. Atherton (E).

6 times: S. B. Doull (NZ); G. A. Gooch (E); B. M. McMillan (SA); C. A. Walsh (WI).

5 times: N. J. Astle (NZ); C. L. Cairns (NZ); R. Dravid (I); Inzamam-ul-Haq (P); C. D. McMillan (NZ); Wasim Akram (P).

4 times: Azhar Mahmood (P); Basit Ali (P); K. C. G. Benjamin (WI); I. R. Bishop (WI); A. R. Caddick (E); D. J. Cullinan (SA): P. A. J. DeFreitas (E); S. P. Fleming (NZ); C. L. Hooper (WI); A. H. Jones (NZ); G. Kirsten (SA); B. C. Lara (WI); D. N. Patel (NZ); S. M. Pollock (SA); K. R. Rutherford (NZ); R. G. Samuels (WI); R. A. Smith (E); P. C. R. Tufnell (E).

3 times: Aamir Sohail (P); J. C. Adams (WI); P. R. Adams (SA); Akram Raza (P); C. E. L. Ambrose (WI); K. L. T. Arthurton (WI); M. A. Butcher (E); S. Chanderpaul (WI); P. A. de Silva (SL); P. S. de Villiers (SA); M. W. Gatting (E); D. Gough (E); C. Z. Harris (NZ); Ijaz Ahmed (P);

P. N. Kirsten (SA); C. R. Matthews (SA); A. C. Parore (NZ); Rameez
Raja (P); J. N. Rhodes (SA); Saeed Anwar (P); M. L. Su'a (NZ);
P. M. Such (E); S. R. Tendulkar (I); D. L. Vettori (NZ); K. C. Wessels
(WI); G. P. Wickremasinghe (SL).

Twice: G. I. Allott (NZ); Aqib Javed (P); A. M. Bacher (SA); W. K. M. Benjamin
(WI); T. E. Blain (NZ); J. P. Crawley (E); A. A. Donald (SA);
D. P. M. D. Jayawardene (SL); J. H. Kallis (SA); R. S. Kaluwitharana
(SL); C. C. Lewis (E); M. J. McCague (E); D. E. Malcolm (E);
Mohammad Akram (P); D. K. Morrison (NZ); M. B. Owens (NZ);
B. A. Pocock (NZ); M. R. Ramprakash (E); A. Ranatunga (SL); Rashid
Latif (P); S. J. Rhodes (E); R. B. Richardson (WI); Saqlain Mushtaq (P);
N. S. Sidhu (I); H. H. Streak (Z); P. L. Symcox (SA); H. P. Tillekeratne
(SL); W. P. U. J. C. Vaas (SL); Waqar Younis (P); G. J. Whittall (Z);
P. J. Wiseman (NZ); B. A. Young (NZ).

Once: Abdur Razzaq (P); S. D. Anurasiri (SL); M. S. Atapattu (SL);
M. Azharuddin (I); C. O. Browne (WI); S. L. Campbell (WI);
U. D. U. Chandana (SL); R. D. B. Croft (E); M. D. Crowe (NZ);
R. P. de Groen (NZ); N. A. Foster (E); S. C. Ganguly (I); H. H. Gibbs
(SA); M. W. Goodwin (Z); T. R. Gripper (Z); U. C. Hathurasinghe (SL);
G. A. Hick (E); A. J. Hollioake (E); B. C. Hollioake (E); A. C. Hudson
(SA); R. D. Jacobs (WI); H. H. Kanitkar (I); L. Klusener (SA);
M. N. Lathwell (E); V. V. S. Laxman (I); M. W. R. Madurasinghe (SL);
M. P. Maynard (E); Mohsin Kamal (P); Moin Khan (P); N. R. Mongia (I);
M. Muralitharan (SL); Mushtaq Ahmed (P); J. R. Murray (WI);
M. S. K. Prasad (I); S. Ramesh (I); Saleem Malik (P); R. J. Shastri (I);
P. V. Simmons (WI); M. S. Sinclair (NZ); R. P. Snell (SA); J. Srinath (I);
R. G. Twose (NZ); S. L. Watkin (E); W. Watson (NZ); D. Williams (WI);
S. C. Williams (WI); J. G. Wright (NZ); Zahid Fazal (P);
D. N. T. Zoysa (SL).

MASTERIES (1)

(Players dismissed most often by Warne in a series)

THREE-TEST SERIES:

Five: N. J. Astle (New Zealand), 1999–2000

Four: W. J. Cronje (South Africa), 1997–98; Azhar Mahmood (Pakistan),
1999–2000

FOUR-TEST SERIES:

Two: W. K. M. Benjamin (West Indies); C. A. Walsh (West Indies), 1994–95

FIVE-TEST SERIES:

Five: G. P. Thorpe (England), 1994–95

SIX-TEST SERIES:
Six: N. Hussain (England), 1997
Five: G. A. Gooch (England), 1993

MASTERIES (2)
(The best player *never* dismissed by Warne)
A. Gurusinha (SL)

DISMISSALS SUMMARY
Warne's wickets have been obtained as follows:
Bowled   64 (17.5%)
LBW   67 (18.3%)
Caught   217 (59.3%)
Stumped   18 (4.9%)
Total   366

ON-FIELD PARTNERSHIPS
MOST DISMISSALS BY A WICKETKEEPER FROM WARNE'S BOWLING
49   (34 c & 15 st) Ian Healy*

*The wicketkeeper–bowler record is held by Australians Rodney Marsh and
Dennis Lillee, who shared in 95 dismissals in 69 games.

MOST CATCHES BY A FIELDSMAN FROM WARNE'S BOWLING
51   Mark Taylor (Test record)*
25   Mark Waugh
11   Greg Blewett
11   David Boon
11   Steve Waugh

*The previous fielder–bowler record was held by West Indians Gary Sobers and
Lance Gibbs, who shared in 39 dismissals in 60 matches.

LEFT-HANDERS
Of Warne's 366 victims, 75 (20.49 per cent) have been left-handers. Left-handed
batsmen he has dismissed most often are G. P. Thorpe (9), Wasim Akram (5),
S. P. Fleming (4), G. Kirsten (4), B. C. Lara (4), R. G. Samuels (4), Aamir Sohail (3),
J. C. Adams (3), C. E. L. Ambrose (3), K. L. T. Arthurton (3), M. A. Butcher (3),
S. Chanderpaul (3), C. Z. Harris (3), Saeed Anwar (3), D. L. Vettori (3);
K. C. Wessels (3).

Top order dominance

Batsmen dismissed in each position of batting order

Pos.	Wkts	% of total
1	20	5.46
2	31	8.46
3	30	8.19
4	43	11.74
5	42	10.82
6	39	10.47

Total dismissals positions 1 to 6: 205 (56%)

7	33	9.01
8	37	10.10
9	34	9.28
10	34	9.28
11	23	6.28

Total dismissals positions 7 to 11: 161 (44%)

Total   366

Most expensive bowling

1/150   v India, Sydney, 1991–92
0/147   v India, Calcutta, 1997–98
1/122   v India, Chennai, 1997–98
1/116   v West Indies, Sydney, 1992–93
1/110   v England, Edgbaston, Birmingham, 1997
0/107   v Sri Lanka, Colombo (SSC), 1992–93

Most runs from an over

18   Muhammad Azharuddin (all 18), India v Australia, second Test, Chennai, 1998 (second innings)

15   Navjot Sidhu (14 & one no-ball), India v Australia, first Test, Chennai, 1997–98 (first innings)

14   Navjot Sidhu (all 14), India v Australia, third Test, Bangalore, 1997–98 (second innings)

14   Aamir Sohail (all 14), Pakistan v Australia, second Test, Rawalpindi, 1994–95 (first innings)

Wicketless tests

1   v India, Adelaide, 1991–92
2   v Sri Lanka, Moratuwa, 1992–93

3   v West Indies, Perth, 1992–93
4   v Pakistan, Hobart, 1995–96 (did not bowl because of injury)
5   v South Africa, Centurion, 1996–97
6   v India, Calcutta, 1997–98
7   v West Indies, Port-of-Spain, 1999
8   v Sri Lanka, Colombo (SSC), 1999–2000

TEST BOWLING & HOW AUSTRALIA HAS PERFORMED

	Games	Wkts	Runs	Ave	BB	5wl	10wM
Winning Tests	46	242	5508	22.76	8/71	9	3
Losing Tests	20	72	2040	28.33	7/56	4	1
Drawn Tests	18	52	1957	37.63	6/136	2	0

Winning Tests 54.8%, losses 23.8% and draws 21.4%

WHEN SHANE WARNE PLAYS . . .

Opponent by opponent

	Won	Lost	Drawn	Total	% won
v England	11	4	3	18	61.11
v India	5	2	1	8	62.50
v New Zealand	8	1	3	12	66.66
v Pakistan	5	2	2	9	55.55
v South Africa	5	3	4	12	41.66
v Sri Lanka	4	1	3	8	50.00
v West Indies	7	7	2	16	43.75
v Zimbabwe	1	–	–	1	100.00
Total	46	20	18	84	54.76

WHEN SHANE WARNE PLAYS . . .

Home & away

	Won	Lost	Drawn	Total	% won
In Australia	26	7	8	41	63.41
In England	7	3	2	12	58.33
In India	1	2	–	3	33.33
In New Zealand	4	1	1	6	66.66
In Pakistan	–	1	2	3	0.00
In South Africa	3	2	1	6	50.00
In Sri Lanka	1	1	3	5	20.00
In West Indies	3	3	1	7	42.85
In Zimbabwe	1	–	–	1	100.00
Total	46	20	18	84	54.76

HOW WARNE COMPARES WITH THE GREATS

AUSTRALIA'S LEADING TEST WICKET-TAKERS
(qualification: 100 wickets)

	Tests	Balls	Runs	Wkts	Ave	Best	5wl	10wM	Balls/ wkt	Runs/ 100 balls
1. S. K. Warne	84	23,501	9505	366	25.96	8/71	16	4	64.21	40.00
2. D. K. Lillee	70	18,467	8493	355	23.92	7/83	23	7	52.01	45.99
3. C. J. McDermott	71	16,586	8332	291	28.63	8/97	14	2	56.99	50.23
4. G.D. McGrath	62	14,863	6458	288	22.42	8/38	17	2	51.60	43.45
5. R. Benaud	63	19,108	6704	248	27.03	7/72	16	1	77.04	35.08
6. G. D. McKenzie	60	17,681	7328	246	29.78	8/71	16	3	71.87	41.44
7. R. R. Lindwall	61	13,650	5251	228	23.03	7/38	12	–	59.86	38.46
8. C. V. Grimmett	37	14,513	5231	216	24.21	7/40	21	7	67.18	36.04
9. M. G. Hughes	53	12,285	6017	212	28.38	8/87	7	1	57.94	48.97
10. J. R. Thomson	51	10,535	5601	200	28.00	6/46	8	–	52.67	53.16
11. A. K. Davidson	44	11,587	3819	186	20.53	7/93	14	2	62.29	32.95
12. G. F. Lawson	46	11,118	5501	180	30.56	8/112	11	2	61.76	49.47
13. K. R. Miller	55	10,461	3906	170	22.97	7/60	7	1	61.53	37.33
14. T. M. Alderman	41	10,181	4616	170	27.15	6/47	14	1	59.89	45.33
15. W. A. Johnston	40	11,048	3826	160	23.91	6/44	7	–	69.05	34.63
16. W. J. O'Reilly	27	10,024	3254	144	22.59	7/54	9	3	69.61	32.46
17. H. Trumble	32	8099	3072	141	21.78	8/65	9	3	57.43	37.93
18. M. H. N. Walker	34	10,094	3792	138	27.47	8/143	6	–	73.14	37.56
19. A. A. Mallett	38	9990	3940	132	29.84	8/59	6	1	75.68	39.43
20. B. Yardley	33	8909	3986	126	31.63	7/98	6	1	70.70	44.74
21. R. M. Hogg	38	7633	3503	123	28.47	6/74	6	2	62.05	45.89
22. M. A. Noble	42	7159	3025	121	25.00	7/17	9	2	59.16	42.25
23. B. A. Reid	27	6244	2784	113	24.63	7/51	5	2	55.25	44.58
24. I. W. Johnson	45	8780	3182	109	29.19	7/44	3	–	80.55	36.24
25. P. R. Reiffel	35	6403	2804	104	26.96	6/71	5	–	61.56	43.79
26. G. Giffen	31	6457	2791	103	27.09	7/117	7	1	62.68	43.22
27. A. N. Connolly	29	7818	2981	102	29.22	6/47	4	–	76.64	38.12
28. C. T. B. Turner	17	5179	1670	101	16.53	7/43	11	2	51.27	32.24

LEADING TEST WICKET-TAKERS
(qualification: 300 wickets)

	Tests	Balls	Runs	Wkts	Ave	Best	5wl	10wM	Balls/ wkt	Runs/ 100 balls
1. C. A. Walsh (WI)	114	25,186	10,983	435	25.24	7/37	17	2	57.89	42.59
2. Kapil Dev (Ind)	131	27,740	12,867	434	29.64	9/83	23	2	63.91	46.38

LEADING TEST WICKET-TAKERS continued

	Tests	Balls	Runs	Wkts	Ave	Best	5wl	10wM	Balls/ wkt	Runs/ 100 balls
3. R. J. Hadlee (NZ)	86	21,918	9612	431	22.29	9/52	36	9	50.85	43.85
4. Wasim Akram (Pak)	92	20,350	8858	383	23.12	7/119	22	4	53.13	43.52
5. I. T. Botham (Eng)	102	21,815	10,878	383	28.40	8/34	27	4	56.95	49.86
6. C. E. L. Ambrose (WI)	90	20,300	7965	377	21.12	8/45	22	3	53.84	39.23
7. M. D. Marshall (WI)	81	17,584	7876	376	20.94	7/22	22	4	46.76	44.79
8. S. K. Warne	84	23,501	9505	366	25.96	8/71	16	4	64.21	40.00
9. Imran Khan (Pak)	88	19,458	8258	362	22.81	8/58	23	6	53.75	42.44
10. D. K. Lillee (Aust)	70	18,467	8493	355	23.92	7/83	23	7	52.01	42.44
11. R. G. D. Willis (Eng)	90	17,357	8190	325	25.20	8/43	16	–	53.40	47.18
12. L. R. Gibbs (WI)	79	27,115	8989	309	29.09	8/38	18	2	87.75	33.15
13. F. S. Trueman (Eng)	67	15,178	6625	307	21.57	8/31	17	3	49.43	43.64

ECONOMY & STRIKE RATES COMPARISON
Australians only
(qualification: 100 Test wickets)

Economy rates:		Runs/100 balls	Strike rates:		Balls per wkt
1.	C. T. B. Turner	32.24	1.	C. T. B. Turner	51.27
2.	W. J. O'Reilly	32.46	2.	G. D. McGrath	51.60
3.	A. K. Davidson	32.95	3.	D. K. Lillee	52.01
4.	C. V. Grimmett	34.04	4.	J. R. Thomson	52.67
5.	W. A. Johnston	34.63	5.	B. A. Reid	55.25
6.	R. Benaud	35.08	6.	C. J. McDermott	56.99
7.	I. W. Johnson	36.24	7.	H. Trumble	57.43
8.	K. R. Miller	37.33	8.	M. G. Hughes	57.94
9.	M. H. N. Walker	37.56	9.	M. A. Noble	59.16
10.	H. Trumble	37.93	10.	T. M. Alderman	59.89
11.	A. N. Connolly	38.12	11.	R. R. Lindwall	59.86
12.	R. R. Lindwall	38.46	12.	K. R. Miller	61.53
13.	A. A. Mallett	39.43	13.	P. R. Reiffel	61.56
14.	S. K. Warne	40.00	14.	G. F. Lawson	61.76
15.	G. D. McKenzie	41.44	15.	R. M. Hogg	62.05

Economy rates:	Runs/100 balls		Strike rates:	Balls per wkt
16. M. A. Noble	42.25	16.	A. K. Davidson	62.29
17. G. Giffen	43.32	17.	G. Giffen	62.68
18. G. D. McGrath	43.45	18.	S. K. Warne	64.21
19. P. R. Reiffel	43.79	19.	C. V. Grimmett	67.18
20. B. A. Reid	44.58	20.	W. A. Johnston	69.05

STRIKE RATE COMPARED TO OTHER SLOW BOWLERS

(qualification: slow bowlers with 100 Test wickets)

	Debut	Style	Wkts	Balls per wkt
J. Briggs (Eng)	1884–85	SLA	118	45.18
C. Blythe (Eng)	1901–02	SLA	100	45.46
R. Peel (Eng)	1884–85	SLA	101	51.64
H. Trumble (Aust)	1890	OB	141	57.43
M. A. Noble (Aust)	1897–98	OB	121	59.16
J. C. Laker (Eng)	1947–48	OB	193	62.31
Mushtaq Ahmed (Pak)	1989–90	LBG	172	62.75
M. Muralitharan (SL)	1992–93	OB	253	63.80
S. K. Warne (Aust)	1991–92	LBG	366	64.21
J. H. Wardle (Eng)	1947–48	SLA/SLC	102	64.67
W. Rhodes (Eng)	1899	SLA	127	64.81
B. S. Chandrasekhar (Ind)	1963–64	LBG	242	65.96
Saqlain Mushtaq (Pak)	1995–96	OB	110	66.90
C. V. Grimmett (Aust)	1924–25	LBG	216	67.18
A. Kumble (Ind)	1990	LBG	276	69.30
W. J. O'Reilly (Aust)	1931–32	LBG	144	69.61

Key: LBG = right-arm leg break & googly; OB = right-arm off break; SLA = left-arm orthodox spin; SLC = left-arm chinaman. List includes all Tests up to 4 April 2000.

Note: The definition as to what constitutes a slow bowler is not always clear. Noble and Trumble could be described as medium pace bowlers, as could Chandrasekhar. Wardle bowled in two styles according to pitch conditions. Comparisons are not strictly valid as players from earlier periods benefited from bowling on uncovered pitches. Among purely wrist-spin bowlers, Warne ranks second in terms of strike rate, behind Mushtaq Ahmed.

WORKLOAD & STRIKE RATE PER TEST
(qualification: Australian bowlers who bowled at least 10,000 balls)

	Tests	Balls	Balls/Test	Wkts	Wkts/Test
C. V. Grimmett	37	14,513	392	216	5.84
W. J. O'Reilly	27	10,024	371	144	5.33
R. Benaud	63	19,108	303	248	3.94
M. H. N. Walker	34	10,094	296	138	4.06
G. D. McKenzie	61	17,684	289	246	4.03
S. K. Warne	84	23,501	279	366	4.35
W. A. Johnston	40	11,048	276	160	4.00
D. K. Lillee	70	18,467	263	355	5.07
A. K. Davidson	44	11,587	263	186	4.23
T. M. Alderman	41	10,181	248	170	4.15
G. F. Lawson	46	11,118	241	180	3.91
G. D. McGrath	62	14,863	239	288	4.64
M. G. Hughes	53	12,285	231	212	4.00
C. J. McDermott	71	16,586	230	291	4.09
R. R. Lindwall	61	13,650	223	216	3.74
J. R. Thomson	51	10,535	206	200	3.92
K. R. Miller	55	10,389	188	170	3.09

FIRST-CLASS CRICKET

DEBUT: 1990–91 Victoria v Western Australia, Junction Oval, St Kilda

BATTING & FIELDING

RECORD SERIES BY SERIES

	Mts	Inns	NO	Runs	HS	Ave	50s	Ct
1990–91	1	2	0	20	20	10.00	–	0
1991–92 (Zimbabwe)	2	3	2	53	35*	55.00	–	1
1991–92	9	11	4	120	30*	17.14	–	2
1992–93 (Sri Lanka)	3	4	0	67	35	16.75	–	1
1992–93	9	13	1	172	69	14.33	2	5
1992–93 (New Zealand)	4	5	2	51	22*	17.00	–	1
1993 (England)	16	15	4	246	47	22.36	–	8
1993–94	10	12	2	151	74*	15.10	–	10
1993–94 (South Africa)	5	8	1	84	34	12.00	–	1
1994–95 (Pakistan)	4	5	0	73	33	14.60	–	2
1994–95	7	14	1	101	36*	7.76	–	5
1994–95 (West Indies)	6	6	0	51	23	8.50	–	5
1995–96	9	9	2	132	36	18.85	–	9

	Mts	Inns	NO	Runs	HS	Ave	50s	Ct
1996–97	7	10	0	159	30	15.90	–	8
1996–97 (South Africa)	5	7	0	101	44	14.42	–	4
1997 (England)	12	17	1	293	53	18.31	1	5
1997–98	9	12	2	138	36	13.80	–	7
1997–98 (India)	5	8	1	129	35	18.42	–	3
1998–99	5	7	2	98	38	19.60	–	8
1998–99 (West Indies)	6	10	0	190	33	19.00	–	6
1999–2000 (Sri Lanka)	5	7	1	55	27	9.16	–	5
1999–2000 (Zimbabwe)	2	3	1	8	6	4.00	–	0
1999–2000	6	7	1	187	86	31.16	2	7
1999–2000 (New Zealand)	4	5	0	60	24	12.00	–	6
Total	151	199	28	2739	86	16.01	6	109

SUMMARY

	Mts	Inns	NO	Runs	HS	Ave	50s	Ct
Tests	84	117	12	1613	86	15.36	4	64
Victoria	29	38	6	545	69	17.03	2	21
Australian XI (in Aust.)	2	2	1	7	6*	7.00	–	0
Australians (overseas)	36	42	9	574	44	17.39	–	24
Total	151	199	28	2739	86	16.01	6	109

FIRST-CLASS FIFTIES (6)

See Test match section for details of the four instances in Tests.

In addition, Warne has made two fifties for Victoria:

69   v Western Australia (St Kilda) 1992–93

52   v New South Wales (Sydney) 1992–93

HIGHEST PARTNERSHIPS

See Test match section for details of two century stands. In addition, Warne has shared in the following notable stands for Victoria:

103   8th wicket, with Tony Dodemaide, Victoria v Western Australia, St Kilda, 1992–93

90   2nd wicket, with Wayne Phillips, Victoria v New South Wales, Sydney, 1992–93

BOWLING

RECORD SERIES BY SERIES

	Mts	Overs	Mdns	Runs	Wkts	Ave	Best	5wI	10wM
1990–91	1	37	13	102	1	102.00	1/41	–	–
1991–92 (Zimbabwe)	2	97.4	28	207	11	18.81	7/49	1	–
1991–92	9	312	81	853	20	42.65	4/42	–	–
1992–93 (Sri Lanka)	3	38.1	8	158	3	52.66	3/11	–	–
1992–93	9	309.5	57	983	27	36.40	7/52	2	–
1992–93	4	187.5	81	337	19	17.73	4/8	–	–
(New Zealand)									
1993 (England)	16	765.5	281	1698	75	22.64	5/61	2	–
1993–94	10	574.2	176	1255	63	19.92	7/56	5	1
1993–94 (South Africa)	5	278	96	552	24	23.00	4/86	–	–
1994–95 (Pakistan)	4	210.4	59	598	23	26.00	6/136	2	–
1994–95	7	373.2	123	814	40	20.35	8/71	3	1
1994–95 (West Indies)	6	178	46	553	23	24.04	4/70	–	–
1995–96	9	449.5	131	1057	42	25.16	7/23	2	1
1996–97	7	314.1	87	795	27	29.44	4/95	–	–
1996–97 (South Africa)	5	169	60	397	16	24.81	4/43	–	–
1997 (England)	12	433.4	112	1154	57	20.24	7/103	4	–
1997–98	9	498.5	115	1381	47	29.38	6/34	3	1
1997–98 (India)	5	209	43	739	12	61.58	4/85	–	–
1998–99	5	178.1	32	631	10	63.10	2/80	–	–
1998–99 (West Indies)	6	162.5	37	509	11	46.27	3/26	–	–
1999–2000 (Sri Lanka)	5	102.5	31	272	15	18.13	5/52	1	–
1999–2000	2	92.1	27	238	10	23.80	3/50	–	–
(Zimbabwe)									
1999–2000	6	256.5	71	705	20	35.25	5/110	1	–
1999–2000	4	158.2	37	519	17	30.52	4/68	–	–
(New Zealand)									
TOTAL	151	6382.2	1832	16507	613	26.92	8/71	26	4

RECORD FOR TEAMS

	Mts	Overs	Mdns	Runs	Wkts	Ave	Best	5wI	10wM
In Australia:									
Tests	41	1909.4	544	4635	188	24.65	8/71	11	4
Victoria (Sheffield Shield):									
v New South Wales	9	429.4	94	1286	30	42.86	5/77	2	–
v Queensland	5	240	47	693	13	53.30	3/70	–	–

RECORD FOR TEAMS continued

	Mts	Overs	Mdns	Runs	Wkts	Ave	Best	5wI	10wM
v South Australia	5	232.1	61	651	15	43.40	4/119	–	–
v Tasmania	4	165.1	50	413	15	27.53	5/104	1	–
v Western Australia	6	257.1	73	658	24	27.41	6/42	2	–
Total for Victoria	29	1324.1	325	3701	97	38.15	6/42	5	–
Australian XI	2	70.3	17	240	12	20.00	4/42	–	–
Total in Australia	72	3304.2	886	8576	297	28.87	8/71	16	4

In England:

	Mts	Overs	Mdns	Runs	Wkts	Ave	Best	5wI	10wM
Tests	12	677	247	1454	58	25.06	6/48	2	–
Australians (non-Test)	16	522.3	146	1398	74	18.89	7/103	4	–
Total in England	28	1199.3	393	2852	132	21.60	7/103	6	–

In India:

	Mts	Overs	Mdns	Runs	Wkts	Ave	Best	5wI	10wM
Tests	3	167	37	540	10	54.00	4/85	–	–
Australians (non-Test)	2	42	6	199	2	99.50	2/88	–	–
Total in India	5	209	43	739	12	61.58	4/85	–	–

In New Zealand:

	Mts	Overs	Mdns	Runs	Wkts	Ave	Best	5wI	10wM
Tests	6	288.2	105	670	32	20.93	4/8	–	–
Australians (non-Test)	2	57.5	13	186	4	46.50	2/21	–	–
Total in New Zealand	8	346.1	118	856	36	23.77	4/8	–	–

In Pakistan:

	Mts	Overs	Mdns	Runs	Wkts	Ave	Best	5wI	10wM
Tests	3	181.4	50	504	18	28.00	6/136	2	–
Australians (non-Test)	1	29	9	94	5	18.80	3/42	–	–
Total in Pakistan	4	210.4	59	598	23	26.00	6/136	2	–

In South Africa:

	Mts	Overs	Mdns	Runs	Wkts	Ave	Best	5wI	10wM
Tests	6	323.5	116	618	26	23.76	4/43	–	–
Australians (non-Test)	4	123.1	40	331	14	23.64	3/1	–	–
Total in South Africa	10	447	156	949	40	23.72	4/43	–	–

In Sri Lanka:

	Mts	Overs	Mdns	Runs	Wkts	Ave	Best	5wI	10wM
Tests	5	94.2	28	273	11	24.81	5/52	1	–

RECORD FOR TEAMS continued

	Mts	Overs	Mdns	Runs	Wkts	Ave	Best	5wl	10wM
Australians (non-Test)	3	46.4	11	157	7	22.42	3/74	–	–
Total in Sri Lanka	8	141	39	430	18	23.88	5/52	1	–
In West Indies:									
Tests	7	221.5	53	674	17	39.64	4/70	–	–
Australians (non-Test)	5	119	30	388	17	22.82	3/21	–	–
Total in West Indies	12	340.5	83	1062	34	31.23	4/70	–	–
In Zimbabwe:									
Test	1	53.1	13	137	6	22.83	3/68	–	–
Australians (non-Test)	3	136.4	42	308	15	20.53	7/49	1	–
Total in Zimbabwe	4	189.5	55	445	21	21.19	7/49	1	–
TOTAL	151	6388.2	1834	16,507	613	26.92	8/71	26	4

RECORD ON AUSTRALIAN GROUNDS

	Mts	Overs	Mdns	Runs	Wkts	Ave	Best	5wl	10wM
Adelaide Oval	10	457	129	1159	31	37.38	4/31	–	–
Brisbane Cricket Ground	7	428.2	137	978	48	20.37	8/71	2	2
Hobart, Bellerive Oval	8	290	77	840	39	21.53	6/31	3	–
Melbourne:									
Melbourne Cricket Ground	19	922.2	241	2324	83	28.00	7/52	5	–
St Kilda Cricket Ground	3	115.3	24	332	10	33.20	5/49	1	–
Perth, WACA Ground	10	341.3	83	967	25	38.68	4/64	–	–
Sydney:									
North Sydney Oval	1	58	9	195	3	65.00	2/78	–	–
Sydney Cricket Ground	14	691.4	186	1781	58	30.70	7/56	5	2
TOTAL	72	3304.2	886	8576	297	28.87	8/71	16	4

RECORD IN FIRST AND SECOND INNINGS

	Overs	Mdns	Runs	Wkts	Avge	Best	5wl
FIRST INNINGS:							
In Australia:							
Tests	1045.4	283	2612	91	28.70	7/23	4

RECORD IN FIRST AND SECOND INNINGS continued

		Overs	Mdns	Runs	Wkts	Avge	Best	5wl
Victoria		739.1	180	2067	65	31.80	5/49	3
Australian XI		38.1	9	118	7	16.85	4/104	–
	TOTAL	1823	472	4797	163	29.42	7/23	7
Overseas:								
England	Tests	280	98	645	28	23.03	6/48	1
	Other	280.4	85	706	39	18.10	5/57	2
	TOTAL	560.4	183	1351	67	20.16	6/48	3
India	Tests	112	24	338	7	48.28	4/85	–
	Other	42	6	199	2	99.50	2/88	–
	TOTAL	154	30	537	9	59.66	4/85	–
New Zealand	Tests	122.5	43	271	17	15.94	4/8	–
	Other	30	3	113	2	56.50	2/53	–
	TOTAL	152.5	46	384	19	20.21	4/8	–
Pakistan	Test	90.3	30	255	10	25.50	6/136	1
	Other	10	3	42	3	14.00	3/42	–
	TOTAL	100.3	33	297	13	22.84	6/136	1
South Africa	Tests	203.2	67	431	13	33.15	4/92	–
	Other	63.5	19	211	6	35.16	3/49	–
	TOTAL	267.1	86	642	19	33.78	4/92	–
Sri Lanka	Tests	79	21	239	8	29.87	5/52	1
	Other	28	6	80	3	26.66	2/37	–
	TOTAL	107	27	319	11	29.00	5/52	1
West Indies	Tests	136.5	36	427	10	42.70	3/83	–
	Other	55	15	181	9	20.11	3/21	–
	TOTAL	191.5	51	608	19	32.00	3/21	–
Zimbabwe	Test	23	2	69	3	23.00	3/69	–
	Other	59	17	133	2	66.50	1/40	–
	TOTAL	82	19	202	5	40.40	3/69	–
Total Overseas	Tests	1047.3	321	2675	96	27.86	6/48	3
	All first-class	1616	475	4340	162	26.79	6/48	5
Overall total		3439	947	9137	325	28.11	7/23	12

SECOND INNINGS:

In Australia:

		Overs	Mdns	Runs	Wkts	Avge	Best	5wl
	Tests	864	261	2023	97	20.85	8/71	7
Victoria		585	145	1634	32	51.06	6/41	1

RECORD IN FIRST AND SECOND INNINGS continued

		Overs	Mdns	Runs	Wkts	Avge	Best	5wl
Australian XI		32.2	8	122	5	24.40	4/42	–
	TOTAL	1481.2	414	3779	134	28.20	8/71	8
Overseas:								
England	Tests	397	149	809	30	26.96	5/82	1
	Other	241.5	61	692	35	19.77	7/103	2
	TOTAL	638.5	210	1501	65	23.09	7/103	3
India	Tests	55	13	202	3	67.33	2/80	–
New Zealand	Tests	165.3	62	399	15	26.60	4/63	–
	Other	27.5	10	73	2	36.50	2/21	–
	TOTAL	193.2	72	472	17	27.76	4/63	–
Pakistan	Tests	91.1	20	249	8	31.12	5/89	1
	Other	19	6	52	2	26.00	2/52	–
	TOTAL	110.1	26	301	10	30.10	5/89	1
South Africa	Tests	120.3	49	187	13	14.38	4/43	–
	Other	59.2	21	120	8	15.00	3/1	–
	TOTAL	179.5	70	307	21	14.61	4/43	–
Sri Lanka	Tests	15.2	7	34	3	11.33	3/11	–
	Other	18.4	5	77	4	19.25	3/74	–
	TOTAL	34	12	111	7	15.85	3/11	–
West Indies	Tests	85	17	247	7	35.28	4/70	–
	Other	64	15	207	8	25.87	3/42	–
	TOTAL	149	32	454	15	30.26	4/70	–
Zimbabwe	Test	30.1	11	68	3	22.66	3/68	–
	Others	77.4	25	175	13	13.46	7/49	1
	TOTAL	107.5	36	243	16	15.18	7/49	1
Total Overseas	Tests	959.4	328	2195	82	26.76	5/82	2
	All first-class	1468	471	3591	154	23.31	7/49	5
Overall total		2949.2	885	7370	288	25.59	8/71	13

RESULTS OF FIRST-CLASS MATCHES IN WHICH WARNE HAS APPEARED

Won	75	(49.7%)
Lost	29	(19.2%)
Drawn	47	(31.1%)
Total	151	

First-Class matches in which Warne has appeared continued

By country:

	Won	Lost	Drawn	Total	% won
Australia	34	13	25	72	47.22
India	1	3	1	5	20.00
Sri Lanka	3	1	4	8	37.50
West Indies	6	3	3	12	50.00
New Zealand	6	1	1	8	75.00
England	15	5	8	28	53.57
South Africa	6	2	2	10	60.00
Pakistan	–	1	3	4	0.00
Zimbabwe	4	–	–	1	100.00
Total	75	29	47	151	49.66%

TEN WICKETS IN A MATCH (4)

See Test match section for details.

HAT-TRICK (1)

See Test match section.

THREE WICKETS IN FOUR BALLS (2)

See Test match section. Additionally:

Australians v Border, East London, 8 March 1997

– Steven Pope, Dion Taljard (first ball), Makhaya Ntini (second)

TEN WICKETS IN A MATCH (4)

See Test match section.

FIVE WICKETS IN AN INNINGS (26)

See Test match section for details of the sixteen instances in Tests. He has performed the feat on ten other occasions, as follows:

7/49   Australians v Zimbabwe (Harare) 1991–92
7/103   Australians v Derbyshire (Derby) 1997
6/42   Victoria v Western Australia (Melbourne) 1993–94
5/42   Australians v Leicestershire (Leicester) 1997
5/49   Victoria v Western Australia (St Kilda) 1992–93
5/57   Australians v Somerset (Taunton) 1997
5/61   Australians v Gloucestershire (Bristol) 1993
5/77   Victoria v New South Wales (Sydney) 1993–94
5/104   Victoria v Tasmania (Melbourne) 1994–95
5/122   Victoria v New South Wales (Melbourne) 1995–96

MOST MAIDENS IN A ROW
7   Victoria v Western Australia, Melbourne, November 6, 1993

LONGEST SPELL
30 overs   Victoria v Western Australia, Perth, 1994–95

MOST OVERS IN AN INNINGS
48   Victoria v New South Wales (1st innings), Melbourne, 1995–96
46   Victoria v Queensland (2), Melbourne, 1995–96
45   Victoria v New South Wales (1), Melbourne, 1995–96
43   Victoria v South Australia (1), Adelaide, 1993–94

MOST OVERS IN A MATCH
68   Victoria v New South Wales, Sydney, 1993–94
65.4   Victoria v Western Australia, Melbourne, 1993–94
64   Victoria v Western Australia, Perth, 1994–95

MOST EXPENSIVE BOWLING
1/122   Australians v Worcestershire, (2nd innings) Worcester, 1993
1/117   Victoria v New South Wales (2), North Sydney, 1997–98
0/111   Australians v Mumbai (1), Bombay, 1997–98
1/106   Victoria v Queensland (2), Melbourne, 1997–98

MOST RUNS OFF AN OVER
19   Graeme Hick (19), Worcestershire v Australians, New Road, Worcester,
       6 May 1993 (2nd innings)
19   Graeme Hick (19), Worcestershire v Australians, New Road, Worcester,
       7 May 1993 (2)
18   Tom Moody (18), Western Australia v Victoria, WACA Ground, Perth,
       16 November 1998 (2)
17   Michael Bevan (17), New South Wales v Victoria, Melbourne,
       16 February 1992 (2)
17   Greg Matthews (17), New South Wales v Victoria, Sydney,
       9 November 1992 (2)
17   Dale Benkenstein (17), Natal v Australians, Durban,
       20 February 1997 (1)
17   Nimesh Perera (15) & Chamara Silva (2), Sri Lankan Board XI
       v Australians, Colombo (PSC), 5 September 1999 (2)
16   Greg Matthews (16), New South Wales v Victoria, Sydney,
       8 November 1991 (1)

18   Trevor Bayliss (16), New South Wales v Victoria, Sydney,
        9 November 1992 (2)

16   Tony Murphy (16), Surrey v Australians, The Oval, London,
        26 May 1993 (1)

16   Keith Arthurton (16), West Indian President's XI v Australians, Castries,
        St Lucia, 27 March 1995 (1)

16   Dene Hills (16), Tasmania v Victoria, Bellerive Oval, Hobart, 22 December
        1997 (2)

16   Sachin Tendulkar (16), Mumbai v Australians, Brabourne Stadium,
        Mumbai, 25 February 1998 (1)

THE DISMISSALS

Warne has dismissed 307 different batsmen in first-class cricket:

10 times: G. J. Thorpe.

9 times: A. J. Stewart.

8 times: W. J. Cronje; N. Hussain; D. J. Richardson.

7 times: M. A. Atherton.

6 times: S. Chanderpaul; P. A. J. DeFreitas; S. B. Doull; R. Dravid; G. A. Gooch;
            C. L. Hooper; B. M. McMillan; C. A. Walsh.

5 times: N. J. Astle; M. G. Bevan; M. A. Butcher; A. R. Caddick; C. L. Cairns;
            Ijaz Ahmed; Inzamam-ul-Haq; B. C. Lara; C. D. McMillan;
            R. A. Smith; Wasim Akram.

4 times: J. C. Adams; J. Angel; Azhar Mahmood; Basit Ali;
            K. C. G. Benjamin; I. R. Bishop; D. J. Cullinan; S. P. Fleming;
            C. Z. Harris; A. H. Jones; G. Kirsten; D. N. Patel; S. M. Pollock;
            K. R. Rutherford; R. G. Samuels; M. A. Taylor; P. C. R. Tufnell;
            M. E. Waugh.

3 times: Aamir Sohail; P. R. Adams; Akram Raza; C. E. L. Ambrose;
            K. L. T. Arthurton; P. A. de Silva; P. S. de Villiers; P. A. Emery;
            M. W. Gatting; D. Gough; W. J. Holdsworth; P. N. Kirsten;
            M. N. Lathwell; C. R. Matthews; T. M. Moody; M. B. Owens;
            A. C. Parore; Rameez Raja; M. R. Ramprakash; J. N. Rhodes;
            R. B. Richardson; Saeed Anwar; J. D. Siddons; M. L. Su'a; P. M. Such;
            S. R. Tendulkar; D. L. Vettori; K. C. Wessels; G. P. Wickremasinghe.

Twice: C. J. Adams; G. I. Allott; Aqib Javed; A. M. Bacher; W. K. M. Benjamin;
            T. E. Blain; N. Boje; E. A. Brandes; J. A. Brayshaw; J. Cox; J. P. Crawley;
            R. D. B. Croft; M. J. Di Venuto; A. A. Donald; D. A. Fitzgerald;
            N. A. Folland; D. R. Gilbert; A. C. Gilchrist; M. W. Goodwin;
            M. L. Hayden; D. L. Hemp; A. G. Huckle; D. P. M. D. Jayawardene;
            B. P. Julian; J. H. Kallis; R. S. Kaluwitharana; J. L. Langer;
            V. V. S. Laxman; C. C. Lewis; M. J. McCague; R. J. J. McLean;

J. P. Maher; D. E. Malcolm; G. D. Mendis; Mohammad Akram;
Mohsin Kamal; D. K. Morrison; P. A. Nixon; B. P. Patterson;
B. A. Pocock; A. Ranatunga; Rashid Latif; S. J. Rhodes; P. E. Robinson;
R. C. Russell; Saqlain Mushtaq; W. A. Seccombe; N. S. Sidhu;
P. V. Simmons; M. J. Slater; B. F. Smith; H. H. Streak; P. L. Symcox;
H. P. Tillekeratne; R. J. Tucker; S. D. Udal; W. P. U. J. C. Vaas;
M. R. J. Veletta; Waqar Younis; G. J. Whittall; S. C. Williams;
P. L. Wiseman; B. A. Young; S. Young; T. J. Zoehrer.

Once: Abdur Razzaq; H. A. G. Anthony; S. D. Anurasiri; K. J. Arnott;
J. M. Arthur; M. S. Atapattu; Ata-ur-Rehman; M. Azharuddin;
M. D. Bailey; T. J. Barsby; T. H. Bayliss; J. E. Benjamin; I. D. Blackwell;
G. S. Blewett; D. C. Boon; A. R. Border; B. C. Broad; C. O. Browne;
M. L. Bruyns; M. G. Burmester; R. Q. Cake; A. D. R. Campbell;
S. L. Campbell; U. D. U. Chandana; R. Chee Quee; V. P. Clarke;
S. H. Cook; P. A. Cottey; G. R. Cowdrey; M. D. Crowe; B. A. Cruse;
A. C. Cummins; R. J. Cunliffe; A. Dale; R. P. Davis; R. I. Dawson;
R. P. de Groen; S. I. de Saram; L. P. C. de Silva; T. M. Dilshan;
D. B. D'Oliveira; B. J. Drew; S. C. Ecclestone; A. Flower; G. W. Flower;
G. I. Foley; N. A. Foster; I. S. Gallage; S. C. Ganguly; S. P. George;
H. H. Gibbs; T. R. Gripper; A. Habib; T. H. C. Hancock; R. A. Harper;
A. J. Harris; U. C. Hathurasinghe; A. N. Hayhurst; R. C. Haynes;
I. A. Healy; P. R. Hewage; G. A. Hick; D. J. Hickey; D. F. Hills;
R. I. C. Holder; A. J. Hollioake; B. C. Hollioake; N. P. Hough;
D. L. Houghton; A. C. Hudson; G. A. Hughes; K. C. Jackson;
R. D. Jacobs; M. P. Jarvis; H. P. W. Jayawardene; D. M. Jones;
P. S. Jones; L. Joseph; H. H. Kanitkar; M. S. Kasprowicz; G. J. Kersey;
L. Klusener; K. M. Krikken; G. Lamb; M. P. Lavender; S. Lee;
D. S. Lehmann; R. N. Lewis; A. L. Logie; G. B. T. Lovell; M. A. Lynch;
N. C. McGarrell; S. C. G. MacGill; G. D. McGrath; P. E. McIntyre;
N. A. M. McLean; G. I. Macmillan; M. W. R. Madurasinghe;
Manzoor Akhtar; G. R. Marsh; J. A. H. Marshall; D. R. Martyn;
C. D. Matthews; G. R. J. Matthews; M. P. Maynard; Moin Khan;
N. R. Mongia; R. R. Montgomerie; B. D. Moore-Gordon; M. P. Mott;
M. Muralitharan; A. J. Murphy; Mushtaq Ahmed; J. R. Murray;
P. C. Nobes; M. Ntini; J. Ormond; N. R. G. Perera; W. Phillip;
A. R. K. Pierson; B. T. Player; J. C. Pooley; S. C. Pope; M. S. K. Prasad;
A. J. Pycroft; P. J. L. Radley; D. Rampersad; S. Ramesh; B. A. Reid;
S. J. Renshaw; A. S. Rollins; J. S. Roos; Saleem Malik; J. C. Scuderi;
K. F. Semple; O. A. Shah; R. J. Shastri; S. F. Shephard; M. G. Sinclair;
M. S. Sinclair; A. M. Smith; D. Smith; R. P. Snell; N. J. Speak;

313

D. J. Spencer, J. Srinath, A. M. Stuart; A Symonds; D. Taljard;
C. J. Tavaré; R. G. Twose; A. van Troost; S. D. Thomas;
M. E. Trescothick; T. R. Ward; S. L. Watkin; D. J. Watson; W. Watson;
S. R. Waugh; P. N. Weekes; V. J. Wells; J. J. Whitaker; B. N. Wigney;
J. R. Wileman; D. Williams; W. K. Wishart; K. A. Wong; A. J. Wright;
J. G. Wright; Zahid Fazal; D. N. T. Zoysa.

DISMISSALS SUMMARY

Warne's wickets have been obtained as follows:

Bowled	106 (17.3%)
LBW	106 (17.3%)
Caught	357 (58.2%)
Stumped	44 (7.2%)
Total	613

ON-FIELD PARTNERSHIPS

MOST CATCHES BY A FIELDSMAN OR A WICKETKEEPER FROM WARNE'S
BOWLING

56	Mark Taylor
42	Ian Healy
29	Mark Waugh (incl. 1 as substitute)
14	Steve Waugh
13	David Boon
12	Greg Blewett
11	Ricky Ponting
8	Darren Berry, Paul Reiffel, Michael Slater, Glenn McGrath (incl. 1 as sub)
7	Justin Langer
6	Allan Border, Michael Bevan, Dean Jones and Darrin Ramshaw

In addition, Warne has held 24 catches from his own bowling.

The wicketkeepers to perform stumpings are I. A. Healy (25),
D. S. Berry (11), T. J. Zoehrer (4), A. C. Gilchrist (2), P. A. Emery (1) and
D. R. Martyn (1).

LEFT-HANDERS

Of his 613 victims, 141 (23%) have been left-handers. Left-handed batsmen
he has dismissed most often are:

G. P. Thorpe (10), S. Chanderpaul (6), M. G. Bevan (5), M. A. Butcher (5),
B. C. Lara (5), Wasim Akram (5), J. C. Adams (4), J. Angel (4),
S. P. Fleming (4), C. Z. Harris (4), G. Kirsten (4), R. G. Samuels (4), M. A. Taylor (4),
Aamir Sohail (3), C. E. L. Ambrose (3), K. L. T. Arthurton (3), M. A. Butcher (3),
P. A. Emery (3), Saeed Anwar (3), D. L. Vettori (3) and K. C. Wessels (3).

REPRESENTATIVE LIMITED-OVERS CRICKET

ONE-DAY INTERNATIONAL CRICKET
DEBUT: 1992–93 Australia v New Zealand, Wellington
HONOURS: Australian ODI vice-captain 1997–98 to 1999–2000; has taken
most wickets for Australia at ODI level.

BATTING & FIELDING – ALL MATCHES

	Mts	Inns	NO	Runs	HS	Ave	50s	Ct
Aust ODIs	146	84	24	753	55	12.55	1	50
Victoria 15	15	11	2	162	32	18.00	–	8
Aust XIs	17	10	3	67	18	9.55	–	5
Prime Minister's	1	1	1	2	2*	–	–	–
Total	179	106	30	984	55	12.94	1	63

BOWLING – ALL MATCHES

RECORD SERIES BY SERIES

	Mts	Overs	Mdns	Runs	Wicks	Ave	BB	4wI	RpO
1991–92 (Zimbabwe)	3	26	3	102	2	51.00	1/32	–	3.92
1991–92	2	20	0	84	3	28.00	2/37	–	4.20
1992–93	1	5.5	0	31	3	10.33	3/31	–	5.31
1992–93 (New Zealand)	2	18	2	75	2	37.50	2/40	-	4.16
1993–94	12	110	6	385	22	17.50	4/19	2	3.50
1993–94 (South Africa)	9	69	3	285	11	25.90	4/36	1	4.13
1993–94 (Sharjah)	3	29	1	103	9	11.44	4/34	1	3.55
1994–95 (Sri Lanka)	3	28	1	109	7	15.57	3/29	–	3.89
1994–95 (Pakistan)	6	58.2	4	238	6	39.33	4/40	1	4.08
1994–95	8	79	6	299	13	23.00	3/40	–	3.78
1994–95 (New Zealand)	4	40	6	140	5	28.00	2/18	–	3.50
1994–95 (West Indies)	4	39.1	4	204	4	51.00	2/33	–	5.2
1995–96	13	112.1	8	478	16	29.87	3/20	–	4.26
1996 (Ind. & Pak. WC)	7	68.3	3	263	12	21.91	4/34	2	3.83
1996–97	11	105.4	9	432	28	15.42	5/33	4	4.08
1996–97 (South Africa)	8	73.1	2	366	14	26.14	2/36	–	5.00
1997 (England)	5	45	1	186	5	37.20	2/21	–	4.13
1997–98	12	111.3	6	484	17	28.46	3/43	–	4.34
1997–98 (India)	5	49	0	219	5	43.80	2/45	–	4.46
1997–98 (Sharjah)	5	47	2	221	4	55.25	2/28	–	4.70
1998–99	13	120.5	3	555	20	27.75	3/16	–	4.59
1998–99 (West Indies)	7	63	10	254	13	19.53	3/28	–	4.03

	Mts	Overs	Mdns	Runs	Wicks	Ave	BB	4wI	RpO
1999 (Eng. World Cup)	13	114.2	18	423	25	16.92	4/29	2	3.61
1999–2000 (Sri Lanka)	5	40	1	213	6	35.50	2/36	–	5.32
1999–2000 (Zimbabwe)	3	19	1	82	4	20.50	2/40	–	4.31
1999–2000	6	52	4	244	7	34.85	2/31	–	4.69
1999–2000 (New Zeal.)	6	49	4	194	9	21.55	3/50	–	4.72
1999–2000 (South Africa)	3	28	3	98	3	32.66	2/30	–	3.50
Totals	179	1630.3	111	6727	275	24.60	5/33	13	4.14

RECORD FOR TEAMS

	Mts	Overs	Mdns	Runs	Wicks	Ave	BB	4wI	RpO
In Australia									
One-Day Internationals	57	527.1	28	2183	97	22.50	5/33	5	4.14
Australia v Australia 'A'	4	40	5	168	7	24.00	3/40	–	4.20
Australia v World XI	1	10	0	57	0	–	–	–	5.70
Prime Minister's XI	1	10	0	47	1	47.00	1/47	–	4.70
Victoria:									
v ACT	1	10	0	31	2	15.50	2/31	–	3.10
v NSW	3	19	2	83	4	20.75	3/43	–	4.36
v Qld	3	25	1	139	2	69.50	1/36	–	5.56
v SA	3	30	3	113	4	28.25	2/34	–	3.76
v Tas	2	15.5	1	66	8	8.25	5/35	1	4.16
v WA	2	20	2	68	2	34.00	2/17	–	3.40
v India	1	10	0	37	2	18.50	2/27	–	3.70
Total for Victoria	15	129.5	9	537	24	22.37	5/35	1	4.13
Total in Australia	78	717	42	2992	129	23.19	5/33	6	4.17
In England									
ODIs	13	123.2	13	490	21	23.33	4/33	2	3.97
Australians (non ODI)	5	36	6	119	9	13.22	3/35	–	3.30
Total in England	18	159.2	19	609	30	20.30	4/33	2	3.82
In New Zealand									
ODIs	11	99	10	374	16	23.37	3/50	–	3.77
Australians non ODI	1	8	2	35	0	–	–	–	4.37
Total in New Zealand	12	107	12	409	16	25.56	3/50	–	3.82

RECORD FOR TEAMS continued

	Mts	Overs	Mdns	Runs	Wicks	Ave	BB	4wl	RpO
In India									
ODIs	11	107.3	3	424	17	24.94	4/34	2	3.94
In Pakistan									
ODIs	7	68.2	4	296	6	49.33	4/40	1	4.33
In South Africa									
ODIs	17	151.1	8	655	24	27.29	4/36	1	4.33
Australians non ODI	3	19	–	94	4	23.50	2/32	–	4.94
Total in South Africa	20	170.1	5	749	28	26.75	4/36	1	4.40
In Sri Lanka									
ODIs	8	68	2	322	13	24.76	3/29	–	4.71
In UAE									
ODIs	8	76	3	324	13	24.92	4/34	1	4.26
In West Indies									
ODIs	11	102.1	14	458	17	26.94	3/28	–	4.48
In Zimbabwe									
ODIs	3	19	1	82	4	20.50	2/40	–	4.31
Australians non ODI	3	26	3	102	2	51.00	1/32	–	3.92
Total in Zimbabwe	6	45	4	184	6	30.66	2/40	–	4.08
Totals	179	1630.3	111	6767	275	24.60	5/33	13	4.14

BATTING & FIELDING – ONE-DAY INTERNATIONALS

RECORD SERIES BY SERIES

	Mts	Inns	NO	Runs	HS	Ave	50s	Ct
1992–93 (New Zealand)	1	1	0	3	3	3.00	–	0
1993–94	10	6	1	15	9	3.00	–	4
1993–94 (South Africa)	8	3	0	87	55	29.00	1	3
1993–94 (Sharjah)	3	1	0	4	4	4.00	–	1
1994–95 (Sri Lanka)	3	2	0	31	30	15.50	–	1
1994–95 (Pakistan)	6	3	2	39	15*	39.00	–	0
1994–95	4	2	0	26	21	13.00	–	2
1994–95 (New Zealand)	4	2	2	7	5*	–	–	2
1994–95 (West Indies)	4	3	2	22	12	22.00	–	1
1995–96	9	2	1	6	3*	6.00	–	3

RECORD SERIES BY SERIES continued

	Mts	Inns	NO	Runs	HS	Ave	50s	Ct
1996 (Ind. & Pak. World Cup)	7	5	2	32	24	10.66	–	1
1996–97	8	5	1	38	11	9.50	–	3
1996–97 (South Africa)	6	5	1	45	23	11.25	–	3
1997 (England)	3	3	1	20	11*	10.00	–	1
1997–98	10	6	1	35	17	7.00	–	6
1997–98 (India)	5	4	1	27	14	9.00	–	2
1997–98 (Sharjah)	5	3	2	32	19	32.00	–	0
1998–99	12	8	2	43	11	7.16	–	6
1998–99 (West Indies)	7	5	2	84	29	28.00	–	0
1999 (England: World Cup)	10	4	1	34	18	11.33	–	1
1999–2000 (Sri Lanka)	5	4	0	43	21	10.75	–	1
1999–2000 (Zimbabwe)	3	did not bat						1
1999–2000	4	3	2	29	16*	29.00	–	4
1999–2000 (New Zealand)	6	2	0	19	12	9.50	–	2
1999–2000 (South Africa)	3	2	0	32	32	16.00	–	2
TOTAL	146	84	24	753	55	12.55	1	50

RECORD AGAINST INDIVIDUAL COUNTRIES

	Mts	Inns	NO	Runs	HS	Ave	50	Ct
v Bangladesh	1	–	–	–	–	–	–	–
v England	12	8	2	75	21	12.50	–	5
v India	12	12	5	74	19	10.57	–	1
v Kenya	1	1	1	0	0*	–	–	0
v New Zealand	22	8	1	75	24	10.71	–	9
v Pakistan	13	9	2	83	30	11.85	–	6
v Scotland	1	–	–	–	–	–	–	–
v South Africa	35	23	4	248	55	13.05	1	15
v Sri Lanka	19	10	2	57	21	7.12	–	5
v West Indies	21	11	6	125	29	25.00	–	5
v Zimbabwe	9	2	1	16	11*	16.00	–	4
TOTAL	146	84	24	753	55	12.55	1	50

HIGHEST SCORES

55	v South Africa, Port Elizabeth, 1993–94
32	v South Africa, Johannesburg, 1999–2000
30	v Pakistan, Colombo (SSC), 1994–95

HIGHEST PARTNERSHIPS

119   8th wicket, with Paul Reiffel, v South Africa, Port Elizabeth, 1993–94

77	9th wicket, with Michael Bevan, v West Indies, Port-of-Spain, Trinidad, 1998–99
54	8th wicket, with Steve Waugh, v West Indies, Georgetown, Guyana, 1998–99
52	8th wicket, with Ian Harvey, v South Africa, Johannesburg, 1999–2000
50	9th wicket, with Tom Moody, v West Indies, Bridgetown, Barbados, 1998–99

BOWLING – ONE-DAY INTERNATIONALS

RECORD SERIES BY SERIES

	Mts	Overs	Mdns	Runs	Wkts	Ave	Best	4w	RpO
1992–93 (New Zealand)	1	10	0	40	2	40.00	2/40	–	4.00
1993–94	10	90	5	301	22	13.68	4/19	2	3.34
1993–94 (South Africa)	8	69	3	285	11	25.90	4/36	1	4.13
1993–94 (Sharjah)	3	29	1	103	9	11.44	4/34	1	3.55
1994–95 (Sri Lanka)	3	28	1	109	7	15.57	3/29	–	3.89
1994–95 (Pakistan)	6	58.2	4	238	6	39.33	4/40	1	4.08
1994–95	4	39	1	133	6	22.16	2/27	–	3.41
1994–95 (New Zealand)	4	40	6	140	5	28.00	2/18	–	3.50
1994–95 (West Indies)	4	39.1	4	204	4	51.00	2/33	–	5.20
1995–96	9	80.1	7	317	15	21.13	3/20	–	3.95
1996 (Ind. & Pak. W. Cup)	7	68.3	3	263	12	21.91	4/34	2	3.83
1996–97	8	75.4	6	325	19	17.10	5/33	3	4.29
1996–97 (South Africa)	6	54.1	2	272	10	27.20	2/36	–	5.02
1997 (England)	3	29	0	129	1	129.00	1/39	–	4.44
1997–98	10	93.3	3	405	12	33.75	3/48	–	4.33
1997–98 (India)	5	49	0	219	5	43.80	2/45	–	4.46
1997–98 (Sharjah)	5	47	2	221	4	55.25	2/28	–	4.70
1998–99	12	112.5	2	532	19	28.00	3/16	–	4.71
1998–99 (West Indies)	7	63	10	254	13	19.53	3/28	–	4.03
1999 (England W. Cup)	10	94.2	13	361	20	18.05	4/29	2	3.82
1999–2000 (Sri Lanka)	5	40	1	213	6	35.50	2/36	–	5.32
1999–2000 (Zimbabwe)	3	19	1	82	4	20.50	2/40	–	4.31
1999–2000	4	36	4	170	4	42.50	2/52	–	4.72
1999–2000 (NZ)	6	49	4	194	9	21.55	3/50	–	4.72
1999–2000 (S. Africa)	3	28	3	98	3	32.66	2/30	–	3.50
TOTAL	146	1341.4	86	5608	228	24.59	5/33	12	4.18

RECORD AGAINST INDIVIDUAL COUNTRIES

	Mts	Overs	Mdns	Runs	Wkts	Ave	Best	4w
v Bangladesh	1	10	2	18	1	18.00	1/18	–
v England	12	114.5	0	498	14	35.71	3/16	–
v India	14	124.2	2	622	11	56.54	2/36	–
v Kenya	1	10	0	25	1	25.00	1/25	–
v New Zealand	22	203.2	15	750	44	17.04	4/19	3
v Pakistan	13	122.1	14	494	22	22.45	4/33	3
v Scotland	1	10	0	39	3	13.00	3/39	–
v South Africa	35	319.4	18	1330	51	26.07	4/36	3
v Sri Lanka	17	156	7	720	28	25.71	3/20	–
v West Indies	21	194.5	25	792	38	20.84	5/33	2
v Zimbabwe	9	76.3	3	320	15	21.33	4/34	1
TOTAL	146	1341.4	86	5608	228	24.59	5/33	12

RECORD BY VENUE

	Mts	Overs	Mdns	Runs	Wkts	Ave	Best	4w
In Australia:								
Adelaide	6	55.5	3	239	14	17.07	4/25	2
Brisbane	4	39	0	192	2	96.00	2/52	–
Hobart	3	26.2	0	103	6	17.16	3/45	–
Melbourne	19	181.1	14	697	32	21.78	4/19	1
Perth	6	59	2	264	11	24.00	3/53	–
Sydney	19	165.5	9	688	32	21.50	5/33	2
Total in Australia	57	527.1	28	2183	97	22.50	5/33	5
Overseas:								
In England	13	123.2	13	490	21	23.33	4/33	2
In New Zealand	11	99	10	374	16	23.37	3/50	–
In India	11	107.3	3	424	17	24.94	4/34	2
In Pakistan	7	68.2	4	296	6	49.33	4/40	1
In South Africa	17	151.1	8	655	24	27.29	4/36	1
In Sri Lanka	8	68	2	322	13	24.76	3/29	–
In Sharjah (UAE)	8	76	3	324	13	24.92	4/34	1
In West Indies	11	102.1	14	458	17	26.94	3/28	–
In Zimbabwe	3	19	1	82	4	20.50	2/40	–
Total Overseas	89	814.3	58	3425	131	26.14	4/33	7
Overall total	146	1341.4	86	5608	228	24.59	5/33	12

CALENDAR YEAR RECORD

Year	Mts	Balls	Mdns	Runs	Wkts	Ave	BB	4w
1993	5	240	2	127	11	11.55	4/19	2
1994	29	1640	13	1045	50	20.90	4/34	3
1995	12	692	13	497	13	38.23	2/18	–
1996	16	911	9	593	36	16.47	5/33	4
1997	18	1017	8	749	23	32.57	4/37	1
1998	17	897	3	693	17	40.76	3/52	–
1999	36	1975	27	1443	62	23.27	4/29	2
2000 (to April)	13	678	11	462	16	28.88	3/50	–

THREE WICKETS IN FOUR BALLS (1)

v South Africa, Wills Series, Iqbal Stadium, Faisalabad, 18 October 1994
– Eric Simons, Meyrick Pringle (first ball), Clive Eksteen (second)
In this match, Warne also dismissed South Africa's No. 11 Fanie de Villiers for
a second-ball duck, giving him four wickets in six balls.

FOUR WICKETS IN AN INNINGS (12)

5/33	v West Indies (Sydney) 1996–97
4/19	v New Zealand (Melbourne) 1993–94
4/25	v New Zealand (Adelaide) 1993–94
4/29	v South Africa (Birmingham) 1999 (World Cup semi-final)
4/33	v Pakistan (Lord's) 1999 (World Cup final)
4/34	v New Zealand (Sharjah) 1993–94
4/34	v Zimbabwe (Nagpur) 1996 (World Cup)
4/36	v South Africa (Port Elizabeth) 1993–94
4/36	v West Indies (Mohali) 1996 (World Cup semi-final)
4/37	v Pakistan (Sydney) 1996–97
4/40	v South Africa (Faisalabad) 1994–95
4/52	v Pakistan (Adelaide) 1996–97

IMPORTANT MILESTONES

1st wicket	Andrew Jones (New Zealand), Basin Reserve, Wellington, 24 March 1993 (Warne's 1st match)
50th	Roshan Mahanama (Sri Lanka), Colombo (PSS), 13 September 1994 (25th)
100th	Junior Murray (West Indies), Melbourne, 6 December 1996 (60th)
150th	Chris Cairns (New Zealand), Sharjah, 21 April 1994 (94th)
200th	Moin Khan (Pakistan), Lord's, World Cup final, 20 June 1999 (125th)

MOST ECONOMICAL
(10-over stints)

3/11   v West Indies (Manchester), 1999 World Cup
2/18   v South Africa (Wellington), 1994–95
1/18   v Bangladesh (Chester-le-Street), 1999 World Cup
4/19   v New Zealand (Melbourne), 1993–94

MOST MAIDENS
4   v West Indies (Manchester), 1999 World Cup
4   v South Africa (Birmingham), 1999 World Cup

MAN OF THE MATCH AWARDS
1993–94   v New Zealand (Adelaide), New Zealand (Melbourne),
                 New Zealand (Sharjah). Player of preliminary series
1994–95   Pakistan (SSC, Colombo), Zimbabwe (Perth)
1995–96   Player of the Finals (shared with Mark Taylor)
1996 World Cup   Zimbabwe (Nagpur), West Indies (Mohali)
1996–97   West Indies (Sydney), Pakistan (Sydney)
1999 World Cup   South Africa (second final), Pakistan (final)

THE DISMISSALS
Warne has dismissed 133 different batsmen in One-Day Internationals:

8 times: D. J. Cullinan (SA)
7 times: W. J. Cronje (SA)
6 times: C. D. McMillan (NZ)
5 times: J. N. Rhodes (SA)
4 times: J. C. Adams (WI); S. L. Campbell (WI); M. J. Greatbatch (NZ);
            J. H. Kallis (SA); Moin Khan (P); S. M. Pollock (SA); H. P. Tillekeratne
            (SL).
3 times: C. E. L. Ambrose (WI); C. L. Cairns (NZ); D. J. Callaghan (SA);
            M. A. Ealham (E); C. Z. Harris (NZ); Inzamam-ul-Haq (P); A. Jadeja (I);
            R. S. Kaluwitharana (SL); R. S. Mahanama (SL); A. C. Parore (NZ);
            Wasim Akram (P); S. C. Williams (WI).
Twice: N. J. Astle (NZ); K. C. G. Benjamin (WI); T. E. Blain (NZ); H. R. Bryan
            (WI); P. A. de Silva (SL); P. S. de Villiers (SA); A. Flower (Z);
            G. W. Flower (Z); M. W. Goodwin (Z); C. L. Hooper (WI); M. J. Horne
            (NZ); R. S. Kalpage (SL); P. N. Kirsten (SA); N. V. Knight (E);
            B. C. Lara (WI); B. M. McMillan (SA); C. R. Matthews (SA);
            N. R. Mongia (I); J. R. Murray (WI); A. S. A. Perera (SL); Shahid Afridi
            (P); P. V. Simmons (WI); S. A. Thomson (NZ); R. G. Twose (NZ);
            W. P. U. J. C. Vaas (SL); D. L. Vettori (NZ); C. A. Walsh (WI);
            Waqar Younis (P).

Once: Aamir Sohail (P); Abdur Razzaq (P); A. B. Agarkar (I); Akram Khan (Bang); M. G. D. Alingham (Scot); K. L. T. Arthurton (WI); M. S. Atapattu (SL); A. M. Bacher (SA); Basit Ali (P); I. R. Bishop (WI); A. M. Blignaut (Z); J. E. Brinkley (Scot); C. O. Browne (WI); A. D. R. Campbell (Z); U. D. U. Chandana (SL); S. Chanderpaul (WI); P. B. Dassanayake (SL); H. D. P. K. Dharmasena (SL); M. W. Douglas (NZ); C. E. Eksteen (SA); C. N. Evans (Z); N. H. Fairbrother (E); S. P. Fleming (NZ); D. J. Gandhi (I); H. H. Gibbs (SA); O. D. Gibson (WI); G. A. Gooch (E); D. Gough (E); A. J. Hall (SA); G. M. Hamilton (Scot); R. A. Harper (WI); B. R. Hartland (NZ); G. A. Hick (E); R. I. C. Holder (WI); A. J. Hollioake (E); A. C. Hudson (SA); N. Hussain (E); Ijaz Ahmed (P); R. D. Jacobs (WI); W. R. James (Z); S. T. Jayasuriya (SL); D. P. M. D. Jayawardene (SL); A. H. Jones (NZ); R. D. King (WI); G. Kirsten (SA); L. Klusener (SA); A. P. Kuiper (SA); G. R. Larsen (NZ); R. T. Latham (NZ); A. C. I. Lock (Z); N. A. M. McLean (WI); Mohammad Wasim (P); A. D. Mullally (E); D. J. Nash (NZ); C. J. Nevin (NZ); K. Odoyo (Kenya); S. G. Peall (Z); M. Prabhakar (I); M. S. K. Prasad (I); M. W. Pringle (SA); C. P. H. Ramanayake (SL); A. Ranatunga (SL); K. R. Rutherford (NZ); Saleem Malik (Pak); Saqlain Mushtaq (P); N. S. Sidhu (I); L. P. C. Silva (SL); E. O. Simons (SA); M. S. Sinclair (NZ); A. J. Stewart (E); E. L. R. Stewart (SA); H. H. Streak (Z); S. B. Styris (NZ); P. L. Symcox (SA); S. R. Tendulkar (I); D. P. Viljoen (Z); V. J. Wells (E); A. R. Whittall (Z); J. Wilson (NZ); B. A. Young (NZ); Zahoor Elahi (P); D. N. T. Zoysa (SL).

DISMISSALS SUMMARY

Warne's wickets have been obtained as follows:

Bowled	42	(18.40%)
LBW	36	(15.76%)
Caught	112	(49.10%)
Stumped	37	(16.35%)
Hit wicket	1	(0.39%)
Total	228	

ON-FIELD PARTNERSHIPS

MOST CATCHES BY A FIELDSMAN OR A WICKETKEEPER FROM WARNE'S BOWLING

13	Mark Waugh, Ian Healy
10	Michael Bevan
8	Steve Waugh

In addition, Warne has held nine catches from his own bowling.

The wicketkeepers to perform stumpings are Ian Healy (21), Adam Gilchrist (14), Justin Langer and Tim Zoehrer (1 apiece).

LEFT-HANDERS

Of his 228 victims, 54 (23.68%) have been left-handers. Left-handed batsmen he has dismissed most often are J. C. Adams (4); M. J. Greatbatch (4); H. P. Tillekeratne (4); C. E. L. Ambrose (3); C. Z. Harris (3); D. L. Vettori (3); Wasim Akram (3).

TOP-ORDER DOMINANCE

Batsmen dismissed in each position of batting order

Pos.	Wkts	% of total
1	20	8.88
2	16	7.01
3	26	11.55
4	27	12.00
5	30	13.15
6	28	12.37

(Total dismissals positions 1 to 6: 147 (64%))

7	27	12.00
8	20	8.88
9	17	7.55
10	12	5.33
11	5	2.22

(Total dismissals positions 7 to 11: 81 (36%))

Total   228

WHEN SHANE WARNE PLAYS . . .

Results of One-Day Internationals in which Warne has appeared

Won	90	(61.64%)
Lost	53	(36.30%)
Tied	2	(1.36%)
No Result	1	(0.70%)
Total	146	

MOST EXPENSIVE BOWLING

(10 overs, unless otherwise stated)

2/64	v South Africa, Cape Town, 1996–97
1/63	v West Indies, Port-of-Spain, 1995
0/61	v India, Dunedin, 1994–95
0/61	v India, Sharjah, 1997–98
0/59	v West Indies, Port-of-Spain, 1998–99

0/58   v Sri Lanka, Lahore, 1995–96
0/49   v India, The Oval, 1999 (off 6.2 overs)

MOST RUNS FROM AN OVER

22   Vinod Kambli (20 and 2 no-balls), India v Australia, Sharjah, 19 April 1994
21   Robin Singh (15) and Ajay Jadeja (6), India v Australia,
      The Oval, London, 4 June 1999
19   Romesh Kaluwitharana (18) & Aruna Gunawardene (1),
      Sri Lanka v Australia, Melbourne, 7 February 1999
19   Manoj Prabhakar (10) & Sachin Tendulkar (9), India v Australia,
      Carisbrook, Dunedin, 22 February 1995
18   Rudi Bryson (13) & Jonty Rhodes (5), South Africa v Australia, Newlands,
      Cape Town, 2 April 1997
16   Chris Harris (14) & Adam Parore (2), New Zealand v Australia, Sharjah,
      21 April 1998
16   Neil Johnson (16), Zimbabwe v Australia, Lord's, London,
      9 June 1999

DOMESTIC ONE-DAY CRICKET
DEBUT: 1992–93 Victoria v Tasmania, Devonport

BATTING & FIELDING

RECORD SEASON BY SEASON

	Mts	Inns	NO	Runs	HS	Ave	50s	Ct
1992–93	1	1	0	26	26	26.00	–	–
1993–94	2	–	–	–	–	–	–	–
1994–95	1	1	0	32	32	32.00	–	–
1995–96	3	2	0	20	15	10.00	–	1
1996–97	3	2	1	12	12*	12.00	–	6
1997–98	1	1	0	14	14	14.00	–	–
1998–99	1	1	0	24	24	24.00	–	–
1999–2000	2	2	0	31	22	15.50	–	–
TOTAL	14	10	1	159	32	17.66	–	7

HIGHEST SCORES

32   v South Australia, Adelaide, 1994–95
26   v Tasmania, Devonport, 1992–93
24   v New South Wales, Melbourne, 1998–99

HIGHEST PARTNERSHIPS

61   7th wicket, with Paul Reiffel, v South Australia, Adelaide, 1994–95

44   8th wicket, with Matthew Mott, v New South Wales, Melbourne, 1998–99

BOWLING

RECORD SEASON BY SEASON

Mts	Overs	Mdn	Runs	Wkt	Ave	BB	4wM	RpO	
1992–93	1	5.5	0	31	3	10.33	3/31	–	5.31
1993–94	2	20	1	84	0	–	–	–	4.20
1994–95	1	10	2	34	2	17.00	2/34	–	3.40
1995–96	3	22	1	104	1	104.00	1/36	–	4.72
1996–97	3	30	3	107	9	11.88	5/35	1	3.56
1997–98	1	8	1	43	3	14.33	3/33	–	5.37
1998–99	1	8	1	23	1	23.00	1/23	–	2.87
1999–2000	2	16	0	74	3	24.66	2/31	–	4.62
TOTAL	14	119.5	9	500	22	22.72	5/35	1	4.17

BEST BOWLING

5/35   v Tasmania, Optus Oval, Carlton, 1996–97

3/31   v Tasmania, Devonport, 1992–93

3/43   v New South Wales, North Sydney, 1997–98

MOST EXPENSIVE BOWLING

(10 overs unless otherwise stated)

0/60   v Queensland, Melbourne, 1993–94

2/55   v South Australia, Adelaide, 1996–97

0/43   v Queensland, Brisbane, 1999–2000 (6 overs)

SCHOOL & CLUB CRICKET

	Mt	Wkts	Runs	Ave	BB
Mentone Grammar	18	54	703	13.02	6/21
Brighton (VSDCA)					
Firsts	3	3	66	22.00	1/11
Seconds	5	9	187	20.77	4/54
St Kilda (VCA)					
Firsts	46	54	1362	25.22	4/31
Seconds	12	26	437	16.81	6/52
Thirds	16	25	396	15.84	5/49
Fourths	4	6	142	23.66	na
Colts & one-day	5	6	122	20.33	3/44
Glenelg (SACA)					
Firsts	8	26	539	20.73	6/75

Warne has made 540 runs at an average of 23.47 in his 46 first XI games with St Kilda. His highest score and only senior century is 109, against reigning titleholders Melbourne in round 3 of Premier League cricket at the Albert Ground in 1998–99, against an attack including Brad Williams. He batted No. 5. Warne represented University in the W. J. Dowling Under 16 schoolboys competition in January in 1983–84 and 1984–85, scoring 254 runs at an average of 23.08 and taking 11 wickets at 31.96. He was captain in his second year.

FURTHER READING

Allan's Cricket Annual.

Benaud, Richie. *Anything but an Autobiography.* Hodder Headline Australia, 1998.

Browning, Mark. *World Cup Cricket 1975–99.* Kangaroo Press, 1999.

Griffiths, Edward. *Jonty: Fruits of the Spirit.* CAB, 1998.

Hussain, Nasser, and Waugh, Steve. *Ashes Summer.* CollinsWillow 1997.

Malcolm, Devon. *You Guys are History.* CollinsWillow, 1998.

Piesse, Ken. *Warne: Sultan of Spin.* Modern Publishing, 1995.

Reiffel, Paul, with Baum, Greg. *Reiffel Inside Out.* HarperSports, 1998.

Stewart, Alec, with Murgatroyd, Brian, *A Captain's Diary: The Battle for the Ashes 1998–99.* CollinsWillow, 1999.

Taylor, Mark, with Heads, Ian. *Time to Declare.* Pan Macmillan, 1999.

Test Match Grounds of the World. Willow Books, 1990.

Tufnell, Phil, with Hayter, Peter. *What Now?* CollinsWillow, 1999.

Warne, Shane, as told to Ray, Mark. *My Own Story.* Swan Publishing, 1997.

Waugh, Steve. *No Regrets: A Captain's Diary.* HarperCollins, 1999.

— *Steve Waugh's World Cup Diary.* HarperSports, 1996.

Wisden Australia Almanack. Hardie Grant Books.

Wisden Cricketers' Almanack. John Wisden & Co.

INDEX

About the Author

From the age of 10, when he moved his bed into the lounge room so he could hear the cricket broadcasts from the West Indies, Ken Piesse has had a rare passion for the summer game. Australia's longest-serving editor of cricket magazines, Ken has written 16 books on cricket, including his bestselling biography *Warne: Sultan of Spin*, *The Great Australian Book of Cricket Stories* and *Wildmen of Cricket*. He has also collaborated in auto-biographies with ex-internationals Max Walker and Terry Jenner.

Ken contributes to *Wisden Australia*, *The Cricketer International* and *Cover Point* and is heard regularly on Melbourne radio station Sport 927. In 1995 he won the Victorian Cricket Association's Media Award for a two-part series on Shane Warne.

Ken and his wife, Susan, live in Melbourne with their five children.

web site: www.cricketbooks.citysearch.com.au
e-mail: kenpiesse@ozemail.com.au

The Taylor Years
Ken Piesse

When Mark Taylor inherited Australian sport's most coveted position in May 1994, the Australian cricket team was finally able to deliver the ultimate knockout blow against the long-running champions, the West Indies. Taylor and his ambitious XI then embarked on a run of success never before seen in Australian cricket – winning nine series in a row to become the undisputed power of the world game.

Award-winning cricket writer Ken Piesse's *The Taylor Years* celebrates Australia's Test achievements under Mark Taylor's captaincy and captures all the highlights of the period, including:

- Taylor's first months as leader of the team after a decade under Allan Border's rule
- his disastrous batting slump in 1996 and courageous career revival in England in 1997
- his famous 334 not out at Peshawar, which equalled the highest individual Australian Test score, by the legendary Don Bradman.

Here are recollections of the stars of Taylor's team, including Michael Slater, Glenn McGrath, the Waugh twins and Stuart MacGill, as well as memorable photographs and fascinating statistics to please cricket fans of every age.

The Taylor Years is an entertaining, illuminating record of one of the finest periods in the annals of Australian cricket.

The Golden Wallabies: The Story of Australia's World Champions
Spiro Zavos

In 1999 Australia's captain, John Eales, held aloft the Rugby World Cup. The Wallabies had beaten France at Cardiff to win the trophy and become the champions of the world. *The Golden Wallabies* tells the story of this victorious campaign, with match-by-match accounts, and also describes many other triumphs over the years.

Award-winning rugby writer Spiro Zavos recounts the glories of the 1991 World Champion Wallabies, as well as those of yesteryear, including their Gold Medal win in the 1908 Olympic Games. He examines how Australia has come to dominate world rugby, and what makes the game played down under so much superior to that played in Europe. He brings to life the outstanding players and their deeds, so one can almost see Campese streaking for the tryline, or Ella outmanoeuvring his opponent. He also tells of the early years, the first tours, the beginnings of the Bledisloe Cup, the permanent rivalry with the All Blacks, the constant irritation of the Home unions . . .

The Golden Wallabies is an exhilarating celebration of Australian rugby. Packed with fascinating detail, it is a must for every follower of Rugby Union.